Strategic Sustainable Business

Compiled and Edited by:

Jonathan H. Westover, Ph.D.
Utah Valley University

First printed/published in 2015 in the USA
by HCI Press
as part of Leading Innovative Organizations series

Library of Congress Cataloging-in-Publication Data

Strategic Sustainable Business/ Jonathan H. Westover, editor.
       p. cm. -- (Leading Innovative Organizations series)
ISBN-13: 978-0692599273; ISBN-10: 0692599274 (HCI Press)
1. Sustainability. 2. Strategy. 3. Business I. Westover, Jonathan H.

Table of Contents

About the Editor

Dr. Jonathan H. Westover is an Associate Professor of Management and Associate Director of the Center for the Study of Ethics at Utah Valley University, specializing in international human resource management, organizational development, and community-engaged experiential learning. He is also a human resource development and performance management consultant. Already a recipient of numerous research, teaching, and service awards and fellowships early in his academic career, Jonathan also recently was named a Fulbright Scholar and was visiting faculty in the MBA program at Belarusian State University (Minsk, Belarus), and he is also a regular visiting faculty member in other graduate business programs in the U.S., UK, France, Poland, and China. Prior to his doctoral studies in the Sociology of Work and Organizations, Comparative International Sociology, and International Political Economy (University of Utah), he received his B.S. in Sociology (Research and Analysis emphasis, Business Management minor, Korean minor) and MPA (emphasis in Human Resource Management) from the Marriott School of Management at Brigham Young University. He also received graduate certificates in demography and higher education teaching during his time at the University of Utah. His ongoing research examines issues of globalization, labor transformation, work quality characteristics, and the determinants of job satisfaction cross-nationally.

Acknowledgements

This text was compiled, edited, and adapted from open source texts at http://www.saylor.org/books and created under a Creative Commons Attribution-NonCommercial ShareAlike 3.0 License without attribution as requested by the work's original creator or licensee. Please contact me for a free copy of the e-text. I would like to thank the many anonymous individuals who contributed their own wisdom and writing to this edited work, particularly those who contributed to the texts *A Primer on Sustainable Business* and *The Sustainable Business Case Book*. Of course, this text would not be possible without each of their important contributions. Most of all, I would like to publically thank my wife (Jacque) and my six wonderful children (Sara, Amber, Lia, Kaylie, David, and Brayden) for all of their love and support!

Preface

Strategic Sustainable Business provides readers with a broad overview of the core concepts of sustainability and sustainable business practice. It is intended for use in undergraduate business courses and will also be of interest to students in environmental studies, engineering, urban planning, and government. This book is not meant to exhort all business people on the path to sustainability enlightenment but to highlight some of the benefits, opportunities, and challenges associated with sustainable business practices.

What distinguishes this book is that it provides a conceptual foundation to promote understanding of sustainability concepts and frameworks and also discusses real-world business examples of sustainability in action. It is believed that this is the best way to teach sustainability as it applies to the business world—a conceptual foundation with practical application.

Sustainable business involves businesses operating with interest and concern for their long-term economic, environmental, and social impact. For-profit businesses focus first and foremost on their own economic bottom line, oftentimes, with a short-term perspective. However, with a sustainability perspective, businesses also consider a longer-term and broader triple bottom line that takes into account not only company profits but also environmental and social impacts. The economic, environmental, and social perspectives are increasingly interrelated and relevant for businesses.

Chapter 1:
Introduction to Sustainable Business and Sustainable Business Core Concepts and Frameworks

Google Invests $39 Million in Wind Farms

In 2010, Google invested $38.8 million in two North Dakota wind farms built by NextEra Energy Resources. These wind farms generate 169.5 MW of electricity, enough to power 55,000 homes. Google's investment represents a minority interest in the $190 million financing of the projects. The two wind farms had already been built, but Google said that its investment would provide funds for NextEra to invest in additional renewable energy projects. Google's investment is structured as a "tax equity investment" where it will earn a return based on tax credits—a direct offset of federal taxes that Google would otherwise need to pay—for renewable energy projects, Google spokesman Jamie Yood said the energy from the wind farms would not be used to power Google's data centers, which consume large amounts of electricity. Mr. Yood said that Google's primary goal was to earn a return from its investment but that the company also is looking to accelerate the deployment of renewable energy. Renewable energy comes from sources such as solar panels and wind turbines to generate energy as opposed to other sources used such as coal or oil. Renewable energy typically has a much lower impact on the environment depending on the type and often emits little to no pollution. Conscious of its high electricity bills and its impact on the environment, Google has long had an interest in renewable energy. Renewable energy projects at Google range from a large solar power installation on its campus, to the promotion of plug-in hybrids, to investments in renewable energy start-up companies like eSolar. Google has also worked on making its data centers more energy efficient, consume less electricity while still handling the same amount of data requests, and has developed technologies to let people monitor their home energy use. But as of 2010, the company had yet to live up to its promise to help to finance the generation of renewable energy. "We're aiming to accelerate the deployment of renewable energy—in a way that makes good business sense, too," Rick Needham, green business operations manager at Google, wrote on the company's blog.

Source: Miguel Helft, "Google Invests $39 Million in Wind Farms," *New York Times*, May 3, 2010.

1.1 Introduction

LEARNING OBJECTIVES

1. Understand that businesses are increasingly acting with concern for the environment and society.
2. Comprehend that business can play a positive role in helping to solve the world's environmental and social problems.
3. Appreciate that business interest in sustainability has been motivated by profit-making opportunities associated with sustainable business practices.
4. Understand that this book focuses on sustainable business case studies in the United States.

Why would Google invest in wind farms that will not provide any energy for its high-energy-consuming data centers? Founded in 1998, Google runs the world's most popular Internet search engine. It's a position that has earned Google high profits and has given it huge influence over the online world. Then why would it take a risky investment of millions of dollars on an activity outside its core business? And why would the US government provide tax credits to Google and other private companies to invest in renewable energy? Can't the private market and profit-making interests of private businesses ensure that an adequate supply of renewable energy is produced in the United States and globally?

All businesses, including Google, must focus on their economic performance and ensure they are profitable and provide an attractive return on investment for their owners and investors. Without this, businesses cannot continue as ongoing entities. For Google and other companies, their most important "bottom line" is their own economic bottom line, which is their profitability, or revenue, minus expenses. Yet it is clear from Google's investment in wind farms and the activities of private companies all around the globe that many of today's business leaders look beyond their own annual economic bottom line and act with concern for how their business activities affect the environment and the very existence and sustainability of the world's physical and human resources and capabilities. This is what this book is about.

All companies must operate legally and achieve profitability to continue as ongoing entities. All companies also embed and reflect in their decision making and activities the values and priorities of their owners, key managers, employees, and other stakeholders. As will be highlighted in this book, some companies, such as BP prior to the Gulf oil spill in 2010, focus on annual profitability and investment returns to owners more than others. Other companies, including Google, give priority to other values (besides profit making) and take into consideration environmental and sustainability concerns along with concern for annual profits. And other firms, such as Green Mountain Coffee Roasters, Oakhurst Dairy, Simply Green, Timberland, Pax World, Seventh Generation, and Stonyfield Farms, more fully integrate sustainable business practices into their mission and corporate strategy and try to gain a competitive advantage by doing this.

This book describes what it means for a business to be sustainable and to engage in sustainable business practices and why a business would choose to act in a more sustainable manner. The book will be of interest to students who are interested in understanding the role of sustainable businesses in the economy and society, in addressing environmental concerns, and in working for or starting their own sustainable businesses.

The focus of the book is on the experience, opportunities, and challenges for sustainable businesses in the United States. While the book does not provide detailed international examples in its in-depth case chapters, it does discuss the opportunities and challenges of US-based sustainable businesses operating globally. The objective is to expose students in the fields of business, science, public policy, and others to the ideals, opportunities, and challenges of sustainable business practices with examples and lessons from a diverse group of companies in different industries.

Sidebar

What Is Sustainability?

Sustainability is meeting "the needs of the present without compromising the ability of future generations to meet their own needs." This is a commonly referenced definition, developed by the Norwegian prime minister Gro Harlem Brundtland for the 1987 report "Our Common Future," produced by the World Commission on Environment and Development under the direction of the United Nations.

Sidebar

What Does It Mean to Be Green and Is That the Same as Sustainable?

And what does "green" mean and how does it relate to sustainability? Green is a term widely used to describe buildings, products (of all types, including cars, food, computers, etc.), and services designed, manufactured, or constructed with minimal negative impact on the environment and with an emphasis on conservation of resources, energy efficiency, and product safety. Being "green" can help to preserve and sustain society's resources.

KEY TAKEAWAYS

- Businesses are increasingly engaging in activities with concern for the environment and society.
- Businesses are engaging in these activities because they recognize they can play a positive role in helping to solve the world's environmental and social problems.
- Businesses are also interested in sustainability because of market and profit-making opportunities associated with sustainable business practices.
- This book intends to explore the opportunities and challenges for sustainable business in the United States primarily through case studies.

EXERCISES

1. Answer the following questions:
a. Do you think that Google would have invested in the two North Dakota wind energy projects if they did not receive tax credits (a government incentive that reduces the federal taxes that they owe)? Why or why not?
b. Besides tax credits, what are some of the other benefits that Google could obtain by investing in the wind energy projects?
c. Based on this article, do you think that it is wise for Google to continue investing in potential future renewable energy projects given that their core successful business model is based on web searches and not providing energy?
   Search on the web and find three other examples of companies investing in renewable energy projects, even though those companies' core business models do not involve energy production. Describe the business, their core business model, and the type of project they invested in.

1.2 Overview of Sustainable Business
LEARNING OBJECTIVES

1. Explain what it means to be a sustainable business and the relationship of profitability and sustainability.
2. Understand what is meant by the triple bottom line for businesses in relation to sustainability.
3. Describe what is meant by enlightened self-interest and provide an example of how it applies to business.

A focus on sustainability (for private businesses) can be thought of as a management strategy that helps businesses set goals and prioritize resource allocations. Sustainability at the private business level can first be thought of primarily in terms of financial sustainability—that is, the ability of private firms to generate profits and cash flow to sustain business operations. For-profit businesses—first and foremost—must focus on their economic bottom line. A company that earns a profit is providing a good or service that is valued by society. Consumers and businesses do not pay for products and services that do not provide them with value or benefits above the cost of the product or service to them (or else they would not have made the free decision to purchase that product or service). Therefore, at a basic level, if a business is profitable, it is having a net positive social impact. This is assuming that the business has no external impact on the environment or society.

However, there are companies that are profitable in the short term that are having a long-term net negative impact. For example, a lumber company that owns timber reserves could harvest all of its timber resources in one year generating a significant profit for that one year. However, if in doing this the company ignored the costs and losses associated with destroying the forest and the ability of the forest to continue to produce timber, then the net impact could be negative. By depleting the resource base of the company, short-term gain can lead to long-term financial failure for the company. This example highlights the need for sustainable thinking in business. For business to be sustainable in a financial sense, businesses must increasingly consider the longer term and broader consequences of decisions.

Beyond just the company's own bottom line, a "next step" for businesses is to consider not only their own long-term financial performance but also broader societal environmental and social impacts. This so-called triple bottom line (TBL) considers business from economic, environmental, and social perspectives and measures business performance based on net impact on profit, people, and planet. This approach to business will be increasingly relevant to students of business and in other fields as global populations and demand for energy, water, and other resources increase and our planet faces resource shortages. Over the next fifty years, the world's population is expected to grow from 6.8 billion to 9.5 billion, and the demand for energy and other resources will follow.

The primary aspects of sustainability considered in this book are profit and planet. Much of the framework and concepts relevant for environmental sustainability also apply to social sustainability and several of the case study chapters highlight examples of businesses, such as Seventh Generation, Green Mountain Coffee Roasters, Stonyfield, and Simply Green, incorporating social issues into their decision making.

For businesses that consider TBL and sustainable business practices, it is increasingly not about deciding whether to focus on (earning) profits, or (saving) the planet, or (caring about) people. Instead, it's about focusing on all three. When McDonald's reduces the packaging with their food, they help the environment, contribute to public health (by reducing toxics in the atmosphere), and they also help their economic bottom line. Enlightened self-interest occurs when companies (or individuals) help others and, in the process, help themselves. When McDonald's uses less packaging for their hamburgers, French fries, and other food items than in the past, this reduces their costs of materials and disposal costs while at the same time it helps the environment. Reducing packaging is an example of a sustainable business practice that can benefit a private company and also society at large.

In the longer term, all businesses rely on the sustainability of societies' resources, including energy, food, and material resources, for their success and survival. Thus it can be in all businesses long-term interest to act with concern for the sustainability of society's resources.

Sidebar
Doing Well and Doing Good
Companies that act with enlightened self-interest are also commonly referred to as doing well (for themselves) at the same time that they are doing good (good things for others), or "doing well by doing good."

Gulf Oil Spill
The 2010 Gulf of Mexico oil spill—the disaster that quickly became the largest oil spill in US history [1]—offers a vivid

example of how sustainability issues affect profits, people, and planet. The spill (as of June 2010) was estimated to have leaked at least triple the amount of oil as compared to the Exxon Valdez spill in Alaska during 1989.

BP put itself into a very difficult and controversial position. BP had a history of accidents that were harbingers of the Gulf spill, including having to pay $25 million in fines for a spill on the north shore of Alaska in 2006. Then in 2010 under financial and time pressure, BP failed to properly cap it's Gulf Coast well from which they had been drilling. BP hastened through procedures to detect excess gas in the well, skipped quality tests of the cement structure around the pipe, and even assigned an inexperienced manager to oversee final well tests. [2]While most of the company's actions were not best practices, they were within acceptable industry standards and believed by many to be legal. The oil released from the uncapped well threatened the valued ecosystem of the Gulf in very serious ways. The oil adversely impacted populations of fish, marine birds, and other aquatic wildlife and threatened fragile wetland ecosystems.

BP could have at some short-term cost avoided the Gulf oil spill. Instead, the company chose not to put in place some safety features and then delayed responding to signals that there were problems in the pipeline, which resulted in a major pipeline break with catastrophic implications for the environment and significant economic costs to the company. From when the drilling rig exploded on April 20 through June 2, 2010, the company lost a third of its market value, or about $75 billion, and the company had spent almost $1 billion on cleanup efforts. One analyst calculated that in a worst-case scenario, BP's cleanup liability would be around $14 billion, which would account for the entire loss of all fishing and tourism revenues for coastal states closest to the spill. [3]

KEY TAKEAWAYS

- Sustainable business involves making decisions and taking actions that consider the long-term impact of the business on society and the environment while still maintaining profitability.
- People, planet, and profit—also known as the triple bottom line—are the three areas that businesses interested in sustainability measure their impacts. This varies from traditional businesses, which are predominantly focused on profits as their measure of success.
- Enlightened self-interest refers to business as taking actions that are good for the environment and society but that also help make the business better off.
- The Gulf oil spill provides an example of how acting in an unsustainable manner with a short-term focus on profit can have significant long-term negative impact for society, the environment, and the economy—including BP, which was seeking to maximize its profit.

EXERCISES

1. Search the web for an article that discusses an action that a company took that benefited the environment or others outside of the company and that also had a financial benefit for the company. Be prepared to discuss what the action was, the financial benefit the company achieved by taking action, and how that action led to the financial benefit.
2. Some have argued that the purpose of a business is to earn a profit and that is its only goal. Do you agree with that? Discuss what you feel are some pros and cons of a business expanding its focus to consider the effect of its actions on "people" and "planet."

[1] "Estimates Suggest Spill Is Biggest in U.S. History," *New York Times*, May 28, 2010, http://www.nytimes.com/2010/05/28/us/28flow.html?ref=us.
[2] "BP Decisions Set Stage for Disaster," *Wall Street Journal*, May 27, 2010,
http://online.wsj.com/article/SB10001424052748704026204575266560930780190.html?KEYWORDS=It+was+a+ difficult+drill+from+the+start.
[3] Jad Mouawad and John Schwartz, "Cleanup Costs and Lawsuits Rattle BP's Investors," *New York Times*, June 1, 2010.

1.3 What Does It Mean to Be a Sustainable Business?

LEARNING OBJECTIVES

1. Identify what it means to be a sustainable business.
2. Define what constitutes sustainable business practices and provide examples.
3. Describe the main motivations for engagement in sustainable business practices.
4. Discuss the barriers that businesses can encounter in adopting sustainable business practices.

The sustainable business perspective takes into account not only profits and returns on investment but also how business operations affect the environment, natural resources, and future generations. Sustainability at the business level can be thought of as taking steps, such as recycling and conserving nonrenewable material and energy use to reduce the negative impact of a business's operations on the environment. While managing operations to reduce negative environmental impact is an important part of business sustainability, these types of activities are increasingly part of a deeper strategic perspective on sustainability for businesses.

Businesses implement sustainability in their organization for a variety of reasons. The benefits from pursuing sustainability can include the following:

- Reduction of energy and materials use and waste and the costs associated with these. McDonald's reducing the packaging with hamburgers and French fries is an example of this.
- Lowering of legal risks and insurance costs. For example, BP, with some investment in safety features to protect against environmental disaster, could have avoided huge liability costs that will be associated with Gulf of Mexico oil spill.
- Differentiation of product or services and brand. Companies such as Green Mountain Coffee Roasters have differentiated their brands and increased consumer awareness and sales of products with their focus on sustainability.
- Drive toward innovation to create new products and serve new markets. Seventh Generation developed new products to address environmental concerns of households and positioned themselves as the leader in that market, sustainable consumer household products.
- Improvement of company image and reputation with consumers, particularly the increasing numbers of consumers who are concerned about the environment and their own impact on the environment.
- Enhancement of investor interest. Increasing numbers of investors take into consideration company sustainability practices when they make their decisions how to invest. Companies that act with concern for social and environmental matters operate at lower risk and their future growth rates can be positively affected. Both of these are positive factors for investors.
- Increase attraction and retention of employees who care about the environment and sustainability.

The most important factors that motivate companies to become more sustainable are internal. This includes the number one objective of companies—to maximize profits.

The beliefs and personal values of management and employees can also significantly influence engagement in sustainable business practices. Many managers and employees have an interest in sustainability and its benefits to society. They can move the company forward on sustainable business practices because it's the right thing to do—that is, owners, managers, and employees believe that sustainable business practices are the moral and ethically right thing to do. Companies with senior management and owners who are committed to sustainable business practices for ethical reasons are more likely to put in place sustainable business practices even without having a detailed assessment of how it will affect revenue, costs, and profitability.

There are also important external factors that influence a business's decision to become more sustainable, including governmental laws and regulations and consumer and investor interests and expectations. These external factors are strongly influenced by societal trends and values, demographics, new knowledge, and the media.

Sustainable businesses strive to maximize their net social contribution by embracing the opportunities and managing the risks that result from an organization's economic, environmental, and social impacts. In many respects, the best measure of business contributions to society are profits. Profits represent the value of products and services that companies provide (as reflected in the prices that consumers are willing to pay for a company's products and services) minus the direct costs of producing the products or services.

However, private market transactions do not take into account so-called external costs to market transactions. For example, the external costs associated with the production of electricity from coal include climate change damage costs associated with the emissions of carbon dioxide (CO_2) and damage costs (such as impacts on health, crops, etc.) associated with other air pollutants (such as nitrous oxide and sulfur dioxide). These pollutants threaten the future sustainability of natural resources and have a cost, and these costs are not included in the price of energy and not passed on to consumers. Thus market prices do not reflect costs to society perfectly, and this can result in significant differences between profits and the net societal contributions of companies and can present challenges to businesses interested in maximizing their net positive social impact and acting in a sustainable way. Government often acts to address market failure and to reduce the external costs associated with pollution and environmental damage incurred in market activities. Controlling negative externalities is used to justify government restrictions, regulations, taxes, and fees imposed on businesses. Governments at the federal, state, and local level in the United States have acted on this. In general, European nations have been more active in trying to address market failures and trying to control external costs associated with market activities in environmental, social, and other arenas than the United States.

Sidebar

The Role of Government Policies in Sustainable Business Government policies, such as a carbon tax (a tax on pollution), can address externalities by having companies and consumers internalize the costs associated with what were externalities. This can help move private companies focused on profits to activities that better reflect their net social contributions.

The challenge of acting in a sustainable way in a private market economy in which the external costs, including those associated with carbon dioxide emissions, are not included is reflected in the Green Mountain Coffee statement that follows.

> *And while we are committed to achieving greater sustainability in our products and practices, we compete in a marketplace where economic value drives demand. This is the challenge of trying to do the right thing in a commercial system that does not yet fully account for its global impact.* [1]

A challenging task for Green Mountain Coffee and other businesses today is to effectively integrate the traditional business performance objectives (profit maximization) with striving to continuously increase the long-term societal value of their organizations. This challenge is represented by the mission statement from the CEO of Ford Motor Company:

> *To sustain our Company, meet our responsibilities and contribute to tackling global sustainability issues, we must operate at a profit.* [2] *I have long believed that environmental sustainability is the most important issue facing businesses in the 21st century. Fortunately, unlike 20 years ago, or even five years ago, a growing number of people in our industry now agree, and we are doing something about it. Our vision for the 21st century is to provide sustainable transportation that is affordable in every sense of the word: socially, environmentally and economically…I am convinced that our vision makes sense from a business point of view as well as an ethical one. Climate change may be the first sustainability issue to fundamentally reshape our business, but it will not be the last. How we anticipate and respond to issues like human rights, the mobility divide, resource scarcity and poverty will determine our future success.* [3]

How Do Businesses View Sustainability? How Important Is It to Businesses?

The actions and statements of Green Mountain Coffee, Ford Motors, and many leading companies globally demonstrate business interest in sustainability. The interest in sustainability is often written, as with the Ford Motor Company example previously mentioned, in corporate mission or value statements. The exact wording and nature of the commitment to sustainability varies but it is represented in an increasing number of the public documents of corporations.

There is significant variance in how deeply and sincerely companies are committed to their mission and in how much the value statements influence actual company practice. However, just that the statements are made and made public for all to read suggests that sustainability is an important issue for an increasing number of businesses. See the following examples from Hewlett Packard (HP) and Walmart, respectively.

> *Environmental sustainability is one of the five focus areas of HP's global citizenship strategy, reflecting our goal to be the world's most environmentally responsible IT company. This commitment is more than a virtuous aspiration—it is integral to the ongoing success of our business. Our drive to improve HP's overall environmental performance helps us capitalize on emerging market opportunities, respond to stakeholder expectations and even shape the future of the emerging low-carbon, resource-efficient global economy. It also pushes us to reduce the footprint of our operations, improve the performance of our products and services across their entire life cycle, and innovative new solutions that create efficiencies, reduce costs and differentiate our brand.* [4]

> *The fact is sustainability at Walmart isn't a stand-alone issue that's separate from or unrelated to our business. It's not an abstract or philanthropic program. We don't even see it as corporate social responsibility. Sustainability is built into our business. It's completely aligned with our model, our mission and our culture. Simply put, sustainability is built into our business because it's so good for our business.* [5]

> *Sustainability 360 is the framework we are using to achieve our goals and bring sustainable solutions to our more than 2 million associates, more than 100,000 suppliers and the more than 200 million customers and members we serve each week. Sustainability 360 lives within every aspect of our business, in every country where we operate, within every salaried associate's job description, and extends beyond our walls to our suppliers, products and customers.* [6]

These are just a few examples. Among companies from the "Global Top 1,000" that responded to a 2008 survey, about three-quarters (73 percent) have corporate sustainability on their board's agenda and almost all (94 percent) indicate that a corporate sustainability strategy can result in better financial performance. But significantly, only about one in ten (11 percent) of the "Global Top 1,000" are actually implementing a corporate sustainability strategy. [7]

In a separate 2009 MIT study with the Boston Consulting Group (BCG) titled *The Business of Sustainability*, of 1,500 corporate executives surveyed, an overwhelming majority believe that sustainability-related issues are having or will soon have a material impact on their business. Yet relatively few of the companies are taking decisive action to address such issues.

While about 45 percent said their organizations were pursuing "basic sustainability strategies," such as reducing or eliminating emissions, reducing toxicity or harmful chemicals, improving efficiency in packaging, or designing products or processes for reuse or recycling, less than a third of survey respondents said that their company has developed a clear business case for addressing sustainability. The majority of sustainability actions undertaken to date appear to be limited to those necessary to meet legal and regulatory requirements. The MIT research did indicate that once companies begin to pursue sustainability initiatives, they tend to unearth opportunities to reduce costs, create new revenue streams, and develop more innovative business models. [8]

It is not only larger companies that are interested and acting on sustainability. Many smaller and start-up companies are focused on sustainability, with some entrepreneurs, such as Jeffrey Hollender, the founder of Seventh Generation, and Andrew Kellar, the founder of Simply Green, founding their ventures based on their commitment to sustainability.

What Holds Companies Back from Implementing Sustainable Business Practices?

There are many factors contributing to private companies not implementing corporate sustainability practices. There is a learning curve associated with sustainable business practices—ranging from basic compliance to completely changing the business environment—and in many respects a large majority of businesses are just at the initial learning stage.

Three of the major barriers that impede decisive corporate action are a lack of understanding of what sustainability is and what it means to an enterprise, difficulty modeling the business case for sustainability, and flaws in execution, even after a plan has been developed.

The learning curve on sustainable business practices is steep, and it often entails significant risks and uncertainty. Any change in company practice involves taking on some risk and uncertainty, and this is heightened when taking on something for which the benefits are not clear and are dependent on changing laws, regulations, and consumer values and interests. But the risks of failing to act decisively are growing, according to many of the thought leaders interviewed in the MIT study.

Sidebar
Learning Curve
The learning curve refers to a graphical representation of learning. The curve represents the initial difficulty of learning something and how there is a lot to learn after the initial learning. In the case of learning about sustainable business practice, managers often quickly learn enough to be interested in it, but then the learning curve is high (steep), and there is a lot to learn to ensure that the sustainable practice serves the interests of the business entity.

There are many different definitions of and frameworks for considering sustainability, and this can confuse businesses considering engaging in more sustainable practices. The confusion and lack of clear definition can result in inaction or a slow response on sustainability. Over 50 percent of respondents to the "Global Top 1,000" sustainability survey stated a need for a better framework for understanding sustainability. Many companies struggle to model the business case for sustainability and need help in doing this. Some companies are making progress on framing and reporting on sustainable business practices and quantifying the impacts of their sustainability efforts internally and externally.

Another contributing barrier to the implementation of sustainable business practices is the ambitious agenda and enthusiasm of the strongest advocates for sustainability. Since sustainability stresses the interconnectivity of everything, many groups have adopted it. While many of the advocates for sustainability are well intended, they often do not appreciate the difficulties and challenges of implementing sustainable business practices. This leads some businesses to resist the call to put in place sustainable business practices, as the economic and environmental benefits of some of the practices may be exaggerated and oversold, and the commitment asked for by advocates can be perceived as too deep, too costly, and too fast for many companies to accept.

Another contributing factor to corporate inaction on sustainability is that some businesses have acted on sustainability only for public relations purposes and to gain favor with consumers, investors, and government agencies without undertaking any practices with significant benefit to the environment or society. This can discourage businesses that have a sincere interest in sustainable business practice as they fear that they will be branded as greenwashing if they are not successful in their efforts.

Sidebar
What Is Greenwashing?

The term used to describe insincere engagement in sustainable business is *greenwashing*. It was first used by New York environmentalist Jay Westerveld who criticized the hotel practice of placing green "save the environment" cards in each room promoting the reuse of guest towels. The hotel example is especially noteworthy given that most hotels have poor waste management programs, specifically with little or no recycling. The term greenwashing is often used when significantly more money or time has been spent advertising being green rather than spending resources on environmentally sound practices or when the advertising misleadingly indicates a product is more green than it really is. For example, a company may make a hazardous product but put it in packaging that has images of nature on it to make it appear more environmentally friendly than it really is.

Sidebar
Walmart and Accusations of Greenwashing

Walmart has been accused of engaging in greenwashing and has taken actions to deepen their commitment to sustainability to address this accusation. It is very difficult to change a large company, and it has not been an easy task turning Walmart, the world's largest retailer, around. But after a difficult start, the company is making progress on environmental targets. The company has succeeded in opening an energy efficient prototype in every market globally, and since 2005, Walmart has improved its fleet efficiency by 60 percent. The company has also cut emissions generated at its existing stores, clubs, and distribution centers by 5.1 percent since 2005, putting the company at about 25 percent toward its 2012 goal. However, the company's absolute carbon footprint has continued to grow, despite it improving facility performance and reducing its carbon intensity over the last two years. In response, the company set the 2015 goal of avoiding twenty million metric tons, which is about 1.5 times the projected cumulative growth of its emissions over the next five years. [10]

Initial efforts in sustainability in which businesses are just at the initial learning stages and trying to figure out what to do can be confused with greenwashing. This might well have been the case at Walmart and other companies at first. And the steep learning curve and the risks of being accused of being insincere and greenwashing can deter businesses from sustainable business practice.

Another one of the more significant barriers is that sustainability, specifically focusing on factors external to the company, may just not be high on the list of important factors for some businesses. This can be particularly true for businesses that are struggling to keep revenues above expenses and survive economically and for small businesses with limited managerial and economic resources.

And then there are the concerns over the additional costs associated with instituting a commitment to sustainability and undertaking new sustainable business practices. There are often significant upfront costs or investments required that do not have immediate financial return. Many of the potential investments in sustainable practices, including investments in energy efficiency (e.g., installing new insulation in buildings) and renewable energy (e.g., wind power) have payback periods of ten years or longer.

It is the uncertainty associated with sustainable practices that is probably one of the main barriers. For most businesses, there is already so much uncertainty in their operating environment that they do not want to add another source of uncertainty if they perceive that they do not have to. But as with the case of BP and the Gulf Coast oil spill, attention to sustainability could actually reduce uncertainty and risks for businesses.

For example, had BP been more focused on sustainable business practices, they may have asked what are the potential negative environmental and social outcomes that may come from an oil leak. They may have more fully appreciated the disastrous impact on both present and future generations in the Gulf Coast area and also the potential negative financial impacts it would have on their corporate earnings. In conducting this "what-if" analysis, a reasonable outcome of this process may have been to have more rigorous safety controls in place and also to have better disaster response technologies and resources available for their drilling projects.

Among the companies that try to implement sustainable practices, there can be difficulty, and some companies after initial efforts may pull back or resist deeper efforts.

Execution may be flawed, and after failed or costly efforts, it can be difficult to overcome skepticism in organizations.

Internal to the corporation there are significant barriers to effective implementation of sustainable practices. This includes the great difficulty that many corporations experience in trying to change (there can be significant inertia) and the challenge businesses experience in institutionalizing new practices and priorities. The experience highlighted in the cases in this book will show how top-down commitment throughout a business organization is important for businesses to move toward sustainability practices.

Finally, the most significant barrier to adoption of sustainable business practices may be that many companies simply do not adequately understand sustainability and what it could mean to their company and, specifically, how it could impact their economic bottom line.

KEY TAKEAWAYS

- Businesses' main concerns are their own viability and profitability.
- Sustainable businesses also take into consideration how their activities impact society's resources and future generations.
- Examples of sustainable business practices include efforts to reduce energy and materials use and to use renewable and nonpolluting resources.
- Some of the main motivations to engage in sustainable business practice include the legal and regulatory concerns, the potential to lower energy and material costs, the opportunity to improve reputation and sales, the founder or owner's concerns and values, and a competitive advantage.
- Three-fourths of top company boards have given attention to sustainability, but only 10 percent are actually implementing sustainability plans. This highlights a large disconnect between interest in sustainability and actually taking steps for companies to become more sustainable.
- Significant barriers to sustainability include uncertainty involved, lack of understanding of what sustainability is, difficulty making the business case for sustainability, and failure to properly execute sustainability plans.

EXERCISES

1. Find three articles about businesses that have adopted sustainability practices. Find an article that shows a sustainability practice that resulted in lower costs. Find an article that shows a sustainability practice that improved reputation and sales. Find an article that shows a sustainability practice that might preempt government regulation (can be local, state, or federal). Be prepared to discuss the action the company took, the benefit the company received, and how the action resulted in benefit.

2. An industrial company with a history of violating its water discharge permit of pollutants decides to "go green." It switches to a biodegradable cleaning detergent for cleaning its offices and starts a paper recycling program for its offices. The cost of the change is minimal to the company. However, the company does not change any of its water discharge practices. The company then commences a marketing campaign of national television and radio ads claiming that it is now a sustainable company. Do you think this is an example of greenwashing? Why or why not?

[1] "Building Demand for Sustainable Products," Green Mountain Coffee Roasters, http://www.gmcr.com/csr/PromotingSustainableCoffee.aspx.
[2] "For a More Sustainable Future: Connecting with Society, Ford Motor Company Sustainability Report 2006/7," Ford Motor Company, http://corporate.ford.com/our-company/our-company-news/our-company-news-detail/sustainability-reports-archive.
[3] "2007/8 Blueprint for Sustainability," Ford Motor Company, http://corporate.ford.com/our-company/our-company-news/our-company-news-detail/sustainability-reports-archive.
[4] "HP Environmental Goals," Hewlett-Packard, http://www.hp.com/hpinfo/globalcitizenship/environment/commitment/goals.html.
[5] "Walmart 2009 Global Sustainability Report," Walmart, http://walmartstores.com/sites/sustainabilityreport/2009/letterMikeDuke.html.
[6] "Overview," Walmart, http://walmartstores.com/sites/sustainabilityreport/2009/en_overview.html.
[7] M. Van Marrewijk, "Concepts and Definitions of CSR and Corporate Sustainability," *Journal of Business Ethics* 44, nos. 2–3 (2003).
[8] M. Hopkins, "The Business of Sustainability," *MIT Sloan Management Review* 51, no. 1 (2009), http://mitsloan.mit.edu/newsroom/2009-smrsustainability.php.
[9] "Rant: Reinventing the Wheel," *My 4-Hour Workweek* (blog), February 13, 2010, http://www.my4hrworkweek.com/rant-reinventing-wheel.
[10] "Walmart's Sustainability Report Reveals Successes, Shortcomings," Greenbiz.com, http://www.greenbiz.com/news/2010/05/12/walmarts-sustainability-report-reveals-successes-shortcomings%20#ixzz0phcjFwWK.

1.4 What Is Required for a Sustainability Perspective?
LEARNING OBJECTIVES

1. Be able to explain what is required to have a sustainability perspective.
2. Understand what it means to have a systems perspective.
3. Describe why a systems perspective is useful for guiding sustainable business practices.

Sustainability and managing a business that works to contribute to sustainability requires a different perspective than many businesses currently have. Most businesses focus on profits, often with a short-term, annual, or even month-to-month focus. Sustainable business practices require a longer term and a systems perspective on how a business organization's actions impact the environment and society. It requires business managers being mindful and considering not only the traditional business concerns, such as revenues, costs, and profits, but also the effects their actions have on the physical environment and the well-being of future generations.

A systems approach can provide an important perspective on sustainability matters. [1] Societal well-being and the sustainability of societal resources are interrelated and relevant for individual businesses and industries as well as for individuals, cities and towns, nations, and the entire planet. For example, on a local community scale, a resource-dependent community economy (e.g., a fishing community in Newfoundland, Canada) cannot achieve economic sustainability if it depletes its most valuable local natural resource—fisheries. On a global scale, global economic activity (by all individuals, households, and businesses collectively) that contributes significantly to greenhouse gas emissions and global warming cannot be sustained if natural resources and human population and health are adversely affected and not sustained.

Starting with the most simple systems perspective we can consider the interdependence between a single company and society as taking two main forms. Every firm impacts society through its operations in the normal course of business—for example, McDonald's with its packaging and BP with its oil drilling. These are called "inside-out" linkages. [2] Then there are "outside-in" linkages with external environmental and societal conditions influencing businesses. For example, McDonald's depending on the supply of food and BP depending on the oil supply.

Another way of thinking about this system is to first think about the consequences of business, for example, how each business affects the economy, the natural environment, and the people (e.g., consumers and employees), and then to think about the context in which businesses operate in,

including the natural, human, and social resources businesses depend on to operate and the legal and regulatory context businesses operate in. Systems thinking would have businesses be mindful and considerate of their operating context and consequences. And systems thinking could help business managers consider how the consequences (outcomes) of their activities affect the context in which they operate in the long term. So for example, if a timber company is depleting a forest it owns, it can think about how this will affect its operating context including its supply costs in the future.

Business's Place in Larger System: A Simple Depiction

Business and the economy are an important part of the greater social system. Businesses and the economy exist within a broader system of laws, cultures, and customs that make up human society. The global social system exists within the broader context of the earth's environment. Businesses, the economy, and society are dependent on the earth's natural resources.

A more complex and dynamic systems approach or perspective defines a system as a set of things that affect one another within an environment and form a larger pattern that is different from any of the parts. When viewed from a systems perspective, organizations engage in the continual stages of input, throughput (processing), and output in an open or closed context. A closed system does not interact with its environment. It does not take in information and therefore is likely to atrophy—that is, to vanish. An open system receives information, which it uses to interact dynamically with its environment. Openness increases the likelihood of survival and prosperity.

Sustainable business practices require an open systems perspective and consideration of how business actions impact not only internal operations and outcomes (such as costs, sales, and profitability) but also external outcomes—that is, the environment and the sustainability of the natural and social systems that businesses are part of.

Systems Conceptual Model

All the systems perspectives highlight how businesses are part of a larger system, and they all suggest the importance of businesses—as major components of the US social and economic system—being mindful and taking into consideration how their activities affect the larger system.

KEY TAKEAWAYS

- Sustainable businesses require a systems perspective.
- The systems perspective enables businesses to understand their position and relationship in the larger environmental and social system, including their dependence on inputs and how their output and use of resources affects the overall system and the elements of the system.
- Without a systems perspective, businesses would not be able to understand their impact on society and the environment.

EXERCISES

1. Do you agree or disagree with the statement "an open system is sustainable while a closed system is not"? Come up with specific examples to support your assertion.
2. In your own words, define what is meant by outside-in linkages and inside-out linkages in a business context. Provide a specific example of each type of linkage.

[1] C. West Churchman, *The Systems Approach* (New York: Delacorte, 1968).
[2] Michael E. Porter, *Competitive Advantage: Creating and Sustaining Superior Performance* (New York: Free Press, 1985).

1.5 The Business Case for Sustainability

LEARNING OBJECTIVES

1. Understand the social responsibilities of business.
2. Describe the stakeholders in corporations.
3. Explain the role of consumers in motivating sustainable business practice.

While the systems perspective is useful as a conceptual framework, there is a need for more practical (and "business-oriented") guidance on sustainable business practices. A pragmatic approach to sustainable business requires moving away from any extreme position: with one extreme having sustainability as solely an additional cost and the other having that it is always beneficial for business to do more to reduce their environmental and societal impact. Neither is particularly useful to guide business practices.

The framing of corporations and their role in society strongly affects the case for and practice of sustainable business. And there are many views of the corporation and private companies and their role/place in a private market economy. The Nobel Prize–winning economist Milton Friedman from the University of Chicago's School of Economics wrote about the social responsibility of business. He described business responsibility as being the achievement of profit in a legal manner. For Friedman, "There is one and only one social responsibility of business—to use its resources and engage in activities to increase its profits so long as it stays within the rules of the game, which is to say, engages in open and free competition, without deception or fraud." [1]

Working from Friedman's perspective businesses should only engage in sustainable business practices if the practices

can directly contribute to their own economic bottom line or if government mandated that business engage in sustainable practices—that is, it was illegal not to do it. Friedman questioned the logic of corporate social responsibility as it had been developing at the time. He insisted that in a democratic society, government, not business, was the only legitimate vehicle for addressing social concerns. He argued that government was the best vehicle for meeting societal concerns, such as environmental sustainability, but many found it difficult to believe, given Friedman's libertarianism, that such an argument was in good faith.

The response of management thinkers to Friedman was to develop alternative views of corporate social responsibility (CSR). Two are presented as follows: the view of stakeholder management and the model of global corporate citizenship, respectively. While there are relevant differences in these, they share important common ground.

Stakeholder engagement is a formal process of relationship management through which companies or industries engage with a set of their stakeholders in an effort to align and advance their mutual interests. This often involves different stakeholders, such as owners, employees and customers, identifying what is in their collective interest. For example, for BP in the future to practice more effective forms of environmental risk management and for Google to invest in renewable energy innovation.

Corporate citizenship *involves corporate management focusing on the net contribution that a company makes through its core business activities, its social investment and philanthropy programs, and its engagement in public policy to society and a broad set of stakeholders. That contribution is determined by the manner in which a company manages its economic, social and environmental impacts and manages its relationships with different stakeholders, in particular shareholders, employees, customers, business partners, governments, communities and future generations.*

The relationship of the models of corporate social responsibility to sustainability is reflected in the values statement of Johnson & Johnson, a company with a strong reputation for corporate citizenship. (Note the "corporate citizenship, **or** sustainability.")

*We see **corporate citizenship**, or **sustainability**, not as a set of "add-ons" to our business but rather as intrinsic to everything we do. We've long recognized that the sustainability of our business depends on being attuned to society's expectations across many domains—including the environment, access to medicines, advocacy, governance and compliance.* [2]

CSR covers the responsibilities corporations have to a broad set of stakeholders, including the communities within which they are based and operate. More specifically, CSR for many management scholars involves a business identifying its key stakeholder groups and incorporating their needs and values within the business's strategic, day-to-day decision-making process.[3] The stakeholders in corporations and any private company include owners and investors, employees, consumers, and all those affected by the actions of the corporation.

A key stakeholder group relevant to sustainable business practices is consumers. The environmental movement in the United States was ignited in the 1970s as an increasing percentage of consumers began to understand that the environment was at risk. Information about this was enhanced with the 1972 publication of *Limits to Growth*, a research study by the MIT Systems Lab and released by the Club of Rome. The book explained the results of computer models that predicted when the world would run out of certain resources. The study presented what was for many at the time a novel finding that the earth's resources were finite. Thirty years after the *Limits of Growth* was published, public interest and concern for the environment was raised to

another level with the emergence of increased scientific evidence of global warming and the human contribution to global warming and the presentation to the general public of the evidence by former US vice president Al Gore in the 2006 movie *An Inconvenient Truth*. The release of the movie was at the same time as the George W. Bush administration was resisting pressure to move forward on federal policy to address global warming.

Increasing numbers of people in the United States and elsewhere turned to business as both the problem and the solution to global warming. Research findings had heightened recognition of businesses as major users of societal resources and major contributors to environmental problems. And with that, there was increased pressure on businesses to be part of the solution to global warming.

Consumers played a very significant role in raising businesses' interest in sustainability. Consumers can use the market (i.e., their purchases) to send a signal to businesses about their concern for the environment and sustainability. Each and every consumer's decision to purchase or not purchase from a company based on the business entities' environmental or sustainability practices directly impacts a company's bottom line. In this way, consumers can be, and increasingly are, a very powerful external force that can motivate companies to become more sustainable in their practices.

The power of consumers and also the opportunity for corporations to influence consumer demand to benefit their sales is reflected in the corporate statement of Green Mountain Coffee as follows:

We're focusing on building demand for sustainable products and evolving our product line to be more sustainable. Once consumers understand the goals of Fair Trade and sustainability—protecting scarce resources, strengthening communities, reducing poverty, and ensuring equity in commercial relationships—they will want to help build a better world.

A new group of environmentally responsible consumers has emerged. They are the lead adopters and others are following. These consumers take into account a variety of factors before they choose to support a company by buying their product. They consider the impact of materials and processes used to manufacture and package goods, how products are distributed and disposed of, a company's broader corporate philosophy on the environment, and even a company's support of public environmental education programs. These factors, among many others, are becoming increasingly important to consumers and consequently to the companies themselves.

According to a 2006 Mintel Research study, the so-called green marketplace was estimated at somewhere between $300 billion to $500 billion a year. And all indications are that it has grown significantly since then. The same study showed that there were approximately thirty-five million Americans who regularly bought green products and that 77 percent of consumers changed their purchasing habits due to a company's green image. Marketing statistics from many different industries support this. Green homes, for example, are estimated to cost between 2 percent to 5 percent more to construct but are valued at 10 percent to 15 percent more in the marketplace. Likewise, organic dairy products are priced typically 15 percent to 20 percent more than conventional ones, and organic meats are often priced two to three times more than traditional meat. [4]

Many companies that have already incorporated sustainability into their business have received benefits in the form of reduced energy and other costs, increased consumer demand, and improved market share. But despite the growing trend of "green purchasing," approximately one-quarter of Americans still do not consciously purchase goods based on a company's sustainability efforts. There is an even larger segment of Americans (approximately 50 percent) that express some level of concern for the environment but may not have the knowledge or commitment required to purchase goods based on a business's efforts in sustainability.

Environmental organizations have responded to this lack of information by providing consumers with resources to make environmentally responsible buying decisions. For example, Climate Counts (http://www.climatecounts.org/scorecard_overview.php) is a nonprofit organization that evaluates, with numerical scores, more than 140 major corporations on their efforts to reverse climate change. Climate Counts publishes these scores so that consumers may use them to support those companies that are showing serious commitment to the environment. The companies are scored on a scale from zero to one hundred based on twenty-two criteria to determine whether a company has

- measured its climate impact,
- reduced its impact on climate change,
- supported (or blocked) progressive climate legislation,
- publicly disclosed its climate actions in a clear and comprehensive format.

In Climate Counts's Winter/Spring 2010 edition of their scorecard, scores ranged from zero to a high of eighty-three. Climate Counts works extensively to educate consumers on corporate sustainability and to encourage them to support companies with scores as close to one hundred as possible.

While Climate Counts focuses on larger corporations, organizations such as the Green Alliance in New Hampshire (http://www.greenalliance.biz) address local companies and their efforts to incorporate sustainability into their business. Based in the Seacoast region of New Hampshire, Green Alliance represents one of the many organizations that spur environmentally responsible purchasing on a local level. Similar to Climate Counts, Green Alliance scores companies to direct consumers to the most sustainable buying options. Similar types of organizations are located in communities across the country and have affected the sustainable business practices of private companies.

Apart from the stakeholder-driven perspective of CSR, another important concept of CSR is the notion of companies looking beyond profits to their role in society. It refers to a company linking itself with ethical values, transparency, employee relations, compliance with legal requirements, and overall respect for the communities in which they operate. With this perspective, CSR moves closer to the sustainable business perspective, as the focus includes managing the impact businesses have on the environment and society.

A path for businesses to adopt sustainable business practices might be thought of as a continuum (see as follows).

1. It can start with Friedman's perspective that businesses adopt sustainable practices because it is a **legal obligation**—governmental laws and regulations require it.
2. It can include, also from Friedman, the pure **profit-driven motive**—businesses adopt sustainable practices because they clearly contribute to corporate profits; for example, it can contribute to brand name recognition and sales. With this motive there is little systematic search for opportunities or embedding of sustainable practices in business.
3. It can include a **balanced values-based approach** in which businesses adopt sustainable business practices from a search for a balanced solution to optimize economic performance and societal benefits.
4. It can include a **systems approach**. Sustainable business practices are fully embedded into every aspect of the business. Businesses have an understanding of the interconnectivity of their business to society over time

and act on it. The focus is on the sustainability of all critical aspects of the system and the influence of the private company on these elements. Business sustainability is valued along with sustainability of environmental, social, and human resource elements in the system.

KEY TAKEAWAYS

- There are many views of the corporation and private companies and their role or place in a private market economy.
- For economist Milton Friedman, there is one and only one social responsibility of business beyond adhering to society's laws and that is to use its resources and engage in activities to increase its profits so long as it stays within the rules of the game.
- Others view the social responsibility of business to include concern for various stakeholders and for the morality and ethics of their practices and their impact on stakeholders.
- For businesses looking to become more sustainable, it can be thought of as a continuum between legal and ethical actions up to a systems perspective.

EXERCISES

1. Do you agree with Milton Friedman's profit-driven philosophy that the purpose of business is to earn a profit and that should be the sole focus of business, with government being responsible for social and environmental issues? Why or why not?
2. Search the web for an article that provides an example of a business that implemented a social or environmental practice that had negative economic impact on the company. Search the web for an article that provides an example of the business that implemented a social environment of practice that had a positive economic impact on the company. Why do you feel the company with a practice that has a negative impact on the company experienced that result? Based on these two articles, do you think that companies should be concerned with sustainability?
3. It can be challenging to think of operating a business with a systems perspective. Think of one example of a sustainability practice that incorporates elements of a systems perspective. Describe the internal and external environment and the linkages between the two and what healthy practices meet the criteria of being considered sustainable.

[1] J. DesJardins, "Corporate Environmental Responsibility," *Journal of Business Ethics* 17, no. 8 (1998).
[2] "Sustainability Report 2008," Johnson & Johnson, http://www.jnj.com/wps/wcm/connect/ad9170804f55661a9ec3be1bb31559c7/2008+Sustainability+Report.pdf?MOD=AJPERES.
[3] M. Milton Friedman, *Capitalism and Freedom* (University of Chicago Press, 1962).
[4] Jay Hasbrouck and Allison Woodruff, "Green Homeowners as Lead Adopters," *Intel Technology Journal* 12, no. 1 (2008): 42.

1.6 A Strategic Approach to Sustainable Business Practice

LEARNING OBJECTIVES

1. Explain how sustainable business practice can be a source of competitive advantage for businesses.
2. Understand what it means for a business to create shared value.
3. Describe how it can be beneficial for society to have businesses acting to address sustainability concerns.

A useful prospective for sustainable business practitioners will be between the balanced values approach and the systems approach. It would use a systems approach, but it would focus on the system from the inside of the business perspective and focus on the business interaction with the external environment.

But how can this systems perspective be incorporated into real-life business practices? The most useful business guidance can be drawn from arguably the most prominent scholar of corporate strategy, Harvard Business School professor Michael Porter. Porter's strategic corporate social responsibility (CSR) model can be applied to sustainability. He rejects the pure stakeholder approach to CSR because stakeholder groups, he believes, can never fully understand a corporation's capabilities, competitive positioning, or trade-

offs it must make and because the loudness of the stakeholder voice does not necessarily signify the importance of an issue—either to the company or to the world. The stakeholder approach, for Porter, is too often used to placate interests or public relations with minimal value to society and to the company. Greenwashing is an example of this, and it has proven to be a failed approach.

Porter's point about CSR that can be applied to sustainability is that sustainable business practices can be much more than a cost, a good deed, or good public relations for businesses—it can be a source of competitive advantage. In his 2006 article with Mark R Kramer, "Strategy and Society: The Link between Competitive Advantage and Corporate Social Responsibility," Porter proposes a new way to look at the relationship between business and society that does not treat corporate profits and societal well-being (including sustainability) as just a balancing exercise. The authors introduce a framework that individual companies can use to identify the social consequences of their actions, to discover opportunities to benefit society and themselves by strengthening the competitive context in which they operate, to determine which CSR or sustainability initiatives they should address, and to find the most effective ways of doing so.

Perceiving social responsibilities, such as acting with attention to sustainability, as an opportunity rather than as damage control or a public relations campaign requires for most private companies to dramatically shift their thinking to a mind-set, the authors argue, that will become increasingly important to competitive success. The principle of sustainability appealing to company's enlightened self-interest works best for issues that coincide with a company's economic interests and when the company has strategically assessed what actions to address. The example of McDonald's using less packaging that reduces company materials and disposal costs at the same time that it helps the environment illustrates this.

Another example is GE and Jack Welch, the famous former CEO of GE. While he was CEO at GE, Jack Welch was often referred to as the greatest CEO of the last century. G. Michael Maddock highlights that "for all the accolades Welch received, those handing out plaudits missed a huge one: He was the King of Green. Six Sigma, the management style (and manufacturing process) he championed, is all about getting leaner: reducing steps, costs, and materials. And lean is green." [1] Lean manufacturing benefited GE, in particular its competitive position, by reducing the company's costs of manufacturing and operations relative to competitors while providing broader societal benefits.

A few corporations such as Stonyfield Farms stand out even more than McDonald's and GE with their exceptional long-term commitment to sustainability. Gary Hirshberg, who refers to himself as the CE-Yo of Stonyfield in his book *Stirring It Up: How to Make Money and Save the World*, highlights how the company has built its entire value proposition around social issues with a focus on environmental actions. [2]

Sidebar
An Example of a Company Value Proposition Driven by Sustainability Objective

Stonyfield Farms value proposition is to sell organic, natural, and healthy food products to customers who care about food quality and the environment.

What Can Companies Do to Deepen Engagement on Sustainability?
Porter and Kramer suggest that companies do the following:
- First, identify their environmental impact (e.g., contribution to carbon emissions).
- Then determine which impact(s) they can benefit the most from addressing.
- Then determine the most effective ways to do so.

For the economy and society overall, businesses' attention to sustainability has already become a source of social progress, as businesses apply considerable attention and resources to reduce their environmental footprint, which benefits their bottom line and also benefits the environment and society more broadly. But most companies are only at the initial stages of the sustainability learning curve.

Sidebar
Competitive Advantage
When a firm sustains profits that exceed the average for its industry, the firm is said to possess a **competitive advantage** over its rivals. The goal of much of business strategy is to achieve a sustainable competitive advantage. Michael Porter identified two basic types of competitive advantage. The first is when the firm is able to deliver the same benefits as competitors but at a lower cost (**cost advantage**). The second is when a firm can deliver benefits that exceed those of competing products (**differentiation advantage**). Thus a competitive advantage enables the firm to create superior value for its customers and superior profits for itself. [3]

What Porter and Kramer suggest is not easy. To enhance sustainable business practices, it must be rooted in an understanding of the interrelations between a corporation and society while at the same time anchored in the activities and strategies of specific companies. No business and no single industry can solve all of society's environmental problems; instead each company can work on environmental issues that intersect with its particular business.

What should guide each and every sustainable business practice is whether it presents an opportunity to create shared value—that it provides a meaningful benefit to society and that it is also valuable to the business. Each company will have to sort through their own sustainability issues and rank them in terms of potential impact. For example, for Toyota, a focus on fuel efficiency with the development and promotion of the highly fuel efficient hybrid vehicle the Prius provided environmental benefits and has been a source of competitive advantage for the company helping it to increase sales and profits. The same is true of Stonyfield and its focus on providing preservative-free, healthy, organic yogurt produced with manufacturing processes that minimize material and energy use.

A corporate sustainability agenda should look beyond stakeholder demands and desires to strategic opportunities to achieve social and company economic benefits simultaneously. This is the move from a strategic approach to sustainable business practices. As the cases in the book will highlight, it is in each company's best interest to identify a manageable number of sustainability initiatives whose shared benefits—to society and to the company—are significant for the company and also distinctive in helping the company strategically position itself in the competitive marketplace. Stonyfield's response to health and environmental concerns with a single basic product, yogurt, and Toyota's response to the concerns over automobile emissions are examples. Strategic sustainable business practices can lead to shared value creation that strengthens a company's competitiveness. Asymbiotic relationship develops. Companies can do well in profits by doing good things for the environment; it is a "win-win" for society and for business.

How do society and future generations benefit? Private companies addressing environmental issues by creating shared value will lead to self-sustaining solutions that do not depend on goodwill or government subsidies. As Porter and Kramer highlight, "When a well run business applies its resources to problems it understands and in which it has a stake, it can have a greater positive impact on social good than any other institutions or philanthropic organization." And if many hundreds and hundreds of thousands of businesses act this way, it is powerful and can have a large impact on society and the world over time. This is the potential of sustainable business practices, which is why it is important to study and understand.

KEY TAKEAWAYS

- Sustainable business practices can be a source of competitive advantage. A sustainable business practice can position companies to have a cost or benefit (differentiation) advantage.
- Creating shared value means providing a meaningful benefit to society, which is also valuable to the business, through an organizational practice or initiative.
- Private companies can create self-sustaining solutions to environmental problems, and when many companies do this, society can benefit significantly.

EXERCISES

1. Identify a company, other than Stonyfield, that takes a strategic approach to sustainable business practices. Describe the strategic approach by the company and its benefits for the company.
2. Read a couple of articles that describe Six Sigma. Discuss the qualities of this management strategy that lead it to be considered sustainable. If Six Sigma is a successful sustainability strategy for business, what might be some barriers to wider adoption by companies?
3. What are some of the pros of considering the stakeholder approach as a sustainability strategy? What are some of the drawbacks of considering the stakeholder approach as a sustainability strategy? Provide some examples of how a small business might integrate the stakeholder approach into its business practices to make it more sustainable.

[1] G. Maddock, "Going Green's Unexpected Advantage," *BusinessWeek*, February 2, 2010, http://www.businessweek.com/managing/content/feb2010/ca2010021_587893.htm.
[2] Gary Hirshberg, *Stirring It Up: How to Make Money and Save the World* (New York: Hyperion Books, 2008).
[3] Michael E. Porter, *Competitive Advantage: Creating and Sustaining Superior Performance* (New York: Free Press, 1985).

NOTES:

Chapter 2:
The Science of Sustainability

LEARNING OBJECTIVES

1. Discuss the key interrelationships among human, earth, and natural systems and why these are important for sustainable businesses.
2. Explain the main ways that businesses and individuals affect ecosystems and the environment.
3. Understand the energy use by businesses in modern society and why this is relevant for sustainable businesses.

Sustainability involves having an understanding of the relationship between business, humanity, and nature. Clean air, drinkable water, food, clean environment, and shelter are fundamental to human survival and to business existence. Natural resources are often taken as a given and not appreciated for how essential they are to human well-being and survival and to business operations. Think for a moment, what life would be like if we did not have clean air to breathe, clean drinking water, or food to eat. And what would businesses do without all these resources and without healthy and productive people and workers. These are all resources originating from natural systems.

Sustainable businesses are concerned about the impact of their organizations on the environment, society, and future generations. To ascertain how humans and business operations impact the natural environment, it is important to understand basic concepts of earth, atmospheric, and ecological systems as well as social and political systems.

Sustainability has evolved into a broad science integrating earth system (e.g., air, water, agriculture) disciplines with social sciences, including economics and sociology, to understand the complex cultural, environmental, and economic interrelationships that exist among humans,

human organizations, and natural systems. Intergenerational equity, or the concept of fairness and justice between different societal groups and future generations, is a key area of concern in the societal component of sustainability.

This chapter integrates discussion of the environment, society, and economics. It begins by discussing two contrasting perspectives of human economic interaction with the environment. One view highlights the ecological limits to growth, and the other highlights how human invention and ingenuity seeks to remove limits to growth. We suggest that these two views are not mutually exclusive—that there are limits to growth but that some of these limits can be addressed and overcome through human and business innovation and adaptation.

The chapter then gives an overview of how earth and natural systems work. This will include descriptions of earth system components and then a focus on threats to well-functioning earth systems. The chapter concludes with a discussion of sustainability science areas that are particularly relevant to business, including how sustainability concepts are being integrated into the economy.

2.1 Sustainability Economics
LEARNING OBJECTIVES

1. Discuss two common views of growth and be able to describe the key features of both views.
2. Understand how both views of growth are relevant for sustainable businesses.

Limits to Growth Concept
The limits to growth concept posits that unlimited economic growth is not possible—that at some point the world's growing population will consume too great a quantity of natural resources (such as clean water and fossil fuels) for human society to exist. Reverend Thomas Robert Malthus (1766–1834) raised the issue of the growing population in the context of limited food resources in his "An Essay on the Principle of Population." He postulated that "population,

when unchecked, increases in a geometric ratio. Subsistence increases only in an arithmetical ratio." [1] In other words, that human growth would outpace the ability of natural resources to keep up. This was in contrast to the overall positive sentiment of the era of continued human progress and improvement, and he viewed humans to "be condemned to a perpetual oscillation between happiness and misery, and after every effort remain still at an immeasurable distance from the wished-for goal." As a reverend, Malthus sought to explain why there was poverty and misery, and he believed the reason to be directly attributable to shortages of resources (means of sustenance, such as food).

The limits to growth perspective reached the global public with the 1972 publication of *Limits to Growth*, a research study by the Massachusetts Institute of Technology (MIT) Systems Lab, released by the Club of Rome. Since its publication, the book has sold millions of copies in thirty different languages. MIT scientists ran a computer simulation of an integrated global model (called World3) that linked the world economy with the environment. The five main variables in the model were world population, industrial production, food production, resource consumption, and pollution. The authors explored interrelationships and feedback patterns by altering growth trends among the five variables.

The model predicted that continued growth in the global economy would lead to global population and economic collapse in the mid-twenty-first century as a result of increased ecological damage and decreased resources. They also found that collapse could be avoided with changes in policy, behavior, and technology.

The study presented, what was for many at the time, a novel finding that the demands of the human population could exceed the carrying capacity of the earth. The MIT group identified the need to stabilize growth so that humans could live within the ability of the earth's natural system to provide a sustainable yield of resources essential to human life. They found that technology alone could prolong but not prevent a system collapse. In an increased technology scenario in which 75 percent of materials were recycled, pollution reduced to 70 percent of 1970 levels, and agricultural land yields increase 100 percent, world collapse was pushed off to the end of the twenty-first century. [2]

Here is an illustrative example of the concept of limits to growth. Assume that five acres of grassland is required to sustainably feed one cow annually. This means that five acres is able to regenerate itself and support the grazing of one cow and that this same cycle of growth and consumption can occur year after year. In other words, the carrying capacity of five acres of grassland is one cow. If you were a farmer with one hundred acres of grassland and you had one cow, there would be more than enough grass available to feed that one cow and have the grass regenerate itself for perpetuity. The farmer could add up to twenty cows on the one hundred acres and every year the grassland would produce enough grass to feed all twenty cows.

Now suppose the farmer wants to increase his annual profits, and he adds another ten cows to the one hundred acres. There probably is enough grass to feed those cows for that year, but now the overgrazing is compromising the ability of the grass to replenish itself. The resource base degrades because the demands on the grassland are greater than its capacity. Perhaps the next year only 90 percent of the grass grows back, and it is not as healthy as before. Continuous overgrazing further degrades the grassland until it is no longer capable of supporting any cattle.

What would happen instead if the farmer believing that he can push profits even further decided to increase the herd size each year by another ten cows? Then the degradation of grassland will proceed at an even faster rate. Even if the farmer does achieve some short-term profitability increase by exploiting the grassland, it is at the expense of productive grassland in the future. Once damaged, it may take years or decades for the grassland to recover or it may never return to its former productive capacity.

This example illustrates the basic concept of limits to growth—that at some point rising resource demand runs into some very hard resource limitations.

No Limits to Growth Concept

It can be argued that throughout most of the nineteenth and twentieth centuries the dominating paradigm in the United States and Europe and most of the developed world has been that there were few limits to economic growth and that economic growth is always desired.

"No limits to growth" is not an articulated theory per se, but it is, to a significant degree, implicit in modern economic thinking. "No limits" thinking highlights the efficacy of the private market. Underpinning "no limits" is the idea that resource scarcity—a major factor in "limits to growth" thinking—can be effectively addressed by economic laws of supply and demand. Laws of supply and demand do work; as resources become scarce, the market will reduce use by increasing the price of those resources.

The market and laws of supply and demand can serve to reduce demand for scarce resources and guide resource allocation to technology and innovation investments that can help address scarce resource concerns. Technology can help reduce resource demand through more efficient use of those resources. For example, a programmable thermostat can more efficiently heat and cool homes than a traditional thermostat. Increased prices will also favor substitution where another resource may be used in place of the scarce resource. An example of this would be building materials or furniture that no longer are produced using 100 percent real wood, as wood has become more scarce and expensive, but instead use wood-laminate and alternative composite materials.

Julian Simon (1932–98), a professor of business administration at the University of Maryland, is often cited in relation the cornucopia theory—that there are no physical limitations on economic growth or human population. In Simon's book *The Ultimate Resource* (published in 1983), he states, "The supply of natural resources is infinite. Almost all trends in environmental quality are positive…There is only one scarcity: Human brain power 'the Ultimate Resource.'" [3] He argued that human ingenuity combined with the correct market signals (pricing) would allow for humans to continually grow economically and the overall human condition would continue to improve, not worsen. He believed that increased consumption would heighten scarcity, which would translate into higher prices, in the short term. This would in turn stimulate entrepreneurship to seek new ways to satisfy shortages. Society eventually ends up better off than if the original shortage had not occurred.

Neoliberalism is a view of the global economic system that holds to the overall tenets of no limits to growth and cornucopian theory. In this view, the private sector, not government, should determine economic and policy priorities. Consistent with a cornucopian viewpoint, neoliberalism views business entrepreneurship (unfettered from government regulations and trade restrictions) as being able to make society better off by letting the marketplace determine the use of resources.

Related to this view of unlimited economic growth are consumerism and the underlying assumption that more consumption is always better for the economy. Consumerism is the belief that our economic systems should favor consumption and that the consumption should be for goods and services that are in excess of basic material needs for survival. Consumerism not only attempts to meet material needs and wants but allows for continuous economic growth. Christine Frederick (1883–1970), a home economist, discussed the need for planned obsolescence in an industrial economy stating, "The way to break the vicious deadlock of a low standard of living is to spend freely, and even waste creatively." [4] In 1955, economist Victor Lebow observed, "Our enormously productive economy…demands that we make consumption our way of life…we need things consumed, burned up, replaced and discarded at an ever-accelerating rate." [5]

Currently, 70 percent of the $14 trillion US economy is driven by consumer spending. A focus on consumption, however, puts tremendous demand on natural resource systems. Natural resources are required to extract, produce, and transport the goods that we purchase, and the extraction, production, and transportation of these goods often release pollution and toxic chemicals in the process. Consumerism is not just limited to the United States, but as globalization of the economy continues, it is becoming universal across the world. Emerging economies such as China, India, Brazil, and Russia have experienced significantly increased demand for goods and services by consumers.

In the chapter on entrepreneurship, innovation, and sustainability, the market opportunities created by scarce resources are highlighted. The chapter will discuss how market signals regarding scarce resources can provide business opportunities for sustainable businesses.

Reconciling Limits and No Limits to Growth
The two views of limits to growth are both important for the business context of sustainability. Both views, at a fundamental level, influence sustainability discussions at a personal, business, and societal level. The earth does have limited resources and human activity can negatively impact the environment. Market forces are often effective in providing signals to society of resource scarcity and the need to change, innovate, and adapt. But even with the overall efficacy of markets, there are limits to the efficacy of the market perspective. Markets often fail to properly price natural resources that are treated as free goods, and this makes limits to growth a reality. Both arguments make important points that frame discussions of sustainability.

Tragedy of the Commons
An important concept relevant for sustainability is the "tragedy of the commons." This phrase was coined by the ecologist Garrett Hardin in a 1968 article in *Science*. [6] The tragedy of the commons describes a situation where different parties share a common good (such as open public land), and acting independently in their own self-interest, they will ultimately overexploit and deplete or destroy the shared resource. The tragedy is that the individuals acting in a way that they believe is in their own best interest end up acting in a way that is detrimental to their collective and individual long-term best interests.

There are numerous examples of tragedy of the commons in modern life and the environment, including polluting the atmosphere, overharvesting fish stocks (see "What Happened to All the Fish" as follows), and polluting waterways. Related to our cattle example in the limits to growth discussion mentioned previously, tragedy of the commons can be illustrated in a simplified example involving cattle. If several cattle herders share a common (publicly shared) area of land and all herders are entitled to let their cattle graze on that land without restriction, there is the potential for tragedy of the commons to occur.

For each individual herder, it is in their self-interest to maximize their profitability by placing as many cattle as possible on the land. There is no direct incremental resource cost to the herder for each cow they add to the shared land, and the herder has increased revenue through greater cattle sales. If each herder acted in this manner, the quality of the common resource can be either temporarily or permanently damaged as a result of overgrazing if the total cattle population exceeds the carrying capacity of the shared land. Once carrying capacity is exceeded, all are negatively impacted, including, ironically, the herders who added to their cattle stock.

In this system, each herder receives all the benefits from adding additional cattle, while the resource damage to the common land is shared by all herders. What should also be noted is there is no economic incentive in this example for a herder to withhold cattle from the land because even if one herder chose not to add additional cattle over concern about damaging the shared land, there is nothing to prevent another herder from adding more cattle resulting in the same end result of a depleted resource.

KEY TAKEAWAYS

- There are two main views of economics as pertains to sustainability: limits to growth and no limits to growth. Both views have merits in terms of explaining the interaction of society and environment.
- The limits to growth concept argues that our current society is living beyond what Earth is capable of providing and that we must change to live within the context of what Earth can provide.
- The no limits to growth concept argues that market signals and technological innovation can overcome limits to growth in natural systems.
- Tragedy of the commons occurs often in shared environmental resources, and understanding the system dynamics is essential to sustainability of shared natural resources.
- Consumerism is a factor in driving economic growth in modern economies and, as a result, resource depletion.

EXERCISES

1. Discuss the merits of both limits to growth perspectives.
2. In an online journal, find an article that illustrates an example of tragedy of the commons. Identify the "commons," the individual actors, and the consequence of the situation.

[1] Thomas Robert Malthus, *An Essay on the Principle of Population* (London: J. Johnson in St. Paul's churchyard, 1798).
[2] *The Limits to Growth: A Report for the Club of Rome's Project on the Predicament of Mankind* (New York: Universe Books, 1972).
[3] Julian Simon, *The Ultimate Resource* (Princeton University Press, 1983).
[4] Christine Frederick, *The New Housekeeping: Efficiency Studies in Home Management* (Doubleday, Page & Company, 1913).
[5] Victor Lebow, "Price Competition in 1955," *Journal of Retailing*, Spring 1955.
[6] Garrett Hardin, "The Tragedy of the Commons," *Science* 162, no. 3859 (1968): 1243–48.

2.2 Life and Climate System of Earth

LEARNING OBJECTIVES

1. Understand basic concepts of Earth's history and ecology.
2. Identify key natural resources.
3. Understand the interaction between ecosystem services and human well-being.

Brief History

The earth has sustained a wide and abundant variety of life for millions and millions of years, with the origin of life on Earth estimated to have begun 3.5 billion years ago. Humans only arrived in the last 500,000 years, or 0.01 percent of the total history of life on the planet. The forms of life and the climate have changed continuously and sometimes drastically over that time. The earth's history is divided into three geological eras, but the most recent and the one that we currently live in is the Cenozoic, which began 65.5 million years ago. The most significant features of the Cenozoic era are a long-term cooling of the earth, the rise and diversification of mammals, and the evolution of humans.

Previous eras featured a much warmer planet, a different atmospheric system, and a wide variety of life.

A significant feature of the climate over the last 2.6 million years has been "ice ages," which are a continuous fluctuation between relatively cold (glacial) and warm (interglacial) periods. Glaciations are periods of extremely cold climate where a greater portion of the earth is covered with ice and snow. Interglacials are intermittent warming periods between glaciations, which feature a melting and retreat of ice from large portions of Earth. In the last 800,000 years there have seen eight glacial cycles—one occurring about every 100,000 years—with the last glaciation ending about 12,500 years ago. Currently we are in an interglacial time period. This last interglacial period is known as the Holocene and features the rise of modern human civilization and the current climate and earth system.

The glacial cycles are the result of a complex interaction of factors, including atmospheric composition (such as the concentration of carbon dioxide and methane), variations in the earth's orbit, movement of tectonic plates, and changes in solar output. Of the different factors, periodic changes in the earth's orbit, tilt, and precession (wobbling around its axis) are believed to be a major driver for ice ages when they occur in a specific combination that reduce the amount of sunlight reaching the earth. These changes are also known as Milankovitch cycles, named after the Serbian mathematician who theorized that these orbital changes were the cause of the ice ages. It is important to understand natural past climate change in the context of man's impact on global climate change, which will be discussed later on in this chapter.

Ecology

Ecology is the study of life forms and their interaction and their relationship with the environment with a focus on how biological systems remain diverse, healthy, and productive. Ecosystems are the "webs" or complex patterns of interactions among a network of life in a specific place on Earth. Wetlands, forests, grasslands, coral reefs, and coastal estuaries are all examples of ecosystems. They are an interaction of living (biotic) and nonliving (abiotic) elements in a specific geographic area.

Healthy ecosystems are important to human society as they provide life-sustaining goods and services, including clean air to breathe, clean water to drink, plants and animals as food sources, and raw materials for clothing and shelter. The goods and services produced by natural systems that benefit humans are called ecosystem services. These goods and services lack a formal market and are not included in

traditional economic measures like GDP. They are often viewed as "public goods" or societal benefits.

Environmental changes can impact the life that an ecosystem can sustain. Severe or rapid changes can reduce the carrying capacity of an ecosystem and result in the loss of living organisms. Severe and permanent loss of animal species is called extinction. In the history of Earth there have been five major mass extinction events—meaning large number of species have died off dramatically: Ordovician (450 million years ago), Devonian (375 million years ago), Permian (251 million years ago), Triassic (205 million years ago), and Cretaceous (66 million years ago). The worst mass extinction is believed to be the Triassic extinction when over 90 percent of species on Earth died off. Evidence suggests that it can take millions of years for new species to recover after a mass extinction event.

In addition to these more well-defined mass extinction periods, there are many other extinction events that have occurred over the course of Earth's history. Causes of past mass extinction have included dramatic changes in climate (warming or cooling), atmospheric changes, dramatic changes in sea level, changes in oxygen levels in the sea, and changes in land structure.

Currently, the Holocene extinction is occurring. This is a widespread extinction that has been ongoing for approximately the last ten thousand years. It is estimated that currently up to 140,000 species are lost every year. The Holocene extinction is characterized by human-driven activities, including habitat loss, overpredation, and, most recently, human-induced climate change. During the last century the rate of decrease in biodiversity has been increasing. [1]

Ross MacPhee and Clare Flemming of the department of mammalogy at the American Museum of Natural History researched mammal extinctions since 1500 AD. They identified ninety species of mammals that have become extinct during the modern era of European expansion. This is 2 percent of all mammal species on Earth. The natural rate of mammal species extinction is estimated to be one mammal species every 400 years, the loss of 90 species in 500 years is a 7,100 percent increase over the natural rate. [2] Example of animal species that have become extinct due to human activity include the dodo bird, Falkland Islands wolf, Atlas bear, eastern cougar, passenger pigeon, and the western black rhinoceros.

Earth's Resources

A basic understanding of the key resources that support the earth is essential for businesses that are concerned with sustainability. These resources support a healthy planet with rich and diverse plant and animal life. Sustainable businesses consider the impacts of their actions on these key resources.

Energy

The earth system has three primary sources that affect the flow of energy on Earth. They are solar, geothermal, and tidal. The sun (solar) is a powerful source of energy on Earth and life on Earth could not exist without it. Geothermal is the energy from within the earth and includes volcanoes and earthquakes. Tidal movement of the oceans is caused by the orbiting of the moon around the earth.

Energy is defined as the ability to do work. Work is defined as the application of a force over a distance. Energy can be divided into two broad categories: potential and kinetic. Potential energy is stored energy that has the potential to do work, such as the energy stored in a battery or fuel, while kinetic energy is energy in motion, such as waves crashing against a beach. Energy can be transferred from one form to another. Within the broad categories of potential and kinetic energy, energy can come in many different forms, including chemical, nuclear, mechanical, thermal, electrical, solar, and others.

The earth's resources, which man uses to power modern society, are classified as either renewable or nonrenewable. Renewable energy refers to energy, including electricity, generated from sources that will not be depleted if used in a sustainable manner. Although the specific technologies that are considered renewable vary, they are generally considered to include solar, wind, geothermal, biomass, and hydro.

Renewable energy resources provide an alternative to more prevalent means of electrical power generation, including coal, nuclear, natural gas, and oil. These sources of energy are nonrenewable and will be depleted at some point in the future.

Nuclear Energy Promise and Problems

Nuclear energy is an energy source that has tremendous potential for increased global power generation as its fuel source is not fossil fuel based and does not involve combustion. This serves to provide a hedge against volatile fossil fuel prices and has the benefit of no air pollution emissions from power generation (including greenhouse gas emissions). It also is a technology that is capable of generating large amounts of energy. This has led some to claim that nuclear power is a viable clean energy technology for the future. However, this power source is not without issues.

Nuclear power involves hazardous, radioactive materials that can cause cancer and death with exposure. A history of infrequent, but damaging, power plant accidents has historically hampered investment in this technology in the United States. A nuclear meltdown occurred in 1979 at the Three Mile Island power plant in Pennsylvania, which resulted in the release of radioactive gases. In 1986, an explosion at the Chernobyl Nuclear Power Plant in Ukraine released large quantities of nuclear contamination into the atmosphere. And most recently, in 2011, a tidal wave damaged the Fukushima I Nuclear Power Plant resulting in the full meltdown of three nuclear reactors. All of these accidents have come with high economic costs for the damage and subsequent environmental remediation.

An example of how energy is transformed from one form to another can be seen in the operation of a car. It takes work to move a car down a road. The chemical potential energy stored in gasoline is transferred into thermal energy when the gasoline combusts in the car's engine. The thermal energy released in the engine moves pistons in the engine transforming the thermal energy into mechanical energy. Through gears and other mechanical parts on the cars, the mechanical energy in the engine is transferred through the car resulting in the rotation of the tires, which move the car. The potential energy stored in the fuel is transformed into kinetic energy of the moving car.

A common measurement unit of energy is the British thermal unit (BTU). A BTU is the amount of heat energy required to increase the temperature of a pound of water by one degree Fahrenheit. A BTU is approximately equal to the amount of heat given off by burning a kitchen match. As a BTU is a relatively small unit, BTUs are often stated in larger units, therms or MMBTU. Therms or thermal units are equal to one hundred thousand BTUs. MMBTU is equal to one million BTUs. To help provide some context, a typical residential water heater has a heat output rating of about forty thousand BTU per hour. The average commercial boiler in the United States has an output ability of 9.6 MMBTU per hour. [3]

In terms of electricity, the common unit of energy is the kilowatt hour or kWh. However, as the kilowatt hour is a unit of energy, electricity usage can also be expressed in terms of BTUs, with 1 kWh equal to 3412 BTUs. The units for energy used vary by country. For example, in the United States, engine power is related in terms of horsepower (HP) while in other countries it is rated in terms of kilowatts (kW). The 2012 Honda Civic's engine is advertised as 140 HP in the United States and 103 kW in European countries. Both measures indicate the same amount of power.

Biodiversity

Biodiversity is the result of 3.5 billion years of evolution. Biodiversity is an indicator of the health of an ecosystem. Higher degrees of biodiversity imply greater ecosystem health. Biodiversity not only strengthens the overall health of the planet but also provides vital benefits to humans. Biodiversity is important in agriculture as it provides different varieties of plants and animals for human consumption. Biodiversity helps protect other natural resources, including water and soil. A significant portion of medicine is derived directly or indirectly from organic sources. Industry relies on biological inputs, such as timber, paper, and fiber. Biodiversity also provides leisure, cultural, and aesthetic value.

Sidebar

Why Is Biodiversity Important?

"At least 40 percent of the world's economy and 80 percent of the needs of the poor are derived from biological resources. In addition, the richer the diversity of life, the greater the opportunity for medical discoveries, economic development, and adaptive responses to such new challenges as climate change." [4]

Source: Convention on Biological Diversity.

Goods and Services Provided by Ecosystems with High Biodiversity

- Food, fuel, and fiber
- Shelter and building materials
- Purification of air and water
- Detoxification and decomposition of wastes
- Stabilization and moderation of the earth's climate
- Moderation of floods, droughts, temperature extremes, and the forces of wind
- Generation and renewal of soil fertility, including nutrient cycling
- Pollination of plants, including many crops
- Control of pests and diseases
- Maintenance of genetic resources as key inputs to crop varieties and livestock breeds, medicines, and other products
- Cultural and aesthetic benefits

Plant and animal species have been disappearing at a rate at least fifty times greater than the natural rate, and this rate is predicted to rise as human activities continue to put demands on ecosystems. Based on current trends, an estimated 34,000 plant and 5,200 animal species face extinction. Agriculture biodiversity is under extreme pressure due to modern commercial agriculture, which has focused on a few specific species of plant and many farm animal breeds are at risk of extinction. [5]

While the loss of individual species is of great concern, of even greater concern is the continued degradation and loss of some of the world's richest ecosystems, including forests, wetlands, and coral reefs. These ecosystems are host to some of the greatest biodiversity on Earth and the loss of these ecosystems is the greatest threat to biodiversity.

The loss of biodiversity reduces the productivity of ecosystems. It weakens ecosystems and reduces their ability to be resilient to extreme natural events, such as floods, droughts, and human activity stresses. While the loss of species has always occurred as a natural phenomenon, the pace of extinction has accelerated dramatically as a result of human activity. This loss of life not only reduces the ecosystems goods and services available to the current generation of humans but also harms future generations as well.

Water

Water covers more than 70 percent of the earth's surface and is vital to all forms of life. Oceans hold 97 percent of surface waters, glaciers and the ice caps hold 2.4 percent, with lakes, rivers, and other land surface waters making up the remaining 0.6 percent. Water is a vital resource to humans as it is required as drinking water; it is an essential input for agriculture; and it provides for sanitation, transportation, energy generation, food processing, and power generation (through hydroelectric plants or dams). Increases in population and current water use practices are expected to increase water consumption in food production by up to 90 percent. [6]

Currently, one in six people in the world lack safe drinking water, and water-related illness is the leading cause of human sickness and death. In 1989, there were 9,000 cubic meters of freshwater per capita available for human use. By 2000, this had dropped to 7,800 cubic meters, and it is expected to continue to decrease as human population increases. [7] Global per capita figures on water availability are somewhat misleading as the world's available freshwater supply is not distributed evenly geographically, seasonally, or annually. Water distribution is dependent on Earth's hydrological cycle. The movement of water is part of a natural cycle of evaporation into the atmosphere, precipitation, and then runoff across the land and into streams, rivers, and lakes. This cycle is powered by the sun, which serves to move clean water about the planet.

Soil

Soil consists of layers of minerals that vary in characteristics across different geographic regions and ecosystems. Soil consists of both organic and inorganic components. Soil is a primary nutrient base for plants and therefore is important to humans for agriculture. Without soil, the earth would not support a rich base of plant and animal life, and it is an essential resource to consider in human interactions with the environment.

KEY TAKEAWAYS

- Sustainable businesses must have a basic understanding of key resources on Earth and the impact their business activities have on these resources.
- In the earth system, there are many critical resources to consider, including energy, biodiversity, water, and soil.

EXERCISES

1. Find an article from a business publication or website that talks about how a business considered its impact on a natural resource and included its impact on that resource as well as profitability in the action it took on a specific business operation. Describe the operation, the resource involved, and the environmental and economic outcome of the transaction. If you were CEO of that company, would you have made the same decision?

2. Go to the United Nations Environment Programme's website, and read the report "21 Issues for the 21st Century." The report is available at http://www.unep.org/publications/ebooks/foresightreport/Portals/24175/pdfs/Foresight_Report-21_Issues_for_the_21st_Century.pdf. Identify an issue highlighted in the report and discuss a potential business idea that could address that issue. Discuss how the company could generate profits while at the same time addressing a contemporary sustainability issue.

[1] "Biodiversity Loss Accelerating, UN Target Will Be Missed," Environmental News Service, October 13, 2009, http://www.ens-newswire.com/ens/oct2009/2009-10-13-01.html.
[2] Ross D. E. MacPhee and Clare Flemming, "Brown-Eyed, Milk-Giving…and Extinct: Losing Mammals Since A.D. 1500," *Natural History*, April 1997.
[3] "Characterization of the U.S. Industrial Commercial Boiler Population," Oak Ridge National Laboratory, http://www.cibo.org/pubs/industrialboilerpopulationanalysis.pdf.
[4] "The DAC Guidelines: Integrating the Rio Conventions into Development Co-Operation," OECD, Annex 2, 2002.
[5] "Sustaining Life on Earth," Convention on Biological Diversity, http://www.cbd.int/convention/guide/?id=changing.
[6] "Agriculture at a Cross Roads: International Assessment of Agricultural Science and Technology for Development Global Report," UNEP, http://www.agassessment.org/reports/IAASTD/EN/Agriculture%20at%20a%20Crossroads_Global%20Report%20(English).pdf.
[7] United Nations Educational, Scientific, and Cultural Organization (UNESCO), "The Makings of a Water Crisis: Can Supply Keep Up with Demand?" *UNESCO Sources*, no. 84 (1996): 12–13.
[8] http://ga.water.usgs.gov/edu/watercycle.html.

2.3 Human Activity Impacts on Ecosystems
LEARNING OBJECTIVES

1. Identify five threats to ecosystems from human activities.
2. Understand what factors affect climate change and what the current trajectory and implications of climate change are for the next century.
3. Discuss the role of population, affluence, and technology in driving human impacts.

Business and human activities can be direct threats to ecosystems. They can cause destruction, degradation, and the impairment of biodiversity and other natural resources. Ecosystem threats include (1) climate change, (2) pollution, (3) habitat destruction, (4) overexploitation, and (5) introduction of invasive species. Business and human activities can stress the ecosystem they operate in reducing its overall health and at some point the accumulation of all negative impact from human activities can exceed the

ecological threshold of the planet. Driving these human activities are population, affluence, and technology.

Climate Change

Climate change is one of the greatest threats to sustainability. It is a controversial and contested topic. As highlighted in the previous section, the earth's climate does fluctuate over time due to a variety of factors. However, there is a significant body of scientific research that indicates that global temperatures are rising and that rising global temperatures are directly linked to human activities involving the emissions of greenhouse gases (GHG). [1] GHG traps heat in the atmosphere allowing the planet to be a habitable place. The primary GHG of interest is carbon dioxide (CO_2), which is a vital gas in our earth system and is released from various sources, including the combustion of fossil fuels. Over the last two centuries, rapid industrialization and the corresponding increased burning of fossil fuels and deforestation of large tracts of land globally has caused the concentrations of greenhouse gases to increase significantly in our atmosphere. Current atmospheric carbon dioxide levels exceed the natural range observed over at least the last 800,000 years and are rapidly rising.

In January 2012, global carbon dioxide levels reached a high of 393 parts per million (ppm) at the Mauna Loa Observatory in Hawaii. This was up from 391 ppm from January 2011 and continues a long-term trend of rising levels of carbon dioxide in the atmosphere. [2] The Mauna Loa Observatory has been performing continuous monitoring of atmospheric carbon dioxide since 1956.

Some greenhouse gases, such as carbon dioxide, occur naturally and are emitted to the atmosphere through natural processes and human activities. Other greenhouse gases (e.g., fluorinated gases) are created and emitted solely through human activities. Not all greenhouse gases have the same impact. Global warming potential (GWP) is a relative measure of how much heat a greenhouse gas traps in the atmosphere. GWP is standardized to carbon dioxide, which has a GWP of one.

The principal greenhouse gases that enter the atmosphere because of human activities—also called anthropogenic—are as follows:

- Carbon dioxide (CO_2; 72 percent of anthropogenic emissions; GWP of one)—emitted through the burning of fossil fuels (oil, natural gas, and coal), solid waste, trees and wood products, and chemical processes.
- Methane (CH_4; 18 percent of anthropogenic emissions; GWP of twenty-five)—emitted during the production of coal, natural gas, and oil; from livestock and other agricultural practices; and by the rotting of organic waste in municipal solid waste landfills.
- Nitrous oxide (N_xO; 9 percent of anthropogenic emissions; GWP of 298)—emitted during agricultural and industrial activities as well as during combustion of fossil fuels and solid waste.
- Fluorinated gases (< 1 percent of anthropogenic emissions; HFC-23 has a GWP of 14,800)—emitted

from a variety of industrial processes and sometimes used as substitutes for ozone-depleting substances (i.e., CFCs, HCFCs, and halons). Although fluorinated gases are typically emitted in smaller quantities, they are potent greenhouse gases sometimes referred to as high global warming potential gases ("high GWP gases").

Average global temperatures have increased 1.3 degrees Fahrenheit since 1850, with the trend in warming in the last fifty years being almost double that of the prior one hundred years. The twentieth century's last two decades were the warmest in four hundred years. Current projections have global temperature further increasing by a significant two degrees to twelve degrees Fahrenheit by 2100. [3] Temperature increases of this magnitude will adversely affect the planet through rising sea levels, shrinking glaciers, changing of the range and distribution of plants and animals, lengthening of growing seasons, changing of weather patterns, and human health effects. People are affected by climate change through extreme periods of heat and cold, storms, climate sensitive diseases, prolonged and increased levels of smog, and economics (e.g., volatility in retail prices; resource scarcity; and changing work patterns, conditions, and incomes). [4]

Changes in global temperature are impacting the global climate in significant ways, including the following:

- Mountain glaciers and snow cover have declined significantly, contributing to rises in sea level. For example, Montana's Glacier National Park now has only 27 glaciers, versus 150 in 1910. In the Northern Hemisphere, thaws also come a week earlier in spring and freezes begin a week later.
- Sea levels will rise dramatically. Thermal expansion has already raised the oceans four to eight inches (ten to twenty centimeters). There is a possibility for a three-foot sea rise by the end of the century, which would flood many cities along the US seaboard. [5]
- Average Arctic temperatures have increased at almost twice the global rate in the past one hundred years. Arctic ice is rapidly disappearing, and the region may have its first completely ice-free summer by 2040 or earlier. Polar bears and indigenous cultures are already suffering from the sea's ice loss.
- Increased precipitation has been observed in the eastern parts of North and South America, northern Europe, and northern and central Asia.
- An upsurge in the amount of extreme weather events, such as wildfires, heat waves, and strong tropical storms, is also attributed in part to climate change by some experts. Examples of these types of extreme events are

already occurring with greater frequency, including recent flooding in Nashville and extreme droughts in Russia.

- Coral reefs, which are highly sensitive to small changes in water temperature, suffered the worst bleaching—or die-off in response to stress—ever recorded in 1998, with some areas seeing bleach rates of 70 percent. Experts expect these sorts of events to increase in frequency and intensity in the next fifty years as sea temperatures rise. Coral systems are rich ecosystems providing breeding grounds for sea life and are major recreational draws. The loss of these vital resources has a devastating economic impact on local economies.

Current science suggests that to significantly reduce the threats of global climate change, worldwide reductions of carbon dioxide emissions by 80 percent below current levels will be required by 2050. [6]

In 2008, global carbon dioxide emissions were 4.8 metric tons per capita. The highest per capita emission was Qatar with 49 metric tons per capita caused by their high emitting gas production sector and their small populations. The United States was the tenth highest per capita emitter of carbon dioxide emissions at 17.9 metric tons per capita. Even though China had the highest absolute level of emissions, it was ranked seventy-ninth at 5.3 metric tons of CO_2 per capita. [8] Per capita emissions are on average higher in developed economies than emerging economies. Countries that were members of the Organisation for Economic Co-operation and Development (OECD) had average emissions of 10.5 metric tons per capita while countries that were classified by the United Nations as the least developed countries had per capita missions of 0.24 metric tons per capita.

It is important to note that there are those that deny the significance of climate change on the human condition and the impact of human and business activity on climate change. Climate change denial dismisses the scientific consensus on the extent of global warming, its significance, and its connection to human behavior. As will be highlighted in the next chapter, climate change denial has been mostly associated with the energy lobby and free market think tanks, often in the United States.

A 2010 paper in the *Proceedings of the National Academy of Sciences of the United States* (PNAS) reviewed publication and citation data for 1,372 climate researchers and drew the following two conclusions: [9]

1. Of the climate researchers most actively publishing in the field, 97 percent to 98 percent support the tenets of ACC (Anthropogenic Climate Change) outlined by the Intergovernmental Panel on Climate Change.
2. The relative climate expertise and scientific prominence of the researchers unconvinced of ACC are substantially below that of the convinced researchers.

Pollution

Pollution is the contamination, harm, or disruption of the natural environment through the emissions of harmful substances. Pollution is most typically associated with anthropogenic sources but can also occur from natural activity, such as volcanic eruptions. Pollution can impact air, water, and land. Pollutants include domestic, industrial, and agricultural waste. It comes in many different forms and can be chemical substances or noise, heat, or light.

Pollution can be either point source or nonpoint source. Point source is a specific and easily identifiable source of pollution, such as a factory or power plant. Nonpoint sources consist of many small, distributed sources of a pollutant that are difficult to individually identify and on their own may not be that harmful but in aggregate are significant sources of pollution. A classic example of nonpoint source would be soap detergents, fertilizers, and other commonly used chemicals and products from many residences and businesses that then contaminate watersheds with high levels of nitrogen. Nonpoint sources tend to be more complex to regulate for pollution emissions.

Pollution is not just toxic substances; it can be pollutants that are actually part of a healthful ecosystem in the proper quantities, such as nitrogen or carbon dioxide, but that in excessive quantities alter the normal functioning of an ecosystem resulting in harm to the ecosystem. Pollution can range from highly dangerous radioactive materials to airborne dust (a substance that is typically benign) resulting from land erosion.

Air pollution, the contamination of the atmosphere by airborne pollutants, is most often related to combustion of fuel from either stationary or mobile sources. Stationary sources include the smoke stacks of factories, power plants, and furnaces or boilers. Mobile sources refer to motor vehicles, aircraft, and other forms of fossil-fuel-based transportation. Paints, chemicals, and aerosol sprays also can pollute the air. Natural sources of air pollution include dust, methane from livestock, volcanic activity, wildfires, and even vegetation.

Concerns over air pollution are not just a modern occurrence but date back many centuries. In 1272, King Edward I banned the burning of sea-coal in England after the smoke was having deleterious effects on the city of London. In fact, the punishment was pretty steep—death by hanging. And it was a punishment that was enforced. Nowadays, fines are a more typical punishment for any type of pollution.

In the United States, California has led the nation in regulating the emissions of air pollution, primarily because it was one of the first states in the nation to locally observe the detrimental impacts of air pollution. Los Angeles has been the focus point for air pollution in California with severe bouts of smog for at least the past one hundred years. The first "officially" recognized episode of smog occurred in Los Angeles during the summer of 1943. Visibility was reduced to three blocks and people suffered from stinging eyes, difficulty breathing, nausea, and vomiting. [10]

Growing concern over the harmful environmental impacts of industry motivated the US environmental movement in the 1960s and 1970s. The movement resulted in the passage of many major environmental laws that impact the business climate of the United States today.

Pollution continues to be a major focus globally. China, which has become increasingly industrialized, now finds that half of its water can no longer be used for human consumption and over a quarter is so toxic that it is unsafe even for industrial use. [11]

Municipal Solid Waste

Municipal solid waste (MSW) is a waste product that becomes a form of pollution if not properly managed. MSW is more commonly thought of as garbage, refuse, or trash. Solid waste is not necessarily toxic but includes discarded materials that need to be properly processed and disposed. Examples of solid waste include household trash, used tires, discarded appliances, furniture, paints, and construction and demolition debris.

In 2008, the United States generated 389.5 million tons of solid waste. Only 24 percent of the waste was recycled, 6 percent was burned to produce energy, and the remaining 69 percent was landfilled. [12] With 70 percent of waste being sent to landfills, there is still considerable opportunity for waste recovery for recycling or as an energy source.

Energy can be recovered from landfill sites through different forms, such as methane gas. Methane gas can be used to generate electricity or be burned as a heat source. However,

the vast majority of waste is being disposed of, even though it contains resources (metals, plastics, and paper) that could be reused or recycled to reduce the demand on new resources. For example, cardboard that is recycled helps reduce the demand for trees to be cut down to make new cardboard.

The EPA encourages MSW to be managed through source reduction, recycling, and composting. Source reduction involves taking steps to reduce the waste material produced. This can include using materials more efficiently, reusing materials, or switching to substitutes that generate less waste. The average US recycling rate is 24 percent but has the potential to be considerably higher. [13] There are opportunities for new sustainable businesses to better manage solid waste, including increasing the recycling rate and composting.

Ecomovement Consulting Composts Restaurant Leftovers

Portsmouth, New Hampshire, has one of the highest numbers of restaurants per capita in the country and these restaurants generate a large volume of food waste that is expensive to dispose of. Entrepreneurs Rian Bedard and partner Marcel Miranda saw this waste as an opportunity and formed Ecomovement Consulting and Hauling (http://zerowastenow.com/) in 2009. Bedard stated, "I started to find out that no one was offering zero-waste services and everyone wanted it."

Customers pay for compostable bags and put the food waste in a recycling tote outside, which are then collected regularly by Ecomovement. The food waste is then brought to a local farm to be converted to compost, a high-value soil component sought after by gardeners and landscapers. In addition to restaurants, other large food waste generators have signed up with Ecomovement, including hospital cafeterias. In North America, only two cities can boast that all of their restaurants compost, but with an entrepreneurial company finding a niche missed by traditional waste management companies, Portsmouth is well on its way to becoming the third. [14]

Ecomovement Consulting can be followed on Facebook at http://www.facebook.com/pages/EcoMovement-Consulting-Hauling/172316763400.

Habitat Destruction

Habitat destruction brought on by the activity of humans threatens resident species and ecosystems. Two examples of habitat destruction are deforestation and desertification.

Deforestation occurs when a forest or stand of trees is removed, converting the land to a nonforest use. This changes the ecosystem drastically and results in a dramatic loss of biodiversity. Deforestation can be the result of timber harvesting or of clearing land for agricultural, commercial, or residential use. The loss of biodiversity and trees alters the ecosystem and can result in aridity and erosion. It also results in climate change and extinction, and it can lead to desertification if on a significant enough scale. The social impacts can include displacement of indigenous peoples.

Desertification is the degradation of land quality and features low biodiversity, dry conditions, and poor soil quality. Deserts are formed through both natural processes and human activity. However, desertification is occurring at a greater rate than past geological time scales due to human activity. The concept of desertification became well known in the United States in the 1930s, when parts of the Great Plains in the United States turned into the "Dust Bowl" as a result of drought and poor agricultural practices. [15]

Overexploitation

Overexploitation is a major threat to ecosystems and therefore sustainability. It is the consumption of a natural resource at a rate greater than that natural resource can maintain itself. Overhunting of species (see "What Happened to All the Fish" as follows) is one of the clearest examples of overexploitation, but there are other forms. Land degradations are human-induced changes that impair the capacity of the land to sustain life. Deforestation and overgrazing exploit the land and result in the exceeding of sustainable yield.

What Happened to All the Fish?

The Grand Banks along the shores of Newfoundland, Canada, were once so full of cod that explorer John Cabot remarked in 1497 that they appeared so thick that a person "could walk across their backs," and sailors reported to be able to catch them just by throwing buckets over the side of the ship. From 1850 to 1950, the fishing industry yielded an overall annual catch of about 200,000 tons of cod. With new technology in commercial fishing boats, catches of cod increased in the late 1950s and early 1960s, peaking at 800,000 tons in 1968. Commercial fishing was catching cod faster than their stock could replenish itself, and by 1975, the catch had declined to 300,000 tons. The catch continued at approximately this level through the 1990s but only through the use of more damaging fishing techniques. In 1992, the cod fishery off Newfoundland collapsed. It was estimated that the entire cod population in the Grand Banks at that time

was only 1,700 tons. In response, Canada set an indefinite moratorium on fishing in the Grand Banks. This collapse devastated the local economy with the loss of forty thousand jobs in the fishing industry. In response, the federal government put up nearly a $1 billion to assist with social welfare payments and retraining of people employed in the fishery trade.

The case of the cod in Newfoundland illustrates how the unsustainable harvesting of a resource, when the yield reduces the overall base of that resource, is not only bad for the environment but also bad for industry and for the economy. Overfishing and habitat destruction damaged nature's ability to provide fish in the Grand Banks. This resulted in a loss to a significant portion of the eastern Canadian economy and the members of the fishery communities experienced true hardship due to the overfishing. Prior to the overfishing that occurred during the second half of the twentieth century, the fish had supported seaside communities for hundreds of years.

Invasive Species

Invasive species are brought on by transporting species either intentionally or accidentally from other areas of the world. This can be devastating to existing species as invasive species are introduced on a timescale much more quickly than typically would happen with evolution over longer time periods. This can include outcompeting native species in the ecosystem, leading to the decline or extinction of local species, and overpopulation as these invasive species may not have any predators in this new ecosystem. They also can be a major economic cost.

The zebra mussel provides an invasive species that has had significant economic impacts. The zebra mussel is native to lakes in Russia but was accidentally introduced in the United States and Canada through the ballast water of commercial ships that were transporting goods to the Great Lakes region in the 1980s. They have been spreading ever since and have recently been found in lakes in Massachusetts; they attach to recreational boats and are transported wherever the boat may go. They colonize rapidly and have covered the undersides of docks, boats, and other marine structures and can grow so thick that they block municipal water and hydroelectric pipelines. The cost of pest management for zebra mussels at power plants and other water-consuming facilities is approximately $500 million a year in the United States. [16]

IPAT Relationship

Human population growth is a factor in human ecosystem impact. From 0 AD to the present, global population has increased from three hundred million to seven billion. While population growth was once considered to be one of the leading drivers of human impacts on ecosystems, it does not adequately explain all the impacts that come from human activities. One concept that is useful in understanding the multiple factors that interact to impact environmental quality is the IPAT equation. The equation was developed in the early 1970s by scientists John Holdren and Paul Ehrlich to explain the human factors that create environmental impact.

$$I = P \times A \times T$$

Impact (I) was expressed as the product of population (P), affluence (A), and technology (T). This formula doesn't quantify actual impacts, but is meant to state relationships. Also, P, A, and T are not independent variables but are interdependent. It does not show a simple multiplicative relationship among the main factors; research has shown that a doubling of population, for example, does not necessarily lead to a doubling of impact. Affluence is related to consumption where more affluent societies are able to consume more resources than less affluent societies can. Technology is a more complex factor as it can provide the means to extract greater quantities of resources but also can be used to limit consumption of resources.

The IPAT equation does not identify sustainable limits but does assist in increasing understanding of the general factors that increase or decrease environmental impact. By highlighting the interplay among a variety of factors in creating an impact, the IPAT equation demonstrates that there are multiple ways of reducing undesirable effects.

KEY TAKEAWAYS

- There are five major ways that business activity can threaten ecosystems: climate change, pollution, habitat destruction, overexploitation, and introduction of invasive species.
- Climate change from human activity has already had an impact on the climate and is projected to cause significant harm to the earth system over the next century if not mitigated.
- Habitat destruction, overexploitation, and introduction of invasive species all negatively impact local ecosystems and should be considered in sustainable business activities.
- The IPAT relationship is defined as impact is the product of population, affluence, and technology.

EXERCISES

1. Find articles that link businesses with each type of the ecosystem-threatening activities discussed in this chapter. Discuss how the business activity either contributed to the threat or helped mitigate the threat.
2. In class, role play the following scenario: A mining company has discovered a large deposit of oil in a pristine area of South America that features high biodiversity. A native village currently lives on the site of the discovery. Try to reach consensus on what should be done. Groups in the exercise include (1) the mining company who wants to extract the oil, (2) the native villagers who do not use oil currently, (3) the scientists researching the biodiversity of the area, and (4) the construction company in the closest city that would build the oil infrastructure if the mining company can move forward with the project and who would employ three hundred local workers.

[1] "IPCC Fourth Assessment Report, Working Group III, Mitigation of Climate Change," IPCC, http://www.ipcc.ch.
[2] "Trends in Atmospheric Carbon Dioxide," National Oceanic & Atmospheric Administration, http://www.esrl.noaa.gov/gmd/ccgg/trends.
[3] "IPCC Fourth Assessment Report, Working Group III, Mitigation of Climate Change," IPCC, http://www.ipcc.ch.
[4] "Climate Change—Health and Environmental Effects," US Environmental Protection Agency, http://www.epa.gov/climatechange/effects/index.html#ref.
[5] "Warming to Cause Catastrophic Rise in Sea Level," *National Geographic*, April 26, 2004, http://news.nationalgeographic.com/news/2004/04/0420_040420_earthday.html.
[6] "World Needs to Axe Greenhouse Gases by 80 pct: Report," Reuters, April 19, 2007, http://www.reuters.com/article/2007/04/19/us-globalwarming-idUSL194440620070419.
[7] http://www.grida.no/publications/other/ipcc_tar/?src=/climate/ipcc_tar/vol4/english/figspm-10b.htm.
[8] "CO2 Emissions (Metric Tons per Capita)," World Bank, http://data.worldbank.org/indicator/EN.ATM.CO2E.PC/countries/1W?display=default.
[9] William R. L. Anderegg, James W. Prall, Jacob Harold, and Stephen H. Schneider, "Expert Credibility in Climate Change," *Proceedings of the National Academy of Sciences of the United States of America*, April 9, 2010, http://www.pnas.org/content/early/2010/06/04/1003187107.full.pdf+html.
[10] "The Southland's War on Smog: Fifty Years of Progress toward Clean Air," South Coast Air Quality Management District, http://www.aqmd.gov/news1/Archives/History/marchcov.html.
[11] "Over Half of China's Water Polluted Beyond Drinkability," Natural News, http://www.naturalnews.com/030630_China_pollution.html.
[12] "State of Garbage," *BioCycle*, October 2010.
[13] "Wastes—Non-Hazardous Waste—Municipal Solid Waste," US Environmental Protection Agency, http://www.epa.gov/epawaste/nonhaz/municipal/index.htm.
[14] "City Eateries Compost with Eco Movement," Seacoast Online, http://www.seacoastonline.com/articles/20100614-NEWS-6140331.
[15] "Desertification," US Geologic Services, http://pubs.usgs.gov/gip/deserts/desertification.
[16] Center for Invasive Species Research at the University of California, Riverside.

2.4 In-Depth Discussion of Sustainability Topics
LEARNING OBJECTIVES

1. Understand the scale of energy use by businesses in modern society.
2. Discuss how peak oil impacts businesses.
3. Understand how green economy activities relate to business sustainability.

Energy use is one of the fundamental connections between business and sustainability. All businesses require energy to convert inputs into outputs, whether it is a product- or service-based business. This section focuses on modern day use of energy and in particular on oil as one of the most prominent energy sources and a nonrenewable resource.

Modern Energy Use

The United States accounts for 25 percent of world energy use, and its economy is a major driver of economic activity (and therefore energy use) throughout the world. In 2009, ninety-five billion MMBTU of energy was consumed in the United States. The main source of energy was from petroleum (oil), accounting for 37 percent of all energy consumed. Natural gas accounted for 25 percent, coal 21 percent, nuclear 9 percent, and renewable energy 8 percent. The United States was a net importer of energy in 2009, it imported 24 percent of the energy used, with about 85 percent of imports being petroleum based. [1]

The four main demand sectors in the US economy are transportation, industrial, residential and commercial, and electric power generation. In 2009, the largest energy demand sector was electric power generation, consuming 41 percent of the energy supply; the next largest was transportation at 28 percent, then industrial at 20 percent, and finally residential and commercial at 11 percent.

US annual energy consumption peaked at 101.5 billion MMBTU in 2007, with the subsequent decline being primarily attributable to the 2008–9 recession in the United States. While currently below its peak, energy use has remained at high levels in the United States, 12 percent higher than usage in 1990.

In the early history of the United States, wood was the primary thermal energy source. In the late 1800s, coal overtook wood in terms of energy consumption. In the mid-1900s both natural gas and petroleum overtook coal in terms of overall energy consumption.

The current energy usage in the United States is heavily dependent on fossil fuels. Fossil fuels are fuels formed from the decomposition of dead organic material over periods of millions of years. Coal, oil, and natural gas are all forms of

fossil fuels. In 2009, over 80 percent of US energy came from fossil fuels. The benefits of fossil fuels are that they are a relatively inexpensive source of energy, have historically been available in large supplies, and have a very high energy density (making them economical to use for a variety of sectors of the economy).

However, fossil fuels have drawbacks as well. They are considered nonrenewable, meaning that they can't replenish themselves—at least on a human time scale. Also in their extraction from the ground, transportation, and use, they can damage the ecosystem. These two drawbacks are the main factors that raise sustainability concerns for fossil fuels.

Dependence on Imported Energy and National Security Concerns

The United States' current high use of imported energy sources puts the nation at risk for politically motivated restrictions to foreign energy supplies. The risks include threats from repressive regimes in oil-producing Arab and other nations to restrict supply if certain political and economic conditions are not met. Without imported energy, the US economy would suffer. More efficient use of energy and increased production and use of domestically produced renewable and other sources of energy can help to reduce national security risks in the United States.

Peak Oil [3]

The fact that fossil fuels are nonrenewable means that at some point they will run out. Oil production in the United States peaked in 1970. While it is still uncertain as to when world oil production will peak, many sources are indicating a peak in the very near term. [4] Petrobras CEO José Sergio Gabrielli stated that new capacity from new projects is insufficient to head off the decline in production and that to maintain existing production the world needs new oil volumes equivalent to Saudi Arabia's contribution every two years; Saudia Arabia has the world's largest oil-proved reserves at 262.6 billion barrels.[5] Sadad al-Husseini, former Saudia Arabian oil company Aramco executive, and multinational energy company Total's CEO, Christophe de Margerie, both don't see global oil production ever exceeding 89 million barrels per day (mbd). World oil production in the first quarter was 90.6 mbd, up 13 percent from the previous quarter. [6] Other sources believe that oil production hasn't peaked yet, but it is close to peaking. Researchers from

Kuwait University and from Kuwait Oil Company predicted recently that world oil production will peak in 2014. [7]

While world oil production has not peaked as of yet, what has peaked are discoveries of new oil reserves. The peak of world oilfield discoveries occurred in 1965 at around fifty-five billion barrels per year (Gb/yr). The rate of discovery has been falling steadily since. Less than ten Gb/yr of oil were discovered each year between 2002 and 2007. The annual rate of discovery of new fields has remained remarkably constant at fifteen to twenty Gb/yr. [9]

All the relatively easy to find and use oil and gas in the world has pretty much been found. Now comes the hard work in finding and producing oil from more challenging environments and work areas.
  William J. Cummings, Exxon-Mobil company spokesman, December 2005

The actual date of the peak is not highly relevant; most relevant is that there is considerable evidence that world oil production will peak in the relatively near future. Given the high dependence of the US and world economy on oil, peak oil will put significant upward pressure on oil prices with the associated volatility as world demand for oil is expected to rise in the future and supplies begin to decline. The impact of reduced oil will demand some response from business to continue to survive and compete.

Green Economy

This section gives a brief discussion of the green economy and is meant to provide a little more detail on this aspect of sustainable business. The green economy can be thought of as private market efforts to address concerns about sustainability. Here the focus is on industries, while the focus of much of the book is at the individual business level. There is no single or standard definition of a "green job" or "the green economy," but it relates to industries involved in activities that address in some way concerns about sustainability.

The green economy includes a broad number of industry and employment occupational categories. One classification of the green economy divides them into five different major categories of industries: energy efficiency, renewable energy, green transportation, environmental services, and clean or smart technology.

Energy efficiency industries, such as building contractors, insulation installers, and material providers, apply measures or practices to help use energy more efficiently. Environmental service industries, such as waste water treatment facilities, provide services directly or indirectly linked to the sustainability and improvement of the environment. Green transportation industries, such as mass transit operators, provide or produce relatively energy efficient transportation. Renewable energy industries, such as solar panels and wind turbine facilities, produce energy from resources that can be renewed. Clean or smart technology industries provide research, production, or services that directly or indirectly relate to the improvement of technology in the four other green industry categories. They include architectural design and services and energy efficiency control systems design and manufacturing.

Using this definition, in 2007, there were over 3.6 million green jobs in the United States, representing 3.2 percent of total private sector employment. Not only do green jobs represent a significant portion of the US economy, but green jobs also tend to pay well. The average annual wages earned in green employment nationally was $57,000, 40 percent above the national average earnings of $40,400. In the United States, the highest average annual wage green industries were in renewable energy and smart technology ($86,800 and $68,800, respectively) and the lowest average annual pay was in green transportation ($41,600).

Energy efficiency and smart technology were the two leading green industries in the United States, with each accounting for 1.1 million jobs and about 33 percent of overall green industry employment. The third most significant sector was environmental services, accounting for 900,000 jobs and 25 percent of overall green industry employment. Following that was green transportation, accounting for 300,000 jobs and 10 percent of overall green industry employment. The least significant green industry in terms of employment was renewable energy. This industry accounted for 100,000 jobs and about 3 percent of green industry employment.

Two areas of smart technology that deserve specific discussion are biotechnology and "green" chemistry. Biotechnology, also known as "biotech," involves engineering biological systems to develop commercial products. This includes medicines, agricultural products, biofuels, and packaging (such as biodegradable cups). Green chemistry is the design of chemical products or processes that reduce or eliminate the generation of hazardous substances. Many products include toxic substances that are damaging to human health. Computers and other electronic devices contain lead, polychlorinated biphenyls (PCBs), cadmium, and mercury—all of which can cause injury to humans upon exposure. Biotechnology is related to green chemistry as biological processes may provide less environmentally damaging alternatives to conventional chemicals. For example, biodiesel, fuel made from vegetable oils, is nontoxic, while diesel fuel obtained from conventional crude oil is toxic.

Conclusion

This chapter has reviewed a variety of issues related to what we call the science of sustainability. There is little question that humans are putting significant demand on Earth's resources, with negative impacts; however, there remains a certain amount of uncertainty of the long-term consequences. The market system and sustainable businesses can help address environmental challenges, but collective and governmental actions outside the market are also necessary given the scope and scale of challenges and the limitations of the market system.

KEY TAKEAWAYS

- Both the global and US economies are heavily dependent on oil and other nonrenewable sources of fuel for energy.
- Nonrenewable resources will at some point run out as their amounts are finite.
- Peak oil has not yet occurred, but there is considerable evidence that a peak in oil supply will occur in the not too distant future.
- Green economy industries include energy efficiency, renewable energy, clean or smart technology, environmental services, and green transportation.
- The green economy sector makes up about 3 percent of the overall US economy in terms of employment.

EXERCISES

1. Discuss the implications of peak oil in the context of the two limits to growth arguments introduced at the beginning of the chapter. What ways can society react based on the views presented? Which outcome, based on these views, do you feel is most likely?
2. What role can sustainable businesses play in addressing the environmental challenges presented in the chapter?
3. What are the limits of sustainable business in addressing environmental challenges?

Minicase: EnerTrac Saves Businesses Money While Reducing Carbon Emissions [11]

EnerTrac, Inc., is a company based out of Hudson, New Hampshire, that was formed in 2006. The company manufactures a transmitter that can measure the fuel levels of heating oil or propane tanks and, using wireless technology, can send a signal to fuel dealers to let them know the amount of fuel in each customer's tank. Traditionally, fuel dealers have had to estimate when to deliver fuel to customers, and this has resulted in unnecessary trips. Now fuel dealers can use their delivery computer systems to know exactly when to deliver fuel to customers. EnerTrac estimates that it can save fuel dealers $52 per year per customer by avoiding unnecessary deliveries. They can also reduce their truck fleet size because they are able to use a fewer number of trucks more efficiently.

EnerTrac is not only saving their customers (fuel dealers) money, but they are also helping them to reduce their GHG emissions. This is because for every unnecessary delivery trip avoided, there is less fuel the company has to use to service their customers. Fuel dealers can be more efficient in their fuel deliveries, reducing the fuel they use to provide service, which results in less carbon dioxide emissions from their delivery trucks. EnerTrac estimates that a fuel delivery company can reduce the carbon dioxide emissions from their trucks up to 40 percent by using their sensor technology.

Watch a video of Pat Mansfield, vice president of business development, explaining how the EnerTrac monitoring system works on YouTube here: http://www.enertrac.com/support/videos/heatingoil.shtml.

EXERCISE

1. Watch the YouTube video of vice president of business development Pat Mansfield explaining the EnerTrac monitoring system. Write a paper discussing how his company's product and services link business performance with environmental performance. This is described in this textbook as a "win-win" situation for business and the environment. Find an example online of another product that creates this "win-win" situation, and discuss it.

[1] "Annual Energy Review," US Energy Information Administration, http://www.eia.doe.gov/aer.
[2] Figure 1.0 Energy Flow, Annual Energy Review 2009, ftp://ftp.eia.doe.gov/multifuel/038409.pdf.
[3] Energy Perspectives 2011, http://www.eia.gov/totalenergy/data/annual/archive/038410.pdf.
[4] "The Peak Oil Crisis: Protests, Tsunamis & Deficits," *Falls Church News Press*, March 16, 2011, http://www.fcnp.com/commentary/national/8762-the-peak-oil-crisis-protests-tsunamis-a-deficits.html.
[5] "The World Factbook," U.S. Central Intelligence Agency, https://www.cia.gov/library/publications/the-world-factbook/geos/sa.html.

[6] "Home Page," International Energy Agency, http://omrpublic.iea.org.
[7] "Home Page," Hybrid Car Blog, http://www.hybridcarblog.com/labels/peak%20oil.html.
[8] http://omrpublic.iea.org/World/Wb_all.pdf.
[9] "Oil Exploration Costs Rocket as Risks Rise," Reuters, http://www.reuters.com/article/idUSTRE61A28X20100211.
[10] http://en.wikipedia.org/wiki/File:GrowingGap.jpg.
[11] http://www.enertrac.com/services/heatingoil/.

NOTES:

NOTES:

Chapter 3:
Government, Public Policy, and Sustainable Business

LEARNING OBJECTIVES

1. Explain how public policies and government influence markets for sustainable businesses.
2. Explain how private businesses can influence government and public policies to serve their interests.
3. Discuss the key influencers of public policy and why public policymaking does not always serve the public interest.
4. Understand why public policy is important to sustainable business and business more generally.

Why should students study public policy if they are interested in understanding sustainable business but are not necessarily interested in government? What is the role of the government in affecting the market rules and economic potential of sustainable business?

This chapter seeks to answer these questions and provide a foundation for students to understand the important and complex role that government plays with all businesses, including businesses focused on sustainability. The chapter covers the effect of public policy on business, the factors that influence public policy, the different views of the relationship between business and government, and the occurrence of market failures and the role of public policy. The chapter also provides specific examples of US and international policies relevant for sustainable businesses.

Businesses that do not understand the political and public policy contexts that they operate in and are not strategic in their interactions with government are at a competitive disadvantage. For example, wind power providers have to act in the context of a very complex set of local, state, and federal governmental policies that influence their costs of providing wind energy and the price they can charge for their energy. Local zoning laws can prevent the siting of wind turbines because of environmental concerns; concerns about how the turbines will affect local habitats, including bird populations; local noise ordinances; and concerns about potential reductions in local property values due to view disruptions. State laws can determine the market for wind and other renewable energy sources through laws, such as renewable portfolio standards (RPS; see the more detailed discussion that follows), that require state-level electrical energy production to include a certain percentage of energy from renewable sources. And federal laws and programs can provide incentives for investment in renewable energy sources through tax credits and favorable types of tax treatment intended to help to reduce carbon emissions and US dependence on foreign energy sources. All of these public policy considerations and more delayed the Cape Wind

Project in Cape Cod, Massachusetts, from going online. The project was first conceived in 2001, received state and local permitting in 2009 and federal permitting in 2010, and is expected to be operational in 2013 (see the following sidebar).

Sidebar

Cape Wind: Public Policy and Renewable Energy (See http://www.capewind.org/article24.htm)

Cape Wind (in Cape Cod, Massachusetts) will be the site of the first large-scale offshore wind farm in the United States. The private developer for the $2.5 billion project is Cape Wind Associates. The project is located on Horseshoe Shoal in Nantucket Sound, 4.8 miles from the nearest shore. One hundred and thirty wind turbines will harness the wind to produce up to 420 megawatts of renewable energy.

Because the proposed turbines are more than three miles from shore, they are subject to federal jurisdiction. However, nearshore infrastructure including roads and power cables make the project subject to state and local laws and regulations. At the state and local level, the project required a water quality certification from the Massachusetts Department of Environmental Protection; access permits from the Massachusetts Highway Department; a license from the Massachusetts Executive Office of Transportation for a railway crossing; orders of conditions from the towns of Yarmouth and Barnstable Conservation Commissions; and road opening permits from Yarmouth and Barnstable.

At the federal level, Cape Wind originally applied for a permit in 2001 from the US Army Corps of Engineers. With the passage of the 2005 Energy Bill, the federal regulatory authority for offshore energy projects was transferred from the Army Corps to the Minerals Management Service (MMS) within the Department of the Interior. While Cape Wind had expected to obtain approval quickly from the Army Corps, this transfer of authority delayed the project. At the federal level, the Federal Aviation Authority was also involved, out of concern that the turbines could cause interference with radar systems and be a hazard to aviation.

In a market economy, government exerts considerable influence on the activities that businesses undertake and on the revenues, costs, and net earnings of businesses. Government and public policies establish the legal system and also the specific rules under which all businesses operate. And government taxes businesses to reflect businesses' use of public services and to collect revenue to fund government operations.

Businesses are creations of government. Businesses are legal entities created under laws established by government. Government impacts the market economy through not only laws that govern the private market system but also specific policies, regulations, judicial (court) decisions, taxes, and government spending. These government actions are constantly changing and are part of the dynamic operating environment for all businesses. Public policies that address energy use and climate change in the United States and other nations impact all businesses but has specific and important impact on businesses focused on sustainability.

The significant role of government in the private market economy was recognized and highlighted by one of the most frequently mentioned supporters of the capitalist system, Adam Smith. Smith was an eighteenth-century Scottish philosopher and political economy professor. He was the author of *The Wealth of Nations* written in 1776. In *The Wealth of Nations*, Smith highlighted the essential role government plays in creating the legal structure, which defines the rules for business transactions, enforces contracts, and grants patents and copyrights to encourage inventions and new products and services. [1]

Smith also highlighted the key role government plays in providing for the public goods and infrastructure required by all businesses. Smith highlighted the need for common physical infrastructure built with government funding, such as roads and bridges. Public goods extend beyond roads and bridges, there are other public goods shared by all businesses and society more generally including clean air, water, and soil and a sustainable environment for natural resources that businesses depend on.

Many public goods would not be available if their existence depended only on individuals or individual businesses and private markets. For example, it would be too costly for any one business to build an interstate highway to transport its

goods or to build and maintain the Internet or to be responsible for protecting the natural environment.

The private market system in general works well to ensure efficient use of limited resources, with efficiency defined as ensuring the best, most highly valued by society, use of resources. But the private market system is not perfect and does not always ensure the best use of society's resources. The market on its own (without government) works best—and makes the most efficient use of society's limited resources—when public goods and externalities (see the more detailed discussion that follows) are not involved. It also works best when near perfect information about how private market activities affect so-called third parties (those who are not directly involved in the market activities) is readily available. For example, if full information was available about the risks involved in British Petroleum (BP) offshore operations in the Gulf of Mexico, BP might, for investor, consumer market, and public relations purposes, have not assumed the operational risks that they did prior to the Gulf oil spill. When market and information failures occur (see as follows for more discussions), governmental intervention can help to facilitate a more efficient private market economy.

The US and other governments are also important in efforts to ensure an overall strong and resilient economy. A key part of a resilient economy is one based on stable, safe, and secure forms of energy. The attention of government and governmental leaders to a new (what has been called) *energy economy* is reflected in US Secretary of Energy Steven Chu's May 2010 commencement speech at Washington University:

> *In order to meet the energy and environmental challenges we face, we will need nothing less than a second industrial revolution. The first Industrial Revolution supplanted human and animal power with machines powered by fossil fuel. Today, we use the power of two horses to dry our hair. We go to the local market under the pull of hundreds of horses, and fly across our continent with a hundred thousand horses. A second industrial revolution is needed to provide the world's energy needs in an environmentally sustainable way. America has the opportunity to lead in this new industrial revolution and build the foundation of our future prosperity. Alternatively, we can hope that the price of oil will return to $30 a barrel and that climate change is not a serious threat. If we are wrong, we will be importing the new energy technologies developed by Europe and Asia.*

Sidebar

Energy Volatility

Energy volatility is a major source of concern for all businesses. In March 2011, the price of a barrel of oil was up to $115 a barrel. This is significantly higher than prices even just five years ago when they were closer to $50 a barrel and ten years ago when oil traded at around $20 per barrel.

In the United States, macroeconomic efforts are primarily influenced by the executive branch of government, which includes Secretary Chu's US Department of Energy and the Federal Environmental Protection Agency (EPA) and also includes the Office of the President, the Departments of Treasury and Commerce, and the Federal Reserve System.
An example of a US government initiative to bolster the general (macro) economy is the 2009, $787 billion economic stimulus plan, also known as the American Recovery and Reinvestment Act of 2009 (ARRA). The ARRA was approved by federal legislation acted on by the US Congress and supported by President Obama. This stimulus plan sought to stabilize employment and encourage business investment and household spending. It included more than $80 billion to support the generation of renewable energy sources; energy efficiency; expanding manufacturing capacity for clean energy technology; advancing vehicle and fuel technologies; and building a bigger, better, smarter electric grid.

The American Recovery and Reinvestment Act (ARRA) provided all US states with funds for energy efficiency, renewable energy, and weatherization programs. These were one-time funds to be spent or committed within two years. The short-term goals for this funding were to create and retain jobs, to achieve energy savings and greenhouse gas reductions, and to encourage energy efficiency improvements in all sectors of the economy. The long-term goals were to strengthen energy efficiency and renewable energy infrastructure, reduce barriers to increasing efficiency and renewable energy, build professional capacity, educate the public, and lay the groundwork for transforming markets so that energy efficiency and renewable energy efforts would be sustained after the ARRA funding was spent.

Sidebar
Texas Department of Housing and Community Affairs (TDHCA): Weatherization Assistance Program (http://www.tdhca.state.tx.us/ea/wap.htm)
The Texas Department of Housing and Community Affairs (TDHCA) operates the Weatherization Assistance Program with funds from the US Department of Energy (DOE) and the US Department of Health and Human Services' Low Income Home Energy Assistance Program (LIHEAP). WAP is designed to help low-income customers control their

energy costs through installation of weatherization materials and education. The program goal is to reduce the energy cost burden of low-income households through energy efficiency.

The main US federal government agency involved with protecting the environment is the EPA. The EPA's priorities as of 2012 included taking action on climate change, improving air quality, ensuring the safety of chemicals, and protecting America's waterways (http://blog.epa.gov/administrator/2010/01/12/seven-priorities-for-epas-future). The US Department of the Interior is also involved in protecting the environment and managing the nation's environmental resources.

Many of the US states, and in particular California and Massachusetts, have also been very active in energy and environmental policies to address climate change. Colorado became the first US state to create a renewable portfolio standard (RPS) by ballot initiative when voters approved Amendment 37 in November 2004. [2] The original version of Colorado's RPS required utilities serving forty thousand or more customers to generate or purchase enough renewable energy to supply 10 percent of their retail electric sales. Eligible renewable energy resources include solar-electric energy, wind energy, geothermal-electric energy, biomass facilities that burn nontoxic plants, landfill gas, animal waste, hydropower, recycled energy, and fuel cells using hydrogen derived from eligible renewables. As of 2011, thirty-nine states had mandatory renewable or alternative energy standards or goals in place. These typically require or target a certain percentage of energy be procured from renewable sources. This expands the markets for renewable energy providers. States also are involved in environmental protection, with most states having an agency dedicated to protecting the environment, such as Florida's and Massachusetts' Departments of Environmental Protection.

Ten states in the Northeast are participating in the Regional Greenhouse Gas Initiative (RGGI), the first regional initiative to reduce carbon emissions from power generation. RGGI institutes a cap-and-trade system for greenhouse gas emissions from power generators and uses funding from the selling of carbon allowances to promote energy efficiency. And there are similar regional efforts starting in other parts of the nation.

Also some local governments in the United States stand out with regards to policies to address climate change and protect the natural environment. Portland, Oregon, was named the Greenest City in the nation in 2008. [3] The city's policies encourage renewable energy usage, support public transportation and biking, and require building's with low environmental impact. These policies have resulted in half the power used in the city coming from renewable sources; a quarter of the workforce commuting by bike, carpool, or public transportation; and thirty-five buildings certified by the US Green Building Council.

European nations have been more active than the US federal government in the establishment of comprehensive policies to address climate change, and this has implications for sustainable businesses (see more discussion with examples as follows). In Europe, national governments have guaranteed prices for energy from solar and wind. Germany, Spain, and other European nations are now among the leaders in global exports in renewable energy, wind power, and solar power technologies. And recently, China has emerged as one of the most attractive markets for investment in renewable energy. [4]

There are "winners" and "losers" with all public policies. In many US states with increased governmental requirements for the use of renewable energy (such as wind and solar power), incentives and financial support has led to new investment in renewable energy and energy efficiency, which increases business opportunity for companies providing clean technology products and services that enhance energy efficiency benefit. All the while generators of electricity using nonrenewable sources, such as coal, natural gas, and other fossil fuels, have experience decreased sales, increased costs, and declining profits as a result of the same policies.

KEY TAKEAWAYS

- Government creates, defines, and regulates markets, including the private market economy overall and the market for sustainable goods and services.
- Government, at all levels, national (federal), state, and local, can exert considerable influence on the activities that businesses undertake and on the revenues, costs, and earnings of sustainable businesses.
- Government impacts the market economy through laws, regulations, judicial decisions, taxes, and government spending.
- Government actions at all levels are constantly changing and are part of the dynamic environment for sustainable businesses.
- The US government and the governments of many other nations are increasingly focused on policies to reduce energy use and business activities that damage the environment. These policies include targets for use of renewable energy, programs to enhance energy efficiency, and regulations to reduce environmental damage. These all can provide expanded markets and business opportunities for sustainable businesses and can impose additional costs on other businesses and reduce the market demand for some businesses that are not providing sustainable goods or services.
- There are business "winners" and "losers" on different public policy issues. On the same policy issue, there will be businesses in favor and against the policy.

EXERCISES

1. Find a recent article or web posting about a clean energy technology or other sustainable business company that has been affected by a government public policy. What was the policy, and how did the government policy affect the profitability (positively or negatively) of that company?
2. Research the federal government policies that might influence US oil prices and discuss what (if anything) the US government should be doing to try to mitigate the fluctuations in the price of oil. What are some possible actions that the government could take and what would be the market implications for sustainable businesses?

[1] Adam Smith, *The Wealth of Nations* (New York: Modern Library, 1937), http://www.online-literature.com/adam_smith/wealth_nations.
[2] "Colorado," DSIRE, http://www.dsireusa.org/incentives/incentive.cfm?Incentive_Code=CO24R.
[3] "America's 50 Greenest Cities," *Popular Science*, February 8, 2008, http://www.popsci.com/environment/article/2008-02/americas-50-greenest-cities?page=1.
[4] Ernst & Young, Renewable Energy Country Attractiveness Report (2010).

3.1 Factors That Influence Public Policy

LEARNING OBJECTIVES

1. Explain some of the factors that can influence public policy, including public opinion, economic conditions, technological change, and interest groups.
2. Identify ways that different stakeholders can influence the operating context of sustainable business.

Public policy is a complex and multifaceted process. It involves the interplay of many parties. This includes many businesses, interest groups, and individuals competing and collaborating to influence policymakers to act in a particular way and on a variety of policies. These individuals and groups use numerous tactics to advance their interests. The tactics can include lobbying, advocating their positions publicly, attempting to educate supporters and opponents, and mobilizing allies on a particular issue. Perfect policies rarely emerge from the political process. Most often policy outcomes involve compromises among interested parties. When a business considers which policy to support and advocate for, considerations include what is in their best interest—that is, which policy could help the business achieve the greatest profits. Other considerations include the policy's political feasibility, whether a majority of others will support the policy, and also how cost effective and efficient the policy would be in achieving the desired outcome. For an example, the cost of a policy of zero carbon emissions would be prohibitive. While the benefits of zero carbon emissions might be high, it would be impossible to achieve without very high economic cost. In contrast, a phased, for example, 5 percent to 10 percent in five to ten years, reduction in carbon emissions from motor vehicles would be a more reasonable and cost effective policy. Equity is another consideration; is the policy fair, are the benefits from the policy equitably distributed, and are the costs of the policy shared fairly?

Public policies are influenced by a variety of factors. These factors include public opinion, economic conditions, new scientific discoveries, technological change, interest groups, nongovernmental organizations (N GOs), business lobbying, and other political activity.

As a result of the wide variety of influencing factors that tend to pull and push policy in different directions, public policy change often happens slowly. Absent a crisis, and sometimes even during a crisis, the influencing factors can tend to check and counteract each other, slowing the development and implementation of new policy and tending to lead to incremental rather than radical changes in public policy. And often, the influencing agents are more effective in blocking policy change than in having new policies adopted—as has been the case with comprehensive climate change policy at the US federal level and resistance from some large energy companies.

Public Opinion

Public opinion and priorities have strong influence on public policy over time. Relevant to sustainable businesses is the increasing public concern about the environment, volatile energy prices, and global climate change. This is influencing public policy through electoral politics, citizen rallies, and actions that affect governmental decision makers. Also influencing public policy relevant for sustainable businesses are new scientific findings and information, such as new findings about climate change and the human and business impact on climate change.

Economic Conditions

Economic conditions also significantly affect the policy environment and operating context for businesses. The Great Recession at the end of the first decade of the twenty-first century enhanced interest and support for public investments and incentives (including in energy efficiency and renewable energy) that could help to create jobs.

Technological Change

Technology advancements—often motivated by market and business opportunities—also affect public policy. Technology is constantly changing and this affects the business environment directly and also indirectly as public policies change with technological inventions. New, lower-cost, and easier-to-use technologies can increase public support for policies that promote renewable energy and energy efficiency and that reduce environmental damage. Examples of these include new designs and materials for packaging that reduce environmental costs, new technology that achieves mass production of full-spectrum solar cells that reduces the cost of solar energy, and programmable thermostats integrated with mobile communication that make energy efficiency actions by households easier to do.

Interest Groups

Interest groups include business and trade associations, professional organizations, labor unions, environmental advocacy organizations, and cause-oriented citizen groups and lobbies. Individuals and businesses also organize into associations and interest groups for other reasons than to try to influence government. This includes for promotional and educational efforts, to support specific activities that are relevant to members (such as clearing and preservation of hiking trails by the Appalachian Mountain Club), and to provide members with select benefits (such as access to cleared trails). Interests groups advocate for public policies that serve the desires of their members and further the mission of their organizations (e.g., environmental interest groups supporting legislation to improve air quality by reducing carbon emissions).

Business Associations

Business efforts to influence public policy and government include not only individual company efforts but also business associations. These associations act collectively to promote public policies in the best interest of business in general and also in the interest of specific industries and localities. Examples of business associations engaging in efforts to influence public policy include the US Chamber of Commerce, the National Association of Manufacturers, the state-level business and industry associations, and the local chambers of commerce. The US Chamber of Commerce is the world's largest business organization, representing the interests of more than three million businesses of all sizes, sectors, and regions.

Sidebar [1]
Since the Toxic Substances Control Act took effect in 1976, the Environmental Protection Agency (EPA) has tested only two hundred of the eighty thousand chemicals in commerce and has regulated only five.
The American Academy of Pediatrics in 2011 called for an overhaul of the thirty-five-year-old federal law governing toxic chemicals in the environment, saying it fails to safeguard children and pregnant women.
"It is widely recognized to have been ineffective in protecting children, pregnant women and the general population from hazardous chemicals in the marketplace."
Among the American Academy of Pediatrics' recommendations were the following:

- The consequences of chemical use on children and their families should be "a core component" of the new chemical policy.

- Chemicals should meet standards similar to those required for new drugs or pesticides.

- Decisions to ban chemicals should be based on reasonable levels of concern rather than demonstrated harm.

- The health effects of chemicals should be monitored after they are on the market, and the US Environmental Protection Agency should have the authority to remove a chemical from the market if it's deemed dangerous.

"Right now, a company manufactures a chemical and puts it out on the market and reaps the economic reward," said Dr. Jerome Paulson, lead author of the policy statement. "And then the public is responsible for trying to figure out if there is any harm associated with the use of that chemical. And then it's almost a criminal procedure, requiring proof beyond a reasonable doubt."

Individual businesses and different business groups differ on many public policies. For example, the American Academy of Pediatrics differed from the American Chemistry Council (http://www.americanchemistry.com/Membership/Membe rCompanies) on revisions to the Toxic Substances and Control Act. And in the fall of 2009, Nike, Apple, and two major utilities—California's largest utility, Pacific Gas and Electric (PG&E), and New Mexico's largest utility, Public

Service Company of New Mexico—left the US Chamber of Commerce because of the organization's stance against policies to address climate change. [2]

Sidebar
An excerpt from PG&E CEO Peter Darbee's resignation letter to the US Chamber of Commerce read as follows:
We find it dismaying that the Chamber neglects the indisputable fact that a decisive majority of experts have said the data on global warming are compelling and point to a threat that cannot be ignored. In our view, an intellectually honest argument over the best policy response to the challenges of climate change is one thing; disingenuous attempts to diminish or distort the reality of these challenges are quite another...I fear it has forfeited an incredible chance to play a constructive leadership role on one of the most important issues our country may ever face.

In contrast to the US Chamber of Commerce, the United States Climate Action Partnership (USCAP) was a group of businesses and leading environmental organizations that came together to call on the federal government to enact strong national legislation to require significant reductions of greenhouse gas emissions. USCAP had issued a landmark set of principles and recommendations to underscore the urgent need for a policy framework on climate change. [3]

The members of USCAP included some of the largest, best-known, and most highly respected companies in the United States including Alcoa, Chrysler, the Dow Chemical Company, Duke Energy, DuPont, Exelon Corporation, Ford Motor Company, General Electric, General Motors Company, Honeywell, Johnson & Johnson, PepsiCo, PG&E Corporation, Shell, Siemens Corporation, and Weyerhaeuser. The members believed that swift legislative action in 2009 based on the USCAP solutions-based proposal titled *Call for Action* would encourage innovation, enhance America's energy security, foster economic growth, improve our balance of trade, and provide critically needed US leadership on this vital global challenge.

On the other side are those who deny that there has been significant climate change. Climate change denial is a set of organized attempts to downplay, deny, or dismiss the scientific consensus on the extent of global warming, its significance, and its connection to human behavior. Climate change denial has been mostly associated with the energy lobby and free market think tanks, often in the United States.

Nongovernmental Organizations (NGOs)
A nongovernmental organization (NGO) is an organization that is not a private company and does not have formal affiliation or representation with government. These are interest groups (see the preceding definition), and they often

try to influence private business behavior either directly by persuasion or protest or indirectly by being influential in shaping public policy. There are currently thirty thousand to forty thousand NGOs globally, and that number keeps expanding as the groups gain support and legitimacy. This includes many environmental organizations.

There are many NGOs influencing the operating context for sustainable businesses.

KEY TAKEAWAYS

- Public policies are influenced by a variety of factors including public opinion, economic conditions, new scientific findings, technological change, interest groups, NGOs, business lobbying, and political activity.
- NGOs are engaging in a wide variety of activities to support sustainable business to fill in gaps missed by local, state, and federal government that are also missed by the private sector.

EXERCISE

1. Search the Internet and identify NGOs currently trying to influence public policies that relate to sustainable business.

[1] David Martin, "Pediatricians Urge Tougher Chemical Safety Law," CNN Health, http://www.cnn.com/2011/HEALTH/04/25/toxic.chemicals/index.html.
[2] Maria Surma Manka, "Irreconcilable Differences: Utilities Leave U.S. Chamber of Commerce, Cite Climate Change," Earth & Industry, http://bit.ly/MgYDUW.
[3] USCAP, *A Call for Action*, http://us-cap.org/USCAPCallForAction.pdf.

3.2 Business and Government Relations: How Do Government and Business Interact?

LEARNING OBJECTIVES

1. Understand the different types of interactions of businesses with government.
2. Explain how businesses try to influence government and the types of responses by businesses to their legal, social, and political environment.

Since businesses are strongly affected by public policies, it is in their best interest to stay informed about public policies and to try to influence governmental decision making and public policy. There are different general ways that businesses view and act on their relationship with government. One perspective is for businesses to consider business and government on "two sides" and in opposition to each other. Some have argued that this was the prevailing dominant mainstream business view in the aftermath of the Great Recession at the end of the first decade of the twenty-first century. It has been characterized as the "antiregulatory" or "limited government" view, and it has been associated with those who believe that free markets with a minimal government role is best for the workings of the economy. This perspective most often focuses businesses' interactions with government on efforts to minimize government and reduce the costs and burdens on private business and the general economy associated with government taxes, regulations, and policies.

Another business perspective on government is that government should favor businesses and incentivize business performance and investment because businesses are the main source of jobs, innovation, and societal economic well-being, and therefore government should support businesses with grants, tax credits, and subsidies.

A third general view of businesses and government relations is with business in partnership with government in addressing societal matters. This is in contrast to government being the regulator to ensure businesses act in a socially responsible manner.

These views are not mutually exclusive. For example, the same solar business can use some of its interaction with government to try to maximize the benefits, such as favorable tax credits, it receives from government and at the same time work in partnership with government to achieve a social purpose, such as reducing carbon emissions, and then try to minimize its tax obligations. It is also important, as described by Pacific Gas and Electric (PG&E) CEO Peter Darbee previously, that the focus of business and government relationships should be on the type of policies required in response to societal challenges rather than an ideological response about the proper role of government in a free market economy.

Sustainable businesses, such as the companies presented in the case study chapters in this textbook—such as Stonyfield Yogurt, Oakhurst Dairy, and Green Mountain Coffee—tend to focus on their responsibility to the environment and societal impact and also tend to recognize that government policies and programs are often necessary to help them achieve their objectives and therefore are inclined to try to work with and even partner with government to achieve desired ends. It is always important for sustainable businesses to understand how their efforts to achieve profits and to serve a social purpose are both strongly influenced by government policies, and it is always important for sustainable businesses to manage their relationships with government (local, state, national, and international) effectively.

Types of Business Responses

Once a business has an understanding of how government affects their operations and profitability, it can formulate strategies for how best to interact with government. There are three general types of business responses to the public policy environment—reactive, interactive, and proactive.

Reactive responses involve responding to government policy after it happens. An interactive response involves engaging with government policymakers and actors (including the media) to try to influence public policy to serve the interests of the business. A proactive response approach entails acting to influence policies, anticipating changes in public policy, and trying to enhance competitive positioning by correctly anticipating changes in policy. For most businesses, a combination of the interactive and proactive approaches is the best approach.

In meeting challenges from nongovernmental organizations (NGOs) and the media, businesses may respond in a variety of ways, including the following:

- **Confrontation.** It may aggressively attack either the message or the messenger, and in extreme cases, business has felt justified to sue its critics for libel.
- **Participation.** Business may develop coalitions or partnerships with NGOs, as McDonald's did with the Environmental Defense Fund (EDF; see the following discussion) or as Home Depot did with the Rainforest Alliance (see the following sidebar).
- **Anticipation.** Business may adopt issues management programs to forecast emerging issues and to adjust or change business practices in advance of the passage of stringent laws or regulations.

When business is in a *reactive* response mode, it most often engages in confrontation of its adversaries. When it assumes an *interactive* response mode, it participates in dialogues with NGOs and the media and develops partnerships or coalitions to advance new policies and programs. When business behaves in a *proactive* manner, it anticipates future pressures and policy changes and adjusts its own internal corporate policies and practices before it is forced to do so. While a

reactive stance may sometimes work, it often only delays needing to engage in a more interactive or proactive way. An interactive or proactive approach is usually a better way to meet political and societal challenges while also protecting the reputation of the firm.

Sidebar

Home Depot and Rainforest Action Network: From Combative to Collaborative Relationship
Home Depot's relationship with the Rainforest Action Network (RAN) on the issue of preserving old-growth forest began as combative and reactive but wound up being collaborative and interactive. After discussions with RAN, Home Depot agreed to sell only lumber that was certified as grown from sustainable forests.

Tactics That Businesses Use to Influence Government

Businesses often engage in a variety of tactics to influence government policy. This includes lobbying, political contributions, and interest group politics.

Business Lobbying

Businesses lobby in different ways. This can include lobbying of Congress and state legislatures and executive branch agencies directly through its own government relations specialists, through an industry trade association, through consultants, or through a combination of all those avenues. Businesses may also engage in indirect or grassroots lobbying by appealing to its own employees, stakeholders, or the general public to make their views known to policymakers. In order to build a broad grassroots constituency, business may manage "issue advertising" campaigns on top-priority issues, or purchase issue ads in media outlets that target public policymakers or Washington insiders.

Business lobbying has a strong influence on public policies. There are more than 1,500 private companies in the United States with public affairs offices in Washington, DC, and more than 75 percent of large firms employ private lobbyists to make their case for policies that can benefit them. This includes more than 42,000 registered lobbyists in state capitals across the nation.

Business may engage in reactive defensive lobbying (defending its own freedom from government regulation) or interactive lobbying (partnering with interest groups on policies that the firm can benefit from). Businesses can also choose to engage in social lobbying, examples of which include chemical companies with the best environmental track record joining environmental NGOs in lobbying for an increased budget for the Environmental Protection Agency (EPA) and retailers wanting to address consumer concerns joining interest groups in pressuring the Consumer Product Safety Commission to adopt more stringent product safety standards. Corporations showing a willingness to join such public interest coalitions can gain reputational rewards from NGOs, the media, and public policymakers.

Energy Company Lobbying

In 2010. energy companies spent more than $2.5 billion to lobby members of the US Congress, according to the Center for Responsive Politics. While oil, gas, and utility companies spent most of that money, renewable energy lobbying efforts were also sizable.

Source: Stephen Lacey, "Top 25 U.S. Energy Lobbyists of 2010,"*Renewableenergyworld.com*, http://www.renewableenergyworld.com/rea/news/article/2010/12/top-25-u-s-energy-lobbyists-of-2010.

Political Contributions

Businesses also use campaign contributions to support their position and to try to influence public policies that can help them increase profits. Seven of the ten largest corporations in the world are oil companies, based on revenues. Their access to funds for lobbying and campaign contributions gives them a significant voice in the political system and on policies that can impact sustainable businesses.

There are a range of avenues a company might use in making political contributions. The most transparent and legitimate is that of forming apolitical action committee (PAC) to which voluntary contributions of employees are amassed and then given in legally limited amounts to selected candidates. Not surprisingly, larger firms in regulated industries, or in industries exposed to greater risk from changing public policies, such as oil companies in 2010 during and after the British Petroleum (BP) Gulf of Mexico oil crisis, use PACs more often than other firms. Beyond contributing directly to political candidates, firms can also advertise on ballot measure campaigns, and those contributions can come from corporate assets and are subject to no legal limitations.

A 2010 US Supreme Court decision, *Citizens United v. Federal Election Commission* ruled that the government could not ban independent political spending by corporations, as well as labor unions and other organizations, in candidate elections. This has led to rise of what have become known as "super PACS." In the 2012 Republican presidential primary, about two dozen individuals, couples, or corporations gave $1 million or more to Republican super PACs to try to influence the primary election.

Interest Group Participation

Business response can include participation in interest group politics. Interest groups play a key role in all democratic systems of government. However, as an interest group is a group of individuals organized to seek public policy influence, there is tremendous diversity within interest groups. Business is just one of many interest group sectors trying to influence public policy (see the discussion previously mentioned). Businesses will encounter interest groups that may support or conflict with their position on an issue.

Other Business Interactions in the Public Arena

Businesses face a complex array of formal and informal public policy actors beyond (just) government. Business practices can be strongly influenced by citizen actions that bypass the formal institutions of government. Though they lack the economic clout and resources of industry as tools of influence, citizen groups do possess other tools. They can lobby and litigate, and they can get out large groups to demonstrate in public events and use exposure in the news media as a vehicle for getting their perspective heard.

Businesses are influenced by direct citizen activism and protest. Organized interests and nongovernmental organizations (NGOs) have been the source of influence. After their experiences in affecting public policy in the 1960s and 1970s, many citizen activists grew skeptical of the government's ability to respond rapidly and effectively and discovered they could often accomplish their objectives more directly and quickly. Citizen groups have both confronted and collaborated with corporations in order to foster change. Finding that confrontation is often counterproductive and that government lobbying is protracted and ineffective, NGOs often turn to collaboration with business to resolve issues. Indeed, as both sides have matured and grown less combative, business and NGOs have learned to work together to resolve problems. There are many examples of such productive collaboration, the most prominent of which have emerged on the environmental front. For example, the Rainforest Action Network (RAN) has worked with Home Depot, Lowe's, and several timber companies in an initiative to protect old-growth forest. RAN combines elements of activism and even militant protest along with peaceful collaboration.

The EDF is an example of an NGO working cooperatively, in contrast to a confrontational approach, with corporations. The EDF was an early actor in this way. In November 1990, the Fund began to work with McDonald's to help the company phase out its polystyrene clamshell food containers.

It was a collaborative effort to significantly reduce McDonald's negative environmental impact by cutting its solid waste. It was the first major partnership between an environmental group and a *Fortune* 500 company in an era when environmental and business interests were often at odds. EDF and McDonald's worked together to develop a new solid waste reduction plan. The initiative eliminated more than 300 million pounds of packaging, recycled 1 million tons of corrugated boxes, and reduced waste by 30 percent in the decade following the initial partnership, and this was all achieved at no additional cost to the company.

Beyond the traditional political tactics, NGOs also have developed new tactics to pressure business. Ralph Nader pioneered the use of the shareholder resolution to protest such corporate actions as discriminatory hiring, investment in South Africa, nuclear power, environmental impacts, and corporate campaign donations. Since the 1970s, religious organizations, most prominently the Interfaith Center on Corporate Responsibility, have been the chief sponsors of such resolutions. More recently, they have been joined by mainstream shareholder groups, such as large institutional investors and pension funds, in calling for major changes in corporate governance and more recently for more attention to businesses' environmental footprint and contribution to greenhouse gas emissions and global warming.

Businesses have to also understand the importance of another actor in the business and public policy sphere—the news media. The media provides important functions for both society and business. For example, it influences the public policy agenda by filtering the various events and interest-group areas of attention and it can serve as a sort of "watchdog" over both business and government exposing any unethical practices. Business must constantly monitor the media and be ready to respond. In particular, since the media are usually a pivotal actor in any corporate crisis, company "crisis management" plans must include steps for dealing appropriately with the media and other critics.

KEY TAKEAWAYS

- There are three general categories of business responses to the public policy environment—reactive, interactive, and proactive.
- Business efforts to influence public policy and government include not only individual company efforts but also business association efforts.
- For most businesses, some combination of the interactive and proactive approaches with government and other interest groups is most often the best approach.
- Businesses, individually and collectively; citizen interest groups; and NGOs all have influence on government policies. These entities often partner to influence public policy.
- Business practices can be strongly influenced not only by government but by direct citizen and NGO actions that bypass the formal institutions of government. Especially since the 1990s, business has been increasingly influenced by direct citizen activism.
- The media has a strong interest in giving visibility to issues and setting the policy agenda. Businesses must view the media as an important influencing agent affecting their operating environment and must be effective in its relations with the media.

EXERCISES

1. Search the business press and Internet for recent examples of businesses responding to challenges from NGOs or the media in confrontational, participatory, and anticipatory manners. Discuss the benefits and problems associated with the three approaches.
2. Find two recent examples of businesses using lobbying to try to influence government policy, one successful and one not successful. Describe why one failed and one was successful.
3. Pick an environmental or energy policy being considered at a federal or state level. Discuss how businesses, individually and collectively; citizen interest groups; and NGOs all have influence on this policy.

3.3 Market Failures and the Role of Public Policy
LEARNING OBJECTIVES

1. Define market failures.
2. Discuss how government efforts to address market failures can be justified to achieve desired social outcomes, such as sustainability.

Government interventions in a private market economy are intended to correct so-called market failures or to achieve a societal objective. We focus here on government interventions to correct private market failures. Market failures can justify government intervention on market efficiency (economic) criteria. A key type of market failure that government tries to address in regulations and laws are externalities. Government policies are also used to address societal concerns that are associated with private market economies, such as economic inequalities. For sustainable businesses, the most relevant market failures are externalities, and we focus on these as follows.

Externalities

An externality occurs when a so-called third party who is not directly involved in an economic transaction is affected by that market transaction. For example, when pollution produced by a private company negatively impacts the air quality and natural environment and harms the health of others. Externalities typically are considered in a negative context but can have either a positive or a negative impact on the third party. Government can constructively intervene when an externality in a private market transaction has a negative impact on a third party and the third party does not receive any compensation for the negative impact.

In the absence of government intervention, when externalities exist, market prices do not reflect the full costs or benefits in the production or consumption of a good. In the case of external costs, such as pollution, producers may not bear all the societal costs of production, and this would translate to lower prices to consumers than they should pay. For market efficiency purposes consumers should pay the full costs, private and social, of the products and services they consume. If an individual or business does not pay the full (private and social) costs of goods and services they consume, this would cause a good to be overproduced and overconsumed while pushing additional costs on to individuals not involved in the transaction. In the case of pollution, a company could profit by not paying the true cost of managing its waste, and others (i.e., the broader public) would be burdened by the costs—including loss of natural resources, loss of pleasure from the environment because of environmental degradation, and public health problems caused by the pollution.

Oil and oil sales and consumption can have high external costs to society beyond the price charged by the oil company. The pollution from oil use has external costs. And oil use can increase dependency on foreign resources, including on foreign countries with repressive governments.

Public policy through a tax on the use of a product or service that produces a negative externality like foreign oil can work to internalize the cost of the externality and improve the workings and efficiency of the market. Since carbon dioxide contributes to greenhouse gas emissions and global warming, and global warming has costs to society, a carbon tax on a product or service that when produced or consumed emits CO_2 (such as the generation of electricity with high-sulfur coal, gasoline, or oil) can address a negative externality. It does this by putting a price on the externality and by having companies and consumers internalize the costs associated with what were unpriced externalities in the private market. This can help move private companies focused on profits to activities that better reflect their net social value, such as energy companies providing more renewable energy.

On the other hand, if there is an external benefit to a product, the producer may not be able to capture those societal benefits in the price of the product resulting in underproduction and under consumption of the good. In this case, a public policy argument might be made to subsidize the good to help increase consumer demand for the good or help improve the producer's prospects for profitability. An example of such a subsidy would be the government assisting with the development of clean energy or a new technology that helps to reduce greenhouse gas emissions and the societal costs associated with greenhouse gas emissions. The government support could encourage greater entrepreneurial pursuit and investment in innovation and new technologies in renewable energy and energy efficiency, and society could benefit.

Failure to Assign Property Rights

Externality problems often occur in market economies when property rights are not properly assigned. Environmental problems often arise because of a lack of well-defined and enforceable property rights. Climate change is a stark example of this because nobody "owns" the atmosphere and in turn, humans have been able to add greenhouse gases to it without cost. This is now causing rising global temperatures and instability in our climate system.

The challenge is to define property rights for shared resources, such as the natural environment, that are hard to exclude usage of without incurring very high transaction costs and costs to individuals. This can make environmental policy controversial, especially when you take what was a free good—such as the ability to pollute at no cost—and put a price or cost on it.

Environmental policy is often foremost about creating and enforcing property rights for environmental resources at minimum cost. In practice this means that collective or public authorities assume de facto ownership and take action to restrict previously unlimited free access to resources, such as water or air, as places to pollute. Who pays becomes an issue of critical importance and controversy. While restrictions can benefit society at large by improving water and air quality, they can come at a cost. This includes not only transaction costs for implementing, monitoring, and enforcing restricted use but also costs for those individuals and companies that had been polluting at no cost and now have a cost imposed on them or have to change their behavior and find other solutions to their waste disposal.

KEY TAKEAWAYS

- Market failures can justify government intervention.
- Private market failures related to sustainable business that government tries to address are externalities.
- Market failure correction efforts are the most relevant justifications for public policies that address sustainability.
- The absence of property rights for the atmosphere and environmental resources leads to externalities and market failures. While property right assignment to a public authority can help to restrict use and overcome the absence of property rights and the market failure, it often comes with significant costs.

EXERCISES

1. Take the position that the most appropriate role for government is to limit business taxes and regulations. What is the strongest case for limited government? Use http://www.youtube.com/playlist?list=PL44FA19690881B24A as a resource.
2. Take the position that government intervention in a private market economy can be beneficial to achieve sustainability objectives. Why are governmental environmental policies and regulations justified?
3. What is a market failure? Give an example of a market failure. How can government policy help overcome market failures?
4. Why are property rights critical to a market economy? How do resources that are not owned by anyone get used? Do they always get used in the most economically valuable way? Does your local public park get used in a way that optimizes its long-term economic value?

3.4 Public Policy Features and Examples
LEARNING OBJECTIVES

1. Understand the general process and difficulties of policymaking.
2. Describe how policy levers can help shape business sustainability.
3. Discuss effective policy design features.
4. Describe specific policy instruments and their features.

Markets are useful for efficiently allocating certain types of goods and services and not as useful on their own for allocating other goods and services that are subject to market failures, such as externalities as discussed previously. A key question for government policymakers is what policies might help achieve desired outcomes. Here we focus on the desired outcome for a more sustainable future and review different types of policies and policy levers that can help to shape effective policy development in this area.

Sustainability Policy Design Features
In the US context and consistent with the nation's private market principles, most would agree that sustainability policies should strive to achieve desired environmental objectives with the greatest positive economic benefit or at least cost. Another key principle is to strive for fairness and justice—that is, to try to ensure that polices work to reduce inequities or at a minimum do not make current inequities in our society any worse than they currently are. An example of injustice is using low-income neighborhoods or countries as the location for hazardous waste collection to reduce hazardous waste generated in higher-income neighborhoods or nations.

After these principles, most of the pragmatic proponents of sustainability would be supportive of the following policy design features:

1. **Use an incremental approach.** Policy proponents should recognize that there will be supporters of existing policies who will resist change. An incremental approach respects what exists now; however, it should not be an excuse for either inaction or diversion from longer-term desired objectives.

2. **Be ready to change or adjust policies.** Policies must be able to adapt to changed conditions. Policies are evaluated once they are vetted and tested after they are implemented; experience provides opportunities for learning and adjustment. The process of adaptive management should guide policy design and implementation.

3. **Address problems institutionally on the same scale as the problem.** It is desirable to deal with a problem at the smallest domain in which it can be solved. Problems should be addressed by institutions on the same scale as the problem. For example, garbage and recycling collection is mostly a local problem and requires local policies. Garbage disposal and the reuse of recycled materials is a wider area issue and would require multilocal or regional entities to address. Climate stability and energy use are global problems and require global policy instruments and institutions.

4. **Address uncertainty by erring on the side of reducing risk of environmental damage when dealing with the possibility of significant environmental damage that is irreversible.** Policies should leave a margin of error when dealing with the biophysical environment. Ecosystem dynamics involve considerable uncertainties and could involve irrevocable negative changes. Adopting a precautionary approach would establish a safety margin between the demands placed on ecosystems and best estimates of their capacities.

Policy Instruments

What follows are some of the governmental policy instruments available to address issues related to sustainability.

Taxes (Taxing "Bads")

Taxes are a powerful, frequently used, policy instrument used to collect revenue to support government policies and programs. And they are also used to discourage societal "bads" that can harm individuals and impose costs on society. This includes the use of taxes to discourage smoking and alcohol use.

With regards to environmental and energy issues, taxes, such as a carbon tax (a tax on the carbon content of fossil fuel, e.g., coal, oil, gas) can send market signals that the free market does not send and can improve the efficiency and effectiveness of the market system. Carbon taxes can help to correct for the market failures associated with externalities and the difficulties of establishing property rights with natural resources.

Sidebar

Carbon Tax

Several nations have established carbon taxes, including Finland, Sweden, and the Netherlands. An informal coalition of economists led by Harvard University professor Greg Mankiw have endorsed a US carbon tax as an efficient economic policy to address concerns about climate change. The proponents of the carbon tax point out that research has demonstrated that people respond to taxes—make the taxes high enough and behavior changes—whether it's smoking or polluting. So a carbon tax would shift energy consumption from high carbon producing sources to low carbon producing sources, for example, from coal to solar power.

Tax Credits

The flip side to taxing is tax credits. Tax credits that reduce tax liabilities can encourage different forms of investment and different types of business activity. Tax credits are a popular policy instrument for sustainable business in the United States.

Federal and state renewable energy and energy efficiency investment tax credits reduce the after-tax cost and encourage businesses and households to invest in renewable energy and energy efficiency. An example is the US federal business energy investment tax credit available for eligible energy systems placed in service on or before December 31, 2016. For solar, small wind turbines, and fuel cells, the credit is equal to 30 percent of expenditures, with no maximum credit. For geothermal systems, microturbines, and combined heat and power, the credit is equal to 10 percent of expenditures, with no maximum credit limit. The original use of the equipment must begin with the taxpayer, or the system must be constructed by the taxpayer. The equipment must also meet any performance and quality standards in effect at the time the equipment is acquired, and the energy property must be operational in the year in which the credit is first taken.

Regulations

A *regulation* is a rule or order prescribed by an authority that controls or directs some activity, often in relation to a standard or target. Environmental awareness in the twentieth century led to a large number of regulations to protect people and the environment. Bans, quotas, and standards of various sorts have been ordered by governments, and fines or penalties are generally prescribed for violations.

DDT (Dichlorodiphenyltrichloroethane), a synthetic pesticide, was one of the earliest substances banned; individual paper factories have limits or quotas set for the amount of wastes they can discharge into a river; and emission standards have been prescribed for many industries. Other regulations require the use of prescribed technologies—for example, best available control technologies (BACTs) may be required to reduce pollution—and the type of equipment used to harvest fish may be prescribed to limit habitat destruction. Regulations can be quite effective at limiting pollution and are helpful in managing renewable resources. But command and control mechanisms are not always the most efficient ways of achieving the desired ends. Regulations have their own limitations as well. There are the issues of administrative costs of microcontrol and threats and potential violations of private property rights. In addition, once regulatory goals are achieved there may be no incentives for additional improvements.

Bans

A *ban* is a regulation that removes a substance from circulation, thereby eliminating throughput of a particular type. A ban is the simplest and best solution when an emitted substance cannot be absorbed or broken down through natural processes; it accumulates in the environment where it causes damage. DDT, leaded gasoline, and CFCs (chlorofluorocarbons; organic compounds that contain carbon) were all found to cause damage to critical ecosystems and all have been banned in the United States and many other developed countries.

Some of the earliest bans can be traced back more than 2,500 years, when hunting certain animals was banned in India. Bans can take many forms: they can be total or partial, they can focus on production or consumption, they can be temporary or permanent, they can be graduated in time or magnitude, or they can be supported by incentives or penalties. Many substances have been banned, and bans are used in a wide variety of situations—from local seasonal bans on hunting and fishing to global treaties imposing bans on specific compounds or activities.

Quotas

Quotas are partial bans. They are a way to establish the maximum allowable throughput of a substance and could be very effective in ensuring specific substances only enter the economy at a sustainable level. Quotas, such as quotas on fishing, may be preferable to a complete ban if there is evidence that some levels of throughput can be safely absorbed by the ecosystems they affect. This safe level of throughput allows the benefits of the substance to be made available. Quotas should not be used unless there is adequate

proof that safe levels are indeed possible; often there are disputes about this issue.

Rationing

Rationing is similar to quotas. While not used currently in the United States, rationing is a public policy that has been used in the past. It has been used most frequently during times of war in the United States to allocate food and consumer goods in short supply to households and businesses. Rationing was used in a nonwar situation in the 1970s in the United States during the OPEC oil embargo. Gasoline was rationed by designating odd and even days for the purchase of gasoline based on the last digit or letter on license plates. In a context of limited reserves of nonrenewable energy sources, rationing is one tool that may become necessary.

Standards

Standards are prescribed levels of performance enforced by law. A wide range of such standards were enacted in the latter part of the twentieth century as a response to growing awareness and concern over environmental pollution. Ambient standards regulate the amount of pollutant present in the surrounding (ambient) environment, such as parts per million (ppm) of dissolved oxygen in a river, sulfur dioxide (SO_2) in an air shed, or ground-level ozone levels. Measures are often an average (e.g., over a twenty-four-hour period or per year), as concentrations vary by time of day and by season (e.g., due to weather changes). The level itself cannot be directly enforced; therefore, the sources of the pollution must be found and regulated to be sure that the ambient standard is met. The US Clean Air Act, for example, sets ambient standards for six criteria pollutants in a region. If a region is in violation, they must come up with a plan to attain compliance.

Emissions standards regulate the level of emissions allowed, such as emissions rates (pounds of SO_2 per hour), concentration (ppm of biochemical oxygen demand [BOD] in wastewater), total quantity of a pollutant, residuals per unit of output (SO_2 per kWh of electricity), residual content per unit of output (sulfur content of coal), or percentage removal of pollutant (90 percent of SO_2 scrubbed). Emissions standards do not guarantee a specific ambient level of pollution.

Technology standards require polluters to use certain technologies, practices, or techniques. While emissions standards require polluters to meet a goal for the level of pollution, they give the polluter freedom to choose the technology used. Technology standards require a specific technology. For example, until 1990, electric utilities were required to install scrubbers with 90 percent efficiency ratings. Another example is the United States requiring catalytic converters in autos. The 1972 Water Pollution Control Act Amendments set a goal of zero discharges by 1985 and used technology-based effluent standards (TBES)—this was a combination of a ban and a standard. The Environmental Protection Agency (EPA) determines the "best practicable technology" and sets standards assuming that firms are using that standard. Often, as in the Clean Air Act, the government mandates that the best available control technology (BACT) be used. However, BACT is often not clearly defined.

Banning certain technologies or processes is another way of establishing a standard. Clear cut logging has been banned in certain jurisdictions and long line drift nets have been banned for certain fisheries. The generation of electricity with nuclear fission has been banned in some European countries.

Like the many other policy tools, standards can be very effective at reducing pollution of various types; they are often used in conjunction with other policy instruments such as bans or quotas. There are many flexible approaches to standards, and considerable experience has occurred with regard to their use. One of the potentially negative aspects of standards is that they have often been of a command and control nature; that is, they prescribe not only, or even necessarily, a goal but a specific means of achieving that goal. This "one size fits all" approach is not always the most effective or cost efficient.

Significant financial resources have been used by business and industry to comply with environmental standards by retrofitting existing infrastructures. In addition to resisting the imposed costs these standards require, business and industry have also objected to being told precisely how to achieve the desired goals. If standards can be set in terms of clear, measurable goals, business and industry prefer to have the flexibility of working out the methods for achieving those goals.

Another problem with the command and control standards is that once achieved there is no incentive for exceeding the standard and providing even greater environmental protection even when this is possible. Incentives to exceed standards can be used to this end.

Standards have been used successfully with a range of local and regional environmental problems. However, the level at which standards are set can have dramatic impacts on other levels. For example, setting standards at the national level for vehicle fuel efficiency can lead to increased vehicle use

(known as the rebound effect), exacerbating the problems at the regional and global levels through increased levels of throughput.

Cap and Trade

A cap-and-trade system is a public policy tool where the government issues permits allowing firms to emit a certain amount of a pollutant—each permit might allow, say, one ton of carbon dioxide. Regulators then limit the amount of emissions by imposing a cap on the total number of permits.

Sidebar
Acid Rain Cap-and-Trade Program
The first cap-and-trade program in the United States (1995) was the innovative, market-based sulfur dioxide (SO2) allowance trading component of the Acid Rain Program (ARP). Affected utilities were required to install systems that continuously monitored emissions of SO2, nitrogen oxides (NOx), and other related pollutants in order to track progress, ensure compliance, and provide credibility to the trading component of the program. In any year that compliance was not achieved, excess emissions penalties would apply, and sources either would have allowances deducted immediately from their accounts or were required to submit a plan to the EPA that specified how the excess SO2 emissions would be offset. Overall the program has been hailed as successful by the EPA, the industry, economists, and certain environmental groups, such as the Environmental Defense Fund. Estimates are that emissions of sulfur dioxide have been reduced by 8 million tons, nitrous oxide by 2.7 million tons, and mercury by 10 tons (from 52 to 42). However, it is difficult to estimate the emissions, which would have occurred without the ARP. Since the 1990s, SO2 emissions have dropped 40 percent, and according to the Pacific Research Institute, acid rain levels have dropped 65 percent since 1976. The EPA estimates that by 2010, the overall costs of complying with the program for businesses and consumers will be $1 billion to $2 billion a year, only one-fourth of what was originally predicted.

The general cap-and-trade system can allow firms to "bank" permits, borrow permits, and buy and sell permits from each other, creating a new form of property rights, basically the right to pollute a certain amount. Some companies might find that they could operate using less than their allotment of permits, leaving those firms with extras to sell. Other companies, in contrast, might produce more pollution than would be allowed by their allotment of permits and have to buy additional permits from those companies with extras to sell.

The economic logic of cap and trade is that the firms that can most cost effectively reduce their pollution (e.g., reduce a given level of pollution at the lowest cost) would do so and then sell their pollution permits or rights to firms that had relatively high cost of reducing pollution. The efficient pollution reducing firms would keep ratcheting down their pollution in an effort to free up more permits to sell, and inefficient ones would buy their permits. For businesses, if it were less costly for them to install abatement technologies than buy permits, they would do that. But if that was more costly, they would purchase permits.

Over time, the government could reduce the number of permits allocated and thus cut the total amount of pollution. As that would occur, the market value of the permits would rise creating an even greater incentive to reduce emissions. A cap-and-trade system can potentially harness the private incentives of the market to motivate innovation in pollution abatement technology and reduce pollution over the long term at the least amount of cost.

Cap-and-trade programs are more flexible than other pollution control instruments as they do not put any type of limit on emissions for individual polluters. Regulated sources can design their own compliance strategies to obtain all the allowances they require. These strategies include sales or purchases of allowances, installation of mitigating technologies, fuel switching, and efficiency measures. A cap-and-trade program provides a system for regulated sources to choose the lowest cost approach to managing their emissions. This allows pollution to be reduced at a lower overall cost than more traditional command-and-control approaches.

While cap and trade has been promoted as an effective market based solution to pollution reduction, taxing pollution instead may require less bureaucracy than a cap-and-trade system. Cap and trade requires someone to issue permits, oversee their exchange, and monitor emissions. After all, the United States already has a significant tax collector in the Internal Revenue Service. Finally, by setting a specific price for carbon pollution, a tax would make it easier for firms to plan for the future.

In a cap-and-trade system, the price of permits fluctuates with demand and supply, just like stock prices do. A tax, in contrast, sets a single explicit price. Carbon trading creates new financial markets, with intermediaries like brokers who would assist in the exchange of permits.

Renewable Portfolio Standard

A renewable portfolio standard (RPS) is a public policy designed to help influence the amount of electricity generated from renewable energy resources. RPS policies are meant to encourage the development of new renewable energy resources and to help maintain existing renewable energy resources. An RPS is a "pull" type mechanism because it provides an incentive for the development of renewable energy facilities.

Renewable energy facilities, such as wind turbines and solar panels, are issued separate tradable credits, called renewable energy credits (RECs), for each megawatt hour (MWh) of electricity they generate. Businesses can either voluntarily purchase these credits to "green" the electricity they use or, in an RPS, utilities are required to purchase a specific amount of these credits each year based on a percentage of overall customer electricity use. For example, an RPS may require that the utility provide 5 percent of energy from renewable sources, and the RECS are the accounting system to track compliance with that requirement.

Information

Dissemination of information by a government body is an example of a policy instrument that is often relatively simple and does not impose high cost on businesses. The US government provides information on food and drugs through the US Department of Agriculture and the Food and Drug Administration (FDA). This information can help consumers choose the food and drugs they consume on an informed basis and can use the private market to regulate the quality of beef and other food products. Information dissemination by government and nongovernmental organizations (NGOs) and by private businesses related to carbon emissions, toxic waste disposal, and other environmental factors can influence consumer choices and business practices in similar ways.

KEY TAKEAWAYS

- Efforts to establish new policies that address environmental concerns must take into account the resistance that will occur.
- There are benefits with environmental policies that adapt to changing conditions and that take action to prevent activities that have significant risk of harming the environment in ways that cannot be reversed.
- There are a range of policies that can address concerns about the environment, from outright bans of chemicals to market pricing (e.g., with the imposition of taxes) of activities that cause social harms.

EXERCISES

1. Why is it beneficial for government to encourage business innovation to address environmental concerns? What are the different ways government policies can encourage innovation?
2. What are some of the benefits and problems of using market-based systems, such as cap and trade, to reduce pollutants?

3.5 Environmental and Energy Policies

LEARNING OBJECTIVES

1. Explain the history of US federal government engagement on environmental issues and how it has changed over time.
2. Understand the most important US government environmental policies.
3. Understand the connections between environmental and energy policies.
4. Compare US policies to address climate change with those in other nations and discuss the implications for sustainable businesses in the different nations.

In the United States, there are many environmental policies, laws, and regulations at the federal, state, and local levels that affect sustainable businesses. Some of these are easy to understand and transparent to a large segment of the population. Others are not. For example, local, state, and federal tax credits (credit against taxes owed) for purchases of hybrid vehicles, home weatherization, and renewable energy use are pretty simple to understand—many individuals and households are aware of these policies, and these policies affect sustainable businesses. In contrast, renewable portfolio standards (see the following for a detailed discussion) are not easy to understand, and only a small segment of the population are aware of these policies. [1]

Environmental policies have developed over time, and they have been supported by both Democratic and Republican administrations in Washington, DC, and also in state houses and local governments across the nation. The start of significant federal government involvement with the environment was the early twentieth century conservation movement, associated with President Theodore Roosevelt. During this period in 1905, the Forest Service was established and it is still an agency of the US Department of Agriculture. The Forest Service acts as a steward over some of the nation's most treasured natural resources. The Forest Service manages public lands in national forests and grasslands. Gifford Pinchot, the first chief of the forest service, summed up the mission of the Forest Service as "to provide the greatest amount of good for the greatest amount of people in the long run." [2]

The origins of the modern environmental movement occurred over half a century later with the publication of Rachel Carson's controversial *Silent Spring* in 1962, which pointed out the perils of pesticide use and rallied concern for the environment. This was the precursor to what became known in the United States as the *environmental decade*. On January 1, 1970, President Richard M. Nixon signed the National Environmental Policy Act (NEPA). NEPA created the Council on Environmental Quality, which oversaw the environmental impact of federal actions. Later in the year, Nixon created the Environmental Protection Agency, which consolidated environmental programs from other agencies into a single entity. The Environmental Protection Agency (EPA) is a public authority that can be thought of as assuming some ownership of the atmosphere to help to protect it. The legislation during this period was concerned primarily with pollutants in the air, surface water, groundwater, and solid waste disposal. Air pollutants, such as particulates, sulfur dioxide, nitrogen dioxide, carbon monoxide, and ozone, were put under regulation and restricted use.

The standards that the EPA put into place called mainly for state implementation. Each state prepared state implementation plans (SIPs), requiring EPA approval, and each state had to request permits from the EPA to emit pollution into any surface water. Congress also provided for a massive public works program to assist in the construction of water and waste treatment plants for municipalities. The 1970 Clean Air Act also enacted deadlines and penalties for automobile emission standards in new cars, resulting in the development and adoption of catalytic converters and other new energy efficiency enabling technologies.

Since the environmental movement of the 1970s, the focus of environmental issues has changed. While the initial emphasis was on conventional air and water pollutants, which were the most easily measurable, newer issues are long-term problems that are not easily discerned and can be surrounded by controversy, such as global climate change. Underlying the policy decisions made by the United States is the concept of risk control, consisting of two parts: risk assessment and risk management. The science behind risk assessment varies greatly in uncertainty and tends to be the focus of political controversy. For example, animal testing is often used to determine the toxicity of various substances for humans. But assumptions made about expected dosage and exposure to chemicals are often disputed, and the dosage given to animals is typically much larger than what humans normally consume. While industry groups tend to take a risk-tolerant position, environmentalists take a risk-averse position, following the precautionary principle.

Another issue is the effect that chemicals can have relative to lifestyle choices. Cancer, for example, typically surface decades after first exposure to a carcinogen, and lifestyle choices can be more important in causing cancer than exposure to chemicals. The governmental role in mitigating lifestyle-choice risks can be very controversial, such as was the case with smoking in the United States and threats to American household use of private automobiles that contribute to pollution that affects population health. The threat to the latter can come if gasoline taxes were to be significantly increased in the United States to levels closer to those in European nations.

Finally, the way that threats are presented to the public plays a large role in whether those threats are addressed or not. During the administration of President Jimmy Carter (1976–80), the United States undertook a risk-averse policy, acting through the EPA and Council on Environmental Quality (CEQ) to research and control the pollutants suspected to cause acid deposition even in the face of scientific uncertainty. The Reagan administration (1980–88) was more risk tolerant. It argued that, given the scientific uncertainties about harm and exposure levels, new expenditures should not be undertaken that could curtail economic growth. During George H. W. Bush's presidential campaign (1988), he called for new Clean Air Act legislation to curtail sulfur- and nitrogen-dioxide emissions. In 1990, after he was elected, amendments to the Clean Air Act were passed that cut emissions by more than twelve million tons per year, set up a market-like system of emissions trading, and set a cap on emissions for the year 2000. These goals were achieved to some degree by the installation of industrial scrubbers.

While the initial costs in cutting emissions levels were expected to be more than $4.6 billion for utilities and a 40 percent rise in electricity costs, the impact ended up being only about $1 billion and a 2 percent to 4 percent rise in electricity costs. Part of the reason for the relatively low costs is the availability of low-sulfur coal and new technologies to cut emissions at lower costs than anticipated.

Since the major environmental legislation of the 1970s was enacted, great progress has been made in some areas and progress has been more limited in other areas. On the progress side, between 1970 and 1996, air pollutants declined 32 percent while the population grew by 29 percent. There has been less progress made in addressing concerns about global climate change as was highlighted in the chapter on the science of sustainability. One reason of this is concern for the potential costs of addressing global climate change.

The overall cost of environmental regulation currently in the United States is estimated to be about 2 percent of the gross domestic product. This is similar to many other countries, but calculating the cost is challenging both conceptually (deciding what costs are included) and practically (with data from a broad range of sources). [3] Critics of environmental legislation argue that the gains made in environmental protection come at too great a cost. The cost of meeting OSHA workplace exposure standards, for example, can be as high as $3 million per life-year for benzene protection in Coke and coal factories or $51 million per life-year for arsenic protection in glass manufacturing plants. The benefits of environmental and energy programs are also hard to fully quantify. So while cost-benefit analysis is important to try to determine the net economic consequence of policies, and it is frequently used, the analysis can be very difficult. The challenges include quantifying all the benefits and identifying all the affected parties.

Sidebar
Cost-benefit analysis is done to determine how well economically, or how poorly, a considered action, such as public policy, will turn out. The analysis finds, quantifies, and adds all the positive factors. These are the benefits. Then it identifies, quantifies, and subtracts all the negatives, the costs. The difference between the two indicates whether the considered policy is advisable on a net economic basis. The challenge to doing a cost-benefit analysis well is making sure you include all the costs and all the benefits and properly quantify them.
Cost-benefit analysis does not take into consideration the distribution of costs or benefits, does not consider noneconomic factors, nor does it address nonquantifiable factors.

Environmental issues, such as air quality and acid rain, began to influence energy policy in the last decades of the twentieth century, and this is increasingly the case in the United States and other nations. The interaction of climate change and energy production and consumption requires closer links between environmental and energy policies. More recently, environmental and energy policies are also being linked with economic policy (see the following).

The objectives at the intersection of environmental, energy, and economic policies include

- reducing the dependence on impacted energy,
- promoting less energy use,
- increasing the efficiency in the use of energy,
- increasing the share of renewable energy used,
- using innovation to achieve all the previously mentioned goals.

In 2010, reflective of President Obama's interest in policy actions at the intersection of the environment, energy, and economy was his administration's posting on their official website [4] of the following:

The nation that harnesses the power of clean, renewable energy will be the nation that leads the 21st century. Today, we export billions of dollars each year to import the energy we need to power our country. Our dependence on foreign oil threatens our national security, our environment and our economy. We must make the investments in clean energy sources that will put Americans back in control of our energy future, create millions of new jobs and lay the foundation for long-term economic security.

After a comprehensive energy bill that included a cap-and-trade market on greenhouse gas emissions failed in the US Senate in 2010, President Obama determined that "climate change policy would have to be achieved in smaller chunks." [5] These "chunks" proposed by the Obama administration included

- a target for power plants to produce mostly clean electricity by 2035—including power from sources like clean coal and natural gas,
- federal government support and investment in clean technologies,
- asking the US Congress to eliminate billions of dollars in subsidies for oil companies.

While President Obama directed pointed action at oil companies, in general, he sought a centrist message on energy issues that had sharply divided the discussion on energy, saying nuclear power and two fossil fuels, clean coal and natural gas, would be needed to meet a goal of 80 percent clean energy in fewer than twenty-five years. "Some folks want wind and solar. Others want nuclear, clean coal, and natural gas," Obama said. "To meet this goal, we will need them all and I urge Democrats and Republicans to work together to make it happen." [6]

As of 2012, there was no federal cap-and-trade program for greenhouse gas emissions in the United States; however, as discussed previously, the Clean Air Act amendment of 1990 created a successful federal cap-and-trade program for sulfur dioxide and nitrogen oxides. Three regional cap-and-trade initiatives have started: the Regional Greenhouse Gas Initiative (RGGI) in the Northeast; Western Climate Initiative (WCI) along the west coast; and the Midwestern Greenhouse Gas Reduction Accord (MGGA) in the central United States. The twenty-four states involved in the three initiatives include over 50 percent of the US population and 40 percent of overall carbon dioxide emissions. [7]

An example of one of the regional initiatives is the Regional Greenhouse Gas Initiative (RGGI), which is an agreement among ten Northeast and mid-Atlantic states to participate in a cap-and-trade program to reduce carbon dioxide (CO_2) emissions from fossil-fueled power plants (plants that use coal, oil, or natural gas). The total cap set for the ten states participating in RGGI was initially set at 188 million tons annually. Total annual emissions in the RGGI states cannot exceed the annual cap from 2009 to 2014 and then must fall by 2.5 percent per year through 2018, so that by 2019 they must be at least 10 percent below the projected 2009 level.

A large majority of US states have renewable portfolio standards (RPS) or the equivalent and these standards are helping to drive the demand for new renewable energy. In addition, federal legislation has been proposed that requires electric utilities to meet 20 percent of their electricity demand through renewable energy sources and energy efficiency by 2020, and the enabling policy mechanism in the legislation is a federal RPS. However, currently there is no federal RPS.

International Environmental and Energy Policies

Even with the environmental decade of the 1970s and the initiatives of the Obama administration, many countries are well ahead of the United States with public policies to address global warming and other sustainability concerns.

The Kyoto Protocol adopted in 1997 in Kyoto, Japan, is an example of an international effort by world leaders to address global carbon dioxide emissions. It illustrates the complex economic, social, political, and technical challenges embedded in addressing GHG emissions globally. For instance, the Kyoto Protocol, among other items, set binding targets for thirty-seven industrialized countries and the European community for reducing GHG emissions over a five-year period from 2008 to 2012. [8]

Although the United States is the second largest emitter of GHG, it is not a participant in the Kyoto Protocol. One hundred and ninety-one countries including China (as a developing country) have signed and ratified participation in the treaty. The Kyoto Protocols, however, are set to expire in 2012 and there is little optimism for a new treaty.

The United States has had varying support for participation in international agreements to address climate change. Vice President Al Gore was a main participant in putting the Kyoto Protocol together in 1997. President Bill Clinton signed the agreement in 1997, but the US Senate refused to ratify it, citing potential damage to the economy and job loss and that it excluded some developing countries from having to comply with the standards. George W. Bush made campaign promises in 2000 to regulate carbon dioxide as a pollutant. However, in 2001, he withdrew the United States from the Kyoto agreement as one of the first acts of his presidency. Bush believed that the Kyoto Protocol was too costly and would harm the US economy. Affecting the policy landscape was the general resistance among those who questioned the validity of the science behind global warming. And even among strong supporters of the need to take action on climate change, there is resistance to participate in global agreements. In the Cancun Climate Change meeting in November 2010, representatives from the Obama administration insisted that before signing off on a global agreement that fast-emerging economies, such as India and China, commit to reducing emissions and to an inspection process that will verify those actions.

European countries have been leaders in addressing global warming. Many of the European nations have very limited fossil fuel of their own and have high costs of energy so that measures to increase energy efficiency and to develop renewable energy make good environmental, and also very good economic, sense. Germany and Spain are global leaders in wind power. Portugal in 2010 will get 45 percent of its energy from renewable sources. By 2025, Ireland, Denmark, and Britain will get 40 percent or more of their electricity from renewable sources. In contrast, the United States in 2009 generated less than 5 percent of its power from newer forms of renewable energy and has a current target for 2025 to reach 16 percent (or just over 20 percent, including hydroelectric power).

European nations increased use of renewable sources has been supported by public policies. In the early 1990s, Scandinavian countries were the first nations to introduce a CO_2 tax. [9] More recently, in 2007, the Netherlands introduced a waste fund that is funded by a carbon-based packaging tax. This tax encourages producers to create packaging that is recyclable and was implemented to help reach the goals of recycling 65 percent of used packaging by 2012. [10]

Sidebar

Extended Producer Responsibility

The European continent has also been the leader in extended producer responsibility (ERP). ERP is policy to promote total life cycle environmental improvements of product systems by extending the responsibilities of the manufacturer products to various parts of the product's life cycle and especially to the take back and final disposal of the product. A principal reason for allocating responsibility to producers is their capacity to make changes at the source to reduce the environmental impacts of their product throughout its life cycle. It is essentially the producers that decide the features of the products they manufacture at the design phase of products. Rational manufacturers, when made responsible for end-of-life management of their products financially or physically, would presumably try to find a way to minimize the costs associated with end-of-life management by changing the design of their products. The establishment of such feedback loops from the downstream (end-of-life management) to the upstream (design of products) is the core of the EPR principle that distinguishes EPR from a mere take back system. Assigning responsibility primarily to one actor would also avoid the situation where everyone's responsibility becomes no one's responsibility.

While most of the European nations have been ahead of the United States in trying to address climate change with public policies, it was much more recently that some leading Asian nations have begun to take initiatives. With its rapidly growing economy and industrialization, China passed the United States as the world's largest emitter of greenhouse gases in 2006. That milestone came not only because of China's rapid growth and industrialization but also because of its heavy reliance on coal, an especially dirty fossil fuel in terms of emission of gases contributing to global climate change.

Under scrutiny globally, Chinese president Hu Jintao in 2009 called for China to reduce its carbon emissions per unit of economic output by 40 percent to 45 percent by 2020, compared with 2005 levels. China has started to move away from fossil fuels. In 2010, China along with other Asian nations that were initially slow to respond to climate change—Japan and South Korea—increased support of money into research and development of clean technologies. Because of these strategic investments, China is positioned to emerge as a global clean tech leader and perhaps diminish the United States' chances of capitalizing on clean tech manufacturing jobs and the fruits of technological innovation. [11]

However, even with research and development investments and even if China meets its energy efficiency goal this year

and its carbon goal by 2020, its total carbon emissions are still on track to rise steeply in the next decade; according to forecasts by the International Energy Agency, that is because of factors including rapid growth in the Chinese economy, growing car ownership, and rising ownership of household appliances. [12]

KEY TAKEAWAYS

- Modern US environmental policy began in the late 1960s and early 1970s as a reaction to rising levels of air and water pollution and featured the creation of the Environmental Protection Agency and passage of the Clean Air and Clean Water Act.
- The United States does not have any type of federal public policy in place to reduce greenhouse gas emissions or a national RPS. Many US states have developed programs to fill in the gap occurring at the federal level.
- The United States is the second largest emitter of GHG emissions in the world, only surpassed by China.
- European and Asian countries have more progressive policies in regards to energy use and climate change and are emerging as leaders in clean technology as a result.

EXERCISES

1. How would you characterize the US government's response to global climate change? How does it compare with the European nations' response?
2. Find an article in an online newspaper about how the United States is supporting clean technology investment in its country. What policy instruments is the United States using to support the technology investment? What implications does this have for sustainable businesses in the United States?
3. Complete the previous assignments for China and compare China's efforts to efforts in the United States.

Summary

Understanding government is not only for political science majors. Government and public policies have strong impact on all businesses. It is important for sustainable business owners and managers to understand government policies, their objectives, and how they are implemented. The best approach for many sustainable businesses in their relations with government is to be interactive and when appropriate to partner with government to achieve desired social objectives, such as stewardship of the environment.

This chapter has highlighted public policy programs and concepts that are especially important for businesses that are focused on sustainability.

Minicase 1: British Petroleum 2010 Gulf Oil Spill: As a Case of Government Failure

The Gulf of Mexico British Petroleum (BP) oil spill of 2010 is the largest oil spill in the history of the United States. While the spill was most directly linked to British Petroleum's drilling practices, the role of government, both before and after the spill, has come into question following the accident. To some the spill reflected that the industry had taken over a regulatory agency, so the agency acquiesced to industry interests. To others it represented how government had failed, both in its role to prevent the spill and in its inadequate response to the spill. Many factors contributed to this

apparent government failure and the subsequent environmental damage.

Regulations passed by the government may have contributed to short-sighted decision making within BP. After the Exxon Valdez spill in 1989, the US Congress capped an oil company's financial liability for a spill (over and above the cleanup costs) at $75 million. [13] Although BP, accepting responsibility for the spill, eventually waived the cap, this law could have contributed more to BP (and other oil companies) undertaking riskier drilling practices than if a liability cap had been in place. Without a cap, BP may have more closely weighed the potential revenue of drilling against the possible costs associated with a spill.

Another aspect of the government failure was related to conflicts of interest. Many federal employees experienced conflicts of interest associated with the oil business in years leading up to the spill. This was specifically the case at the Minerals Management Service (MMS), which is the federal agency under the US Department of the Interior that managed the US oceanic oil resources prior to the spill. US government auditors had warned of corrupt operations within the MMS that suggested inappropriate relationships and interactions with members of the oil industry. In particular, MMS personnel were found to have accepted gifts from oil company employees. [14] Another source of conflict of interest was with the lawmakers on the congressional committees that oversaw the MMS. Some committee members represented states in which oil companies had a significant economic presence and members of the Senate Energy and Natural Resource Committee, for example, received, on average, double the amount of campaign support from the oil and gas industry as did other members of the Senate. [15]

The MMS seemingly ignored federal regulations surrounding oil drilling compliance. The National Environmental Policy Act (NEPA) was enacted to ensure that federal agencies completed thorough and adequate assessments before approving projects that carried significant environmental risk, including offshore drilling. The MMS, however, had been bypassing this regulation and granting hundreds of drilling permits without due process. Specifically, the well associated with the Gulf spill was granted exemption from the NEPA process because BP officials ensured that the well was safe.[16]

The management of former MMS director Elizabeth Birnbaum has also come into question after the oil spill. She did very little during her one-year term to solve the issues of corruption and inefficiency at the MMS. Many staff members, especially at remote offices, claim to never have even seen her during her term. Birnbaum had very little experience in the oil and gas industry before she took office.

Her lack of experience with the industry may have contributed to the agency's inattention to regulations. [17]

The government also received criticism for how it responded after the incident. In fact, one poll cited that two-thirds of Americans viewed the government's actions negatively, a higher percentage than a similar poll in the aftermath of Hurricane Katrina. [18] Many critics argued that the government relied too heavily on BP's assessment of the spill and the company's suggested methods for cleanup. However, analysts suggest that neither party could have completed the task on its own. The government required the assistance of BP's available equipment and BP needed the government's scientific expertise and logistical management. [19]Consequently, collaboration was crucial to the success of cleanup efforts.

The 2010 Gulf oil spill exposed many organizational problems and concerns within the agencies managing offshore drilling. The MMS was described as having a "culture of lax oversight and cozy ties to [the oil] industry." [20] In response to this criticism and the many others during the spill, the US government chose to reorganize the MMS into a new agency—the Bureau of Ocean Energy Management, Regulation, and Enforcement. It is hoped that this will lead to reforms that will help to prevent some of the government failures in the BP oil spill. [21]

EXERCISES

1. What could US government agencies have done to prevent the BP oil spill? What government policy options were available and what would be the benefits and problems associated with different approaches (e.g., bans, quotas, regulations)?
2. In what ways can businesses, such as BP and other companies, benefit from government policies?
3. In what ways can businesses be harmed and progress on sustainability be limited by government?
4. Can progress on sustainability be achieved without government? Can it be achieved without businesses?

Minicase 2: Apple Suppliers in China [22]
In 2011, a Chinese environmental group accused Apple and the company's Chinese suppliers of discharging polluted waste and toxic metals into surrounding communities and threatening public health. The group, the Institute of Public and Environmental Affairs in Beijing, released a forty-six-page report documenting what it said was pollution from the dozens of "suspected" Apple suppliers throughout China.

The report, which the group said was based on visits to many of the factories' regions, said that factories that the group suspected were Apple suppliers often "fail to properly dispose of hazardous waste" and that twenty-seven of the suppliers had been found to have environmental problems. Also, earlier in 2011, Apple acknowledged that 137 workers

at a Chinese factory near the city of Suzhou had been seriously injured by a toxic chemical used in making the signature slick glass screens of the iPhone.

An Apple spokesman said that the company had been aggressively monitoring factories in its supply chain with regular audits.
"Apple is committed to driving the highest standards of social responsibility throughout our supply chain. We require that our supplier provide safe working conditions, treat workers with dignity and respect, and use environmentally responsible manufacturing processes wherever Apple products are made."

Supply chain experts say brand-name companies generally do a better job of monitoring and auditing their supply chain than smaller companies in China. But most experts agree that while conditions have improved at many work sites, labor violations and the discharge of toxic waste continue to be major problems.

EXERCISES

1. Should the damage done to the environment by Apple suppliers be of concern to Apple management? What are the risks and benefits of having suppliers in China?
2. Should Apple try to partner with the Institute of Public and Environmental Affairs, with other US companies with suppliers in China, with the Chinese government, or with the US government to address the issue of the environmental damage done by suppliers in China?

[1] "Supportive Public Policies," The Sustainable Scale Project, http://www.sustainablescale.org/AttractiveSolutions/SupportivePublicPolicies.aspx#four.

[2] US Forest Service, http://www.fs.fed.us/aboutus/.

[3] *Wikipedia*, s.v., "Environmental Policy of the United States," last modified February 23, 2012, http://en.wikipedia.org/wiki/Environmental_policy_of_the_United_States#cite_note-5.

[4] "Clean Energy Economy Fact Sheet," The White House, http://www.whitehouse.gov/the_press_office/Clean-Energy-Economy-Fact-Sheet.

[5] Timothy Gardner, "Obama Sets 2035 Clean Electricity Target," Environmental News Network, http://www.enn.com/environmental_policy/article/42276.

[6] Timothy Gardner, "Obama Sets 2035 Clean Electricity Target," Environmental News Network, http://www.enn.com/environmental_policy/article/42276.

[7] Based on 2005 carbon dioxide emissions provided by the US Environmental Protection Agency, states that have signed on to participate in a regional cap-and-trade program emitted 2.399 billion metric tons of carbon dioxide out of total US emissions of 5.996 billion metric tons of carbon dioxide.

[8] Kyoto Protocol, http://unfccc.int/kyoto_protocol/items/2830.php.

[9] *Wikipedia*, s.v., "Carbon Tax," last modified April 4, 2012, http://en.wikipedia.org/wiki/Carbon_tax#cite_note-65.

[10] *Wikipedia*, s.v., "Carbon Tax," last modified April 4, 2012, http://en.wikipedia.org/wiki/Carbon_tax#cite_note-83.

[11] Joan Melcher, "Throwing the Race for Green Energy," *Miller-McCune*, March 18, 2010, http://www.miller-mccune.com/business-economics/throwing-the-race-for-green-energy-10976.

[12] Keith Bradsher, "In Crackdown on Energy Use, China to Shut 2,000 Factories," *New York Times*, August 9, 2010, http://www.nytimes.com/2010/08/10/business/energy-environment/10yuan.html?scp=1&sq=china%20closes%20plants&st=cse.

[13] David Leonhart, "Spillonomics: Underestimating Risk," *New York Times*, June 1, 2010, http://www.nytimes.com/2010/06/06/magazine/06fob-wwln-t.html?emc=eta1.

[14] John M. Broder, "Reforms Slow to Arrive at Drilling Agency," *New York Times*, May 30, 2010, http://www.nytimes.com/2010/05/31/us/politics/31drill.html?pagewanted=1.

[15] John M. Broder and Michael Luo, "Reforms Slow to Arrive at Drilling Agency," *New York Times*, May 30, 2010, http://www.nytimes.com/2010/05/31/us/politics/31drill.html?pagewanted=1.

[16] John M. Broder and Helene Cooper, "Obama Vows End to 'Cozy' Oversight of Oil Industry," *New York Times*, May 14, 2010, http://www.nytimes.com/2010/05/15/us/politics/15obama.html?pagewanted=1&sq=Obama%20Vows%20End%20to%20'Cozy'%20Oversight%20of%20Oil%20Industry&st=cse&scp=1.

[17] Gardiner Harris, "Crisis Places Focus on Beleaguered Agency's Chief," *New York Times*, May 25, 2010, http://www.nytimes.com/2010/05/26/us/politics/26birnbaum.html.

[18] Andy Barr, "Poll: Oil Response Worse than Katrina," Politico, http://www.politico.com/news/stories/0610/38246.html.

[19] "'Cap-and-Trade' Model Eyed for Cutting Greenhouse Gases," *San Francisco Chronicle*, December 3, 2007.

[20] "'Cap-and-Trade' Model Eyed for Cutting Greenhouse Gases," *San Francisco Chronicle*, December 3, 2007; Ian Burbina, "Inspector General's Inquiry Faults Regulators," *New York Times*, May 24, 2010, http://www.nytimes.com/2010/05/25/us/25mms.html?scp=1&sq=Inspector%20General%20Faults%20Minerals%20Management%20Service&st=cse.

[21] Bureau of Ocean Energy Management, Regulation, and Enforcement, "Salazar Swears-In Michael R. Bromwich to Lead Bureau of Ocean Energy Management, Regulation and Enforcement," news release, http://www.mms.gov/ooc/press/2010/press0621.htm.

[22] David Barboza, "Apple Suppliers Causing Environmental Problems, Chinese Group Says," *New York Times*, September 1, 2011.

NOTES:

NOTES:

.

Chapter 4:
Accountability for Sustainability

LEARNING OBJECTIVES

1. Discuss business and organizational accountability.
2. List the factors that are influencing an increase in interest and activity in business accountability.

Accountability is a concept in corporate governance that is the acknowledgement of responsibility by an organization for actions, decisions, products, and policies that it undertakes. A customer of a business expects that a product manufactured and sold by a business has been designed, tested, and produced so that it is safe to use. An investor in a business expects that the managers of the company are working to maximize shareholder return and to not be wasteful of corporate resources. The federal government expects that a business pays its taxes properly and promptly. These are all examples of the expectations that stakeholders have of businesses to act in a responsible manner.

Rising stakeholder expectations are motivating organizations to consider the impacts of their actions in a broad, transparent, and systematic manner. Businesses are a major actor in modern society, and stakeholders expect that businesses be a positive contributor to societal well-being. Stakeholders want companies to be more than purveyors of a product or a service; they expect them to fulfill a more positive societal role.

Consumers are showing increasing concern for the environmental and societal impacts of the products and services they purchase. [1] Many investors are starting to use a company's performance in sustainability as an indicator of business value and of management strength. A recent example of increased investor sustainability accountability expectations is when twenty-four institutional investors wrote to thirty of the world's largest stock exchanges asking that they address inadequate sustainability reporting by companies.[2]

"Shooting the Elephant"

There are numerous examples of companies' social or environmental actions affecting consumer purchasing behavior both positively and negatively. In March 2011, Bob Parsons, the CEO of GoDaddy, the world's largest provider of web hosting and domain name registrations, posted a video of him shooting an elephant in Zimbabwe, Africa, on the Internet. The video showed the elephant being killed and local villagers stripping flesh from the carcass of the dead elephant to a score of rock band AC/DC's "Hells Bells." While Parsons claimed the elephant was destroying the villagers' crops and that he was actually providing a service to the local African community, his actions—and specifically the callous way that he documented his actions—spurred outrage from customers with many cancelling their accounts as a result. This is an example of how the social conduct of the CEO of a company carried over to the brand image of the company and resulted in a loss in revenue.

Sidebar
"Ethical Jewelry"
In June 2011, Jewelers' Circular Keystone (JCK), the jewelry industry's leading trade publication, reported on the results of a survey that found 78 percent of consumers said they cared about sustainability and 60 percent of consumers said they were willing to pay a premium for "ethical jewelry." Rebecca Foerster, the US vice president at Rio Tinto Diamonds, stated, "This generation that is up and coming is more concerned about where the products they are buying come from, and they are becoming activists about it." [3] Consumer demand for ethical jewelry is increasing sales for products, such as recycled gold and conflict-free-certified diamonds.

"Conflict" diamonds, also known as "blood" diamonds, are defined by the United Nations as those that originate from areas controlled by forces opposed to legitimate and internationally recognized governments. Angola and Sierra Leone in Africa are examples of two countries that are sources of conflict diamonds. Diamonds have often been used by rebel forces in these countries to finance arms purchases and other illegal activities. Conflict-free diamonds do not look any different from conflict diamonds but have proof of origination showing that were produced in more peaceful regions of the world.

Ethical jewelry is an example of how consumer concern for sustainable products is transforming the offerings from the jewelry industry. By customers "voting" with their purchases

they are supporting conflict-free diamonds, which helps reduce a source of funding available to rebel forces with the expectation that this will either shorten wars or prevent their occurrence.
Source: Wikimedia,
http://commons.wikimedia.org/wiki/File:Alluvial_diamond_miner_Sierra_Leone_2005.jpg.

Organizations also need to prepare for anticipated regulation and new government measures related to environmental and social impact. Governments continue to pass legislation to change or end business practices that are harmful to the environment, consumers, or employees. Governments also provide programs and incentives to support voluntary efforts by business to improve their impacts on the community and the environment.

The response by many businesses has been an increase in transparency on the reporting of the economic, ecological, and social impacts of their activities. This allows for credibility and operational integrity in a company's business activities. Businesses need to clearly communicate the positive and measurable impact that they have on all the stakeholders impacted by their operations.

Triple bottom line (TBL) reporting, also known as sustainability reporting, has emerged as the primary vehicle to communicate this information from businesses to stakeholders. This type of reporting goes beyond profit (financial) information and discloses the planet (environmental) and people (social) impact of a business. Sustainability reporting is a tool to communicate to society the actions a company is undertaking to fulfill its broad responsibilities to society.

A goal of sustainability reporting at the society level is to identify uneconomic growth. Uneconomic growth is a concept from human welfare economics and is economic growth that results in a decline in the quality of life. Only measuring financial activity would not identify uneconomic growth, but with the inclusion of social and environmental performance, stakeholders have a better indication of the quality of economic activity.

Quite often sustainability reporting is driven not only by external stakeholder forces but by the internal core values of the companies. Some companies are founded by social entrepreneurs who want to incorporate aspects of social change or environmental stewardship into their business operations. Sustainability reporting provides a way of documenting efforts by these organizations and communicating that to customers and other stakeholders.

Some companies hope that by publicly disclosing successes and failures related to their sustainability initiatives that they can provide lessons learned to help other companies become more sustainable.

Businesses are facing new risks that need to be managed and this is leading them to actively manage their sustainability profile. Resource depletion, increased toxicity, and climate change are all examples of risks that can decrease profitability through either increased cost or decreased revenue. Sustainability reporting can help a company measure and quantify its economic risk associated with different environmental or social threats that may be overlooked in traditional financial reporting. At the same time, all of these factors provide for new business opportunities, and the companies that can successfully manage their businesses from a sustainability perspective can build competitive advantage, mitigate risk, and capitalize on innovation.

Currently, larger-size companies, such as Ford, are leading efforts in sustainability reporting as they have greater financial resources available to cover the additional costs of sustainability reporting. It can be challenging for smaller companies to replicate the efforts of the largest and most resourceful companies. These larger company efforts in sustainability reporting, which are the focus of this chapter, provide examples of the types of information that could be useful for businesses of all sizes to report on and provide details about processes that business of all sizes can establish in sustainability reporting.

Sidebar
Sustainability Reporting at Ford
Ford's "12th Annual Sustainability Report" provides a performance summary with measures that are important to Ford in its pursuit of sustainability. Ford chose to publish their report as an interactive website that allowed stakeholders to quickly jump to the areas of sustainability that were of interest to them.
Source: "Sustainability Report 2010–2011," Ford Company,
http://corporate.ford.com/microsites/sustainability-report-2010-11/overview-performance.
Highlights from the Twelfth Annual Sustainability Report

- Reduced CO_2 emissions from Ford's global operations by 5.6 percent on a per-vehicle basis, compared to 2009.
- Set a goal to reduce global facility CO_2 emissions by 30 percent by 2025 on a per-vehicle basis.
- Listed water as one of the top sustainability concerns; Ford aims to reduce 2011 global water use by 5 percent per vehicle compared to 2010. This is in addition to the 49 percent per vehicle reduction since 2000.

To read Ford's complete sustainability report, go to http://corporate.ford.com/microsites/sustainability-report-2010-11/default.

Sidebar

Rocky Mountain Flatbread

Rocky Mountain Flatbread is owned by Dominic and Suzanne Fielden, who "care deeply about…community, food and celebration." The Canadian-based business operates two carbon neutral restaurants and a pizza wholesale business, which distributes to over two hundred health and grocery stores throughout western Canada. Their company exists to generate a profit but also to create positive societal change. They engage in a wide variety of sustainability activities, including partnering with local schools on healthy cooking classes, using Canadian-grown ingredients, and fueling their clay oven with salvage wood or fallen timber. They have taken a simplified approach to sustainability reporting and have calculated a carbon footprint and keep track of some key metrics. For example, 90 percent of their food ingredients are produced locally, and they compost 100 percent of their food. [4] They have found the right balance of tracking information to help inform progress on sustainability goals without hindering business operations. Public reporting of their sustainability efforts includes videos on YouTube (http://www.youtube.com/watch?v=8PSIPWavu0o) and sustainabilitytv.com, Facebook, and a page on their website called "Going Green."

KEY TAKEAWAYS

- Accountability is the acknowledgement of responsibility by an organization for actions, decisions, products, and policies that it undertakes.
- Stakeholders expect that businesses will act in a responsible manner.
- Sustainability is a business philosophy in which a company considers its accountability for its social and ecological impacts.
- Triple bottom line, also called sustainability reporting, is a mechanism to communicate accountability activities to stakeholders.
- Larger-size companies are leading efforts in sustainability reporting as they have greater financial resources available to cover the costs of sustainability reporting.

EXERCISE

1. Visit Rocky Mountain's website at http://www.rockymountainflatbread.ca/goinggreen/carbonneutral.html. What activities are they undertaking to be carbon neutral? Do you think the web page is an effective tool to communicate with their customers? What other stakeholders might benefit from this web page?

[1] BBMG, *Conscious Consumers Are Changing the Rules of Marketing. Are You Ready?*, http://www.bbmg.com/pdfs/BBMG_Conscious_Consumer_White_Paper.pdf.
[2] United Nations Global Compact, "Investors Representing US$1.6 Trillion Call for Sustainability Disclosure from Listed Companies," news release, February 2011, http://www.unglobalcompact.org/news/103-02-22-2011.
[3] Rob Bates, "JCK Las Vegas: Consumers Want Sustainable Products," *JCK Magazine*, June 4, 2011, http://www.jckonline.com/2011/06/04/jck-las-vegas-consumers-want-sustainable-products.
[4] American Institute of CPAs, *SMEs Set their Sights on Sustainability: Case Studies of Small and Medium-Sized Enterprises (SMEs) from the UK, US and Canada*, http://www.aicpa.org/interestareas/businessindustryandgovernment/resources/sustainability/downloadabledocuments/sustainability_case_studies_final%20pdf.pdf.

4.1 Sustainability Reporting

LEARNING OBJECTIVES

1. Discuss the value of sustainability reporting.
2. Explain the phrase "You can only manage what you measure."
3. Identify the core areas that are part of sustainability reporting.
4. Explain radical transparency and how it pertains to sustainability.

How do an organization and its stakeholders know how "sustainable" it is? This is not an easy question to answer. As all human activity have economic, social, and ecological impact, it is very difficult to determine whether the sum of the total impact of all activities of a company makes it "sustainable" or "unsustainable." A more useful approach is to consider an organization's actions on a continuum with a goal of continuous improvement in decreasing its negative overall societal impact and improving its positive overall societal impact. Any change in any organization can be challenging to implement, and viewing business operations from a triple bottom line perspective—especially in organizations that typically have been only financially focused—can be extremely challenging. Progressive and small changes when approaching sustainability often will be a more effective strategy than implementing more widespread changes.

There is an axiom in business that "you can only manage what you measure." Measurement is at the core of performance-based management. This statement is true whether the business is a small sole proprietorship or a large multinational company. In order for any organization to understand its current status and progress on its business activities, it is essential that it has clearly defined business metrics that can be collected, analyzed, evaluated, and acted upon.

Businesses have traditionally focused on their performance on financial and accounting information. It is only in recent years that the business community has shifted to additional metrics—in terms of environmental and societal impact—to assess their business performance. Over the past decade, sustainability reporting has been increasingly adopted by corporations worldwide. In 2008, nearly 80 percent of the largest 250 companies worldwide issued some form of reporting that incorporated environmental or societal impact; this is up over 50 percent from 2005. [1]

Sidebar
Sustainability reporting continues to become more mainstream in the corporate world. In June 2011, global consulting and accounting firm Deloitte expanded its sustainability service offerings by acquiring DOMANI Sustainability Consulting, LLC, and ClearCarbon Consulting, Inc. Large accounting firms are recognizing the business opportunity to shift from single bottom line accounting to triple bottom line accounting.
Chris Park, principal at Deloitte Consulting, LLP, and national leader of Deloitte's sustainability services group, said Deloitte's "focus is on working with clients to further embed sustainability into everything they do, helping companies drive growth and innovation, mitigate risk, reduce cost and improve brand—using energy, water, resources and emissions as levers for creating value." [2]

Sustainability reporting is for the most part a voluntary activity with two main goals currently:
1. Documentation and assessment of an organization's environmental and social impact
2. Communication of a company's sustainability efforts and progress to stakeholders

Sustainability reporting typically focuses on comparing performance in the current year to the previous year and comparing it to specific goals and targets. It can also include a longer-term focus and comparisons to other companies in similar industries and in the same geographic areas.

Sustainability reporting is also referred to as "triple bottom line" reporting, meaning that it takes into account not only the financial bottom line of a company but also the environmental and social "bottom lines" for a company. Sustainability reporting reflects the interrelated progress of a company in the three areas—also referred to as people, planet, and profit.

For businesses to understand and improve corporate sustainability performance, organizations need accurate carbon, energy, toxics, waste, and other sustainability data. While traditional business financial statements—such as balance sheets and net income statements—may help a business determine if it is financially sustainable (an important part of business sustainability), they are alone inadequate in measuring a company's environmental and social progress.

Just as there are accounting standards, such as generally acceptable accounting principles (GAAP), to provide organizations with a common "language" of reporting financial information, there are also standards and processes that have been developed for organizations to measure and communicate their position and progress on sustainability.

One of the most important aspects of sustainability reporting is the communication of the information so that it can be evaluated by stakeholders. For most businesses, the most visible form of sustainability information communication is in their annual corporate sustainability report. This has become an increasingly common document released by major companies and is typically featured on their websites. Many companies will have a section of their website specifically dedicated to highlighting their initiatives and outcomes relating to sustainability. Sustainability information can be included on consumer packaging or other marketing pieces to help brand the sustainability efforts of the company and assist consumer choice.

Sidebar
Coca-Cola's Sustainability Efforts
Coca-Cola Enterprises' *2009/2010 Sustainability Review* report provides an example of an annual sustainability report. It discusses goals and performance for areas including beverage benefits, active healthy living, community, energy efficiency and climate protection, sustainable packaging, water

stewardship, and workplace. These areas encompass economic, ecological, and social performance in a way that fits and is meaningful to Coca-Cola's business and strategy. The report is available online at http://www.thecoca-colacompany.com/citizenship.

While metrics are important, quantitative information is only one aspect of sustainability reporting; what is also important is qualitative information that provides context for a company's sustainability efforts and discussion of how sustainability integrates into an organization's short-term and long-term mission and business activities.

Sustainability reporting can be challenging. Sustainability efforts can be difficult for organizations for reasons including

- lack of internal expertise and understanding of sustainability,
- dispersed and difficult to access or incomplete data,
- the need to coordinate across various functional units within an organization, and
- lack of a clear vision and management strategy in regards to sustainability.

Information systems, labor, and other organizational resources must be devoted to measuring and analyzing sustainability information. In addition, sustainability is a complex topic and reporting on specific economic, ecological, and social metrics that are quantifiable may not be sufficient to give a full picture of a company's "true" societal impact.

One of the greatest challenges for businesses is the actual collection, compilation, and validation of data necessary for sustainability reporting. Businesses need to collect information in an accurate and timely manner and business processes must be in place to compile and analyze collected sustainability data.

But even if an organization has the best data collection systems in place and a robust and accurate sustainability reporting process, organizations must also act on that information—that is, use the information to inform and influence subsequent actions. This leads to the next major challenge, which is integrating the information collected and analyzed into the management decision-making process. It is not beneficial to produce a great sustainability report and then stick it on a shelf or a website. A business must be able to "sense" its external environment through effective data acquisition and reports, and it must be able to learn from what it perceives from that information to improve its practices using that information.

Radical Transparency

Radical transparency is an emerging concept that complements sustainability and represents a departure from the current business environment that—while slowly becoming increasingly more transparent—still relies heavily on closed decision making and limited disclosure of business activities and the consequences of those activities.

Radical transparency is a voluntary transparency that exceeds what is required by law or regulation and involves providing a clear picture to the public of "the good, the bad, and the ugly" about the company. Sustainability reporting is one component of radical transparency as it allows a more public and honest view of the company. Radical transparency is based on the concept that the truth is far easier to sustain than hidden information or a lie. The belief is that customers and other stakeholders will want to engage and support organizations that are built on full disclosure.

Radical transparency has been supported by the rise of social media, including Facebook, Twitter, blogs, and other forms of Internet-based communication that expose the truth and that can provide a low-cost way to reach a global audience with information.

Sidebar
Kashi Controversy
In April 2012, Kashi, a brand of cereal owned by Kellogg's, learned the importance of transparency with its customer base. The cereal markets its products as natural and healthy. But customers felt betrayed when they learned that genetically modified soy was being used in the product but was not disclosed by Kashi. Social media, including Facebook and Twitter, allowed customers to immediately and with great impact express their outrage as many of Kashi's customers believe genetically modified food products are not healthy. Kashi's callous initial response did little to appease customers as David Desouza, Kashi's general manager, stated they had done nothing wrong as "the FDA has chosen not to regulate the term 'natural.'" [3] The rise of social media has allowed anyone to gain the attention of the world and highlights the companies to be aware of potential "firestorms" that can arise from customers posts; however, had Kashi been transparent about their use of this product and engaged their customers on their products—through social media and open dialog—they could have not only avoided alienating their customers but also built better relationships and trust with their customers.

Sidebar
Seventh Generation's List

In contrast to Kashi's failure to be transparent, Seventh Generation provides an example of how being transparent can build customer relationships. Jeffrey Hollender, cofounder of Seventh Generation, posted a list on the company's website several years ago of all the things that were wrong with their products and how they fell short of what the company's mission, which is to "restore the environment, inspire conscious consumption and create a just and equitable world." The list included packaging that compromised their values and use of certain less-desirable ingredients because they were unable to use preferable alternatives.

Jeff's sales manager was concerned that this level of transparency would be exploited by their competitors leading to a loss in market share and revenue. In fact, competitors did provide their customers with the list of Seventh Generation's shortcomings. However, competitors'

customers did not use this information against Seventh Generation, but instead they asked Seventh Generation's competitors to now share their own list. Most competitors were not willing to do this. This level of radical transparency resulted in Seventh Generation's customer loyalty becoming even stronger. The bottom line, according to Hollender, is that "you can't judge your own level of sustainability or responsibility, you can only be judged by others."[4]

Businesses have become increasingly more sophisticated in their aspirations and approaches to sustainability—including an embrace of greater transparency—which has translated into tools and sustainability evaluation methods that continue to improve and expand over time. The remainder of this chapter will provide examples of and insights on various metrics, frameworks, and processes of sustainability reporting.

KEY TAKEAWAYS

- Sustainability reporting is increasing at businesses throughout the world.
- Sustainability reports on the triple bottom line of people, planet, and profit.
- Global climate change, stakeholder requirements, corporate values, economic risks, and government regulations are all factors driving the increase in sustainability reporting.
- Traditional financial metrics are insufficient in addressing sustainability challenges and opportunities; ecological and social metrics are also necessary.
- Radical transparency is an emerging trend in which organizations publicly display the positives and negatives of their companies.

EXERCISES

1. Visit the website of a company that you like to purchase products from. Look for a section of the website that documents their sustainability efforts. Create a list and record actions that the company is taking to improve environmental performance or social impact. Look for specific measures that document the impact of their environmental or social impacts.
2. Watch Jeff Hollender's video on radical transparency at http://www.youtube.com/watch?v=annLX3uRVjQ. What are the benefits of radical transparency? What might be some of the drawbacks? How does it relate to the concept of continuous improvement and sustainability?

[1] KPMG, *KPMG International Survey of Corporate Responsibility Reporting 2008*, http://www.kpmg.com/EU/en/Documents/KPMG_International_survey_Corporate_responsibility_Survey_Reporting_2008.pdf.
[2] "Acquisitions, Hirings Expand Deloitte's Sustainability Service Offerings," Inaudit.com, http://inaudit.com/consulting/acquisitions-hirings-expand-deloittes-sustainability-service-offerings-6705.
[3] "The Kashi GMO Controversy: Will You Stop Buying the Crunchy Cereals?" Well & Good NYC, May 1, 2012, http://www.wellandgoodnyc.com/2012/05/01/the-kashi-gmo-controversy-will-you-stop-buying-the-crunchy-cereals/.
[4] R. P. Siegel, "Radical Transparency: Seventh Gen's Hollender Puts His Money on the Truth," *Triple Pundit* (blog), July 2010, http://www.triplepundit.com/2010/07/radical-transparency-seventh-generation%E2%80%99s-jeffrey-hollender-puts-his_money-on-the-truth.

4.2 Sustainability Reporting Process

LEARNING OBJECTIVES

1. Identify the four steps in the sustainability reporting process.
2. Describe what sustainable performance indicators are and be able to provide examples of them.
3. Discuss the organizational resources necessary for sustainability reporting.
4. Provide examples of tools and techniques used in sustainability reporting.

The process for sustainability reporting is similar to all performance-based business management processes. It involves the same steps, including goal setting, measurement, analysis, and action, but differs in the type of information collected. As with any business initiative, it is essential that management be supportive—in this case of sustainability—and that management provides the necessary financial, technical, and human resources to support each step of the process. The success of sustainability reporting depends on the commitment of the senior management in the organization.

Information technology is a major consideration in sustainability reporting. Businesses should be prepared to effectively manage the large amount of information related to sustainability and need to have information systems that can help to integrate sustainability information into their existing corporate reporting systems. These information systems must be designed to communicate performance metrics to decision makers throughout the organization. Large corporate software vendors, such as SAP and Oracle, which provide traditional business software, have integrated sustainability modules that help businesses with measuring their social and environmental performance data. In addition, a variety of custom software applications are available to assist businesses with measuring their environmental and social impact.

Define Performance Goals and Metrics

The first step is to define the sustainability goals of the company. This is an important action and should guide the rest of the process. While sustainability reporting is meant to be broad and comprehensive to provide a full "360 degree" view of the company or documentation of the complete ecological and societal impact of a company, it must be bound at a level that is pragmatic and appropriately focused for a company. Typically resource limitations will require a company to take a phased in approach where it focuses on the areas of higher impact and importance and gradually expands to areas of lower impact and importance. Organizations should put their resources into collecting the information that is most relevant to their sustainability efforts.

The company should have an overall vision of why it wants to integrate sustainability efforts into its business operations. Is the goal of the company to "change the world"? Or is it more simply to document the company's progress on environmental and social impacts? Is the audience for the reporting internal, external, or both? A company will need to evaluate whether its focus is on continuous improvement in its own individual actions or if it is measuring its performance

relative to a broader target, such as a reduction in greenhouse gas (GHG) emissions.

The next step is to develop key performance indicators (KPIs) that will be used to measure progress toward those goals. A key performance indicator is a performance measure from operational data that is used by organizations to track a particular activity.

There are different methods for establishing KPIs, but one typical method is the SMART criteria. In SMART, a measure has a **s**pecific business purpose and is **m**easurable, **a**chievable, and **r**elevant to the success of the organization and can be measured over a specific period of **t**ime.

Companies need to take into account their financial, human, and information technology resources when selecting KPIs. Data collection cost must be factored into performance metric selection. This includes the availability of data and cost to integrate into existing information systems and existing business processes. For some metrics, the business cost may be too high to justify the changes necessary to collect the data required.

In sustainability reporting, a KPI is referred to as a sustainable performance indicator (SPI). SPIs are used as a tool to measure a company's sustainability performance and to monitor and report on future progress. SPIs can be further categorized into the three areas covering either the economic, ecological, or social aspects of sustainability.

For example, a company may select annual net income, annual workplace accidents, and annual water usage as SPIs. Annual net income is an economic performance indicator to measure the financial progress of the company. Annual workplace accidents are a social performance indicator to measure a company's progress in providing a safe work environment for its employees. Annual water usage is an ecological performance indicator to record the progress a company is making in reducing water usage as a way of protecting the environment.

Goal and SPI selection can become overwhelming to an organization given the wide reach of sustainability reporting; fortunately, there are well-developed resources available on sustainability goals and metrics. Companies do not need to "reinvent the wheel" in regards to performance indicator selection. Common sustainability frameworks are available (discussed later in the chapter) that can help companies choose important SPIs. Companies can also contract with consultants who specialize in sustainability reporting to assist with prioritization and goal establishment.

Sidebar

Annual organizational energy use is one of the most common SPIs in sustainability reporting. GHG emissions, another very common SPI, can be calculated from energy usage. Utility bills, such as natural gas or electricity, are the typical data source for energy use. Utility bills provide both cost and quantity of fuel consumed during the billing period (typically one month). Organizations typically are already recording energy cost information into their financial information systems but usually do not enter any information on the amount of energy used.

Information on energy used is necessary to calculate an annual energy use SPI. Therefore organizations interested in tracking energy and GHG emission information need to modify their business processes and information systems to not only collect energy consumption information. Organizations should take into account the cost and effort required to modify business processes to accommodate the new data requirements when deciding what SPIs to measure.

SPIs can be used in determining the projects that a business undertakes. Under traditional business finance, a project—such as the purchase of a new piece of equipment—would be considered using financial measures, such as payback or return on investment. SPIs can be used to calculate a sustainable return on investment (SROI). SROI determines the full value of a project by assigning monetary values to environmental and social indicators. This allows for the calculation of full costs and benefits of a project to be evaluated and may result in approving projects that would fail traditional financial tests or in not moving forward with projects even though their traditional financial measures would support the project.

Measure Performance

Once SPIs are established and business processes are modified to allow for the necessary data to be captured and recorded, the process of measurement begins. Data needs to be collected, validated for accuracy, and stored (typically using database technology or computer spreadsheets). Data collection processes must be straightforward and data must be collected systematically and consistently. Sometimes multiple data sources may be required to offset limitations in any one source of data.

In this phase, it is important to assign responsibility of data collection to ensure that it is being collected correctly. This includes quality control to ensure that data are accurate. For example, errors in measurement devices or communication can lead to false data being collected. As the popular saying goes, "Garbage in, garbage out," which means that that the quality of the analysis is only as accurate or insightful as the quality of the information analyzed.

Evaluate Performance

The goal of the evaluation phase is to convert raw data into useful performance information and knowledge so that organizations can make informed decisions. Key components of the evaluation phase are data compilation, data analysis, and communication. The evaluation phase includes organizing, synthesizing, and aggregating data. Data analysis is then performed to provide insight by converting data facts into useful knowledge. This includes calculation of SPIs. Analysis of data is required before performance can be interpreted. Reporting and communication, a component of performance evaluation, is the dissemination of information to stakeholders in a form that they can understand results and their implications and realize what actions are needed.

Data Analysis

Data analysis can include a variety of techniques including database-driven reporting, spreadsheet analysis, and statistical tests. A business analyst is typically involved in managing this aspect of the sustainable reporting process, and they require both business and technical skills to perform their job. Often the data analysis involves looking for trends when analyzing SPIs. It can also include comparing performance with a goal or standard or to competitors or peers? This typically involves comparing a performance measure to a baseline.

While there are many different tools and techniques that can be applied to analyze data and SPIs, two that have specific relevance to sustainability reporting are normalization and benchmarking.

Normalization

Normalization is the process of removing the impact of factors that may influence direct comparison of SPIs. For example, weather impacts the energy use of a building and varies from year to year. Frequently, an annual energy use SPI will be normalized for weather (e.g., controlled for the coldness of a winter season) to allow for relevant comparison of energy use from one year to the next.

Another frequent application of normalization for companies is to document GHG emissions on the basis of unit of output rather than an absolute number. Growing companies with increasing activities may have rising absolute GHG emissions, even as they are successfully taking actions to reduce their environmental impact on a per unit or consumption basis. Normalizing GHG emissions for output, such as pounds of CO_2 per unit produced, can highlight the impact of companies efforts to reduce energy that otherwise would be masked by just considering absolute emissions. Other examples of factors that can be normalized for include the occupancy level in a hotel, volume of sales at a retail location, square feet of a building, or number of employees at an office.

Benchmarking

One useful strategy to use in analyzing sustainability performance is to compare SPIs with those of other organizations. This can help an organization gauge the potential and success of its sustainability efforts relative to other companies in their industry and peer organizations. In the process of benchmarking, the best firms in a company's industry or industries with similar business processes are targeted, and the company then compares its own results and processes with the results and processes of the targeted organizations. This provides insight into how well the organization compares to an industry's top performers and can provide insight into the business processes and practices that explain why these firms are the "best." Benchmarking can also include assessing an organization's relative position to that of other organizations. Is an SPI below average, average, or above average? For example, a company may use benchmarking to see how its GHG emissions compare with those of other companies in its industry. If a company's emissions are above average, it would indicate that they have the potential to reduce their emissions. The business benefit is that—as GHG emissions are linked to energy usage—the company has potential cost savings by implementing measures to reduce its energy consumption.

Reporting and Communication

The final step in the evaluation process is communicating analyzed information so that stakeholders can understand and learn how a company is performing in relation to its sustainability efforts. The information communicated is different depending on the target audience for the information. Management would look for information in a different format than would an investor, consumer, or other stakeholder.

Communication outside of the company through company websites, annual sustainability reports, and other forms of disclosure about organizations environmental and social performance has become standard business practice. There is no universal method of external communication of sustainability performance, although many standards do exist. The trend in sustainability reporting has been moving toward standardized reporting using frameworks, such as the Global Reporting Initiative (GRI) or the Greenhouse Gas Protocol (GHG Protocol), discussed later in this chapter. Standards allow for meaningful comparisons between sustainability information reported by different organizations.

Reporting should include a meaningful assessment of environmental and social risks as well as an analysis of past sustainability performance and an outlook for the future. Reports should communicate performance both quantitatively and qualitatively and should communicate sustainability information in a way that represents a complete and accurate picture of the organization. While not required, it is common for information reported to be independently verified. Independent verification and standards assist with accountability, as public reporting is typically voluntary and helps reduce the potential for organizations to misuse sustainability reporting, such as for "green washing."

Corporate Annual Sustainability Report

The corporate annual sustainability report has become a common way for businesses to report out annual progress on sustainability initiatives. Companies may not always call this document an annual sustainability report; it could also be called a corporate social responsibility report, corporate responsibility report, global responsibility report, or many other variants, but they all represent an annual report that discusses the ecological, economic, and social impacts of the company. While each company's annual sustainability report are different and tailored to the organization, there are often several key common features in a sustainability report.

Key common features of an annual sustainability report include the following:

- **Executive introduction.** A statement from the CEO or other prominent officials at the company discussing the importance of sustainability for their company and discussing how sustainability integrates into their organization.
- **Performance summary.** A summary of goals, SPIs, and key events related to sustainability over the past year. Many sustainability reports base their presentation of information on the Global Reporting Initiative (GRI).
- **Detailed sections.** These sections provide more in-depth discussion of areas of sustainability highlighted in the performance summary. At a minimum, reports will typically discuss economic, environmental, and social impacts. But there may be dedicated sections for specific areas, such as the supply chain or corporate governance.

Eco-Labels

Eco-labels are a form of communication to consumers of an organization's products or services. Eco-labels provide an indicator of the sustainability of a product or service to the customer. Eco-labels are typically voluntary, although there are some government required eco-labeling programs. For example, in the United States, the EPA requires new cars to be sold with an environmental label listing the fuel economy of the vehicle and many appliances in the United States are required to display yellow EnergyGuide labels estimating annual energy use and cost. Many other countries, such as the European Union, also have mandatory eco-labeling requirements.

Example of Government Required Eco-Labels

A new fuel economy labeling system has just been announced by the EPA beginning for model year 2013 motor vehicles. These labels are required for gasoline vehicles, plug-in hybrid electric vehicles (PHEV), and electric vehicles.

Source: "Home Page," Fueleconomy.gov,
http://www.fueleconomy.gov/feg/label/docs/EPA_FE_Label-052311.pdf.

Example of Labeling for US Appliances [1], [2]

Appliance manufacturers are required by law to use standard test procedures developed by the US Department of Energy (DOE) to record the energy use and efficiency of their products. The results from these tests are printed on yellow EnergyGuide labels, which manufacturers are required to display on most appliances. This label estimates how much energy the appliance uses, compares energy use of similar products, and lists approximate annual operating costs.

The EU Energy label is required for light bulbs, cars, and most electrical appliances (e.g., refrigerators, stoves, washing machines) in member nations of the European Union. They have grades from A+++ to D depending on the efficiency of the appliance.

Registry

Registries are organizations that allow companies, government agencies, and other organizations to report sustainability information. Reporting to registries can be voluntary or mandatory depending on the laws applying to the organization; however, at this time, most registries are voluntary. Typically registries have involved environmental reporting, specifically GHG emissions, but registries can be a way for companies to report both social and environmental performance measures. Examples of GHG registries include the Climate Registry, CRC Energy Efficiency Scheme, Climate Disclosure Project (CDP), National Greenhouse and Energy Reporting System (NGER), and Electronic Greenhouse Gas Reporting Tool (e-GGRT).

To participate in a registry, an organization must join the registry. Some registries are free while others charge a fee to be a member. Registries provide guidelines about the type of information that they collect and protocols for data submission. Some registries require that the information submitted by an organization be independently verified by a third party. Registries may also provide the opportunity for companies to benchmark their SPIs with those of other companies that are using the registry. Registries can include some form of award or recognition program. Registries range from small to large in terms of membership, and some have relatively simple reporting requirements while others have more sophisticated reporting requirements.

An example of a small-scale voluntary program is Maryland's Green Registry. The Maryland Green Registry provides recognition—such as listing on the registry's website, window decals, and leadership awards—to Maryland companies who document five of their environmental practices and submit at least one SPI to the registry.

An example of a large-scale voluntary program is the Carbon Disclosure Project (CDP). The Carbon Disclosure Project is an independent not-for-profit organization holding the largest database of primary corporate climate change information in the world with over three thousand organizations in sixty different countries around the world. Organizations utilizing this registry measure and disclose their greenhouse gas emissions, water management, and climate change strategies through CDP so that they can set reduction targets and make performance improvements. Data submitted to this project is made available for use by a wide audience including institutional investors, corporations, policymakers and their advisors, public sector organizations, government bodies, academics, and the public. [3] This program does not have any form of recognition awards but is meant to drive organizational excellence through benchmarking and reporting best practices.

Manage Performance

The final step of sustainability reporting is action and this is executed by management. Management should be prepared to react to sustainability performance with all the basic management functions: planning, organizing, controlling, and leading.

Management should review sustainable performance information routinely. The frequency of the reviews depends on the organization and its ability to act on information learned through sustainability reporting.

Management is the final step in the sustainability reporting process, if management does not react and change based on the insight provided by the sustainability reporting, there is little value to the entire process. The reporting process is a cycle and the management phase then proceeds back into the first step of defining goals and establishing SPIs. Management activity allows an organization to continually improve on its sustainability performance.

KEY TAKEAWAYS

- Sustainability reporting is based on performance-based management and is a cycle to promote continuous improvement.
- There are four steps in the sustainability reporting process: (1) define performance goals and metrics, (2) measure performance, (3) evaluate performance, and (4) manage performance.
- Companies need to take into account their financial, human, and information technology resources when selecting SPIs. Management must be supportive of integrating sustainability reporting into business operations and be prepared to act on information learned from the reporting.
- SPIs are used as a tool to measure a company's sustainability performance and to monitor and report on future progress. SPIs are categorized into economic, ecological, and social.
- Annual reports, eco-labels, benchmarking, and balanced score cards are examples of tools and techniques used in sustainability reporting.

EXERCISES

1. Go to the websites of one of the registries discussed in this chapter. What are the membership requirements? What type of information is collected and how is it reported to the registry? Discuss the business value for a company to participate in this registry and how it would assist the company's sustainability reporting efforts.
2. Discuss the four steps of the sustainability reporting cycle. Why is it important that the process is a cycle?
3. Search the web for an eco-label for a product that interests you. Describe the information communicated through the label and how it relates to sustainability. Do you feel that the eco-label influences your likelihood to purchase the product?

[1] "Energy Guidance: Appliance Shopping with the EnergyGuide Label," Federal Trade Commission, http://www.ftc.gov/bcp/edu/pubs/consumer/homes/rea14.shtm.
[2] http://ec.europa.eu/energy/efficiency/labelling/labelling_en.htm.
[3] "Carbon Discloser Project," CDP, https://www.cdproject.net/en-US/Pages/HomePage.aspx.

4.3 Sustainability Reporting Guidelines and Frameworks

LEARNING OBJECTIVES

1. Discuss the features of the Global Reporting Initiative (GRI) G3 reporting framework.
2. Understand how more than one reporting framework may help inform the reporting of sustainability efforts by an organization.

Voluntary frameworks or guidelines have emerged to help businesses determine how to report on their sustainability performance. These tools provide structure that can help businesses get started with sustainability reporting or help businesses that are already reporting on sustainable performance improve or expand their reporting.

There are many different sustainability reporting guidelines and frameworks for businesses to choose among. The Global Reporting Initiative (GRI) is one of the most common and encompasses the three spheres of sustainability: economic, environmental, and social. In this section, the GRI G3 Sustainability Guidelines will be discussed in greatest detail to help the reader understand the type of information in a reporting framework.

Global Reporting Initiative

The Global Reporting Initiative (GRI) was started in 1997 by the NGO the Coalition of Environmentally Responsible Economies (Ceres) and today collaborates as an independent entity with the United Nations Environmental Program and the UN Secretary General's Global Compact. Ceres developed the Global Reporting Initiative to help companies report sustainability performance in a similar way as financial information.

The GRI provides a consistent way for companies to voluntarily measure and report progress on economic, ecological, and social performance of their businesses. In 2009, 1,400 GRI based reports were registered by reporting entities.

GRI first released the guidelines in 2000, and the current version, G3, was published in 2006. The framework is continuously improved as knowledge of sustainability issues evolves and the priorities of reporters and report users change. In March 2011, GRI released the G3.1 guidelines (https://www.globalreporting.org/reporting/guidelines-online/G31Online/Pages/default.aspx), which is an update and revision to the G3 guidelines.

The G3.1 guidelines provide seventy-nine performance indicators. Fifty of these indicators are "core" and twenty-nine are "additional."

KEY TAKEAWAYS

- Organizations do not need to "reinvent the wheel" when selecting sustainable performance indicators and goals; they have many reporting guidelines and frameworks to choose from and can choose to implement the standards that are most meaningful and relevant to their business operations.
- The GRI G3.1 standard is one of the most common and comprehensive sustainability reporting protocols.

EXERCISES

1. Download a copy of the G3.1 guidelines at https://www.globalreporting.org/reporting/guidelines-online/G31Online/Pages/default.aspx. Select one sustainable performance indicator (SPI) from their economic, environmental, and social category. Discuss the steps needed and type of information required to calculate that SPI.
2. Search the web for another reporting framework related to sustainability. An example of another framework would be ISO 14000. Be prepared to discuss the features of the reporting framework.

4.4 Certification

LEARNING OBJECTIVES

1. Discuss the role of certification in relation to sustainability reporting.
2. Understand why businesses are pursuing certifications such as Leadership in Energy and Environmental Design (LEED).

Certification is an important and growing component of sustainability reporting and corporate accountability. Certification is the process by which individual facilities and organizations undergo assessment by a third-party auditor. If the facility meets the requirements set out in the standard or code, it can earn a certificate attesting to its compliance.

Many organizations are providing certifications of products to provide an indicator to customers that a product or service meets minimum requirements in regards to its sustainability impact. Quite often, it can be very difficult for a customer to understand the differences in conditions that occurred in producing a product, such as a t-shirt. A certification can provide a tangible way for consumers to discern products that were produced with lower societal impact, such as through SA8000 organizations, versus products that were produced at a sweatshop. The quality and appearance may or may not be similar.

Certification can help purchasing agents of companies select a supply chain that uses sustainable practices. An example of this could be Fair trade. Fair trade certifies that suppliers for agricultural products—such as coffee beans and cacao—pay farmers a "fair" amount for their product and have met specific environmental and labor standards.

Fair Trade Certification [1]

Fair trade (a.k.a. Fair Trade Certified in the United States) is an alternative approach to conventional trade. Fair trade offers producers (such as small coffee bean farmers) improved terms of trade. This provides producers with additional income by paying a "fair" amount for the commodity they produce. A commodity is a marketable item produced in significant quantities. Examples include agricultural products (corn, soybeans, etc.), metals (gold, iron, etc.), and fuel (coal, oil, etc.). Fair trade offers consumers a powerful way to reduce poverty through their everyday shopping.

Over the last twenty years, sales of Fair Trade Certified products have increased significantly. Many farming communities in the *developing* world now benefit from fairer terms of trade. The Fair Trade Certification system covers a growing range of products, including bananas, honey, oranges, cocoa, coffee, shortbread, cotton, dried and fresh fruits and vegetables, juices, nuts and oil seeds, quinoa, rice, spices, sugar, tea, and wine. In 2009, Fair Trade Certified sales amounted to $4.8 billion worldwide up 15 percent from the previous year. Fair trade distributed an additional $74 million for community development. It is estimated that six million people directly benefit from fair trade. [2]

Leadership in Energy and Environmental Design Certification

A popular certification standard for organizations is the Leadership in Energy and Environmental Design (LEED). LEED is an internationally recognized environmental building certification system that was developed by the US Green Building Council (USGBC) in 2000. According to the US Department of Energy, buildings use 39 percent of the energy and 74 percent of the electricity produced each year in the United States; therefore, efforts to improve building sustainability can have a significant impact.

Organizations that are constructing new buildings or renovating building can use the LEED sustainable building design program. The organization can pick and choose different sustainable practices to undertake (although some projects are required for certification) and earn points for those projects. Organizations participate in LEED certification for a variety of reasons, including to help brand their organization as sustainable and to reduce building operational cost.

Up to one hundred points is possible in the LEED 2009 Certification for New Construction and Major Renovations with different levels of certification possible based on the total number of points. If a project achieves forty points and meets all minimum requirements, it will be certified. The next level up is silver certification if fifty minimum points are achieved. The next highest level is gold certified, and the highest possible level is platinum certification.

Johnson Controls Builds Corporate Headquarters LEED Platinum [3]

Johnson Controls, traded on the New York Stock Exchange under JCI, is a global diversified company in the building and automotive industries with $34 billion in sales and 142,000 employees in 2010. Johnson Controls was ranked number one company in the 2011 *Corporate Responsibility Magazine* "100 Best Corporate Citizens" list. The Johnson Controls headquarters campus at Glendale, Wisconsin, has the largest concentration of buildings on one campus to ever receive LEED (Leadership in Energy and Environmental Design) platinum certification.

The company recently expanded their corporate campus by160,000 square feet, but even with the expansion, Johnson Controls has been able to reduce their energy use by 21 percent. Additionally, the company has reduced its greenhouse gas emissions by 375 metric tons of carbon dioxide equivalent and reduced its water use by 600,000 gallons annually. These reductions were achieved using on-site solar electricity generation, a rainwater collection, and a recycling system.

Employees have control over the temperature, lighting, airflow, and ambient noise levels at their individual workspaces. And if they're not at their workspace for ten minutes or more, their individual environmental systems are automatically shut off to save energy.

"As a company that's been in the energy efficiency business for 125 years, we believe it was important to set an example and demonstrate the benefits of incorporating the latest green technologies, including many of our own, into a multibuilding campus setting," said Stephen A. Roell, chairman and chief executive officer of Johnson Controls. "We're delighted that the US Green Building Council has recognized our efforts with its highest award of LEED Platinum certification. Hopefully, it will encourage others to improve the energy efficiency and sustainability of their properties, be it for one building or several."

KEY TAKEAWAYS

- Certification is a growing component in sustainability reporting and accountability.
- Companies are pursuing certification for a variety of reasons, including to brand their companies as sustainable, to increase business opportunities, and to improve their business operations.

EXERCISES

1. Go to the Fairtrade International website to learn more about how fair trade benefits producers. What is the benefit of fair trade to a company that purchases commodity crops such as coffee beans? How does it impact their sustainability? List two sustainable performance indicators (SPIs) from the Global Reporting Initiative (GRI) G3.1 guidelines that would be impacted by an organization that uses a fair trade producer.
2. Search the web for three product certification standards, what spheres of sustainability do they influence and how? Try to be specific by relating them to GRI G3.1 performance indicators.

3. Find out if your school has had any LEED certified buildings and talk with your sustainability or energy management office to find out (1) the level of LEED certification, (2) the number of points received, and (3) what building measures were performed to earn LEED certification.

[1] http://www.fairtradeusa.org/what-is-fair-trade.
[2] "Facts and Figures," Fairtrade International, http://www.fairtrade.net/facts_and_figures.html.
[3] "LEED Platinum Certification for Johnson Controls Headquarters Campus Buildings," Johnson Controls, Inc., http://www.johnsoncontrols.com/publish/us/en/about/our_company/featured_stories/glendale_campus_now.html.

4.5 Life Cycle Management and Sustainability

LEARNING OBJECTIVES

1. Describe life cycle management.
2. Discuss the phases of a product life cycle.
3. Understand the role that life cycle assessment can have in sustainability reporting.
4. Discuss the key considerations in carbon and water footprint analysis.
5. Explain the benefits of assessing the supply chain for sustainability.

Sustainability involves taking a holistic perspective to understand the true short-term and long-term impacts of a business activity. Life cycle thinking has emerged as a useful tool in sustainability to consider the total impacts of an activity, product, or service from its origin to its end. This differs from conventional business practices in which the focus has traditionally been on more immediate factors, such as cost, quality, and availability in the supply chain. Life cycle thinking still takes into account these factors but considers them over a product's lifetime. While conventional business practices have given limited consideration to disposal costs, life cycle thinking considers the impacts of disposal to be an important part of the overall process of product or service provision.

Life cycle thinking in a business context considers business activities using a "cradle to grave" perspective. Cradle to grave starts by considering the impacts of raw material extraction and other inputs. It considers transportation of inputs to the organization and the impacts of the transformation process into a useful product or service that occur at the organization. It then considers transportation from the organization through the use of the product or service up to the ultimate disposal. Each step in the life cycle features a specific focus on inputs and outputs, such as raw materials and waste.

Life cycle thinking came into attention in the 1960s, when life-cycle-based accounting was first used to account for environmental emissions and economic costs associated with various energy technologies over their life cycle. Life cycle thinking has evolved as a sophisticated method for businesses to consider their environmental and social impacts.

Life Cycle Management

The management philosophy that integrates a comprehensive life cycle approach for organizations in managing their value chain is called life cycle management (LCM). A value chain is the connected activities that an organization undertakes in providing a product or service, with each interconnected activity adding value. LCM is a systematic progress of organizing, analyzing, and managing of sustainability impacts throughout the entire life cycle of a product, process, or activity. LCM can occur at the product or service level or at the entire company level. For example, a company may be interested in managing the life cycle of one of its products to improve sustainability, or it may take a more comprehensive look at the portfolio of activities that it engages in as part of a more far-reaching approach to sustainability. One of the key benefits of life cycle management is that it can alert management to potential "hot spots," or areas that may be ecologically or socially problematic.

Sidebar

So how might LCM play out in real life? For example, if a company is selecting raw materials for the production of a product, they may have several material options to consider. The company can have a goal of choosing materials that have a higher degree of sustainability, meaning less negative societal impact or greater positive societal impact.

For example, if a product could be produced with three pounds of plastic material or two pounds of wood material, which material selection would result in lower pollution emissions per unit of product produced? Which would use less water? The impacts may vary depending on what other materials are required; for example, wood may require paint, while plastic would not. What about the quality of labor conditions for where the wood is harvested versus where the plastic was produced?

Materials that do not have environmental and social impact do not exist; every material has some form of impact. LCM can be used to manage for ecologically and socially preferable products and services.

Phases of a Life Cycle

The following figure illustrates three key phases in a life cycle. Cradle is the resource extraction or impacts of elements that serve as inputs to the process. Throughout the business activity or process, there are inputs and outputs, including water, energy, emissions, and waste. Upon completion of the activity, the finished output of the activity is at the gate. The gate is the defining point when a business output activity is completed and it moves beyond the organization to the next step in its life cycle. For example, the gate at a factory that produces tablet PCs is when the manufactured tablet is boxed and ready to be shipped from the factory. Between the gate and up until the grave is the active use phase of the output of the organization, with the grave being the ultimate disposal of the output.

Two terms that are associated with the life cycle are upstream and downstream processes. Upstream refers to activities occurring before the organization (supply chain) and downstream refers to activities occurring after the organization (product distribution and product use and disposal). Upstream and downstream can also be in reference to a specific point in the life cycle. For example, a company might be interested in the impacts of all activities "upstream" of a specific supplier. While business life cycles frequently are focused on products or tangible goods, it can also apply to services.

Life cycle management does not need to consider the entire life cycle, but instead, it can consider discrete phases or parts. This depends on the needs of the organization. Sometimes, the greatest opportunities for reducing environmental or social impacts may exist outside a company's own operations and in its supply chain, in which case, life cycle management would focus on its supply chain. Or the assembly of a product might be quite complex, and life cycle management is focused on one specific part of the assembly process.

Different types of life cycle management include the following:
- Cradle to grave includes the whole product life cycle from beginning to disposal.

- Cradle to gate focuses on the phase from input extraction through the organization output, but not downstream impact.
- Cradle to cradle specifically focuses on the end-of-life step being recycling. This type of life cycle management is becoming more in focus where considerable attention is paid in designing products so that they can become part of another beneficial use and not be disposed of as waste.

Life Cycle of a Cheeseburger

An example of a life cycle would be a hamburger from a fast food restaurant. There are economic, social, and environmental impacts associated with the harvesting of the wheat, vegetables, and beef required as inputs to the burger. Other impacts would be associated with the napkins, packaging, condiments, and other supplies. There are also impacts associated with the transportation of these inputs to the restaurant. These impacts would be considered upstream. As part of the transformation process, inputs—such as water, electricity, and raw ingredients—are required. Waste is generated in the process of producing the burger and pollution emissions are generated—for example, carbon dioxide and other forms of air pollution are generated depending on the type of power plant that generated the electricity.

The gate would be the customer receiving the burger at the checkout counter. All impacts after this point would be considered downstream. The useful life of the burger would be the customer eating the burger and the grave would be the disposal of the packaging for the burger in to a trash or recycle bin.

Energy Use for a Cheeseburger [2]

One sustainable performance indicator (SPI) that could be used in life cycle thinking is to consider the total energy used in the production of a product. A 500-calorie cheeseburger requires about 1,700 calories of energy from oil and electricity to make it from the farm to the finished product at a restaurant. This means that it takes more energy to make a burger than we receive from eating the burger. This negative energy flow and its dependence on fossil fuels has its own implications for the sustainability of eating cheeseburgers, but from the restaurant owner perspective, they would be most interested in the areas where changes to their business practices would have the most impact in reducing energy use. One option for the restaurant owner is to consider which ingredients of the burger have the greatest energy impact in their life cycle. Almost 80 percent of the energy in a cheeseburger comes from all the steps associated with producing, preparing, and cooking of the hamburger meat. This would be an area for the restaurant owner to focus on. Cheese and bread are also two ingredients that require a significant amount of energy in the cheeseburger life cycle.

Another option for the restaurant owner would be to consider which steps have the greatest energy impact in the life cycle of a cheeseburger. The area with the biggest impact on the energy use of a cheeseburger is agricultural activities, or the activities that occur at the farm. This suggests that the biggest impacts on energy use that a restaurant owner can make actually occur in his supply chain and not at his own facility. This might be a finding that the owner may never have expected or have known about without considering his operations from a life cycle perspective. Only about 10 percent of the energy in the entire cheeseburger life cycle is generated on-site in the cooking of the burger; the other 90 percent comes from various upstream activities.

Cheeseburger life cycle phase energy requirements.

Carbon Footprint

One of the key drivers for sustainability reporting relates to greenhouse gas emissions reporting. A popular and specific application of life cycle management is to calculate a carbon footprint. A carbon footprint measures all greenhouse gas (GHG) emissions associated with the life cycle of a product, service, or business operation, including carbon dioxide, methane, and nitrous oxide.

To help organizations, standards have emerged to assist with the complexities of calculating carbon footprints. As carbon footprints involve the complex interaction of organizations, supply chains, retail activities, and consumers, there is often imperfect data and uncertainty in the total emissions impacts of a business activity. These standards help provide organizations with a consistent way of reporting and addressing common problem areas, such as the double counting of emissions and system boundaries.

Organizations are calculating their carbon footprints to
- forecast future emissions,
- provide data for allowances management to allow organizations to manage voluntary or mandatory emissions trading programs,
- provide data for carbon offsets and clean energy projects,
- provide sustainability information to their stakeholders, including customers,

- provide carbon registration and reporting (such as for the Carbon Disclosure Project).

Greenhouse Gas Protocol [3]

The Greenhouse Gas Protocol (GHG Protocol) Corporate Standard is the most widely used international accounting tool for government and business leaders to understand, quantify, and manage greenhouse gas emissions. This standard was developed by the World Resources Institute and the World Business Council for Sustainable Development, whose working committee includes the World Wildlife Fund, the United Nations, Ford, BP, PricewaterhouseCoopers, the US EPA, and other organizations. The standard was originally released in 2001, with a revised version released in 2004.

The GHG Protocol Corporate Standard focuses on the accounting and reporting of emissions. Entities using this accounting system include the European Emissions Trading program and California's voluntary Climate Action Registry Protocol.

The GHG Protocol Corporate Standard considers three different scopes. Scope one consists of direct emissions from an organization's operations. An example of scope one would be emissions from fuel consumed to heat a building. Scope two emissions are emissions from energy purchased by the organization that are generated outside of the organization. Typically, this would be the emissions from power plants for the electricity used by an organization. Scope three emissions are emissions from sources outside of the organization but related to an organization's business activities. Supplier emissions and emissions related to transportation not directly owned by the organization would fall under scope three emissions.

Water Footprint

Another common application of life cycle management is to calculate a water footprint. The water footprint is an indicator of water use that looks at both direct and indirect water use. A product or corporate water footprint is the first step toward identifying the processes and activities, which significantly influence an organization's water use. The water footprint of a product (good or service) is the volume of fresh water used to produce the product, summed over the various steps of the value chain. The water footprint of a business consists of its direct water use for producing, manufacturing, and supporting activities plus its indirect water use—that is, the water used in the business's supply chain. [4]

As freshwater becomes an increasingly scarce resource—especially in some parts of the world—companies that are able to understand, measure, and manage their water footprints and water scarcity risks can gain competitive advantage over those organizations that do not.

A water footprint has three components:

1. **Green water footprint.** Use of rainwater stored in the soil as moisture.
2. **Blue water footprint.** Use of surface and ground water.
3. **Grey water footprint.** Use of freshwater required to absorb pollutants based on water quality standards.

Applications of a water footprint are as follows:

- Measurement of corporate water use and wastewater discharge both in direct operations and in the supply chain
- Assessment of local and regional water resources
- Water risk assessment to map vulnerable watersheds, ecosystems, and communities

Water Footprint Accounting at Coca-Cola [5]

In 2008, Coca-Cola Enterprises undertook a water footprint assessment for the company's most popular beverage, Coca-Cola. They evaluated the water used in a 0.5-liter PET bottle of Coca-Cola produced at CCE's Dongen bottling plant in the Netherlands.

Direct and indirect water footprint components.
Source: Coca-Cola Enterprises, Inc.

The accounting process began with the water used in the supply chain to produce ingredients and other components (e.g., bottles, labels, and packing materials). Ingredients include sugar made from sugar beets grown in the Netherlands, carbon dioxide (CO_2), caramel, phosphoric acid, and caffeine. The supply chain water footprint also included overhead, which accounts for water used to produce the energy that powers the plants; building materials; office paper; vehicles; fuel; and other items not directly related to operations.

Source: **Water Footprint of a 0.5 liter of Coca-Cola,** *Coca-Cola Enterprises, Inc.*

Coca-Cola found that to produce a 0.5 liter of Coca-Cola, 15 liters of green water, 8 liters of blue water, and 12 liters of grey water were required. A key finding of the assessment was that the water footprint of sugar was a significant component of the overall water footprint of Coca-Cola. More than two-thirds of the total water footprint of a 0.5-liter PET bottle came from blue and green water used in the supply chain to

grow sugar beets. The operational water footprint only accounted for 1 percent of the total water footprint.

This study resulted in Coca-Cola taking a closer look at the water use associated with sugar beet production and supported the business value of conducting a water footprint. [6]

Sustainable Supply Chain Assessment

Assessing the sustainability performance of an organization's supply chain is an essential part of life cycle management and can be instrumental in strategy and managing long-term business risks and opportunities. Supply chain assessment can provide a comprehensive view of risk associated with specific suppliers. A supplier may have low pricing but highly irresponsible environmental or labor practices. An organization's reputation and brand can be damaged by poor performers in its supply chain. By evaluating risks—such as low eco-efficiency or poor social practices in the supply chain—organizations can identify "hot spots" and opportunities for process improvements and cost savings.

Sidebar

In 2007, toy manufacturer Mattel recalled one million children's toys that were manufactured using lead paint. These products were made by a contract manufacturer in China. Lead paint is banned in the United States and can cause children to suffer from lead poisoning, which can lead to learning and behavior problems. Mattel had safety measures in place to prevent contaminants in toys including independent audits of facilities, but the contaminated toys were still produced and distributed. [8]

Failure to effectively manage its supply chain allowed for the introduction of dangerous and illegal substances into its products. If the company had had the appropriate information systems and sustainability reporting protocols in place, they could have been in a better position to avoid this situation, which not only damaged its brand but hurt financial profitability.

Supply chain assessment can be challenging. While large companies may have the economic clout to mandate suppliers to provide information about their business practices, smaller companies may experience difficulty with supplier compliance. There also is the risk of overburdening the relationship with an organization's suppliers if the information required is too high or onerous.

Supplier questionnaires are one of the most common forms of supply chain assessment. Third-party certification can be another useful component in supply chain assessment. An example of certification for use in supply chain assessment is Fair Trade Certification.

Walmart Supplier Sustainability Assessment [9]

Walmart is the world's largest public corporation by revenue and exerts a tremendous impact on US and global economic structures. Any initiative that Walmart undertakes can have significant social and environmental consequences, both positive and negative.

In recent years, Walmart has put significant focus on sustainability in its business operations. Walmart produces an annual social responsibility report, as do many other major multinational companies, but their recent efforts extend far beyond reporting on sustainability performance. Part of this initiative is the construction of a sustainability index. Walmart's goal is to communicate to customers the safety,

quality, and social responsibility of the products they purchase from Walmart.

The first step in developing the sustainability index has been to analyze the impact of their supply chain. This upstream analysis has involved surveying and scoring suppliers according to a fifteen-question supplier sustainability assessment. These questions are divided into four categories: (1) energy and climate, (2) material efficiency, (3) nature and resources, and (4) people and community. Walmart provided more than one hundred thousand global suppliers with the brief survey to evaluate their own sustainability, and the survey was required to be completed by their top-tier suppliers.

The next steps in their development of a sustainability index are to develop a life cycle analysis database for products and to develop a simple tool to communicate sustainability performance from suppliers to customers. [10]

KEY TAKEAWAYS

- Life cycle management is a philosophy that integrates a comprehensive life cycle approach for organizations in managing their value chain.
- Life cycle thinking considers the impact of a product or service from its "cradle to grave."
- Carbon and water footprinting are specific applications of life cycle management.
- Supply chain assessment serves as a valuable tool. For many organizations, the life cycle impacts of a product or service are upstream of the organization.

EXERCISES

1. Go online and find the Walmart Supplier Assessment Survey. Review the questions in the survey. Do you think these questions are sufficient to allow Walmart to assess the sustainability of its suppliers? Based on the frameworks discussed in this chapter can you highlight any shortcomings to this approach?
2. Visit the GHG Protocol website and review the corporate standard posted at http://www.ghgprotocol.org/standards/corporate-standard. Identify and discuss three examples of how the standard provides guidance to organizations on how to account for emissions. (An example is employee commuting.)

[1] http://www.unep.fr/shared/publications/pdf/DTIx1208xPA-LifeCycleApproach-Howbusinessusesit.pdf.
[2] Swiss Federal Institute of Technology, *Energy Use in the Food Sector: A Data Survey*, http://www.infra.kth.se/fms/pdf/energyuse.pdf.
[3] http://www.ghgprotocol.org/files/ghgp/public/ghg-protocol-revised.pdf.
[4] Institute for Water Education, *Water Neutral: Reducing and Offsetting the Impacts of Water Footprints*, http://www.waterfootprint.org/Reports/Report28-WaterNeutral.pdf.
[5] http://www.thecoca-colacompany.com/presscenter/TCCC_TNC_WaterFootprintAssessments.pdf.
[6] Coca-Cola Company and Nature Conservancy, *Product Water Footprint Assessments: Practical Application in Corporate Water Stewardship*, http://www.thecoca-colacompany.com/presscenter/TCCC_TNC_WaterFootprintAssessments.pdf.
[7] "Changing Course: A Global Business Perspective on Development and the Environment," MIT Press, April 1992.
[8] Louise Story, "Lead Paint Prompts Mattel to Recall 967,000 Toys," *New York Times*, August 2, 2007, http://www.nytimes.com/2007/08/02/business/02toy.html.
[9] http://www.walmartstores.com/download/4055.pdf.
[10] "Sustainability Index," Walmart, http://walmartstores.com/sustainability/9292.aspx.

4.6 Conclusion

Sustainability reporting builds on existing business management tools and concepts and applies them in a

broader context in response to a complex and highly interactive social, environmental, and economic environment. It builds on conventional business management techniques—such as key performance indicators—but applies them with a focus on triple bottom line and life cycle management. It requires a sophisticated approach of integrating nonfinancial, sustainable performance measures into the traditional reporting of an organization.

The challenge of sustainability for business organizations is to extract value from sustainability reporting so that it constructively guides and transforms their business operations. Sustainability reporting without strategic purpose may result in information that is nice to know; costly to obtain; and of little benefit to the company, the environment, or society.

Sustainability reporting in the hands of a proactive organization that learns, adapts, and continuously improves can give a competitive advantage in dealing with the challenging environment that businesses face. Sustainability reporting allows companies to identify business risks or "hot spots" that were previously undetected and also to alert management to business opportunities related to new markets, products, and services.

While sustainability reporting is still maturing, there is considerable guidance and expertise available to help guide management in incorporating sustainable practices into their organizations. The tools, frameworks, and guidelines discussed in this chapter can assist a company in its progression to sustainability.

The resources needed to implement aspects of sustainability reporting can be significant. Therefore many of the concepts in this chapter are most relevant for medium and large businesses and can be particularly challenging to smaller organizations. Many of the tools and processes discussed in this chapter are geared toward small, incremental change as a part of continuous improvement. All businesses, small or large, new or mature, can implement aspects of sustainability reporting into their organization to achieve improved operating results while minimizing negative societal impacts and emphasizing positive societal impacts.

NOTES:

NOTES:

Chapter 5:
Entrepreneurship, Innovation, and Sustainable Business

LEARNING OBJECTIVES

1. Discuss what is meant by entrepreneurship and why it is important to sustainable enterprise.
2. Discuss the relationship between innovation and sustainable business.
3. Understand the key factors affecting entrepreneurial viability.
4. Explain the different motivations for sustainable business entrepreneurs.
5. Discuss the main challenges facing entrepreneurs.

Today's world faces significant challenges. This includes environmental challenges, such as climate disruption caused by man-made greenhouse gas emissions, and societal challenges, including rising income inequality and other forms of social injustice. There are several ways that businesses are responding to these challenges. Some organizations are accepting deteriorating environmental, economic, and social conditions and are managing through the decline by adapting to limitations. Other organizations speak to the need to make choices between what is good for the environment and society or doing what is good for the economy. However, there are also more proactive, positive responses, including ones that champion business as a force for positive societal change.

Sidebar

Entrepreneurs Find Solutions to Societal Problems
"Deep down, philosophically, we believe that most problems in society—most environmental problems—exist because business hasn't made their solutions a priority," says Gary Hirshberg, founder and CEO of Stonyfield Yogurt. "Our idea is that these problems will go away only if business makes finding solutions a priority."

Addressing ecological and social concerns can create business opportunities that benefit both the economy and society. This is one of the core philosophies of sustainable business practices and a focus of this textbook. Sustainable businesses can help address society's concerns while providing profit-making opportunities for business owners.

Sustainable business is in large part about changing business practices. Successful sustainable businesses are focused on the creation of new products, services, or practices that address or mitigate environmental and social concerns in new ways. Success in implementing sustainable business practices relies on entrepreneurship and innovation.

Entrepreneurship and innovation are relevant in many different sustainable business contexts. They are fundamental for the success of start-up companies that are providing innovative solutions to meet environmental or social challenges. Entrepreneurship and innovation are also highly relevant for established businesses. This applies all the way up to multinational companies, such as General Electric (GE) or Microsoft, and all the way down to small- to medium-sized companies, such as Timberland, Green Mountain Coffee, Oakhurst, and Stonyfield (which are highlighted in cases in this textbook).

Companies undertake sustainability entrepreneurship for a variety of reasons, including to enhance their brand name and reputation and to benefit financially by being market leaders in business practices that reduce environmental and societal impacts in their sphere of operating influence. They also engage in sustainability entrepreneurship to affect positive societal change.

This chapter provides an overview of entrepreneurship and innovation as it relates to sustainable business and specifically focuses on entrepreneurial innovators who forge new paths and break with accepted ways of doing things in new or existing businesses. The chapter begins by discussing some broader topics related to entrepreneurship and innovation and then relates these concepts in a sustainable business context.

5.1 Overview of Entrepreneurship

LEARNING OBJECTIVES

1. Discuss what is meant by entrepreneurship.
2. Discuss the relationship between opportunity and entrepreneurship.
3. Understand the key factors affecting entrepreneurial viability.
4. Explain the different motivations for entrepreneurs.
5. Understand what intrapreneurship is and how it relates to entrepreneurship.
6. Discuss the challenges facing entrepreneurs.

What Is Entrepreneurship?

Entrepreneurship is to a large degree a mind-set, always striving to do new things in an innovative and better way. The meaning of entrepreneurship is derived from the French seventeenth-century term for someone who "undertakes" and more specifically someone who undertakes a specific project or activity. In the nineteenth century, the French economist Jean Baptiste Say refined the meaning of entrepreneurship to individuals who create value by shifting resources from lower- to higher-valued activities. The higher value activities can be activities that bring value to both individuals and society.

It is the twentieth-century thought on entrepreneurship from Joseph Schumpeter, an Austrian born and then Harvard University–based economist and sociologist, which has most influenced contemporary thinking about entrepreneurship. In Schumpeter's view, entrepreneurs are innovators who drive the "creative destruction" process, reforming or revolutionizing the pattern of production. In many respects, sustainable businesses are significantly changing, if not revolutionizing, the patterns of production and service delivery, transforming business practices in ways that benefit the environment and society.

Sidebar

More Than Half Million New Businesses a Month Created in the United States

According to the Kauffman Index of Entrepreneurial Activity, [1] a leading indicator of new business creation in the United States, 3.4 of every 1,000 American adults created a business per month in 2010, or 565,000 new businesses, a rate that remained consistent with 2009 and represents the highest level of entrepreneurship over the past decade and a half.

Another helpful view of entrepreneurship is provided by the twenty-first-century management scholar Peter Drucker. Drucker suggests that entrepreneurs always search for change, respond to it, and exploit it as an opportunity. Entrepreneurs take risks in starting new activities and take on

significant personal responsibility. Many sustainability entrepreneurs perceive opportunities emanating from increased public concern about the environment and climate disruption and are responding to this opportunity with profit-making ventures that address these concerns.

Putting these perspectives together, entrepreneurship can be viewed as

- recognizing change,
- pursuing opportunity,
- taking on risk and responsibility,
- innovating,
- making better (higher value) use of resources,
- creating new value that is meaningful to customers,
- doing it all over again and again.

And entrepreneurship is an attitude and drive to pursue opportunity and create something new and of value.

Entrepreneurial Opportunities

Many different conditions in society can create entrepreneurial opportunities for new goods and services. Opportunity conditions arise from a variety of sources. At a broad societal level, they are present as the result of forces—such as changes in knowledge and understanding, the development of a new technology, shifting demographics, political change, or changing attitudes and norms—that give rise to new preferences and concerns. These forces constantly open up new opportunities for entrepreneurs.

Related to sustainability concerns, certain demographic shifts and pollution challenges create opportunities. For example, with 50 percent of the world's population, for the first time in history, now living in urban areas, city air quality improvement present opportunities for entrepreneurs.

The entrepreneur must first recognize the opportunity and then innovate by proposing a business solution that provides an attractive alternative to customers. A solution is just the first step in the process, the entrepreneur must also investigate the economic value of and business proposition emanating from that opportunity. They must research the market to understand how their potential product or service provides value to a customer and whether the amount a customer is willing to pay, which reflects the value of the product or service to the customer, exceeds the costs to provide that value, product, or service to the customer. In this way, the entrepreneur is contributing to economic growth and society by providing customers with goods and services whose costs to provide are less than their value to consumers.

An entrepreneur can come up with a new approach that meets a customer's need or want, but if not enough customers are willing or able to pay a price above the cost of that product or service, it will not be financially viable. Therefore the opportunity becomes a true business opportunity when it is of sufficient scale and value—that is, revenues will cover costs and promise to offer net revenue above operating costs after the initial startup investment expenditures are repaid.

Entrepreneurial Resources

Successful entrepreneurial efforts require the mobilization of a wide array of resources quickly and efficiently. All entrepreneurial ventures have to have resources such as capital, talent and know-how (e.g., accounting and finance, operations, management, legal, and regulatory), equipment, and facilities. Breaking down a venture's required resources offers a picture of the components required and when they are needed. Resource needs change over the growth stages of a venture; at each stage, the entrepreneur should be clear about the priority resources that enable moving to the next stage of venture development.

While management teams must be recruited relatively quickly, typically there are one or two individuals who initially drive the entrepreneurial process through hard work and determination to succeed. As the business grows, the business team becomes the key factor. The entrepreneur's skills, education, and capabilities must be augmented and complemented by the competencies of other team members. It is essential to have adequate financial resources when starting any new entrepreneurial activity; this is no different for sustainable business activity. Funding can come from a variety of sources including personal savings, credit lines of entrepreneurs, family members, friends, and other sources. Depending on the type of business, venture capital or other investors may be an option. Typically, a company might acquire investors if there are expectations for high growth in the industry. Clean technology is an industry sector that can potentially attract investors for this reason.

All the previously stated resources in the entrepreneurial process are important, but the single most important factor is the individual entrepreneur—that is, their ability to identify a market opportunity and develop a creative response to that opportunity with market potential, to get a product or service out, to sell to customers, to organize an organizational team, and to garner the confidence of potential investors. Entrepreneurs must have passion, drive, excitement, and unique capabilities to do what they do.

Entrepreneurship is not constrained to starting a private for-profit company. While the definition of entrepreneurship is commonly assumed to be individuals creating new for-profit enterprises and pursuing private benefit, entrepreneurship and entrepreneurial innovation can occur in a variety of settings including small or large companies, nonprofits, and government agencies. And entrepreneurship can be focused on a local, national, or global marketplace. Entrepreneurship focused on bringing value to society is often referred to as social entrepreneurship, while entrepreneurship focused on individual and private enhancement of value is simply called entrepreneurship.

Why Do Entrepreneurs Do It?

The only factor found to be associated consistently with becoming an entrepreneur is that one or both of your parents were entrepreneurs. [2] This suggests that if the entrepreneurial path is familiar to you, then you are more likely to follow that path yourself.

Beyond having the common trait of having parents who were entrepreneurs, there are many personal reasons why individuals decide to become entrepreneurs. Becoming an entrepreneur can be motivated by personal interests and values, the prospects of financial rewards, or lifestyle preferences. It is also sometimes driven by "necessity" when there is a paucity of other employment or income-earning opportunities.

The motivations for being an entrepreneur include the ability to pursue a passion or interest that is exciting and one feels deeply about. It can include the opportunity to create something new, enhance one's personal reputation, and make an impact or a difference in customers' and employees' lives and in society in general. All of these are motivations for many sustainability entrepreneurs.

The motivation for becoming an entrepreneur can also be driven by a desire to be independent, to be your own boss, to make your own decisions, and to make your own schedule. This moves into the so-called lifestyle motivations for being an entrepreneur—to have a more flexible work schedule that allows time for other activities including more time for family and recreational and creative pursuits.

Intrapreneurship

While entrepreneurship is normally thought of as starting a new business, it applies to applying innovation to existing organizations. Often, this type of entrepreneurial activity is distinguished as intrapreneurship (meaning entrepreneurship from within). Intrapreneurship applies the entrepreneurial mindset characterized by innovation, risk taking, and flexibility to an established firm. The objective is to enhance the ability of an established firm to react to market opportunities in a timely and effective manner much like start-up ventures do. Large established companies like General Electric (GE) often encourage intrapreneurship to foster innovation and accelerate new product development, to take advantage of a new opportunity, or to assess feasibility of a new process or design.

Sidebar

Jack Welch at GE: An Industry Leader as an Intrapreneur
Some of the greatest business leaders of the past century made their early mark in business as intrapreneurs. For example, former General Electric (GE) chairman Jack Welch made a name for himself by building GE's engineering plastics business as if he were starting his own company.
GE invested about $1.8 billion in 2010 on research and development of clean technologies. This investment helped lead to the development in 2010 of twenty-two new products and solutions such as WattStation, a user-friendly charging station designed to accelerate the adoption of plug-in electric vehicles, and Nucleus, a smart meter technology that helps homeowners manage energy use. The program called "ecomagination" is a competitive force for growth across GE's businesses. With $85 billion in sales and services since 2005, ecomagination is a business strategy that represents an area of continued strength for the company. GE's ecomagination report is available at http://www.ecomagination.com/progress.

Entrepreneurial Risk and the Importance of Resilience and Persistence

Being a successful entrepreneur is not easy and there is no guarantee of success. It requires broad competence across a range of functional areas—including finance, accounting, strategy, marketing, management and operations, and strong interpersonal skills. There are also significant risks and significant likelihood of failure. Part of being an entrepreneur is assessing and managing risk.

Also part of being an entrepreneur is being resilient and persistent. As an entrepreneur, there will always be challenges and difficult times and being able to endure through the tough times and being persistent in working to achieve success is critical for entrepreneurs. Remember that even Steve Jobs got removed from his position at Apple before he came back to transform the company with the introduction of innovative new products including the iPod, iPhone, and iPad.

Sidebar

What Is a Business Plan?
A business plan for an entrepreneur, in its simplest definition, will define where the entrepreneur expects the business to be within a certain period of time and how the entrepreneur plans on getting there. It can serve as an effective tool to manage entrepreneurial risk. It should include details about financing, target market and customers, competitors, and organizational development, including staffing. A business plan is for starting a business as blueprints are for building a home—they are essential.

More business start-ups fail before four years than make it to their fifth year according to the US Small Business Administration. The risks and failures can come from internal factors—such as limited access to funding, poor planning and decision making, or the idea just simply being a bad idea for a business. Failure can also be a result of external factors beyond the entrepreneur's influence, such as weak economic conditions and changing public policies, that can have profound market implications. Also with entrepreneurship—and with ownership, independence, and decision-making authority—comes significant responsibility and the potential for high personal stress and possible burnout.

While this chapter highlights several entrepreneurial success stories, it is important to understand that not all ideas for businesses are good business opportunities. Potential customers have to perceive that the product has value to them (above its cost and better than the products or services provided by competitors) and have the means and desire to purchase it. Furthermore, the pricing options have to cover expenses, and funds have to be available to finance the start-up of the business before revenue from sales cover expenses. These various dimensions must be explored rigorously before a business is launched. While business plans can serve multiple purposes, the first and most important reason for writing a business plan is to test whether an idea is truly an economically promising market opportunity.

KEY TAKEAWAYS

- Entrepreneurship is the introduction of a new product or service through the creation of a new company or the innovation of an existing organization.
- Entrepreneurs search for change, respond to the change, and seize on the change as an opportunity.
- Entrepreneurship requires hard work, dedication, passion, resilience, and persistence.
- Entrepreneurship is to a large degree a mind-set, always striving to do new things in an innovative and better way.
- Entrepreneurs require access to capital, equipment, land, talent, and business know-how.
- Intrapreneurship refers specifically to entrepreneurial activity that originates from within an existing company.
- The key elements of entrepreneurial success include recognizing change, identifying market opportunities inherent in that change, and delivering value to customers by addressing customer needs or problems associated with the change.

EXERCISES

1. Search online for a recent article discussing an entrepreneurial venture, a start-up company. Describe the venture, the motivation for the start-up, and the background of the entrepreneur.
2. Reflect on your personal experiences. Have you had personal experience with an entrepreneur or have you thought about starting your business?
3. Search online for an article about sustainability entrepreneurship in an existing business. Write a paper discussing the activity, the role that innovation and entrepreneurship played in the activity, and the tangible business benefits the company experienced from the new sustainability activity.

[1] Ewing Marion Kauffman Foundation, "'Jobless Entrepreneurship' Tarnishes Steady Rate of U.S. Startup Activity, Kauffman Study Shows," news release, March 7, 2011, http://www.kauffman.org/newsroom/jobless-entrepreneurship-tarnishes-steady-rate-of-us-startup-activity.aspx.

5.2 The Keys to Successful Sustainability Entrepreneurship

LEARNING OBJECTIVES

1. Understand the role of entrepreneurship in sustainable business.
2. Discuss what is meant by providing value to customers and how this concept applies to sustainability practices.
3. Understand what is meant by social entrepreneurship.

All the factors that are important to the entrepreneur in a standard business are critical to the successful sustainable business. Sustainability entrepreneurship builds on the basics of entrepreneurship and extends it to encompass addressing ecological and social concerns through the creation of new enterprises and innovation in existing enterprises.

Sustainable businesses *recognize change* in the form of the increased scientific evidence about the effects of ecological disruption on human populations and the environment and increasing evidence of rising social inequities that are disruptive to the business environment and global society. Sustainable businesses recognize change by understanding that the consuming public is becoming increasingly concerned about these challenges to a sustainable world. These changes create *market opportunities* for sustainability-focused businesses. The market opportunity includes the opportunity to address concerns about sustainability by providing new products and services that reduce energy and natural resource use.

Sidebar

Stonyfield Yogurt: Tapping into Consumers Taking Responsibility for Their Health and for Society

Stonyfield's [1] start-up years were 1983 to 1987—before the era of broad interest in organic agriculture and products. The company tapped into the post-1960s, maturing baby boomer generation. "People were looking to take greater responsibility for their own health and also wanted to have their purchases count for something more than just a purchase," says Gary Hirshberg, the company's CEO. "They liked the idea that their grocery dollars could go to causes that they cared about." Ten percent of Stonyfield's profits are donated, primarily to environmental causes.

Stonyfield Farms has been a success on an international basis by many different measures. By the time Groupe Danone, S.A., a French conglomerate, purchased a 40 percent stake in the company in October 2001, Stonyfield had $80 million in annual sales and was America's number four brand of yogurt. The company in 2010 exceeded $100 million in annual revenue and is expected to rank number three nationwide in yogurt sales very soon. Underneath it all, Gary Hirshberg says, is the constant creation of new strategies. "We never knew what was really going to work because there were no models for us," he explains. "We led with the only things we really knew—our yogurt and our causes."

The opportunities to address sustainability concerns are worth pursuing if new ways of addressing the concerns can be conceived and delivered in ways that bring net value to significant numbers of consumers in the marketplace. A key for successful sustainability entrepreneurs is to make sure that the new way of doing things they create provide value to their potential customers.

An example of the value from a better and more sustainability-oriented product coming from an entrepreneur can be seen with the Nest Learning Thermostat, also known as the Nest (http://www.nest.com/reviews). Thermostats and even programmable thermostats have been around for a long time. But they have been hard to use and hard to achieve energy efficiency with. The Nest thermostat was created by Silicon Valley start-up Nest Labs, whose cofounder Tony Fadell used to be in charge of iPods at Apple and wanted to start up a venture to fill an unmet need. And not surprisingly, the Nest thermostat has been described as the thermostat that Steve Jobs would have loved and the thermostat can be accessed and set using the iPhone and iPad.

The innovative thermostat learns from household behavior and automatically programs the thermostat settings to reflect household routines and preferences to achieve maximum energy efficiency. The Nest thermostat adjusts to household patterns. The Nest thermostat gets smarter over time based on the way households raise or lower the temperature and how household members come or go at different times. In a week's time, the Nest thermostat will automatically turn down heating or cooling when household members are not around. The Nest product was introduced in 2011, and in early 2012, the company was sold out and could not meet demand for its product even though the price was well above conventional and other programmable thermostats.

Consumers that purchase a Nest thermostat pay a premium above the cost of conventional thermostats due to the higher cost of the technology in the Nest product. The benefit consumers derive is that over time they can more effectively and more easily manage their home heating and cooling, use less energy, and reduce their costs and greenhouse gas emissions. Customers receive value in lowered costs and the personal satisfaction of knowing that their carbon footprint

has been reduced, and they can also demonstrate their environmentalism to visitors in their home. A bit of conspicuous conservation can help sell "cool" new products like the Nest.

Sidebar
Making the World a Better Place with Invention and Entrepreneurship

To understand why Tony Fadell is building the world's most high-tech thermostat with a team that includes several former iPod and iPhone engineers and an artificial intelligence researcher who's won a MacArthur Genius Grant award, you have to imagine that you're him: flush with cash after nine years leading mobile devices at Apple, and wandering the world with your family. You've just spent six months in Paris on a whim. You're building an ultra-green home in Lake Tahoe, with a $15,000 heating and cooling system. When your architect shows you the archaic $350 thermostats that control the system, you're not only genuinely offended by their lack of innovation, but you have the ability, time, and means to make your own.

The amazing thing about Tony is that he tells this story as though it's the most natural thing in the world—as though anyone faced with a similar set of circumstances would immediately start trying to build a thermostat. Actually, that's not the amazing thing. The amazing thing is that after a while you start to believe him.

"Most thermostats are built by plumbing companies," Fadell tells me. "But you really need to understand how to build a phone to make them better." His pitch to Nest co-founder Matt Rogers and their other team members was simple: a breakdown of how much energy a thermostat controls (50 percent in a typical home), the size of the potential market (150 million residential thermostats in the US alone, and another 100 million commercial units) and how much technology would be needed to make an impact (lots). "In a span of 25 to 30 seconds people are like 'how couldn't I do this?'" It's 20 minutes into our meeting and now I'm fired up about thermostats too. Let's change the world, one leaf icon at a time.

Source: Nilay Patel, "Inside the Nest: iPod Creator Tony Fadell Wants to Reinvent the Thermostat," *The Verge*, November 14, 2011, http://www.theverge.com/2011/11/14/2559567/tony-fadell-nest-learning-thermostat.

Since there are always people pursuing market opportunities, to be a successful entrepreneur requires constant innovation and effort, continuously figuring out new ways to service customers' needs and wants in cheaper, faster, and better ways. That is what Tony Fadell's Nest efforts are all about. The opportunities to address sustainability concerns are worth pursuing if new ways of addressing the concerns can be conceived and delivered in ways that bring value to a significant numbers of consumers in the marketplace and that are capable of generating revenues higher than costs over time for the enterprise.

Entrepreneurship as a mind-set, or kind of behavior, lends itself well to sustainable business practices. For sustainable business practice, entrepreneurship is about constantly looking for innovative ways to protect the environment or improve societal conditions by providing new goods, services, or methods that reduce detrimental activities while also generating profits for the entrepreneur. By always thinking about doing things in new and better ways, entrepreneurship is highly relevant to individuals and organizations interested in sustainability.

From the business perspective, entrepreneurship and an entrepreneurial mind-set can be advantageous. It can allow for quicker response to market opportunities, such as those emerging for sustainable business. It can also allow for the ability to focus on particular customers, such as the households most interested in minimizing their environmental footprint even if that means having to purchase a product or service at higher cost than a similar product or service.

Sidebar
The Entrepreneurial Process of Sustainable Entrepreneurs
Choi and Gray [2] examined the entrepreneurial processes of sustainable entrepreneurs. They identified successful sustainable entrepreneurial companies in various industries ranging from apparel to biotechnology that were exemplary in their pursuit for sustainability. They examined their key decisions and activities in their "entrepreneurial process," collecting most of the relevant information from published or self-developed case studies. They found that most sustainable entrepreneurs are an unusual breed with limited business backgrounds. Most obtain financing from nonconventional sources and employ unorthodox, yet sound, human resource management practices. They are shrewd in their marketing strategies and effective in running efficient, environmentally sound operations. Also they find innovative methods for balancing their financial goals against their objectives of making a difference in their environment and society.

International Entrepreneurship
China is the "place to be" for many clean technology companies. China is the fastest-growing market for all products and services and also for wind and nuclear power. It is the leader in solar power modules. In addition, the nation has a commitment to expand in the development of electric vehicles and carbon capture from coal plants.

With markets for sustainability goods and services in China and in some other nations growing faster than in the United States, there are significant opportunities and incentives for international entrepreneurship. This can, however, be very challenging, particularly for small start-up ventures. To enter global markets requires knowledge of different laws and regulatory requirements and also of foreign exchange. It also requires knowledge of historical, economic, political, social, and cultural differences among nations.

In China, for example, contracts are more of a memorandum of understanding than a legal binding contract. Business arrangements are commonly built on the foundation of a relationship instead of the law. Chinese companies are used to a rapidly changing business environment. They expect their business partners to be flexible to deal with changing conditions as they occur. This can be a good match for the entrepreneurial mind-set but difficult for entrepreneurial ventures relying on relations and "changing on the ground" while they are physically located thousands of miles and many time zones away from the Chinese market. Also for sustainable business ventures introducing new technologies, China can be a particularly difficult environment for protecting intellectual property. This issue has kept many technology companies from doing business in China. There is a real possibility that Chinese competitors will copy a Western product and nullify the patent or other intellectual property that is protected by law in the home country. Some entrepreneurs might not take this as a barrier. An example is if a US software company operating in China actually tracked down the hackers that had been infiltrating their system and talked them into joining their team as security experts. This is an example of an entrepreneurial company turning a threat into an international market opportunity.

Most entrepreneurs, especially first-time and relatively inexperienced entrepreneurs, would benefit from first focusing on home markets before entering global markets. The challenges of entrepreneurship are hard enough without also trying to figure out entry into global markets. Yet the reality is that China's and other nations' high growth rates and large populations make it an important market for sustainable products and services. Before engaging in global markets, however, entrepreneurs must prepare and recognize how global markets vary and how they may require different strategies and practices. If done right, the Chinese and other global markets could be significant opportunities for entrepreneurs focused on sustainability.

Social Entrepreneurship

Many of the for-profit entrepreneurs engaged in sustainable businesses might be characterized as social entrepreneurs—enterprising individuals who apply business practices to addressing societal problems, such as pollution, poor nutrition, and poverty, and are interested in social change. Social change involves social processes whereby the values, attitudes, or institutions of society, including businesses, become modified. It includes both the natural process and action programs initiated by members of society. Entrepreneurship can be a process that contributes to social change.

Many social entrepreneurs are engaged in nonprofit organizations. An example is Kiva (http://www.kiva.org/about), a nonprofit organization with a mission to connect people through lending to alleviate poverty. Leveraging the Internet and a worldwide network of microfinance institutions, Kiva lets individuals lend as little as $25 to help create opportunity around the world. Since Kiva was founded in 2005, it has engaged nearly six hundred thousand lenders worldwide providing more than $200 million in loans to microenterprises in sixty different countries.

Sidebar

Profile of a Successful Social Entrepreneur
Jessica Jackley was a cofounder of Kiva, the world's first person-to-person microlending website. Jackley and Matt Flannery founded Kiva in October 2005. Jessica obtained an MBA from the Stanford Graduate School of Business, with certificates in public and global management, as well as a BA in philosophy and political science from Bucknell University.

Social entrepreneurs engaged in for-profit ventures are concerned with creating shared value—for their companies and also for society. Creating both private and societal value aligns well with the interests of the large percentage of consumers. Edelman (http://www.edelman.com), the public relations firm, has identified that 87 percent of Americans believe that companies should place at least as much value on societal interests as on business interests. And many thought leaders on entrepreneurship have recognized the potential of social enterprises. For example, Bo Fishback, vice president of entrepreneurship at the Kauffman Foundation in Kansas City believes that "it's not all pie in the sky....Many social entrepreneurs have shown they can accomplish their mission....They can deliver a social good and report a positive cash flow." [3]

The concept of building a profitable business model in which doing good and contributing to social change is an intrinsic part of the business and not just a sideline has been gaining ground in recent years. Social entrepreneurs total more than thirty thousand and are growing in number, according to B Lab, a nonprofit organization that certifies these purpose-driven companies. Together, they represent some $40 billion in revenue.

Sidebar

Certified B (Benefit) Corporation
Certified B (Benefit) Corporations are a new type of corporation that use the power of business to solve social and environmental problems. B Corps (http://bcorporation.net/about) are unlike traditional businesses because they meet comprehensive and transparent social and environmental performance standards and meet higher legal accountability standards.

Sidebar

Private Foundation Support for Social Entrepreneurs
The idea of blending a social mission with business is not new. One of the founding forces behind the movement, the Ashoka Foundation (http://www.ashoka.org), since its inception in 1981, has granted multiyear living stipends to support more than two thousand fellows dedicated to finding answers to a host of social ills through business ventures.

Examples of Sustainability Entrepreneurs (from the Textbook Case Studies)

Case chapters in the textbook document sustainable businesses and how they addressed consumer concerns about ecological and social matters in new ways across different industries. An entrepreneur was the key driver in four of these cases. Simply Green, Green Mountain Coffee, Seventh Generation, and Stonyfield Yogurt have provided fuel, coffee, household products, and yogurt to customers, respectively, with product options that have lower carbon and environmental footprints and higher attention to social justice. We summarize one of the case examples and its founder entrepreneurs here.

Green Mountain Coffee Roasters (GMCR)

Bob Stiller opened his first coffee shop in 1981 in Waterbury, Vermont, selling high-quality coffee. His concept was simple: sell only high-quality coffee to ordinary people every day. When demand for his coffee outstripped his small store, he started bagging his coffee and sold it to wholesalers, supermarkets, and through mail order. Then recognizing and experiencing the challenges brought on by fierce competition in the specialty coffee segment of the industry, Stiller became an early advocate that his business—and all businesses for that matter—could help make the world a better place by committing to sustainable business practices. Green Mountain Coffee Roasters (GMCR), under Stiller's entrepreneurial leadership, saw an opportunity to create a competitive advantage by embedding sustainability in its products and practices. Stiller was passionate about this commitment and was convinced that this would lead to financial success. By adopting innovative sustainable business practices, GMCR met customer demand while having a positive impact on the environment and society. GMCR implemented a fair trade procurement model that improved the quality of life for the farmers in the coffee bean supply chain and their families. At the same time, fair trade helped GMCR monitor quality and lower costs. By lowering dependency on traders and other supply chain intermediates in procuring its coffee, the company lowered supply chain costs and was able to respond more quickly to customer preferences. The company's entrepreneurial success is seen in Green Mountain's stock price with $100 invested in company stock in September 2004 valued at $1,600 by March 2009. In 2009, the company was listed as number eleven on *Fortune*'s "100 Fastest Growing Companies" and number five in *Forbes*'s "Best Small Companies." The company sales and net income for year-end 2009 were $803 million and $55.8 million, respectively.

KEY TAKEAWAYS

- Addressing environmental and social concerns can create business opportunities that can benefit the economy and society.
- Successful sustainable businesses are focused on the creation of new products and services that address ecological and social concerns in new ways.
- Sustainability entrepreneurship can involve starting a new business or creating a new product or service in an existing business.
- Sustainable entrepreneurship can impact companies of all sizes, from the very small to the world's largest.
- The entrepreneur is the key driver in sustainability efforts at both new and established companies.
- To be successful in sustainable business practices often requires entrepreneurship and innovation.
- Social entrepreneurship specifically utilizes a business as the vehicle to tackle a societal problem.
- Green Mountain, Stonyfield, and Oakhurst all provide examples of how entrepreneurship led to innovation in regards to sustainability at existing organizations.

EXERCISES

1. Generate a list of possible sustainable new business opportunities that you might be interested in undertaking. What innovations are critical to the success of each of the new business opportunities that you identified?
2. In the sidebar on Peter Drucker's interpretation of entrepreneurship (from Section 5.1 "Overview of Entrepreneurship"), discuss how that view applies to sustainability entrepreneurship.
3. Search for a blog on social entrepreneurship. Write a paper reflecting on what you learn from the blog and answer the question, "Why do you think social entrepreneurs do what they do?"

[1] "Everybody Must Get Stonyfield," *Reveries*, June 2002, http://www.reveries.com/reverb/cause_marketing/hirshberg/index.html.
[2] David Y. Choi and Edmund R. Gray, "The Venture Development Processes of 'Sustainable' Entrepreneurs," *Management Research News* 31, no. 8 (2008): 558–69.
[3] Stacy Perman, "Making a Profit and a Difference," *Businessweek*, April 3, 2009, http://www.businessweek.com/smallbiz/content/mar2009/sb20090330_541747.htm.

5.3 Innovation and Sustainability

LEARNING OBJECTIVES

1. Understand the role of innovation in sustainable business.
2. Discuss the relationship between technology and innovation in sustainable business.
3. Discuss the relationship between social networks and innovation in sustainable business.

Innovation in business involves a change in a product offering, service, business model, or operations that meaningfully improves the experience of a large number of stakeholders. There are two particularly important words in the previous definition—"meaningfully" and "stakeholders."

Sidebar
Apple: The World's Leading Innovating Company
Consistently since 2006, *Fortune* surveys have ranked Apple number one in innovation and the company is also frequently mentioned as the most admired company in the United

States. In August 2011, Apple also became the world's most valuable company at $349 billion based on stock market valuation. Apple's innovations have revolutionized the way we use computers and phones and play music and movies. One innovation in particular, the iPod was the start of a trend of products with broad consumer market appeal. The iPod combined technical knowledge with a new online music concept to become the most influential new product in decades. That was followed by Apple's introduction of the iPhone and iPad. All these products combine technological innovation with attention to design, usability, and content delivery in new and innovate ways to transform the way billions of consumers use music, use their phones, use their computers, and access the Internet.

If a company redesigns its packaging to be more environmentally friendly, that's a change. It's new. But does it *meaningfully* reduce the materials and energy use of consuming or using the product? There are many types of changes that can be made, but the question of whether it's an innovation rests on how significantly it improves what is being targeted to be improved. This aspect of the definition raises the bar to avoid classifying meaningless changes as innovations. What is meaningful is contextual on a per innovation basis.

And for an invention to be more than something new and creative, it should have broad impact. The term *stakeholders* acknowledges that the beneficiaries of an innovation can vary widely—consumers, shareholders, employees, and any subset thereof. All of these stakeholders can potentially benefit from different types of innovations meant to address sustainability.

Responding to an opportunity often requires innovation; for example, finding a new way to solve a problem or address a concern that is cheaper, faster, or better than the old way of doing things. The innovation can range from a relatively simple process (way of doing things) change to a highly complex new technology, such as those introduced by General Electric (GE) in their ecomagination program (discussed in the previous sidebar titled "Jack Welch at GE: An Industry Leader as an Intrapreneur").

Sidebar
Commercialization and Its Phases
The process by which a new product or service is introduced into the general market is called commercialization. Commercialization is broken into phases, from the initial introduction of the product to its mass production and its adoption. It takes into account the production, distribution, marketing, sales, and customer support required to achieve commercial success. As a strategy, commercialization requires that a business develop a marketing plan, determine how the product will be supplied to the market, and anticipate barriers to success. Read more at http://www.answers.com/topic/commercialization#ixzz1PvcRgIo5.

To help illustrate the concept of innovation, two companies will be discussed. Both companies are innovators in two entirely different areas at two entirely different price points. However, both companies are connected to sustainability in that they are providing a product to help reduce the consumption of fossil fuels for energy.

Enertrac (http://enertrac.com) provides low-cost smart sensors to track energy use so households and businesses know when they need refills. The smart sensors allow fuel distributors to electronically monitor the amount of oil in a tank. The sensors send information to a software-as-a-service interface that integrates into fuel dealers delivery scheduling systems. This allows business owners to make their delivery methods more efficient while reducing greenhouse emissions by 30 percent or more. The same sensors can also monitor other energy and natural resource use, including water, and can help with regulating use and conservation efforts. The basic smart sensor device is priced at less than $30. From early 2010 to early 2012, Enertrac went from 200 monitors installed to 25,000 monitors in place with 140,000 units on order.

On the other end of the technological spectrum is SustainX Energy Storage Solutions (http://www.sustainx.com/), a company started by the former dean of the engineering school at Dartmouth College. SustainX has invented a new technology to cost-effectively and efficiently store energy from renewable and other sources. The technology being pioneered by SustainX compresses and expands gas resulting in seven times the reduction in storage cost as compared to traditional methods. This could profoundly change the economics of energy generation from both renewables and conventional sources. The storage systems that SustainX is developing for utility companies will cost more than $1 million.

Technological Innovation and Sustainable Business
Fundamental to many sustainable businesses, including Enertrac and SustainX, are so-called clean energy technologies or sometimes called clean tech. These include technologies that generate energy from renewable sources, store energy, conserve energy, monitor and regulate energy

usage and the pollution it generates, and efficiently manage water and other natural resources.

Technological advancement relies on investment in research and development. This can range from relatively small investments for Enertrac and other sustainable businesses pursuing low-cost technology solutions to millions of dollars for companies like SustainX, which are pursuing more radical (so-called game-changing) inventions.

Public policy can play a role in encouraging the development and adoption of new technology, which serves to jump-start market development and demand and reduce start-up risks for sustainability entrepreneurs. Research and development tax credits can reduce the costs of innovation and new products and services, offering development for entrepreneurs. And public programs offering tax advantages and rebates to customers, such as the California Solar Initiative (http://www.gosolarcalifornia.ca.gov/csi/index.php), can lower the cost and increase the rate of customer adoption of new products and services.

Sidebar
Financial Incentive from Government to Innovate: The Research and Development Tax Credit
The Research and Development (R&D) tax credit is for businesses of all sizes, not just major corporations. Any company that designs, develops, or improves products, processes, techniques, formulas, inventions, or software may be eligible. In fact, if a company has simply invested time, money, and resources toward the advancement and improvement of its products and processes, it may qualify. The company receives a credit that can be used against taxes owed for their investment in qualifying research and development. The credits are available in the United States at the federal level at 14 percent (as of 2011), and additional R&D tax credits are available in some states.

Also important in the development of new technologies are the industry standards the government defines and regulates. Examples of public policy initiatives that have pushed forward technological innovations are energy efficiency standards for appliances and for buildings.

Innovation in turn can lower the barriers and costs of public policy standards on emissions and efficiency, and this can also be true for some policies to address social injustices (e.g., technologies that improve the productivity and output of workers and that can lower the costs of increasing the minimum wage). So from a systems perspective, there is

feedback going in both directions between innovation and public policy.

Sidebar
Energy Efficiency Standards and Clean Tech Innovations
Minimum standards of energy efficiency for many major appliances were established by the US Congress in various legislations including the Energy Policy and Conservation Act (EPCA); the National Appliance Energy Conservation Act; and the Energy Policy Act of 2005, Public Law 109-58 (http://www1.eere.energy.gov/buildings/appliance_standards/pdfs/epact2005_appliance_stds.pdf). [1] Regulations are issued by executive branch agencies to carry out federal laws, such as the standards laws, and are available in the Code of Federal Regulations. [2] Proposed and recently adopted rules and regulations may be found in the Federal Register (http://www.gpoaccess.gov/cfr/).

The end users of clean energy technology are diverse. They include private households, businesses, public agencies, and utilities. End users can take advantage of public incentives and they can also influence the public discourse and policies concerning investment, standards, mandates, and incentives. Most importantly, the choices end users make influence decisions by green producers and sustainability entrepreneurs regarding new products and services. For example, as end users are becoming more conscious about the environmental impact of a product from production to discontinued use (from "cradle to cradle"), consumers are demanding cleaner production processes and recycling services for the end of the product's life. And this provides an entrepreneurial opportunity.

Innovation and Social Networks
To compete in the sustainability arena, entrepreneurs must frequently go beyond what has worked in the past and seek new and different perspectives and connections. One important area of innovation is new associations, networks, and partners that can provide new resources and information and foster new ways of doing things. Facebook is an example of a social network that has been innovative in creating new connections and relationships on a global scale that otherwise would not have existed through applying existing technology. People from the same circles tend to share the same pools of information and contacts. Research indicates that the longer the duration of these direct connections, the more similar the perspectives and resources. Under normal circumstances, this is fine. However, when entrepreneurs want to take action in an arena outside the familiar terrain—such as launching a new sustainable enterprise—it is likely that information from

existing relationships will not be enough. Instead they must search outside of their traditional network of relationships.

For new entrepreneurs, it will be beneficial to seek information and resources from new relationships and contacts. These new relationships can be formed with a range of individuals and organizations—including academics, consultants, nonprofit research institutes, government research organizations, and nongovernmental organizations (NGOs). NGOs have often been business's harshest critic on environmental and social issues. It is for this reason that businesses are increasingly forming relationships to these groups to engage them in thinking strategically about solutions and new venture opportunities. The most innovative ideas may well come from those quarters most critical of how business has traditionally been done. An example of this is McDonald's benefitting from collaboration with the Environmental Defense Fund, which was one of the company's harshest critics before their working together. In consultation with the Environmental Defense Fund, McDonald's has reduced their use of materials in packaging, replacing polystyrene foam sandwich clamshells with paper wraps and lightweight recycled boxes, replacing bleached with unbleached paper carry-out bags, and making dozens of other packaging improvements behind the counter in McDonald's restaurants and throughout the company's supply chain.

Ronald Burt [3] and other network theorists add useful and interesting constructs to the discussion of entrepreneurship, which is relevant to understanding the benefits of weak ties to sustainable businesses. Burt's focus is on what he calls "structural holes." Structural holes are defined as the gaps between nonredundant contacts, stated more simply for our purposes here: it is individuals not connecting with resources that would be very helpful to them.

For sustainable business focused on producing green products or services, structural holes often take the form of engineers aspiring to start businesses based on new technologies they have conceived but that are not connected or don't know how to get connected to well-qualified (1) marketing professionals (who can help them identify specific market opportunities) and (2) management professionals (who can help them effectively develop and implement business plans and to potential funders).

Burt suggests the value of processes at the "local" level, which help to fill structural holes for entrepreneurs. An example of what Burt suggests is the Green Launching Pad (GLP; http://greenlaunchingpad.org/about/overview) at the University of New Hampshire. The GLP works with aspiring entrepreneurs and connects the entrepreneurs with qualified marketing and management professionals and potential funders. The program works with entrepreneurs to accelerate the development of new sustainable businesses that will directly reduce energy use and carbon emissions while creating new jobs and economic opportunities in the state of New Hampshire. In a short time period, just more than one year (from May 2010 to June 2011), the GLP helped to launch eleven companies, including Enertrac and SustainX.

The GLP's focus is on helping entrepreneurs enter new social networks that are critical to their success. The GLP helped Enertrac gain the support of state and federal government officials and helped the company to expand the markets they target and reach. The GLP is helping SustainX, which is dominated by highly skilled engineers, connect with market development expertise. Without GLP, both these companies would not have been able to establish these connections to new resources and to develop their businesses as fast and as effectively.

KEY TAKEAWAYS

- Innovation is a new change in a product offering, service, business model, or operations that meaningfully improves the experience of a large number of stakeholders.
- Responding to an opportunity effectively often requires innovation.
- Clean tech includes technologies that generate energy from renewable sources, store energy, conserve energy, monitor and regulate energy usage and the pollution it generates, and efficiently manage water and other natural resources.
- Innovation can lower the barriers and costs of public policy standards on emissions and efficiency, and this can also be true for some policies that address social injustices.

EXERCISES

1. Search online for a clean tech product. Describe the product and discuss how it is innovative compared to conventional alternatives.

2. Search online for the example of a social network that specifically applies to sustainability, such as the Green Launching Pad. Provide detail of how this social network is specifically useful in forming new relationships for a sustainability entrepreneur.

[1] To access these laws establishing federal appliance and equipment standards and Department of Energy's authority to review, revise, and issue standards, see Energy Conservation Program for Consumer Products Other Than Automobiles, 42 USC § 6311.

[2] For the regulations pertaining to appliance and equipment standards, see Energy Conservation Program for Consumer Products, 10 CFR Part 430 (http://www.gpo.gov/fdsys/pkg/CFR-2011-title10-vol3/pdf/CFR-2011-title10-vol3-part430.pdf) and Energy Efficiency Program for Certain Commercial and Industrial Equipment, 10 CFR Part 431.

[3] Ronald S. Burt, *Structural Holes: The Social Structure of Competition* (Cambridge, MA: Harvard University Press, 1995).

5.4 Conclusion

To be successful in sustainable business practices often requires entrepreneurship and innovation. This chapter provides an overview of entrepreneurship and innovation as it relates to sustainable business. The discussion is most relevant to sustainable businesses focused on offering new products and services in response to societal concerns. The importance of entrepreneurship and innovation also applies to companies that change how they produce products and services. The latter companies can use innovative practices and entrepreneurship to establish their brand name and to be market leaders in doing things that create shared value for society and their companies and also, over time, contribute to changes in practices in their industry.

KEY TAKEAWAYS

- To be successful in sustainable business practices often requires entrepreneurship and innovation.
- Entrepreneurship and innovation are relevant in for-profit and nonprofit ventures.
- Entrepreneurship can be viewed as recognizing change, pursuing opportunity, taking on risk and responsibility, innovating, making better use of resources, creating new value that is meaningful to customers, and doing it all over again and again.
- Being an entrepreneur requires taking on significant responsibility and comes with significant challenges and potential rewards.
- Entrepreneurship is a mind-set, an attitude; it is taking a particular approach to doing things.
- The motivations for becoming an entrepreneur are diverse and can include the potential for financial reward, the pursuit of personal values and interests, and the interest in social change.
- For innovation to be relevant for sustainable businesses, it has to be meaningful and affect a large number of stakeholders.
- Successful entrepreneurship often requires creativity and innovation in addressing a new opportunity or concern in a new way.

EXERCISES

1. Interview an entrepreneur in your city or town. Identify why the individual started their business and what has been most important to their success. Then investigate why Mark Zuckerberg became an entrepreneur and founded Facebook. What motivated him to start a new venture? What keeps him motivated to grow Facebook? What do you attribute his success to? Has he been an agent for social change?

2. Assess your likelihood of becoming an entrepreneur. Were your parents entrepreneurs? Are they presently entrepreneurs? Do you have the mind-set, attitude, and way of thinking of an entrepreneur? If not, could you change to pursue a business interest? What passions or interests do you have that could translate to an entrepreneurial pursuit? Do you readily take on new challenges? Are you a risk taker? Are you interested in making a lot of money? Are you interested in social change?

3. Identify the role model entrepreneur for you. Is there any entrepreneur that you are familiar with who you think of as a role model or as a model that other entrepreneurs should emulate? Describe the entrepreneur and why you think of them as a role model.

4. Using the business media, identify a for-profit enterprise that has a strong social mission. Then using a nonprofit media source, identify a nonprofit organization that has strong similarities to a for-profit entrepreneurial venture.

5. Think of three new types of innovations that are needed to help address ecological and social concerns. Have any ventures been started to commercialize these types of innovations?

6. Investigate public polices in your state or city (using government websites) that work to promote sustainable business entrepreneurship. And identify new policies that could be established to help support sustainable businesses.

NOTES:

Chapter 6:
Sustainable Business Marketing

6.1 What Is Sustainable Marketing?

LEARNING OBJECTIVES

1. Describe sustainable marketing and how it differs from traditional marketing.
2. Define the size of the sustainable product and service market and its growth potential.
3. Explain the key challenges in sustainable marketing and how they can be overcome.
4. Identify key growth drivers of sustainable marketing.

There is significant and increasing interest and demand by both consumers and companies in being more sustainable. The sustainability market includes an increasingly wide range of companies, products, and services, all in some way intending to address sustainability concerns.

Why do companies adopt sustainability principles? Sustainable practices are good business practices. Not only does it help the greater good by improving a company's ecological footprint, but it can reduce waste, increase consumer engagement and loyalty, and provide a competitive edge, all contributing to the bottom line. Unlike more traditional companies that focus almost solely on the bottom line alone, sustainable companies focus on the triple bottom line, which includes (1) people, (2) planet, and (3) profits.

Sustainable marketing involves developing and promoting products and services that meet consumer and business user needs utilizing society's natural, human, and cultural resources responsibly to ensure a better quality of life now and for future generations to come. The focus of this chapter is to help students better understand what is meant by sustainable marketing and how it differs from traditional marketing.

Sustainable marketing is not just about taking steps to appear more environmentally friendly or more socially conscious and advertising that fact to consumers. It is more substantive and meaningful. Sustainable marketing draws on traditional marketing methods and in addition requires the following:

*   Understanding of consumer's values, emotions, and buying behavior related to sustainability
*   Knowledge of the evolving sustainability marketplace
*   Organizational commitment to sustainability and to positive relationships with their customers, communities, and the planet

An increasing number of consumers base their purchases in some way on the environmental and social impact of the product and services they buy and the companies from which they purchase. In an October 2011 study, Cone Communications and Echo Research identified that 81 percent of respondents said that companies had a responsibility to "address key social and environmental issues" and 76 percent of respondents said they had bought a product with "an environmental benefit" in the last twelve months. [1]

The size of the sustainable market (defined by Mintel, a research company, as "healthy products/healthy planet") is significant and is expected to grow to $922 billion by 2014. [2] This represents an increasing but still relatively small portion of the US and world economy, with the size of the US economy being approximately $15 trillion and world economy being about $60 trillion in 2010. New sustainable product launches are continuing to grow with consumer demand. In the food and beverage category alone, Mintel Global New Products Database (GNPD) has tracked more than thirteen thousand new sustainable food and drink products since 2005. [3]

Sidebar

Survey of Global Consumers on Environmental Issues of Concern

According to Nielsen's 2011 Global Online Environment and Sustainability Survey (http://www.nielsen.com/us/en/insights/press-room/2011/global-warming-cools-off-as-top-concern.html) of more than 25,000 Internet respondents in fifty-one countries, three out of four global consumers rated air pollution (77 percent) and water pollution (75 percent) as top concerns, both increasing 6 percentage points compared to 2009. The areas where concern is mounting fastest is over the use of pesticides, packaging waste, and water shortages, with reported concern increasing 16, 14, and 13 percentage points, respectively. Top environmental concerns among Asia Pacific consumers include water shortages and air pollution. Water pollution was the main concern for Latin Americans, Middle Easterners, Africans, Europeans, and North Americans.

The following are key drivers of sustainable marketing:

- Consumers increased demand for socially responsible products and actions, as consumers worldwide are increasingly concerned about what is included in products and their environmental footprint
- Large corporations—such as Walmart—demanding sustainability initiatives from their suppliers
- The ability to gain a competitive edge and customer loyalty in a growing market for sustainable goods and services
- Regulations and public policies requiring and encouraging more sustainable products and practices
- The increasing cost and volatile prices of natural resources

Sidebar

One Company's Approach to Sustainability: P&G

More and more companies are realizing the importance of incorporating sustainability principles into their business model. Keys to success are (1) complete integration and adoption of sustainability into the company's vision and business strategy; (2) clear transparency and honest communication to the consumers, stakeholders, and community at large; and (3) measureable progress against well-defined sustainability goals.

In 2010 one of the largest consumer packaged goods company in the world, Procter & Gamble (P&G), announced a new long-term sustainability vision. P&G's "Purpose-inspired Growth Strategy" is about "improving the lives of more consumers, in more parts of the world, more completely."

As P&G describes it, [4]

We developed this vision over the course of a year, partnering with external experts and soliciting input from hundreds of P&G employees at all levels and functions.

Our complete visionary end-points are outlined below. These end-points are long-term in nature because some of them will take decades to come to fruition.

- *Using 100 percent renewable or recycled materials for all products and packaging*
- *Having zero consumer waste go to landfills*
- *Designing products to delight consumers while maximizing the conservation of resources*
- *Powering our plants with 100 percent renewable energy*
- *Emitting no fossil-based CO_2 or toxic emissions*
- *Delivering effluent water quality that is as good as or better than influent water quality with no contribution to water scarcity*
- *Having zero manufacturing waste go to landfills*

KEY TAKEAWAYS

- Sustainable marketing involves developing and promoting products and services that meet consumer needs utilizing resources responsibly to ensure a better quality of life now and for future generations to come.
- The sustainability market is of significant size and growing due to increased consumer and customer demand, rising resource costs, and increased governmental regulations.
- Sustainable marketing draws on traditional marketing methods and applies them specifically to environmental and social initiatives and products and services.

EXERCISES

P&G has made a serious commitment to sustainability.

1. Do you think this will negatively or positively affect their products and their bottom line? Explain how.
2. Which of their goals do you believe will be their biggest challenge and why?
3. What sustainable practices might cause P&G product prices to increase, and which ones might cause pricing to decrease? Why?
4. Would this make you more favorable or less favorable to buying P&G brands? Why?

[1] "2011 Cone/Echo Global CR Report," Cone Communications, http://www.coneinc.com/2011globalcrreport.

[2] "Consumers Claim They Are Willing to Pay Extra for Green," *eMarketer Green*, last modified April 1, 2010, accessed April 1, 2010, http://www.emarketergreen.com/blog/index.php/consumers-pay-extra-green; "Definitions of Healthy Products, Healthy Planet ('HP2') Sectors," *Nutrition Business Journal*, last modified May 15, 2008, http://newhope360.com/business-directory/definitions-healthy-products-healthy-planet-hp2-sectors.

[3] Mintel, "Sustainable Food and Drink Category," press release, October 2010, http://www.mintel.com/press-centre/press-releases/614/sustainable-food-and-drink-lovers-attracted-by-perceived-superior-quality.

[4] "Environmental Sustainability," Procter & Gamble, http://www.pg.com/en_US/sustainability/environmental_sustainability/index.shtml.

6.2 Green Marketing Strategy and the Four P's of Marketing

LEARNING OBJECTIVES

1. Explain green marketing strategy and how to best incorporate a green strategy into a company's overall vision.
2. Define how sustainability works in the marketing mix.
3. Understand consumer market segmentation.
4. Describe marketing tools to help promote a brand.

Kermit the frog may have had it right—"It's not easy being green." There is a lot to consider when creating a sustainable marketing strategy. It is not simply adding "green" to your brand platform or announcing that you support a worthy cause. To be most successful, a commitment to sustainability should be part of the company's overall vision and an integral part of the company's values and fundamental beliefs. For example, Seventh Generation, a Vermont-based company that makes personal and household cleaning products, adheres to a model of deeper business purpose. The company's founder, Jeffrey Hollender, had a vision to create and nurture a company with sustainability at the core. Everything that the company does focuses on the triple bottom line of people, planet, and profit for the greater good. From their products—which are made using only natural, recycled, or renewable materials—to their philanthropic efforts that seek to help create a sustainable community, Seventh Generation employs a well-integrated sustainability vision and strategy.

A strong sustainability strategy includes understanding how the company impacts the people and environment in which it operates and consciously applies sustainable practices throughout *every* element of its business. Companies such as Timberland and Procter & Gamble have adopted sustainability practices and have set specific and measureable goals—both short and longer term—to reduce their company's carbon footprint. This includes actively examining the carbon lifecycle of their products—from the raw materials used in manufacturing all the way through to the recycling phase to ensure that they are meeting these goals.

Inherent in this practice is the concept of radical transparency, whereby everything the company does is transparent and visible to the consumer and community at large, which contributes to the credibility of the sustainable brand. Measureable goals contribute to radical transparency as they provide clear and actionable goals to which the company can commit and progress against. For example, Unilever's sustainable strategy commits to aggressively reducing their environmental impact and enhancing livelihoods by the year 2020. Unilever has made sustainability the cornerstone of their mission with clear, transparent goals against which they will be measured. [1]

To view Unilever's Sustainable Living Plan, visit http://www.unilever.com/images/UnileverSustainableLivingPlan_tcm13-239379.pdf and go to page seven.

Sidebar
Radical Transparency
Radical transparency involves everything a company does being completely transparent and visible to the consumer and all stakeholders.

A marketing plan is derived from the company's vision and integrates an organization's overall goals and marketing objectives (what goals they want to achieve) and strategies (how they are going to achieve them) into a cohesive plan, typically on an annual basis. The green marketing plan focuses on the ideal marketing mix to achieve maximum profit potential while adhering to sustainability principles.

The key elements of the marketing plan are as follows:
- **Corporate goals.** These are the overall company goals that should be in line with the company's vision and long-term strategic plan.
- **Objectives.** Determine marketing objectives. Objectives should be stated clearly and should stem from the overall company's vision and goals. Objectives should have specificity, such as to grow to 5 percent market share.
- **Strategies.** After objectives are determined, strategies (which are how you are going to achieve the objectives) should be developed. An example is to convert all product ingredients to those that are locally sourced to help meet the objective of minimizing the company's carbon footprint.
- **Tactics.** Tactics are the specific means or programs to achieve the strategies and this includes the four Ps (see the following). One example is identifying the local suppliers and costs to achieve a buy local strategy.
- **Market.** Determine what market you are participating in and what stage your product or service is in its life cycle: development, introduction, growth, maturity, or decline (see the following sidebar titled "Product Life Cycle"). For green products especially, there may be opportunity to add a new dimension to a mature category with a new

product benefit. For example, in the mature category of yogurt, Stonyfield Yogurt was able to breathe new life into the category when they first launched in 1984 with an organic product. Adding credibility to their sustainable brand was their "Profits for the Planet" program tactic, which commits 10 percent of annual profits to individuals and organizations working to restore and protect the environment.

- **Consumer target audience.** Identify who is your potential customer. In a study conducted by OgilvyEarth, there are varying degrees of how "green" consumers are. From die-hard "super greens" to "green rejecters," marketers need to determine who best to target to achieve their marketing objectives.

There are several keys to creating an effective *green marketing strategy*:

- Understand the market and the underlying values and beliefs of your consumers and other key stakeholders, and develop a marketing plan that aligns well with these values and beliefs.
- Make sure that the products and services balance the needs of meeting consumer's desires for quality, convenience, and affordability with sustainability goals.
- Be genuine and radically transparent throughout the marketing mix. In marketing communication and promotion efforts, actively engage consumers with issues that are meaningful to them, and listen to them. Give them a voice.
- Create alliances. Look for sustainable business partners, such as those from whom you source ingredients or other materials; nongovernmental organizations (NGOs) that complement your business; and sustainable industry leaders and other like-minded businesses.
- Measure performance against key metrics and communicate progress. Radical transparency includes being able to share progress against sustainability goals with consumers and the community at large.

Sidebar
Product Life Cycle
There are basically five stages of the product life cycle, including the development, introduction, growth, maturity, and decline stages. Customers will only be able to purchase products in the latter four stages because the product typically has not yet been placed on the market in the development stage. Some companies, however, like computer software companies, do release a limited number of products during the development phase to help with their beta testing.

Sustainable Marketing Mix
The *marketing mix*, also known as the **four Ps of marketing**, is the combination of product, price, place (distribution), and promotion. Marketers develop strategies around these four areas in marketing to enhance branding, sales, and profitability. The marketing mix forms the foundation for creating a sustainable marketing strategy. Sustainability marketing, unlike traditional marketing, needs to adhere well to sustainability principles throughout the marketing mix. This helps to (1) strengthen the brand identity; (2) provide credibility; and (3) ensure honest, truthful communications and radical transparency with stakeholders, one of the cornerstones of good sustainability marketing principles.

Product
A **product** is a tangible good or an intangible service that is marketed to a consumer. A tangible good is something that can be seen, heard, tasted, felt, or seen. Products such as coffee, milk, biofuel, laundry detergent, and outdoor apparel are all examples of tangible goods.

Intangible products are mostly service based and provided by someone directly in contact with customers, such as mutual fund investment services, health care services, and consulting services. Sometimes the intangible service results in a tangible product, such as a lawyer providing legal advice in filing for a product patent. The intangible product is the lawyer's services, and the tangible product is the patent itself.

When looking at a sustainable-marketed product, consideration should be made for sourcing of materials, ingredients used, and the manufacturing of the product. This includes using all natural and organic materials, sourcing local and through fair trade suppliers, utilizing environmentally friendly materials, and using lean manufacturing and distribution methods that minimize the company's carbon footprint. For example, Unilever (the corporate owner of Ben & Jerry's) has committed that all ingredients in Ben & Jerry's ice cream be sourced through fair trade suppliers and certified as such by 2013.

Sidebar
Fair Trade
Fair trade is a global trade system that ensures producers get a fair price for their goods. It is the cornerstone of a sustainable economy. Starbucks began purchasing Fair Trade Certified coffee in 2000, helping to grow the market for Fair Trade Certified™ coffee in the United States. Fair Trade Certified™ coffee empowers small-scale farmers organized in cooperatives to invest in their farms and communities,

protect the environment, and develop the business skills necessary to compete in the global marketplace.[2]

Companies, both large and small, are undertaking sustainability initiatives. The most successful companies in doing this sincerely embrace sustainability principles at its core; set clear and measurable goals; and clearly, transparently, and truthfully communicate with their stakeholders about the ecological and social impacts of their products and services. These companies use the four Ps to enhance and fulfill their sustainable positioning to be true to the vision throughout their marketing mix.

Seventh Generation is a pioneer in sustainability marketing and a leader in natural household cleaning products. Deriving its name from the Great Law of the Iroquois that states, "In our every deliberation, we must consider the impact of our decisions on the next seven generations," Seventh Generation has long been practicing sustainability throughout its marketing mix for over twenty years. Their entire product line of household and personal care products—from laundry detergents to baby wipes—are carefully designed and manufactured to minimize their impact on the environment. Using all natural, renewable, and recyclable resources, Seventh Generation is working to "help protect human health and the environment." [3]

Timberland's Earthkeepers product line is the company's most visible effort to put their environmental values into their products and market it. Products produced under the Earthkeepers label feature (1) reduced use of harmful chemicals, including no PVC and water-based adhesives; (2) use of recycled materials, including plastic bottles made into linings and laces and recycled rubber sole boots made with up to 30 percent recycled rubber; (3) use of organic materials, including organic cotton; and (4) use of recycled packaging materials, with all boxes made of 100 percent postconsumer recycled packaging cardboard. Timberland has implemented eco-labels to communicate information to consumers about the impacts of their products and has implemented life cycle management to quantify the environmental impacts of the products that it produces.

Another example is General Electric. The company committed to utilizing clean technologies and reducing their environmental footprint in 2005 with their ecoimagination program. Since then, a hybrid engine train has been put into development, a state-of-the-art wind turbine blade has been manufactured, and a superefficient washing machine and coal-gasification technology have been introduced. General Electric, in particular, is noteworthy for its pledge to double

its investments in the research and development of environmentally friendlier technologies. The total budget for research and development went from $700 million in 2004 to $1.5 billion in 2010. General Electric has been consistently named in the top ten of Global 100 Most Sustainable Corporations.[4]

In the garment industry, Earthtec is an emerging sustainability product marketing clothing manufacturer. Using postconsumer recycled polyethylene terephthalate plastics (such as discarded water bottles), Earthtec converts landfill-bound bottles into high-performance fabrics and clothing. The company is dedicated to using recycled or renewable materials in every single article of clothing they make. Beyond their product line focused on sustainability, the company has incorporated a streamlined manufacturing model that is designed to minimize their carbon footprint. [5] An example of sustainable intangibles is the services provided by the mutual fund company Pax World. Pax World is a recognized leader in the field of sustainable investing—the full integration of environmental, social, and governance (ESG) factors into investment analysis and decision making—in its mutual fund offerings. [6] Pax World provides the intangible service of investment advice with a strong sustainability conscience.

Consumer Target Market Segmentation

A consumer target market (often referred to as a target audience) is a defined set of consumers who are particularly interested in a product or market, would have access to it, and are able to purchase it. Market segmentation divides these audiences into homogenous groups of customers, each of them reacting differently to promotion, communication, pricing, and other variables of the marketing mix. Market segments should be formed in a way that differences between consumers within each segment are as small as possible. This is especially helpful to optimize marketing budgets, targeting dollars to those most interested in your product to allow a more effective and efficient marketing plan.

Segmentation can be further defined using demographic, geographic, psychographic, and behavioral segmentation. Demographic segmentation divides the market into groups based on variables, such as age, marital status, household income levels, education, children in household, and occupation. Geographic segmentation divides a market by location and includes such variables as population density (urban, suburban, and rural areas) and climate. Psychographic segmentation classifies consumers based on individual lifestyles, attitudes, and beliefs. Behavioral segmentation divides consumers by such variables as attitude toward the product, user status, or user rate.

Within the green market segment, it is important to understand which consumers to target. Once strictly limited to "tree huggers," the market is growing. According to a 2011 study by OgilvyEarth titled "Mainstream Green," consumers can be subdivided and segmented *behaviorally and psychographically* by their level of "green intensity." Hardcore green consumers who only purchase sustainable products are called "super greens" and represent about 16 percent of the market. On the other extreme are "green rejecters," those not looking for or interested in green products, which represent 18 percent of the market. Most of America (66 percent) is in the green middle ground—not hardcore green but not completely unaware or unappreciative of issues surrounding sustainability. [7]

Companies who market to green consumers look at those on the spectrum as well as determine which consumers will provide the greatest volume potential. But with so many consumers firmly entrenched in the middle green, there exists opportunities to create products with mass appeal.

For consumer packaged goods purchases, women are typically the primary target audience as they still do the bulk of today's household shopping. Seventh Generation, a sustainable personal care and household cleaning products manufacturer, targets the middle green as well as new moms, whom they find to be especially interested in making the world a better place for their newborns.[8]

Sidebar
Consumer Packaged Goods
Consumer packaged goods are a type of good that is consumed every day by the average consumer. The goods that compose this category are ones that need to be replaced frequently, compared to those that are usable for extended periods of time. Examples are laundry detergent, food, shampoo, soap, and beverages.

Other companies target the super green. Super green consumers may undertake costly actions in order to signal themselves as such; this has been called conspicuous conservation. [9] Car ownership decisions are one of the most visible consumption decisions households make. Since the introduction of the Toyota Prius in the United States in 2001, a growing number of vehicle models have been introduced with features that reduce environmental impacts. The Prius was the only model that provided a unique exterior shape and a design that stood out and announced that it was different

than standard vehicles. The Prius has emerged as the clear leader among twenty-four different hybrid models available in the United States, with 48 percent of the 290,271 hybrid cars sold in the United States in 2009. Prius's success is particularly pronounced in communities with high percentages of super greens, such as Berkeley (California), Boulder (Colorado), and Portland (Oregon), who want to make public their environmental practices and beliefs. The Prius with its unique product design has successfully provided the vehicle for owner's to signal their affinity for the environment allowing super greens to make a conspicuous statement about their conservation efforts.

Packaging
Packaging plays a critical role in the product's sustainability. Consumers have increasingly been made aware of environmental packaging choices and are changing their behavior as a result. A leading example of this is with water bottles. Many consumers have made the switch from purchasing single-use plastic water bottles to using refillable water containers. In 2008, 2.5 million tons of plastic bottles and jars were thrown away. [10] The extremely slow decomposition rate of plastic bottles leaves them to sit in landfills or litter oceans for years. As a result of increased consumer awareness and consumer demand, sales of reusable water bottles from environmentally friendly producers such as Sigg and Kleen Kanteen have come onto the market. Consumers still want clean, filtered water, and companies, such as Brita and PŪR, makers of water filters, have seen a 22.2 percent and 15.2 percent increase in sales during 2009, respectively. [11]

Another strong consumer packaging trend is the use of reusable shopping bags at grocery stores. Americans use one hundred billion plastic shopping bags every year and over five hundred billion are consumed globally. Of this, four billion become general litter. [12] Consumers and retailers are recognizing this, encouraging new behavior, and now it is almost fashionable to bring your reusable shopping bags to your local store. As of 2011, more than two-thirds of consumers indicated that they now use reusable shopping bags.

Another one of the keys to sustainable packaging is to ensure that the product-to-packaging ratio is "right-sized"—meaning that the product tightly fits in the packaging and there is no wasted use of packaging materials or "air space." This is not only for the package itself but also for the packing case, which houses multiples of the products for shipping. This is often referred to as "cube optimization." Cube optimization means right-sizing packages and fitting orders into packaging dimensions that are as small as possible without threatening the integrity of the order. Tight packaging-to-product ratios accomplish two things: (1) they reduce use of packaging materials and (2) they reduce energy costs as the pallet loads are more condensed and the manufacturer is not paying to transport "air." Additionally, as more and more products are being shipped globally in containers by ocean, air, trucks, and rail, every inch of transport space and fuel usage is significant. This is an example of a win-win situation for the business and the environment, as shipping more in the same volume of space cuts shipping costs, impacting the business bottom line, while reducing the amount of energy (and associated greenhouse gas [GHG] emissions) needed, positively impacting the environmental "bottom line."

Using renewably sourced materials is another way companies can create more sustainable packaging. Renewable materials are those that utilize forest, fiber, and agriculture products. Nonrenewable materials are those like plastic or Styrofoam, which are derived from petroleum and other fossil fuels.

Sidebar
Walmart's Packaging Sustainability Initiative

Walmart has pledged to eliminate twenty million metric tons of GHG emissions from their global supply chain by the end of 2015. That is 150 percent of the company's estimated global carbon footprint growth over the next five years. [13] As part of this initiative, Walmart is planning to reduce its packaging globally by 5 percent versus their 2008 baseline. Through a sustainable packaging scorecard that Walmart has developed and put in place to help monitor their suppliers' efforts, Walmart can track and use their immense weight to push suppliers to help them achieve their goals. The following are some of their notable successes with their suppliers to date: [14]

- The transition of all liquid laundry detergents to concentrated versions has saved more than 125 million pounds of cardboard, 95 million pounds of plastics, and 400 million gallons of water.
- Packaging of Apple iPods was changed to 100 percent renewable, recyclable, and more sustainable materials.
- By reducing the packaging size of its Kid Connection line of toys, Walmart claims to have saved over $2.4 million in freight costs.
- The apple juice sold under the Member's Mark label at Sam's Club now uses 35 percent renewable energy in producing half the corrugated box packaging, and 50 percent of that corrugated packaging is from 100 percent recycled corrugated cardboard.

- All of Walmart's cut fruit and forty-ounce vegetable trays and some of the nine-ounce trays are packaged with NatureWorks PLA, a biodegradable polymer. According to the company, by making that change to PLA in 2005 on just four produce items, they saved about eight hundred thousand gallons of gasoline and avoided more than eleven million pounds of GHG emissions.

Price

Price is the monetary (or bartered) amount a consumer pays for a product or service based on the product or service's value or worth. For sustainable products, pricing has often been an issue limiting a product's or service's mass acceptance and market growth. Green products tend to be more expensive because the ingredients may cost more than their conventional counterparts. For example, organic food grown with natural fertilizers may be more expensive than those foods not utilizing natural fertilizers. Manufacturing and transportation costs can also be higher. For example, if the transport costs use a higher cost but lower polluting renewable energy fuel source, this will contribute to a higher price point. This creates a price gap between conventional products and those that are sustainable, which is often referred to as the "green pricing gap." The higher price can be a barrier to wide market acceptance for many green products, as some consumers may want to purchase products that are better for the environment but either do not want or are financially unable to pay a higher price. For the large majority of consumers, if they do not receive additional value from a sustainable product, for example, in the form of reduced energy costs or longer product lives, they will not pay a premium for the sustainable product. If a product is competitive in terms of price, as well as product, place, and promotion, with traditional products and services, sustainability can give that product a competitive edge particularly among consumers with some interest in sustainability such as the middle green.

Marketers need to minimize the price barrier either by reducing the price point to be closer to its conventional counterparts or through marketing efforts to raise the perceived value to command a premium. Products, such as organic food brands, Earth's Best, and Starbucks with their fair trade coffee, have done a commendable job in creating greater perceived value, thus commanding premium pricing. Some green product marketers use effective targeting to minimize the green price gap by targeting either people who are better off financially (those who can better afford to take environmental factors into their consumption decisions) or particular market or consumer groups, such as super greens and green regional markets (e.g., Portland, Oregon), with concentrations of potential customers who derive value in conspicuous conservation and demonstrating their environmentalism. [15]

Sidebar
When Price and Quality Are the Same, Preferring to Support a Worthy Cause
A 2011 Cone/Echo Global Study revealed that when price and quality are about the same, consumers will pick the brand that is supporting a worthy cause like sustainability. [16]
To view data about switching brands, visit http://www.echoresearch.com/data/File/pdf/Cone_pdfs/2011%20Cone_Echo%20Global%20CR%20Opportunity%20Study.pdf.

To that end, consider the American family of four who spends an average $115.60 per week on groceries. [17] If the green products cost 10 percent to 25 percent more, their $115.60 per week yields significantly less purchasing power. This is even more pronounced in a weak economy. Yet many sustainable business practices, such as using materials with longer life, can save consumers money in the long term. Pricing is key in the marketing mix and marketers of sustainable products and services need to ensure the price and value equation is right for maximum success.

Sidebar
What Really Motivates Consumers: Green Earth or Green Cash?
Marketers take notice. One way to create a so-called win-win for consumers of sustainable products is to capitalize on what can help really motivate consumers to use green products—cost savings from using green products. Some consumers recognize this benefit as some green products save them money in the long run, such as driving a hybrid car saves at the gas pump; energy efficient light bulbs, refrigerators, washers, and dryers save on energy costs; water conservation shower heads save on the water bill; and using refillable water bottles is much cheaper than buying plastic water bottles at the store. Combining a concrete benefit like saving money with a sustainable benefit strengthens the brand messaging and may help to minimize the green pricing gap.

Place
Place is where the product can be purchased and includes how the product is distributed to the purchase location. Place can be a physical store as well as a virtual store on the Internet, also known as an e-tailer. Amazon is probably one of the best and biggest examples of an e-tailer as it has no "brick and mortar" storefronts.

Some sustainability focused retailers with brick and mortar storefronts are moving toward more sustainable practices. Retailers like Kohl's are implementing solar energy panels in some of their stores. Walmart is building more energy-efficient stores, using more alternative fuels in its trucks, and reducing packaging. [18]

A place-related sustainable marketing area of increased interest is buying locally. According to the 2011 Nielsen global online consumer survey, belief in the positive impact of local products is highest in North America, where 65 percent of consumers reported that local goods have a positive impact on the environment.
Consumers are increasingly concerned about the environment and carbon emissions from transporting goods over long distances. Increasing numbers of local retailers are promoting themselves as local with the associated environmental and community economic benefits associated with local residents buying from local businesses compared to national and international companies. Some larger companies are recognizing the interest in buying local by increasing their use of local suppliers. This includes Whole Foods stores buying from local farmers and fisheries.

Sidebar [19]
Whole Foods: Buy Local Strategy
We are permanently committed to buying from local producers whose fruits and vegetables meet our high quality standards, particularly those who farm organically and are themselves dedicated to environmentally friendly, sustainable agriculture. We are greatly increasing our efforts in this regard by further empowering our individual store and regional buyers to seek out locally grown produce.
What is local? Local produce is by definition seasonal. In spring in California, that means artichokes; summer in Michigan means blueberries and autumn in Washington means apples. We value this natural diversity, and each of our 11 regions has its own firm guidelines for using the term "local" in our stores. While only products that have traveled less than a day (7 or fewer hours by car or truck) can even be considered for "local" designation, most stores have established even shorter maximum distances. Ask a team member for your store's definition of "local."
Source: Whole Foods Market, http://media.wholefoodsmarket.com/multimedia/image-library.

Retailers are increasingly scrutinizing their suppliers and demanding that the products that they sell meet higher sustainability standards. Walmart has implemented a sustainability scorecard that scrutinizes their suppliers' and vendors' entire product development cycle to ensure that they are implementing sustainable practices and continually looking to improve on these practices. If they are not, Walmart has stated that they will not carry the products. Other retailers are also beginning to demand that their suppliers meet sustainability hurdles including Safeway, Kroger, and Target.

The distribution channel is a significant consideration for sustainable marketing practices. Companies that are sustainability-minded are looking at ways to reduce their carbon footprint through a variety of efforts. Transportation with fuel-efficient loads, using alternative energy sources, and optimizing distribution routes are a few of the examples that can favorably impact the distribution channel in a sustainable way.

Promotion

Promotion is the communication tools and tactics that a company uses to promote and market their product. There are many ways to communicate a company's products and benefits. Branding is the cornerstone of the communications platform.

A brand is an image in the consumer's mind for a particular product or service. Strong sustainable brands should have a brand image of the product or service having a positive impact on people and the environment. Stonyfield's brand positioning of "healthy food, healthy people, healthy planet" stems directly from the company's strategic vision.

Advertising, public relations, personal selling, consumer and trade promotion, social media, digital marketing, and mobile marketing are all marketing promotion tools. When determining which mediums to utilize, marketers need to consider (1) marketing objectives, (2) effective reach of mediums among identified target audiences, and (3) budget. It is best to use a mix of promotion vehicles to most effectively and efficiently reach the target market and consistently apply the branding and messaging to maximize awareness. The messaging is best when it elicits a call to action on the consumer's part—that is, purchase, engagement, and loyalty.

- **Advertising** encompasses communications designed to increase awareness and encourage the purchase of a particular product or service and is a paid medium. Advertising methods are more interruptive versus permission based (see the following description) and include television, print (newspapers and magazines), Internet advertising (such as banner ads), radio, billboards, and cinema advertising.

Nike recently made a big splash with its marketing focused on creating a better world through sports. Their efforts included the first 100 percent recycled television advertising, reusing and remixing film from their previous campaigns over the years to create a new spot to introduce their Better World campaign. The digital mash-up showcases the inspiration and history of the brand while bringing attention to the sustainability concept of reuse and reducing resources. This is also a good example whereby utilizing sustainability principles actually benefits the bottom line. By reusing existing film, Nike did not have to spend the thousands of dollars to produce a new television commercial nor expend energy costs for a production shoot. For perspective, an average television commercial cost exceeds $300,000, [20] and an average television shoot is two to three days depending on how many locations are required.

Utility company the Denver Water Company created an advertising campaign that visually highlighted their campaign message of "Use Only What You Need." This campaign was run on outdoor billboards, print ads, and bus and taxi ads.

Sidebar

Shipping Giant Befriends a Forest: FedEx Sustainable Solutions
FedEx recently launched a charming new ad campaign that highlights their sustainability initiatives. When consumers think of FedEx, sustainability doesn't usually come first to mind, as it is a shipping and transportation business, which is a large user of fuel, not to mention paper products. But this new commercial highlights FedEx's environmental efforts that help save forests and fuel and does so with Disney-esque charm. And when you strip away the Hollywood fairy tale dramatics, the spot reveals that FedEx is working hard at sustainable solutions for a better planet.
Makes you feel a little bit better when you absolutely have to have it delivered overnight.

- **Public relations** is about influencing, informing, and persuading the consumer and is often not a medium that is directly paid for, such as paying to take out ads in the newspaper, on the radio, or on television. Instead, you earn stories and coverage, which is called "earned media."

There are many tools to use for public relations; among them are press releases, press conferences, fact sheets, letters to the editor, guest columns, radio and television talk show appearances, blogs, white paper publishing, speaker engagements, trade shows, and endorsements.

Toyota, when it launched Prius, one of the first hybrid cars, received endorsements from such influential eco-friendly organizations as the United Nations, the Sierra Club, and the

National Wildlife Federation. These endorsements helped to establish Toyota's green brand image and credibility. Utilizing press releases and print ads, Toyota helped to spread the word of their endorsements to maximize awareness. Prius has gone on to be the number one hybrid car in the United States.

- **Personal selling** includes one-on-one selling, word of mouth, cold calls, sales meetings, product presentations, and demonstrations.

One of Simply Green's (a biofuel company based in Portsmouth, New Hampshire) most successful marketing tools was cold calling (phone calls that are unsolicited and without any prior connection) to music industry performers touring in the region. It was through this personal selling technique that Simply Green landed an account filling famous musicians' tour buses, which earned Simply Green instant fame and credibility.

- **Consumer promotions** are programs that directly help to influence the consumer to purchase the product and typically include some price incentive. For sustainable marketing they often include an incentive or donation that help people and the planet. Items such as free standing inserts (FSIs: the inserts that are typically in Sunday's newspaper), coupons, buy one get one free offers (BOGOs), Groupon offers, in-store sampling, couponing, event marketing, sweepstakes, and other contests are key consumer promotion tactics.

Sidebar

Free Standing Inserts (FSIs)

FSIs are used as a consumer promotion tool and are typically inserted into Sunday's newspapers. FSIs are used primarily to distribute coupons to encourage purchase.

Groupon (group + coupon) is an online digital coupon company (http://www.groupon.com) that provides deal-a-day coupons and price incentives. These deals are activated when a certain number of consumers agree to purchase at a specified discount rate.

Blake Mycoskie started Toms Shoes on the premise that for every pair of shoes sold, one pair would be donated to a child in need. Toms Shoes recognized that consumers want to feel good about what they buy and thus directly tied the purchase with the donation. This consumer promotion is a buy one give one. In just four years, Toms Shoes has donated more than four hundred thousand shoes, evidence that consumers have clearly embraced the cause.

- **Social media** involves the use of sites, such as Facebook, Twitter, Foursquare, LinkedIn, and

YouTube, among others, to help generate awareness and get consumers engaged in a *relationship* with a brand and talking to each other about the brand. Social media are permission-based marketing, and consumers have to engage on their own and give "permission" to marketers to engage with them (e.g., when you "Like" a product or service fan page on Facebook or you view a promotional YouTube video or sign up for a blog RSS feed). This is different than interruptive marketing, which consumers usually have little control over (although DVRs are making it possible for consumers to not have to watch television advertising).

Using the power of social media, two CEOs created a "rap off" contest utilizing YouTube videos, Facebook, and Twitter. CE-YO Gary Hirshberg, of Stonyfield Yogurt, and CEO Seth Goldman, from Coca-Cola's Honest Tea, became dueling rappers to promote organics for Earth month. Hirshberg and the "Stonyfield Moms" created a rap video about eating organic (http://www.youtube.com/watch?v=SCA6P9lsEfw&feature=pyv&ad=8718280378&kw=organic%). Not to be outdone, Goldman, who is a longtime friend of Hirshberg's, thought that they at Honest Tea could do a better rap video and responded with the rap, "Rethink What You Drink" (https://www.youtube.com/watch?feature=player_embedded&v=jeF-65eDLc0#!).

Consumers voted on Facebook for the best rapper team and could upload their own organic rap video to win cash and a supply of Stonyfield Yogurt and Honest Tea. Both Stonyfield and Honest Tea used social media to engage consumers for a sustainable mission and actively encouraged consumer participation. The campaign went viral, receiving many website hits, likes on Facebook, tweets and retweets, and YouTube visits.

Tom's of Maine, a Kennebunk, Maine–based personal care company owned by Colgate and well known for its sustainable positioning, uses social media to engage their consumers. For example, they introduced their new Wicked Fresh toothpaste and mouthwash with ads running on Facebook's newsfeed page, a "Wicked Fresh" sweepstakes, a contest, and an online instant win game. The company also used Twitter to promote the contest.

- **Event marketing** is either the use of an existing event or the creation of an event to engage prospective consumers, build awareness, and market a company's products and services. One of the simplest examples is the use of trade shows and exhibits. Other methods include creating flash mobs, interactive exhibits, pop-up stores, or other means to stage events.

Sidebar
Flash Mobs
Flash mobs are a group of people who assemble suddenly in a public place and perform a choreographed demonstration or performance that catches consumers unaware. Flash mobs are organized via telecommunications or social media.
Pop-up stores are portable store kiosks that are used to catch consumers in high-visibility locations and are only on display for a short period of time. They can be used at sporting events, concerts, or other high-traffic locations. For food and beverage pop-up stores, sampling is often a key marketing tactic used to entice purchase.

Volkswagen creates interactive exhibits in key cities globally to help consumers change their habits to reduce their carbon footprint. Titled "The Fun Theory" (http://thefuntheory.com), they have built interactive exhibits, such as glass bottle recycling bank arcades and piano-based steps in subways that play musical notes when stepped on to encourage more walking versus riding the escalator. By making consumer habit changes fun, Volkswagen is making an impact.

- **Digital marketing** is primarily the use of web-based marketing tools. This would include a company's website, search engine optimization (SEO), pay-per-click, retargeting, e-mail, RSS, blogging, podcasting, and video streams, to name a few. The Internet can be used with push or pull techniques. Digital marketing can be used to "push" a message to the target market via e-mail, IM, RSS, or voice broadcast, and it can also be used to "pull" content via a banner ad and pay-per-click search terms.

Seventh Generation, a national manufacturer and distributor of environmentally friendly household and personal care products, recently has been successfully utilizing digital marketing techniques including SEO, retargeting (generating ads that follow consumers by placing cookies on their site based on previous site visits), and pay-per-click.

- **Mobile marketing** is on the rise, especially with the increasing penetration of smartphones. Currently, the Nielsen Company puts smartphone household penetration at 40 percent, but it is growing quickly.[21] Mobile advertising and the use of QR (quick response) codes is an effective way to engage consumers. QR codes are two-dimensional (2D) matrix barcodes that can hold thousands of alphanumeric characters of

information. When consumers "snap" them on their smartphones, the QR codes can take them to a special mobile-enabled site that provides content and incentives to promote a product. In today's digital world of immediacy, consumers want instant access to what's relevant and mobile marketing techniques are being used to make that possible.

Sea Bags, a Portland, Maine–based company that makes handmade tote bags from recycled sails, is using a strategic approach with QR codes, incorporating them into its marketing strategy. The QR code directs consumers to a mobile-enabled website that shows a video portraying the company story and commitment to recycling, detailing how they use recycled sails to make their product. Future plans are to include bag tags (also made of recycled sails) with QR codes, which tell consumers their sail's history and sailing journey around the world.

- **Grassroots promotion and marketing** combines some of the different promotional approaches in a focused, creative, and low-cost way that is often local or community based. It can be particularly useful for start-up ventures. It uses public relations (such as local press and media stories), blogs, social media, and community event planning and participation to drive qualified leads to company websites and physical locations for purchases.

Andrew Kellar, the founder of Simply Green, used grassroots marketing with a focus on company participation with a nonprofit organization (the New Hampshire Green Alliance) and high-visibility sales with well-known early adopter customers (touring rock band buses) to build up its customer base to over five hundred in just one year at a very low marketing cost.

Sidebar
Honest Tea's Honest Marketing
When Coca-Cola acquired Honest Tea, they began to approach the marketing plan the way the giant marketing behemoth always did—with plenty of national television advertising, deep trade promotion discounts, and slick shelf placement and promotion at retail. The traditional marketing efforts, which normally work well for a more traditional CPG brand, were a flop. Why? Because a big splashy marketing campaign was not in keeping with their "honest" brand image nor did it capitalize on the way that Honest Tea's following had been built. Honest Tea's success had been developed through grassroots marketing, which gave the brand an elite following that said, "We are not like everyone else—we require something special."

Their Honest Cities campaign worked particularly well; Honest Tea set up displays with bottles of tea with a one-dollar collection barrel next to the pallets—purchases on the honor system. They promoted Earth Day by handing out reusable shopping bags with each purchase of Honest Tea. The brand built its presence first in a local market then spread out to the region and then moved to the next local market; the brand then positioned itself to grow into the next region.

In addition, the brand continued to focus on the health food chain channel like Whole Foods—not a stronghold for the traditional Coke beverages. [22] So when the big marketing campaign failed, what did Coke do? Coca-Cola went back to basics to effectively develop and implement a marketing plan that personified the brand image and even reprised the Honest Cities campaign, refreshed, of course, using pop-up stores called "The Honest Stand" and social media. [23]

KEY TAKEAWAYS

- A sustainable marketing strategy works best when it adapts and complements the overall corporate sustainability vision of the company, personifies the brand image, and is clearly and transparently executed throughout all marketing elements.
- For an effective sustainable marketing approach, the four Ps, product, price, place, and promotion, should be based on sustainability principles and should align with overall marketing strategy.
- Consumer target market segmentation is effective to better tailor marketing efforts to those consumer's that align best as potential buyers or customers of a given product or service.
- Physical products can be made more sustainable through considering ways to minimize materials use, minimize the negative impact of the production process, and maximize the efficiency of the distribution process.
- Packaging changes, such as encouraging reusable bags, a tighter packaging-to-product ratio, or cube optimization, can be effective ways to reduce the environmental impact of a product while increasing profitability.
- Sustainable goods can be more expensive to produce than conventional alternatives as a result of potentially higher-cost raw materials, methods of production, and renewable resources. This should be taken into consideration when developing the branding, developing the marketing mix, and focusing on a market segment.
- A mix of promotional mediums is best to effectively and efficiently reach the target market with a consistent branded message and call to action.

EXERCISES

1. Walmart is using their retail power to pressure their suppliers and vendors to help the company achieve its sustainability goals. How do you feel about this approach? Contrast it versus P&G's approach.
2. It has been viewed by some that Walmart's sustainability efforts are a shallow public relations effort to help create a better corporate image, especially after much negative publicity that it is not substantive and meaningful. What do you think?
3. Provide an example of a product or service that adheres to sustainability principles and discuss the four Ps they use in the market. What is working well for them and what would you suggest for them to do to improve?

[1] "Unilever Sustainable Living Plan," Unilever, http://www.unilever.com/images/UnileverSustainableLivingPlan_tcm13-239379.pdf.

[2] "Responsibly Grown and Fair Trade Coffee," Starbucks, http://www.starbucks.com/responsibility/sourcing/coffee.

[3] "Green Cleaning Products," Seventh Generation, http://www.seventhgeneration.com.

[4] "GE and Unilever Step Forth to Write a New Agenda," *New Economy*, http://www.theneweconomy.com/business-and-management/sustainability/ge-and-unilever-step-forth-to-write-agenda.

[5] "Earthtec—Clothing with a Conscience," Earthtec, http://www.earthtec.com/our_story/conscience.

[6] "About Pax World," Pax World, http://www.paxworld.com/about.

[7] Graceann Bennett and Freya Williams, *Mainstream Green*, 2011, http://assets.ogilvy.com/truffles_email/ogilvyearth/Mainstream_Green.pdf.

[8] Romy Ribitzky, "Seventh Generation Embarks on First Ever National Ad Campaign," Portfolio.com, February 11, 2010, http://www.portfolio.com/industry-news/advertising-marketing/2010/02/11/seventh-generation-embarks-on-first-ever-national-ad-campaign.

[9] Much of this paragraph is drawn from Steven Sexton and Alison Sexton, "Conspicuous Conservation: The Prius Effect and Willingness to Pay for Environmental Bona Fides" (unpublished manuscript, April 2011).

[10] "Use-and-Toss Bottle Facts," Reuseit.com, http://www.reuseit.com/learn-more/top-facts/plastic-bottle-facts.

[11] GreenerDesign staff, "Green Product Trends: More Launches, More Sales," GreenBiz.com, April 23, 2009, http://www.greenbiz.com/news/2009/04/23/green-product-trends-more-launches-more-sales.

[12] "Reusable Shopping Bags…What's the Buzz?," Notawaste.com, http://www.notawaste.com/articles/reusable_shopping_bags.html.

[13] Walmart, "Remarks as Prepared for Mike Duke, President and CEO of Walmart Greenhouse Gas Goal Announcement," news release, February 25, 2010, http://walmartstores.com/pressroom/news/9669.aspx.

[14] Kevin Hagen, "The Effects of Walmart's Packaging Scorecard on Environmental Sustainability," Yahoo!, January 22, 2010, http://www.associatedcontent.com/article/2614159/the_effects_of_walmarts_packaging_scorecard_pg2.html?cat=3.

[15] Lindsay Kauffman, "Green as a Status Symbol: Why Increased Prices May Increase Sales," Triplepundit.com, http://www.triplepundit.com/2011/05/green-status-increase-prices-increase-sales.

[16] "2011 Cone/Echo Global CR Report," Cone Communications, http://www.coneinc.com/2011globalcrreport.

[17] Food Marketing Institute, *U.S. Grocery Shopper Trends* (Food Marketing Institute, 2010), 107; "Key Facts," Food Marketing Institute, accessed April 1, 2010, http://www.fmi.org.

[18] Dan Sewell, "Retailers See Green in 'Green' Business," MSNBC.com, April 23, 2010, http://www.msnbc.msn.com/id/36739333/ns/business-going_green/t/retailers-see-green-green-business.

[19] "Locally Grown: The Whole Foods Market Promise," Whole Foods Markets, http://www.wholefoodsmarket.com/products/locally-grown.

[20] Tim O' Leary, "The Latest on How Much It Costs to Produce a TV Commercial," *Bizzy Life*, May 23, 2010, http://bizzylife.com/2010/05/the-latest-on-how-much-it-costs-to-produce-a-television-commercial.

[21] Nielsen, "In US, Smartphones Now Majority of New Cellphone Purchases," *Nielsenwire*, June 30, 2011, http://blog.nielsen.com/nielsenwire/online_mobile/in-us-smartphones-now-majority-of-new-cellphone-purchases; Graceann Bennett and Freya Williams, *Mainstream Green*, 2011, http://assets.ogilvy.com/truffles_email/ogilvyearth/Mainstream_Green.pdf; Stephanie Clifford and Andrew Martin, "As Consumers Cut Spending, 'Green' Products Lose Allure," *New York Times*, April 21, 2011, http://www.nytimes.com/2011/04/22/business/energy-environment/22green.html?pagewanted=2&_r=2; *Wikipedia*, s.v., "Greenwashing," http://en.wikipedia.org/wiki/Greenwashing; Arthur Thompson, A. J. Strickland, and John Gamble, "Five Generic Competitive Strategies," in *Crafting and Executing Strategy*, 17th ed. (New York: McGraw-Hill, 2009); "Seventh Generation's Mission," Seventh Generation, http://www.seventhgeneration.com/seventh-generation-mission; "Seventh Generation," Behind the Brand, http://www.gobehindthebrand.com/498341/Behind-the-Brand-br-Seventh-Generation-br-Jeffrey-Hollender#.TitH0s0xYyM; "'Green' Household Cleaning Products in the U.S.: Bathroom Cleaners, Laundry Care and Dish Detergents and Household Cleaners," Packaged Facts, http://www.packagedfacts.com/Green-Household-Cleaning-2554249; Laurie Burkit, "Seventh Generation Protecting Its Turf," *Forbes*, January 18, 2010, http://www.forbes.com/2010/01/18/seventh-generation-brand-awareness-cmo-network-chuck-maniscalco.html; Kari Lipshutz, "Once You Go Green, You'll Probably Go Back," *AdWeek*, April 22, 2011, http://www.adweek.com/news/advertising-branding/once-you-go-green-you-ll-probably-go-back-130883; "Arm & Hammer's New Cleaners Not Only Greener, They're Cheaper," EnviralMarketing.com, http://www.enviralmarketing.com/2008/10/22/arm-hammers-new-cleaners-not-only-greener-theyre-cheaper; Stephanie Clifford and Andrew Martin, "As Consumers Cut Spending, 'Green' Products Lose Allure," *New York Times*, April 21, 2011, http://www.nytimes.com/2011/04/22/business/energy-environment/22green.html?pagewanted=2&_r=2; "Seventh Generation Corporate Conscious Report," Seventh Generation, http://www.7genreport.com/introduction/performance.php; "Big Changes at Seventh Generation," *7Gen* (blog), June 1, 2009, http://www.seventhgeneration.com/learn/blog/big-changes-seventh-generation; Marc Gunther, "Seventh Generation Sweeps Out Its Founder," *Marc Gunther*, November 1, 2010, http://www.marcgunther.com/2010/11/01/seventh-generation-sweeps-out-its-founder; Alex Goldmark, "Seventh Generation Snags Burt's Bees CEO to Replace Founder," *Good Business* (blog), February 10, 2011, http://www.good.is/post/seventh-generation-gets-a-new-ceo-john-replogle-from-burt-s-bees; Priti Ambani, "Jeffrey Hollender & Seventh Generation: Lessons Learned at the End of a Chapter," *Ecoprenuerist*, June 27, 2011, http://ecopreneurist.com/2011/06/27/jeffrey-hollender-seventh-generation-lessons-learned-at-the-end-of-a-chapter; Jonathan Bardelline, "Clorox Income Falls as Recession Slows Green Brands," GreenBiz.com, May 3, 2011, http://www.greenbiz.com/news/2011/05/03/clorox-income-falls-recession-slows-green-brands.

[22] Denise Harrison, "Honest Tea Teaches Coke a Lesson," *Simplified Strategic Planning* (blog), http://www.cssp.com/strategicplanning/blog/?p=871.

[23] Kyana Gordon, "Honest Tea Campaign Stimulates Sales Growth, Brand Awareness, and Honesty," *PSFK*, March 9, 2011, http://www.psfk.com/2011/03/honest-tea-campaign-stimulates-sales-growth-brand-awareness-and-honesty.html.

6.3 Market Barriers to Sustainability Products

LEARNING OBJECTIVES

1. Understand the market barriers to sustainable products and how they can be addressed with marketing.
2. Identify and discuss the three primary barriers to sustainable product sales growth.

With all the attention given to sustainability, the question remains, why aren't more consumers using green products? There are three key barriers that sustainability marketers need to keep in mind to better position their products for growth:

1. Price
2. Performance
3. Behavioral change

Sidebar

Mainstream America Unmoved by Green Marketing [1]

Green marketing messages targeting mainstream American consumers are missing the mark, according to a study released in 2011 by consultant group OgilvyEarth. The report included research that showed that many of the environmental messages of marketers were not just failing to close what the study called the Green Gap, but were actually cementing it by making green behavior too difficult and costly from a practical, financial, and social standpoint.

"Many of the world's leading corporations are staking their futures on the bet that sustainability will become a major driver of mainstream consumer purchase behavior. Unless they can figure out how to close the gap, there will never be a business case for green," added Freya Williams, Co-Founder and Director of Strategy at OgilvyEarth and co-author of the study.

The study found that 82% of Americans have good green intentions but only 16% are dedicated to fulfilling these intentions, putting 66% firmly in what the report called the "middle green." Considering green behavior on a continuum, most of the dialogue and marketing to date according to the report has focused on "super greens" on the one hand and "green rejecters" on the other. There has been limited success in motivating the masses or the middle green.

Existing green marketing is either irrelevant or even alienating to most Americans, the study asserts. Half of Americans think green and environmentally friendly products are marketed to "Crunchy Granola Hippies" or "Rich Elitist Snobs" rather than "Everyday Americans." The report highlighted that cost continues to be the greatest barrier that holds Americans back from more sustainable purchases.

"One trip to the grocery store and you would see that green products can have as much as a 100% price premium. It's as if we're penalizing virtuous behaviors with a de facto sustainability tax," says Bennett.

But price was far from the only thing preventing consumer behavior change. The super green minority, according to the report, who venture into the green space do so with a relatively high social and emotional cost. They say they feel ostracized from their neighbors, families, and friends. Meanwhile the middle greens say they fear attracting the negative judgment of their peers if they go out on a limb to purchase green products. Until green products and services feel normal and adhere to normative pricing, the middle green are unlikely to embrace them.

Nearly half of Americans claim to feel guiltier "the more they know" about how to live a sustainable lifestyle. Super greens feel twice the guilt as the average American. Even among the green middle, guilt plays a role. As it increases, these consumers want to retreat to the comfort of ignorance.

"Understanding the prevalent misuse of appeals to a sense of guilt, we can see where sustainability marketing has gone wrong," says Williams. "People don't need to know about the state of polar bears in the Arctic to turn off the lights—paradoxically it may be stopping them from doing so."

The barrier to adopting sustainable behaviors is even higher for men. Fully 82% of respondents say going green is "more feminine than masculine." More men identify as Green Rejecters, and the ranks of the Super Greens are dominated by women. This feminization holds men back from visible green behavior like using reusable grocery bags or carrying around reusable water bottles.

Price

Price is a well-recognized hurdle for many consumers in purchasing sustainable products and services. Sixty-six percent of US consumers view environmentally friendly products as too expensive. Whether consumers are looking to purchase an energy saving light bulb or environmentally friendly home cleaning products, these products often cost more than the most popular consumer versions. Often the premium price puts these products out of the reach or interest of the majority of consumers. And the price premium as a hurdle is magnified during economic downturns.

Sidebar
Gap between Concern and the Cash Register
Overall, 83 percent of global online consumers reported in Nielsen's 2011 Global Online Environment and Sustainability   Survey (http://www.nielsen.com/us/en/insights/press-room/2011/global-warming-cools-off-as-top-concern.html) say that it is important that companies implement programs to improve the environment, but only 22 percent say they will pay more for an eco-friendly product. Willingness to pay extra for environmentally friendly goods is highest in the Middle East and Africa, where one-third of consumers are willing, and lowest in North America, where only 12 percent of both Canadians and Americans say they will pay extra for eco-friendly products. Many consumers reported a personal preference for eco-friendly goods, but large percentages of respondents report setting aside this preference and buying whichever product is cheapest, including 48 percent in North America, 36 percent in the Middle East and Africa, 35 percent in Europe, 33 percent in Asia Pacific, and 27 percent in Latin America.

The price premium compared to the conventional alternative needs to be addressed through the three other parts of the marketing mix (product, place, and promotion). But the most effective way to address the price premium is to address it directly—to find ways to reduce it. Reducing the sustainable price premium is a key factor in having a greater percentage of average consumers purchase more environmentally favorable products.

Performance

Marketers need to clearly communicate the product's benefits and sustainable position especially when commanding a premium price. The challenge is that greener products do not have a stellar history of performing well. In the 1970s, green laundry detergents were developed as a result of concerns over phosphates—a chemical that can cause environmental degradation in large quantities—and resulted in gray, dingy clothes. The original organic cereals tasted like cardboard to many consumers and the early versions of energy efficient light bulbs cast a green glow. Many consumers—roughly a third in the United States and around the globe—still question the efficacy of green products versus their regular, nongreen product alternatives despite strides made in product performance.

Sidebar

Going Green Packaging? Go Softly.

In April 2009, Frito Lay introduced a biodegradable bag for Sun Chips with a big marketing effort to play up its environmentally friendly nature as it was made from plants and not plastic and could break down in compost. Sound good?

Well, the stiffer material made the packaging give off a loud annoying noise that measured at roughly eighty to eighty-five decibels. Consumers compared this sound to a noisy busy city street or even a jet engine. The criticism grew so much that within six months, the company was forced to switch back to its original bag. It didn't help that sales dropped 11 percent during that timeframe as well. [2]

Marketers need to stress the traditional benefits of the sustainable good and must demonstrate the product's effectiveness. This can be more important than highlighting the sustainability benefits to overcome inherent consumer skepticism.

A good example of this is Glad Products Company's 2011 introduction of a version of its Glad tall kitchen drawstring trash bag that is made with less plastic. Glad Products, a joint venture of the Clorox Company and Procter & Gamble, spent over $30 million on a campaign to introduce the trash bags. The bags were billed in ads and on packages as "strength with less plastic" and "stronger with less plastic waste." (The bags were made using 6.5 percent less plastic than before, Glad Products executives say, and have what are called reinforcing bands to make the bags stronger.) [3] The company smartly kept the price at parity to more conventional counterparts, thereby eliminating the green pricing gap. They have made it easier for consumers to adopt this more sustainable product. Moreover, they have positioned it correctly by combining an efficacy product

benefit, "stronger," with a sustainable benefit, "with less plastic/less plastic waste." That's a win-win-win.

Behavioral Change

Many sustainable practices require consumers to change their habits and adopt new ones. Recycling, turning off the lights, lowering the thermostat in winter, using recyclable bags for shopping—all require changing behavior. Typically changing a behavior is a slow process as consumers have to be retaught a habit. That is why Generation Y, often referred to as millennials, are quicker to adopt sustainability practices since they are not breaking old habits.

Most behavioral changes are more readily adopted when there is a perceived consumer benefit, for example, using a kitchen bag with less plastic that is stronger and driving a fuel-efficient car that saves money at the gas pump. Using a more energy efficient, longer-lasting light bulb and a programmable thermostat can save on energy costs and conserving water using a more efficient toilet saves on the water bill. Marketers can help consumers more quickly adopt new behavior and buy new products when they highlight the benefits and long-term cost savings in promoting the product.

Sidebar

One Step at a Time

How much are marketers of green products scaling back ambitious efforts to sell eco-friendlier brands as life-changers and planet-savers?

A line of recycled paper products, introduced by Marcal in 2009, has the brand name "Small Steps" rather than something grander like "Giant Leaps." Each Marcal product is promoted on packages with the tagline, "A small, easy step to a greener earth." This provides a much more realistic and manageable tack that diverges from the hyperbole so favored by Madison Avenue and helps consumers feel empowered to make a difference.

KEY TAKEAWAYS

- The three market barriers to sustainable products are (1) price, (2) performance, and (3) behavior change.
- Each of these market barriers must be considered by the marketing professional when developing a marketing strategy.

EXERCISES

1. Consider a "conventional product," such as toothpaste. Develop a marketing mix plan (the four Ps) for making this product "sustainable" while considering the three market barriers discussed. Discuss how your marketing mix addresses each of these three potential barriers.
2. Find examples of sustainable goods or services that encountered the market barriers discussed in this section. Try to find one unique example per barrier.

[1] "Mainstream America Unmoved by Green Marketing," SustainableBusiness.com, http://www.sustainablebusiness.com/index.cfm/go/news.display/id/22277.

[2] "SunChips Bag Proves It Not Easy Being 'Green,'" *Washington Post*, October 7, 2010, http://www.washingtonpost.com/wp-dyn/content/article/2010/10/06/AR2010100606681.html.

[3] Stuart Elliot, "Glad Cuts the Hyperbole for Its New Green Trash Bag," *New York Times*, October 19, 2011.

6.4 Business Risks of Sustainability Marketing

LEARNING OBJECTIVE

1. Discuss the risks associated with sustainability marketing.

Although sustainability continues to grow as an important business concept, focusing on sustainability in marketing entails significant risks that need to be addressed. These risks can cause problems with a company's marketing plan, short and long term.

The sustainable marketing risks can be categorized as follows:

1. Market risks
2. Operating risks
3. Corporate image risks

Market Risks

Addressing market risks are part of a normal strategy and marketing plan development process, but sustainability adds a dimension of uncertainty due to its relative "newness." Marketing sustainability is in its high-risk phase since the consumer appeal for sustainability is still not well defined. It is true that consumers, when polled, will espouse sustainability's benefits and appeal, but a gap currently exists between the consumers' words and actions.

As a result, the following market risks are associated with sustainability initiatives:

1. Weakness in sustainability's consumer appeal, particularly relative to more basic incentives, such as value, convenience, and efficacy
2. Lack of understanding and personal appreciation of sustainability's benefits among consumer groups

In the abstract, consumers easily agree that the coupling of economic and environmental sustainability is a very positive concept. Who would argue that working to ensure that future generations have the resources to enjoy success is a negative idea? This apparent universal appeal has led more than a few marketers to believe that sustainability as a consumer benefit has mass potential. Consumer purchasing behavior to date, however, has not confirmed sustainability's appeal for the majority of potential consumers. When marketers pit sustainability's strength as a benefit against value in a low-price or low-cost provider differentiation strategy, sustainability seems to have only a limited impact. When marketers pit sustainability's strength as a benefit against convenience and effectiveness in a differentiation strategy, sustainability also seems to have very limited impact.

Sustainability marketers need to understand their "pioneer" role in capturing and leveraging sustainability benefits. Consumers still seem to be processing the value of sustainability as a benefit. Most importantly, consumers are still processing how much they would pay for this benefit.

In addition, sustainability often addresses externalities or failures of conventional products or services to fully cost the negative impact they have. Therefore the "price" of sustainability, whether it be an additional financial cost or a time or effort cost, is something that may make society collectively better off, while making an individual worst off for absorbing that additional cost. The marketer must find ways to communicate personal benefit as well as societal benefits. "It's good for the environment" may not be good enough to convince a consumer to justify any personal cost or sacrifice.

Initial attempts to use sustainability as a key marketing benefit have demonstrated the nascent appeal. Niche businesses, such as Simply Green and Seventh Generation, as well as larger-scale companies such as Stonyfield seem to be able to define an industry segment using the sustainability platform. When mass marketers, attracted by the high growth rates in the "good-for-you, good-for-the-planet" segment, attempt to duplicate niche marketers' success on a larger scale, the mass marketers have generated mixed results.

Examples include "green" product launches from Clorox, SC Johnson, and Dwight and Church. Although some products, supported by heavy introductory marketing programs, experienced initial success, the premium pricing for the products with no accompanying added benefit except for sustainability eventually led to a reduction in the size of the business. This was the case with Green Works from Clorox. Sales of Green Works reached $100 million in its introductory year. Clorox spent approximately $25 million in advertising in 2008 and 2009. Due primarily to the recession, which put pressure on premium-priced products, Green Works sales fell to $60 million and Clorox dropped advertising support to approximately $1 million.

Sustainability as a key benefit is still developing, and the strength of the benefit versus established benefits of better value, lower price, more convenience, and more effectiveness is still not measurable or clear. Many consumers will purchase green products that make no compromises in other benefits. But most consumers will not buy when the green benefit comes at the expense of higher price or more conventional benefits.

The marketing discussion has focused on sustainability as a benefit in a product offered to consumers. When companies apply a sustainability focus as a corporate mandate, such as Timberland, the benefit to the business is also still to be determined. The number of consumers willing to buy a product from a "green" company or an outstanding corporate citizen instead of products from other companies with no such mandate is not definitive at this time. Marketers may believe that the "good" company will reap benefits over the "neutral" or "bad" companies, but unfortunately, this may not always be the case.

Nevertheless, current evidence suggests that consumers are finding the sustainability benefit to be appealing and will possibly become more influential for a consumer's buying decision in the future. Sustainability as a benefit appeals to the logical and emotional sides of the consumer, offering potential for the development of a larger opportunity. Marketers must remember that they are still responsible for developing this opportunity by pioneering information dissemination to consumers and education about sustainability. Sustainability does not yet operate in a clearly defined opportunity space that allows companies to launch new products with no pioneering effort for mass success.

Operating Risks

Chasing the opportunity presented by the growing awareness of sustainability also can create operating risks that need to be addressed during marketing plan development and execution. Much discussion on this subject has taken place, and the issues are fairly straightforward. The following operating risks are associated with pursuing sustainability initiatives as part of a marketing plan:

1. Loss in profitability
2. Loss of focus

Just as sustainability would seem to be a rallying cry for consumers, some companies have jumped on sustainability as a rallying cry for employees. By incorporating sustainability into corporate mission statements and adding green to their products, some companies like Timberland believe that they can drive business improvement via a competitive advantage. All this seems to be a reasonable operating assumption, and a growing number of companies including Timberland have

been successful operating under this assumption. Loss of profitability can occur, however, if a company uses more financial and human resources than competitors without gaining a commensurate benefit. As an example, activities designed to protect the environment have costs. If a company cannot price to recover these costs or if the costs do not lead to benefits that make products superior in the minds of the consumer, then the company now operates at a cost disadvantage versus competition. By internalizing these costs and not receiving a real benefit, a company may experience loss of sales, market share, and profitability.

In addition, adding sustainability to the marketing mix can lead to a loss of focus on the primary objective: economic profitability and economic sustainability. Driving activity through marketing to results that are not part of the core economic strategy may lead a company to damage its profitability by loss of focus and misallocation of critical resources.

Corporate Image Risks

The last risk classification deals with the risks to corporate image that can occur when pursuing sustainability marketing activities and goals. Although all marketing activities have implications for corporate image, sustainability marketing activities can create a higher level of positive or negative impact on image. This is probably because sustainability is a more altruistic and noble cause versus other business objectives and also increasingly of interest to the media and general public and therefore a highly visible company activity. The following corporate image risks are associated with sustainability marketing:

1. Negative greenwashing image
2. Magnified negative impact of an inconsistent action

Greenwashing is the use of green marketing to give the incorrect impression that the company's strategy, operations, and products are designed to be beneficial to the environment. The company attempts to market their green credentials to improve their public image to generate greater sales through positive "spin." Companies embarking on this path are taking a significant risk because exposure of the company's true activities and footprint could result in a relatively large negative impact on all elements of the marketing and public relations plan and eventually sales and profitability. Even companies that are sincere but are perceived to be insincere by the public can suffer grave consequences. It is imperative for companies employing sustainability marketing to be genuine in their motivation and effective in its execution. The damage done by even a hint of insincerity or with poor execution is potentially irreversible.

Sidebar

Greenwashing

Environmentalist Jay Westerveld coined the phrase in his 1986 essay regarding the hotel industry's practice of using placards in each room to promote reuse of towels to "save the environment." He wrote that many hotels made little effort toward energy use reduction. The principal goal of this activity was to increase profits.

Since that time, the Federal Trade Commission (FTC) has put some parameters into effect to help minimize greenwashing with its Green Guide, which was first published in 1998 and revised again in October 2010. The FTC Green Guide mandates that companies provide clear substantiation to any environmental claims and that there is specificity surrounding these claims. In particular, the FTC warns of using more generic terms such as "eco-friendly" and "environmentally friendly" without documented and detailed evidence to these claims. Failure to comply can cost a company up to $16,000 per false claim. [1]

To see the "Sins of Greenwashing," visit http://sinsofgreenwashing.org/findings/the-seven-sins/.

Even a company that has demonstrated its commitment to sustainability over time is still vulnerable, if not more vulnerable, to a misstep in its sustainability initiatives and action. Some companies may be able to generate goodwill through their past actions, but some consumers may take a "what have you done for me lately?" mind-set that does not provide the opportunity to generate this equity. As a result, marketers who incorporate sustainability marketing as an integral element of their plan must be aware of the importance in maintaining consistency and effective execution in its approach and commitment.

As an example, Green Mountain Coffee, a company that has sustainability among its core beliefs, has had some setbacks to its public image due to its biggest business success, Keurig coffee cups. Per its mantra, the company is aggressively researching methods to build a recyclable cup, but its current cups are not biodegradable. Green Mountain's history has given it some protection from negative publicity, but this protection may wear down if a solution is not found in the short term. Once the company loses that essential part of their corporate image, Green Mountain runs the danger of becoming just another coffee company.

Although there is some significant disagreement and experience to support that disagreement, there is evidence that marketing that leverages sustainability attributes is relevant and important. Due to the unique and continuously changing positioning of sustainability in consumers' minds, sustainability marketing comes with its own set of rewards and challenges. To be successful in sustainability marketing, a company must recognize and be ready to deal with the risks associated with this relatively new business concept.

KEY TAKEAWAYS

- Marketers and strategists must consider the market, operating, and image risks associated with sustainability marketing to capture this relatively new business concept's power and to minimize its downside.
- Sustainability as a consumer benefit alone may not be enough to motivate the mainstream consumer to purchase. There exists an opportunity for better consumer cognitive balancing between "good for the environment" and "good for the pocketbook."
- Greenwashing practices have potential to inflict long-term damage to a brand and company franchise.

EXERCISES

1. Find an example of a company that undertook a sustainability strategy that was perceived as greenwashing. Do you agree that the company was greenwashing or was its actions sincere?
2. BP (British Petroleum) rebranded itself in 2000 as "Beyond Petroleum." In 2010, the Deepwater Horizon drilling rig was involved in one of the worst oil spills in history. What is your reaction to their rebranding given this event? Have you changed your purchasing habits as a result of the BP oil spill?

[1] Lee van der Voo, "FTC Takes a Swipe at Greenwashing," *Sustainable Business Oregon*, May 8, 2011, http://www.sustainablebusinessoregon.com/articles/2010/10/new_ftc_rules_take_swipe_at_greenwashing.html.

6.5 Keys to Marketing a Sustainable Brand

LEARNING OBJECTIVES

1. Discuss why marketing a sustainable brand is different than a mainstream product.
2. Discuss keys to effectively market a sustainable brand.

Marketing to the "green" or sustainability market is different than marketing mainstream products. The products are held to higher standards, judged not only on the product's effectiveness but also on delivering on societal and environmental responsibilities. When marketing sustainability it is important that dedication be given—from the initial stages of developing the product through to the products end of life—to environmental responsibilities while still delivering financial performance.

The following are guidelines on how to market sustainable products effectively:

- **Make sure your product works.** Ensure the product competitively delivers on *both* traditional and sustainability benefits. If the product doesn't work, it doesn't matter how "green" it is.

- **Be genuine in sustainability efforts.** Fulfill the sustainability message throughout the entire product's lifecycle—from sourcing of ingredients to the recycling process.

- **Market transparently.** Consumers have come to develop a strong relationship with sustainable companies and brands. They demand transparency. Seventh Generation got into trouble with their baby wipes product when they changed the size of the packaging to have less wipes per package and did not effectively communicate the change to their consumers. Consumers felt "cheated" and lost faith in the company, which took some time to rebuild.

- **Strengthen your core.** Corporate social responsibility needs to be at the core of your company's business philosophy permeating the supply chain all the way through to treating employees fairly. Take, for example, Walmart, who has pledged to reduce their carbon footprint yet is getting sued for employee discrimination. [1]

- **Manage any sustainable pricing gap.** The high price of many of the sustainable products discourages consumers from purchasing and actually can be perceived as a sustainability tax or surcharge. Eliminating or reducing the price barrier helps to dispel the notion that green products are not just for the elite and will encourage more people to consume better-for-the-environment products.

- **Don't force the consumer to make big tradeoffs**— whether it is price, performance, convenience, or a noisy package. Most consumers have not proven that they are willing to make significant sacrifices.

- **Have patience.** Most environmentally friendly consumer behavior requires behavioral changes, and behavioral change takes time. Generation Y and millennial consumers are more apt to embrace this change faster. As more and more companies are jumping on the green bandwagon and eliminating some of the barriers, change will evolve quicker to help shape this shift toward a more sustainable future.

KEY TAKEAWAYS

- Sustainable marketing requires additional consideration when compared to marketing traditional products and services.
- Marketers must deliver value and performance on their sustainable goods.
- Marketers need to be creative in their marketing mix to address areas that may be perceived as deficient, such as a higher price, compared to traditional goods.

EXERCISE

1. Find an example of a "green" product. Discuss the current value proposition of the product. Based on the lessons learned in this chapter, what is the company doing right in marketing its product? What is it doing wrong? What suggestions would you provide to the company to change the value proposition and why?

[1] "Plaintiffs in Walmart Suit File New Claim," *Supermarket News*, Oct 27, 2011, http://supermarketnews.com/retail_financial/walmart_plantiffs_1027/?cid=upd.

NOTES:

NOTES:

Chapter 7:
Case: Sustainable Business Entrepreneurship: Simply Green Biofuels

LEARNING OBJECTIVES

1. Understand the motivations of the entrepreneur Andrew Kellar in starting the sustainable business Simply Green Biofuels.
2. Explain the key challenges faced by the entrepreneur and the start-up company and how they were addressed.
3. Understand how the entrepreneur used personal relations and social networks to inform and support his efforts.
4. Discuss the ecological and social values of the entrepreneur and how the business he started reflected those values.
5. Understand the performance of the entrepreneur and the start-up venture from a triple bottom line perspective.
6. Discuss the role of the entrepreneur's public relations efforts in informing and educating potential customers about sustainable business products and services.
7. Explain what an entrepreneur has to do well to have a successful business venture through the start-up phase and into the growth phase.

This case provides the example of a start-up sustainable business venture. Its purpose is to provide the student with a detailed look at the challenges of entrepreneurship and of small company management in a sustainable business enterprise. Students should consider this case in the context of the triple bottom line—people, profit, and planet.

Simply Green Biofuels offers green alternatives to home heating, diesel, and marine fueling in the seacoast New Hampshire and southern Maine area (http://www.simplygreenbiofuels.com). The company's flagship biofuel blends can be used without any changes to a customer's heating system or motor vehicle engine. In four years, from 2007 to 2011, the company grew its customer base to more than 1,400 customers and, according to *Biofuels Digest*, established itself as one of the leading companies in the bioenergy sector nationally. Its founder, Andrew Kellar, was named one the "25 Leaders for the Next 25 Years" by *BusinessNH Magazine* in 2009.

The company's biofuels are locally sourced from waste vegetable oil (WVO). Typically, WVO is collected as recycled vegetable oils from restaurants and distributors. Once it's refined into a petroleum-like fuel, it is combined with traditional petroleum products to make biofuel blends.

The company offers a bio heating oil product called BioHeat and biodiesel for motor vehicle use in three different blends. The only difference between BioHeat fuel and biodiesel motor engine biofuel is that BioHeat is blended with no. 2 heating oil, and biodiesel is blended with diesel fuel. The blends and their environmental attributes and benefits are as follows:

- **B5.** B5 is a blend of 5 percent biofuel and 95 percent no. 2 heating oil or diesel fuel. By using B5, the typical consumer will reduce their CO_2 emissions by 4 percent or the equivalent of planting fifty-two trees.
- **B20.** This blend contains 20 percent biofuel and 80 percent no. 2 heating oil or diesel fuel. By using B20, the typical consumer will reduce their CO_2 emissions by 16 percent or the equivalent of planting 192 trees.
- **B100.** This blend contains 100 percent biofuel and no no. 2 heating oil or diesel fuel. In its purest form, biofuel is a highly solvent product that breaks down any petroleum residue (e.g., sludge) that has built up in a system over time.

Every heating and motor vehicle manufacturer has endorsed the use of B5. However, Simply Green states that after B5 has been run for a sufficient amount of time (typically after a couple deliveries), customers may be able to "bump up" to a B20 blend.

Sidebar
Biofuels Contribution to Reduction of Greenhouse Gas
Biofuels offer the potential to reduce greenhouse gas (GHG) emissions because the carbon in the plant matter from which biofuels are produced comes from the carbon dioxide absorbed by the plants from the atmosphere during their lifetime. This is in contrast to the carbon in fossil fuels, which has been sequestered underground for millions of years and is released into the atmosphere as carbon dioxide when the fuels are burnt. Biofuels can lead to significant GHG emissions savings compared to fossil fuels.

Andrew Kellar

One might think that Simply Green started partly out of necessity and partly out of Andrew Kellar's passion and concern for the environment. Andrew Kellar identified an opportunity—a market niche that was not being filled—and he developed a business to meet that opportunity. But that is not how he or Simply Green got started. In 2003, Simply Green was founded by Andrew as an erosion control and hydro-seeding business. It was a seasonal business that fit well with Andrew's preferred lifestyle. It enabled him to pursue his passion for outdoor activities, including surfing in Mexico with his wife during the cold winter seasons in New Hampshire. His passion for the environment started when he was young. In addition to surfing as a youth, he was constantly doing activities to help protect the environment, including beach cleanups and recycling.

As Simply Green's hydro-seeding business grew, the company required additional trucks and equipment, which, in turn, required the use of more and more diesel fuel. Andrew, with his love for the outdoors, became increasingly concerned about the negative environmental impact of his company's use of diesel. This concern led Andrew to investigate alternatives. Were there options for fuel that could still power his business but reduce his negative impact?

Andrew had heard of people collecting grease from McDonald's or other fast food restaurants and then using it to power their motor vehicles. This intrigued him and he started to see if there was a biofuel alternative to power the vehicles and equipment for his business.

Starting in 2006, Andrew started looking into the biodiesel market more deeply. At the time, there was limited availability in northern New England. He could only locate two gas stations that provided biodiesel, one that was somewhat close to his operating area and one that was two hours away. Also there was only one home heating fuel provider in the area that offered biodiesel, but it was not their main focus; instead, it was a specialty product that they offered.

For Andrew, a personal change was one of the major factors that convinced him to move forward into biofuels. Andrew and his wife, Ginger, received a phone call from the Florida Department of Children and Families. There were three young children that were in need of a home who were relatives of the Kellars. The Kellars took the children in. Andrew's new parenting role and responsibility got him to think about how he could positively impact society and the earth and also how he was going to help support the three

new additions to the family. This convinced him to start the business.

As Andrew describes, fate may have had a hand in the situation: "What really kicked me over was that phone call. The phone call that we were going to be parents instantly…And, call it fate, call it whatever you want, but I had just finished doing a hydro seeding job for this one customer and I was researching online where the supply sources were and it said, for more information on our biodiesel, contact Tim Keaveney. And I looked down, this one evening, and there was a check from Tim K for the hydro seeding I just did."

7.1 Biodiesel

Biofuels have been around as long as cars have. At the start of the twentieth century, Henry Ford planned to fuel his Model Ts with ethanol, and the original diesel engine designed by Rudolph Diesel used peanut oil–based fuel. Discoveries of huge petroleum deposits kept gasoline and diesel at a low cost for the twentieth century, and biofuels were largely forgotten. However, with the rise in oil prices, along with growing concern about global warming caused by carbon dioxide emissions from conventional fuels, biofuels have been regaining popularity recently. Gasoline and diesel are actually ancient biofuels. They are known as fossil fuels because they are made from decomposed plants and animals that have been buried underground for millions of years. Biofuels are similar except that they are produced from plants grown today. [1]

Biodiesel is a product that is derived from a renewable energy source, such as soybeans. The renewable energy source could also be other crops, such as corn, although corn is more typically made into ethanol for use by gasoline engines. It could also be recycled grease that comes from commercial fryers. Biodiesel produced from recycled oils and grease is considered a second-generation biofuel, whereas the soybean would be, if it was grown as a virgin product specifically for it, considered a first-generation biofuel. There also are third-generation biofuels based on algae. [2]

The greenhouse gas (GHG) emission reduction from using biofuels is not 100 percent when compared to fossil fuels. Carbon savings are partially offset by the energy that is needed for cultivation, harvesting, processing, and transportation of biofuels. This can represent a substantial fraction of the total energy released from processed biofuels and varies significantly between crops. In the worst-case scenario, the production process may actually take more energy than can be produced when the biofuels are used, which undermines the potential environmental benefits. [3]

Second, there may be carbon emissions associated with changing the usage of land to biofuel crop cultivation. For instance, if areas that have not been previously cultivated, such as forest land, are converted to produce biofuels, then there may be significant immediate releases of carbon stored in the existing plant life and in the soil and also damage to biodiversity and the ecosystem. These land use–change effects may prevent biofuel plantations from generating an overall reduction in carbon emissions until many decades of crops have been produced.

Public Policy Impact on the Market
The biofuel industry is subsidized by the federal government, like most other US energy markets, such as oil and natural gas. There is a $1 per gallon "blenders'" credit for companies that produce pure 100 percent biofuels and then blend in 0.1 percent heating oil or diesel fuel to produce B99.9 made from either first-, second-, or third-generation sources. This blending triggers the credit and allows the product to be competitive with traditional fossil fuels.

The biofuel industry is significantly impacted by changing public policies due to the highly politicized nature of discussions about climate change and the human influence on climate change in the United States. This has made it difficult to develop a business in the industry. For example, the blenders' credit was repealed in early 2010 and it took almost nine months for it to be reenacted in the US Congress. During this period, many biodiesel factories were either in temporary shut down or in foreclosure, and this resulted in significant job loss in the industry. [4]

[1] "Biofuels: The Original Car Fuel," *National Geographic*, http://environment.nationalgeographic.com/environment/global-warming/biofuel-profile.
[2] For more information on BioHeat and related products, see "Alcohol Can Be a Gas," http://www.permaculture.com.
[3] "Biofuels—The Net Energy Debate," SyntecBiofuel, http://www.syntecbiofuel.com/biofuels_net_energy_debate.php.
[4] Brett Clanton, "New Year, New Troubles: Biofuel Plants Idled by Loss of Tax Credit," *Houston Chronicle*, December 31, 2009, http://www.chron.com/disp/story.mpl/business/energy/6794155.html.

7.2 The Challenges and Overcoming Them
After Andrew's first meeting with Tim Keaveney, he realized quickly that he was facing several different challenges. The first—entering an established, mature home heating oil industry—was going to be extremely difficult. Tim told Andrew, "Nobody starts a fuel business these days. I mean, the youngest fuel company in this area is 10 or 12 years old." Fuel distribution to homes was a challenging industry to get into because traditionally they were multigenerational

businesses with very loyal customers. There was no easy solution to this challenge. Andrew was simply willing to take a leap of faith and try to help transform the industry by offering a new product into the marketplace.

Not only was Andrew entering a mature industry, but he was entering an industry that he had no experience in. While his hydro-seeding business had provided him with experience in a service-based industry and experience running a business, he did not have experience in fuel procurement and delivery. Another challenge was capital. Any new business or business expansion faces this challenge—access to adequate capital. Simply Green was better positioned, in terms of financial position, than many other new businesses. Its new business expansion could be in part self-funded. Andrew Kellar, unlike many other entrepreneurs, was fortunate to have the hydro-seeding business, which, at the time, was one of the largest in the region and was generating positive net revenue of approximately $100,000 annually.

Sidebar
Self-Funding a Business Start-Up
Self-funding involves funding a venture through savings accumulated on one's own or in a previous business. It can also include taking on personal debt through bank loans or loans from friends and family and use of personal lines of credit.

Simply Green started the biofuel home heating side of the business in April 2007. To most fuel providers, this would have seemed to be the worst time of year to start because it was toward the end of the heating season in the Northeast. But for Simply Green it made sense because the company had the ability to softly test the market through early adopter customers and learn from that experience. Andrew's plan was to capture some revenue from the heating season market, go into the summer time, quickly reevaluate what was working and what needed improvement, and then move on into the next heating season.

This soft market entry approach also helped with another challenge—educating their potential customers about their product and value proposition. Simply Green used different types of marketing and public relations to educate the public about their unique product offering. As Andrew describes it,

> *We were not concerned with going to any type of event. We didn't care if it was a first graders' classroom that we were going to, we would go in and talk. We would go to every place we had an opportunity to talk about biofuel and our services. And looking back now, the irony of that is where people remembered*

seeing us, and hearing us, were in some of those obscure places that you wouldn't have normally thought from a marketing standpoint that people would remember you and actually make a decision to buy your product or service.

Sidebar
Early Adopters of Products

An early adopter is a person who embraces new technology before most other people do. Early adopters tend to buy new products sooner than most others. According to a theory called diffusion of innovations, formulated by Everett Rogers, early adopters make up 13.5 percent of the population. Early adopters, while eager to explore new products, are not the first to buy a new offering. That role, according to Rogers, is played by a small minority just under 3 percent of people called innovators. Laggards are at the other end of the spectrum. They are reluctant to embrace new technology because of disinterest, financial constraints, or fear.

Sidebar
Value Proposition for a Business

A value proposition is a business or marketing statement that summarizes why a consumer should buy a product or use a service. The statement should be able to convince a potential consumer that one particular product or service will add more value or better solve a problem than other offerings.

Another challenge was the licensing and the regulatory process of entering the highly regulated fuel industry. While Simply Green was providing biofuel, it was a blended product and it had conventional fuel in it so the company had to be regulated just like any other heating oil or diesel provider. Simply Green had to learn about and undertake many different types of licensing including at the state level, for hazardous material, and from the US Department of Transportation.

Simply Green already had experience with the US Department of Transportation (USDOT) licensing as they had just completed a vehicle audit. Andrew was already familiar with the licensing process, and the USDOT official who was involved with the audit made the audit more of an educational audit. During an audit, as Andrew was considering biofuel sales, the USDOT official was so intrigued by the potential Simply Green entry into biofuel provision that he became a customer and also then became an adviser to the company.

The lesson for Andrew was the importance of relations, contacts, and broader social networks for developing business opportunities. As Andrew describes it, "It was important not to be afraid to ask people that might know somebody or that might have an in with somebody that might have the information we were looking for."

7.3 Getting the Business Off the Ground

When Simply Green's biofuel business commenced in April 2007, Andrew started with family and friends as his first customers. Some of the other initial customers came from contacts from the hydro-seeding side of Simply Green's business, including the USDOT official.

In the first six months, Simply Green expanded its customer base to fifty. Building from the first season's customer base was mostly about education, getting potential customers familiar with Simply Green biofuel products; getting people to understand what biofuels were, its environmental benefits, and how it was easy to use; and convincing them that it was not going to negatively impact their vehicles or their homes. With outreach and education, people started to learn, develop interest, and trust and started to tell their friends. Some took the leap of faith and signed on to try BioHeat.

In its second year, Simply Green grew quickly. It started to grow fast, in part, because of the increased concern about the human influence on climate change after the 2006 release of the movie *An Inconvenient Truth*. As Andrew describes it, "When we were talking to potential customers about the environmental impact of different fuel options, people were seeing it on the big screen. It just helped pave the path a little bit easier for us to get down the education road. And we quickly started to see an increase in our customer base."

Simply Green was entering an established market for fuel that had certain characteristics that the company had to understand and figure how to effectively compete in the context of these characteristics. While most of the competition was based on price, it was also subject to strong customer loyalty to dealers who had been delivering their fuel for a long time. A larger dealer might be making $0.60 a gallon over wholesale, versus $0.40 a gallon for a smaller establishment. Simply Green usually came in anywhere in the middle of these, as it was unknown whether customers would pay a premium for a more environmentally friendly product. Simply Green pegged their price to range from $0.05 to $0.10 on either side of the conventional competition. And in addition to being able to address their customers' environmental concerns, a benefit Simply Green's product had over the conventional competition was that it burned cleaner in furnaces and car engines. It helped the system: either the engine in the vehicle or the heating system in the home or workplace. It allowed engines and furnaces to clean themselves, as the biofuel acted as a natural solvent. And this lowered the customer's maintenance cost, extended the life of the furnace or engine, and increased the burning efficiency of the furnace or engine by about 5 percent. So any relatively small price premium for Simply Green biofuels could pay for itself.

In the first full year, Simply Green grew the customer base to about five hundred customers. In addition, Simply Green continued to engage in creative marketing and outreach. One of the best examples of this was Andrew making cold (unsolicited and without any prior connection) phone calls to music industry performers touring in the region whose fans and the performers themselves were expressing concerns about the environmental footprints of their performance tours. For Andrew this was fun and exciting. He was able to connect with Guster, Dave Matthews, Jack Johnson, and Farm Aid.

In May 2007, as Andrew describes it, "I saw that the band Guster was coming to this area. And I knew that they were pretty environmentally concerned with how they set up their concerts. So I put a call into this organization that was managing their concert venues, called Reverb. And the woman who runs it was the wife of one of the band members. Long story short, she and I grew up in the same town, and we didn't realize, she was friends with my best friend's older brother." Again, Andrew was able to make a personal connection and turn social networking into a business benefit.

The Reverb representative (http://www.reverb.org/about) was very excited that Simply Green could deliver the biodiesel directly to Guster's tour entourage. So Andrew brought the truck filled with biodiesel to their location and filled their tour buses and their tractor trailers. Guster's handlers took a photo of the tour bus being filled from a Simply Green biofuels truck and the photo went viral in many publications and the Internet, the biggest publication being an issue of *Rolling Stone*.

After Guster, Simply Green fueled the tour buses for Dave Mathews, John Mayer, the Beastie Boys, Farm Aid, Kelly Clarkson, the Blue Man Group, Sheryl Crow, Willie Nelson, Jack Johnson, Phish, Coldplay, Maroon 5, and Styx.

Sidebar
Reverb: Helping the Music Industry "Go Green"
Reverb is a nonprofit organization based in Portland, Maine, that was founded in 2004 by environmentalist Lauren

Sullivan and her musician husband, Adam Gardner of Guster. Reverb provides comprehensive, custom greening programs for music tours while conducting grassroots outreach and education with fans around the globe. In addition to their "greening" work with bands and artists, Reverb also works to move forward the sustainable practices of music industry leaders, including venues, record labels, and radio stations. Reverb is an example of a social enterprise.

This instantly gave Simply Green higher credibility and visibility. The perception of the fuel industry in general was the delivery driver that would come to your home, maybe your parents' home, and maybe even your grandparents' home. And that same company came to you every year. But Simply Green was trying to change the standard practice. They wanted it to become something different. They wanted to enable the public to be able to make a purchase motivated by environmental concerns and to have that be "hip and cool." And once they got the *Rolling Stone* exposure, that credibility and market buzz carried through into their local press. A lot of local press started picking up on what Simply Green was trying to do.

As Andrew describes it,
That's really what impacted our business the most…the amount of public relations that we got from Rolling Stone and some of these really fun events, that may not even been the best business decision because we might have driven to the southern part of Massachusetts to deliver 500 gallons of fuel and we might not have covered the cost of getting there and the driver's time. But what that and similar efforts did for us was continually got us in the press. If it wasn't every week, it was probably every other week, or a couple times a month, a few times a month. And then people started to read about us, and that's where the phone calls started to come in. We started to get up the education curve with our potential customers, the credible component to hearing it or reading it in the newspaper, started to multiply, and we really start to see the business pick up.

It was not just the cover of *Rolling Stone*. Simply Green used community engagement and its commitment to serving the community to reach out to potential customers, to get noticed, and to establish its market presence. In April 2008, the company created a not-for-profit subsidiary, the Green Alliance, in the greater seacoast of New Hampshire area as a public relations and marketing division to educate the community on "being green."

Simply Green also used its commitment to serve the community to build its customer base. In February 2008, the company serviced former Veilleux, Peron Fuel, and Price Rite customers after the companies stopped delivering fuel and went out of business in the middle of winter. For this, Andrew Kellar and the Simply Green team won the Environmental Hero award in Maine. Again in May 2008, Simply Green helped out households in need, offering special pricing for Rye Fuel customers that were unable to get deliveries of their prebuy fuel at the end of the heating season. And in July 2008, when fuel prices were peaking at $4 a gallon, Simply Green offered discount prices to large groups, such as neighborhoods, town co-ops, and employees of local businesses.

Staffing the Business

From April 2007 to the end of the year, Andrew operated as a solo entrepreneur and employee. In January 2008, Simply Green added its first employee. Staffing increased steadily along with customers and revenue growing to ten employees in April 2009 and seventeen employees in April 2010. The first hires were fuel truck drivers who became the public face of the company. As Andrew describes it, "We wanted each of our drivers to be the face of the company and be able to educate and handle any onsite customer service concerns. We also wanted them to have a clean and friendly demeanor. We were fortunate to find just the right mix of drivers that supported the brand and our mission."

Simply Green then added to its marketing staff for customer outreach and acquiring new customers. The last area Simply Green added to was operations staff. Operations managed customer relationships after deliveries occurred and also managed the internal relationships of the employees. Simply Green was able to find all their employees, with only two exceptions, through referrals by staff members. Recruited employees wanted to work for a socially and environmentally responsible company that was contributing to the community that they all lived in.

Growing the Business

In the fall of 2008, Simply Green expanded and diversified, adding a biodiesel division, opening up a gas station, and starting to do research into third-generation biofuels with scientists at the University of New Hampshire.

The gas station was a first of its kind. The station located at a busy intersection in Dover, New Hampshire, sold biofuel for automobiles and also included a congreenience store. The concept behind the congreenience store was to be a traditional convenience store with a green twist to it. The store had solar panels on the roof, used bamboo flooring, and sold local food. About 75 percent of all the products in the store came from within a one hundred mile radius, to support the local economy and local vendors. The station had two different types of biodiesel available at the pump, gasoline, which had a 10 percent blend of bio (ethanol), and a fully biofuel product.

With the station, Simply Green had the ability to further promote the sustainability mission and commitment of the company. The station became a highly visible showplace for Simply Green to educate more customers. There were more than one hundred people at the station every day and about 50 percent were new to the store, looking to fuel up their vehicles or get a cup of coffee, and thousands of others drove by every day. So that was an opportunity, every day, to educate.

With the congreenience store, community outreach, and other efforts, Simply Green's customer base continued to grow at a steady pace. By April 2009, Simply Green had one thousand customers. And by September 2009, as Andrew describes it, "We were creeping towards profitability."

7.4 The Keys to Success

Critical to the company's success was its filling of a market niche, focus on core products, and effective messaging and education. Customers could simply, with no or minimal extra cost and very little risk, reduce their carbon footprint and feel good about it by buying Simply Green biofuel.

An important factor in Simply Green's success was the highly creative and energetic market outreach led personally by the founding entrepreneur himself. The educational outreach took the approach that all events and opportunities to get the word out about Simply Green and biofuels were worthwhile. Underpinning it all was the consistent and persistent branding. The branding was about being a sustainable business with a triple bottom line that included concern for the planet and people and was focused on helping customers act on their own concerns about the environment. This was sincere and it came off as such, and customers responded positively. As Andrew describes it, "We were really concerned about how we came across to our customers. We wanted to be as authentic and as transparent about our own practices, so that way our customers felt as though they were buying something from somebody, from a company that truly cared about the environment. We practiced what we were preaching. We were out there at events. We were supporting other businesses that were doing the right thing."

7.5 Why No Profits?

By September 2011, the company had 1,500 heating oil customers and was delivering about a million gallons a year of biodiesel. Customers were concentrated in the seacoast of New Hampshire into southern Maine and down into northeastern Massachusetts. Simply Green's market share within the heating oil industry was 10 percent to 12 percent and had grown fast, especially given the traditional customer to dealer relationship and that their product was a new one. Total revenue at the end of 2011 was more than $4 million. Of the total revenue, 60 percent to 70 percent was BioHeat and 20 percent to 30 percent biodiesel and the balance was the congreenience store (see details as follows).

By many measures, Simply Green could be characterized as successful. Then why, after four years, was it still operating in the red—that is, losing money? One factor was volatile oil prices and changing overall economic conditions. For example, in its second year (winter of 2008) the start-up company was negatively impacted by the unanticipated $4 a gallon oil. As is standard industry practice, Simply Green prebought ahead of the peak heating season from their wholesale fuel suppliers for a select percentage of their customers that wanted to prebuy their fuel.

Simply Green was contractually obligated to pick up those gallons at the fixed price. Historically, there would be some fluctuation in those prices versus what the retail spot pricing would be. But never was there such an exaggerated difference where a customer who had prebought would then call another company to get fuel from them because the market price was so much lower than the prebuy price they had locked in.

Many Simply Green customers locked the price at $4.50 a gallon, and then that winter, heating oil plummeted to $2. Simply Green could not force customers to take the fuel and they had not required their customers to commit to buying a minimum amount of fuel. Some Simply Green customers may have went to another oil dealer to get fuel at its market price, some may have just turned their heat way down and put on a sweater to reduce their oil consumption, and some people may have burned more wood. The loss between what Simply Green had paid for the peak price oil and what it could eventually sell ended up being more than $300,000.

This forced Andrew Kellar to take on two silent business partners. The partners took a 30 percent equity position in the company and contributed $150,000 to the business. Taking on the partners provided Simply Green

with the financial resources that Andrew did not have and did not have access to. The business partners, however, did not have as much of an interest as Andrew in community engagement and the partners shifted the focus more toward the single bottom line of profitability.

The partners had a commitment to the environment and were conscientious of how they operated in the community; however, these were not as much in the forefront of their efforts according to Andrew Kellar. As Andrew describes it, "I get that in businesses sometimes you're forced to get to a place where you really have to focus more on the main bottom line, until you can get to a place where you can have the luxury of expanding that."

Sidebar
Equity Interest in a Business
An equity interest is an ownership interest in a business entity. Shareholders in a publically traded company have equity interest; their purchase of shares of stock in the corporation gives them a share of the ownership of the business. Private equity is a broad term that refers to any type of equity investment in an asset in which the equity is not freely tradable on a public stock market. Categories of private equity investment include business partnership investments, leveraged buyouts, venture capital, and angel investing.

7.6 Limits of Always Focusing on Doing the Right Thing

Andrew Kellar's priority to always do the right thing for the environment and people had implications. As Andrew describes it, "I think my biggest mistake was I stayed so focused on the environmental and social mission of Simply Green, that I failed to stay focused equally on the fundamentals of the business. And the fundamental are the numbers, the profits and the losses and the working capital to operate the business. I didn't do my homework. I didn't have the resources that I needed to effectively sustain the business."

Sidebar
Working Capital and Keeping the Business Ongoing
Working capital measures how much in liquid (readily available) financial assets an organization has available to fund and build its operation. The number can be positive or negative, depending on how much the organization is growing relative to revenue collection and the debt the organization is carrying. In general, companies that have a lot of working capital will be more successful since they can expand and improve their operations. Companies with

negative working capital may lack the funds necessary for growth.

In particular Andrew neglected his need for capital and adequate cash resources (cash flow). He did not adequately anticipate the implications of different potential scenarios beyond his control, such as what if oil went to $4 and then down to $2 or by growing to one thousand customers, how was he going to manage $300,000 in accounts receivable over thirty days? He did not think through these potential scenarios, and he did not have the adequate financial resources on hand when these happened. What he needed to have done was in the early stages have a detailed business plan with "what ifs" for different scenarios and identify risks in his operations.

For Simply Green and any other company in the energy business, price volatility is one of the biggest risks. This is a particularly significant challenge for start-up and small companies with limited financial resources and little operating reserves.

This challenge also has a potential upside for Simply Green and the renewable energy and energy efficiency industries. For example, as fuel prices were rising rapidly again in the early spring of 2011, this again raised awareness about alternative energy, which can be a positive factor for the biofuel industry. But the volatility—the up and down of oil prices—as was experienced in 2008 and again in 2011, makes it a challenging operating environment for new energy companies trying to change the industry and customer preferences.

The final challenge was personal for the entrepreneur. Life became "too crazy," as Andrew put it, and it became increasingly difficult to satisfy both his personal and professional lives. They were no longer aligned for Andrew. The craziness of being an entrepreneur for Andrew included being responsible for 1,500 customers who could call at any time and responsible for drivers on the road twenty hours out of the day delivering customers their fuel. He had taken only one vacation during the four years of his business start-up. And even on the very occasional days off, there was always something that had to be taken care of. As Andrew describes it, "Being the owner, you can have amazing people around you, and most time, they can take care of most of it, but there's always something that comes through that you need to take care of. And that was the craziness, that being pulled in a lot of different directions. At times, when as a young father, you might normally like to be home, going to a baseball game with your son, going to different events with your kids, that wasn't an option."

7.7 Conclusion
What's Next for Simply Green?

Focusing on the core business that drives the bottom line, which for Simply Green is getting the most amount of renewable fuel out onto the market, continues to be an exciting opportunity for Simply Green. The company's focus in 2011 is on developing a marketing plan that gets Simply Green out to the next group of customers beyond the early adopters to the early and late majority customers. Coming up with a strong marketing plan can allow Simply Green to attract that next ring of customers. The growth potential is significant, particularly since more than two-thirds of the population in Simply Green's service territory use heating oil to heat their homes, and a large percentage of commercial vehicles use conventional diesel fuel.

The Entrepreneur's Life Takes a Different Turn

In mid-2010, Andrew Kellar began to realize that, as an entrepreneur, his key strengths were in the creative development end, and he left Simply Green to pursue other opportunities.

As Andrew describes it,

There are some people that are meant to be operators of business long term, and there are people that are meant to be in startups, in the craziness of everything that has to do with starting up a business…I realized that that was where my strength was. While there wasn't a lot of challenge left for me, there was still plenty of challenges for Simply Green in the long term, managing a business with 1,500 customers, and trucks on the road 20 hours out of the day. That skill set was not where I saw my strengths. So it was time for me to make a change. It was time for me to look to my business partners to take over the business.

I felt that Simply Green had helped me to define a new industry in this small community and helped me to do something really special and something unique. While I thought Simply Green was bringing me closer to being that person I wanted to be, and that businessman I wanted to be, it wasn't allowing me to have a balance between being an entrepreneur and other things. I wanted to move on to a different working environment, where I could leverage all the experience that I had gained over those four years.

Between the highs and the lows, and all of the excitement and challenges that we had, I felt that was something that needed to be shared with other entrepreneurs. And I really, really enjoyed being in this kind of green, or now called clean-tech sector, that I wanted to reach out to other younger entrepreneurs that were in that same market, and try to give back to them.

After leaving Simply Green, Andrew became an entrepreneur in residence at the University of New Hampshire's Green Launching Pad (GLP) program (http://greenlaunchingpad.org). The GLP is a business accelerator program focused on assisting new and growing business in renewable energy and energy efficiency. In that role, Andrew is assisting sustainability-focused businesses in their start-up and early growth phases. He also became an advisor and engaged in development efforts for Revolution Energy (http://www.rev-en.com/company/about-us). Revolution Energy was a company that the GLP helped launch in 2010. The company assists in the financing of renewable energy projects with a focus on municipalities, schools, and colleges. Based on this work and his experience with Simply Green, Andrew was selected as a Mel King Community Fellow at MIT in 2012 (http://web.mit.edu/colab/people-mel-king-community-fellows.html). All of these allow Andrew to help others learn from his experience with Simply Green and enable him to continue to act on his commitment to sustainability.

Postscript: What Would Andrew Kellar Want Students to Know?

For Andrew, the next generation has the opportunity to focus on learning from his successes and mistakes and those of others in the first generation of sustainability entrepreneurs. What he suggests to students interested in being sustainable business entrepreneurs is to

- take advantage of the resources available to learn all you can about sustainability science, engineering, and business;
- try to get an internship with a local sustainable business;
- on your own or with a friend, try out a small sustainability project idea at your school and in communities.

As Andrew describes it, "There are a lot of great opportunities for young students, at the undergrad level up to the MBA level, to get involved in different way in sustainable businesses…(a)nd they're not just stuffing envelopes. They're actually getting involved with these businesses. We used to bring in interns, and we had our interns do a lot of in-depth work. It wasn't mindless work, it was actually in-depth market analysis."

KEY TAKEAWAYS

- Success in sustainable business entrepreneurship requires commitment to sustainability and problem solving, creativity, innovation, and "day-to-day" business management skills.
- The entrepreneur, Andrew Kellar, started the company out of concern for the environment and for future generations.
- The entrepreneur entered a mature industry with no experience but with a new product.
- The entrepreneur used personal contacts, relations, and social networks to gather useful information and resources.
- The start-up successfully employed creative marketing and low cost public relations to grow the company, appealing to the public's concern for the environment.
- The company was environmentally and socially focused but had to also focus on core business fundamentals, such as effective management of liquid, or cash, resources and strong customer service to be successful.
- Simply Green focused on the people and planet side of the triple bottom line and had to learn over time how to more effectively manage to achieve the profit side of the triple bottom line.
- The sustainable business founder lacked business training and skills that could have helped him to maintain ownership of the business. Commitment to and passion for sustainability are important and so are financial and other management skills.

EXERCISES

1. What factors contributed to Andrew Kellar starting the biodiesel business? Were you surprised at the reasons that he gave for starting this business? Do you think his decision to start the business was wise? Why or why not?
2. Discuss how Andrew Kellar is a social entrepreneur. What do you think were his strengths in running the company? What do you see as his main weaknesses? Discuss how an action that Andrew undertook was good for both sustainability and the business. Discuss how an action that Andrew undertook may have been good for sustainability but not good for the business.
3. Do you think that Andrew Kellar is well suited to be a successful entrepreneur? Why or why not?
4. What similarities do you think a sustainable business start-up shares with a "normal business" start-up? What differences do you think there are? Give an example of a business challenge that both Simply Green and a conventional fuel dealer share. Give an example of a business challenge that was unique to Simply Green and would not have affected a conventional fuel dealer from the chapter.

5. Discuss the charitable actions that Simply Green took in regards to customer accounts from failed fuel businesses in a triple bottom line context. Was this a smart business move? Why or why not?

6. Explain how Andrew Kellar used low-cost public relations to educate potential customers and promote Simply Green.

7. Describe how you might use personal contacts to start a business venture. What would that involve? How would you start? What type of people would be most useful to draw on for information and resources when starting a sustainable business?

8. Assess your skills and ability to manage a business start-up effectively. Do you have course work, training, or experience in financial and operations management? How are you at leading and motivating others, communicating and getting a message out, and organizing efforts and people at a workplace? Are you task oriented? Are you good with details?

7.8 Appendix: Simply Green Timeline

- **April 12, 2007.** First delivery of BioHeat and biodiesel by Simply Green.

- **May 2007.** First delivery to Guster and Reverb, spurring a flood of fueling services for musicians, which included Dave Mathews, John Mayer, the Beastie Boys, Farm Aid, Kelly Clarkson, the Blue Man Group, Sheryl Crow, Willie Nelson, Jack Johnson, Phish, Coldplay, Maroon 5, and Styx.

- **June and July 2007.** Simply Green finds its way into *Rolling Stone* and *Billboard*.

- **December 2007.** Simply Green is featured in Sundance Film Channel's "Big Ideas for a Small Planet" with Guster and Reverb.

- **January 2008.** Simply Green hires its first employee.

- **February 2008.** Simply Green bails out former Veilleux, Peron Fuel, and Price Rite customers when the companies leave customers out in the cold after they allegedly stopped delivering fuel and went out of business.

- **March 2008.** Simply Green moves out of Andrew's house into an actual office in Portsmouth and hires its second employee.

- **April 2008.** Simply Green creates the Green Alliance as a public relations and marketing division to educate the community on "being green" and hires Sarah Brown as the project director.

- **May 2008.** Simply Green is back to its old ways and starts to offer special pricing for Rye Fuel customers that were unable to get deliveries of their prebuy fuel at the end of the heating season.

- **June 2008.** Andrew Kellar and the Simply Green Team win the Environmental Hero award in Maine along with Governor Baldacci for their rescue mission for the residents of Maine left out in the cold by the Veilleux, Peron Fuel, and Price Rite scandal.

- **June 2008.** Andrew Kellar is invited to give the commencement speech at Berwick Academy.

- **July 2008.** Simply Green starts to offer discount prices to large groups, such as neighborhoods, town co-ops, and employees of local businesses, during a time when oil was on its way to $4 a gallon.

- **October 2008.** Simply Green opens the first biofuels and congreenience store in New England, offering gas and biodiesel at the pump and local products in the store.

- **November 2008.** Simply Green receives the Innovation Rock award by the New Hampshire Department of Resources and Economic Development and is given the first of many commendations by Governor Lynch.

- **November 2008.** Simply Green begins its research and development into third-generation biofuels in conjunction with the University of New Hampshire and starts to apply for grants to study algae as a feedstock to make biofuels.

- **December 2008.** Simply Green is named one of the top fifty hottest companies in the bioenergy sector worldwide.

- **January 2009.** Andrew Kellar is named one of the "25 Leaders for the Next 25 Years" by *BusinessNH Magazine*.

- **April 2009.** Simply Green marks a huge milestone by delivering BioHeat to more than one thousand customers around the seacoast of New Hampshire and Maine, signs on Coca-Cola and Public Service of New Hampshire for onsite fueling services, and hires its fifteenth employee.

- **December 2009.** Simply Green is named one of the top fifty hottest companies in the bioenergy sector worldwide for the second year in a row.

- **January 2010.** Simply Green is back at it again. Flynn's Oil goes out of business on Christmas night and leaves customers without fuel, so another bailout plan is in place to help thousands of customers heat their homes at Christmas.

- **April 2010.** Simply Green announces the purchase of their new office, Regeneration Park in Portsmouth. Once construction is completed, Regeneration Park will be the "greenest" building on the seacoast.

- **June 2010.** Simply Green's customers complete the 2,000,000 lb. "Carbon Challenge," which results in planting the equivalent of 153,000 trees.
- **August 2010.** Simply Green is honored to have Congresswoman Shea-Porter and US Secretary of Labor Solis visit Regeneration Park and hold a press conference praising Simply Green for their efforts in the green movement.
- **September 2010.** Simply Green marks another milestone by delivering BioHeat to more than 1,500 customers around the seacoast of New Hampshire and Maine.
- **November 2010.** Andrew Kellar leaves Simply Green.
- **February 2011.** Andrew Kellar starts work with Revolution Energy, helping with blended (private, public, and tax incentivized) financing of large scale solar projects.
- **May 2011.** Andrew becomes entrepreneur in residence with the University of New Hampshire's Green Launching Pad program.
- **January 2012.** Andrew Kellar begins yearlong activities as Mel King Community Fellow at MIT.

NOTES:

NOTES:

Chapter 8:
Case: Marketing Sustainability:
Seventh Generation Creating a Green Household Consumer Product

LEARNING OBJECTIVES

1. Understand how a coherent and consistent commitment to sustainability in the company's marketing mix—product, promotion, place, and price—enabled Seventh Generation to differentiate itself in a highly competitive industry.
2. Explain how sustainable marketing differs from traditional marketing as reflected in Seventh Generation's experience.
3. Describe the difficulties that large incumbent firms in traditional industries have in selling sustainable ("green") products.
4. Understand the key challenges and opportunities in sustainable marketing for small and large firms.

8.1 Introduction

Sustainable marketing involves developing and promoting products and services that meet consumer and business user needs utilizing society's natural, human, and cultural resources responsibly to ensure a better quality of life now and for future generations to come. Sustainable products and services as they are commonly defined are more sustainable than traditional products and services, without necessarily being environmentally neutral or sustainable in a scientifically valid way.

The size of the sustainable market is significant and is expected to grow to $922 billion by 2014. [1] This represents an increasing but still relatively small portion of the US and world economies, with the size of the US economy being approximately $15 trillion and world economy being about $60 trillion in 2010.

What are some of the marketing strategies that have helped to create this market niche and have helped it to grow? How much can the market grow in the future? This chapter focuses on one company that is a leader in sustainability, Seventh Generation, to address these questions and to gain detailed insight and perspective about sustainable marketing. Seventh Generation is one of the first companies founded on sustainability principles and mission in the United States (http://www.seventhgeneration.com/about)). It is a Burlington, Vermont–based privately held manufacturer and distributor of environmentally friendly household and personal care products. The company's marketing vision and marketing mix known as the four Ps—product, price, promotion, and place—emanated from its founding principles and the ideals and aspirations of its founder, Jeffrey Hollender. Seventh Generation's products are made using only natural, recycled, or renewable materials that use nontoxic ingredients and the company focuses all its operations to minimize its impact on the environment. Initially Seventh Generation started out as a small mail-order company. As of 2011, Seventh Generation was a $150 million brand selling products at eco-focused stores, such as Whole Foods, and also in the broader consumer market at outlets, such as Target and Walmart.

At its core and driving its marketing plans is the company's mission to enable consumers to make a positive difference for the planet and people's health through everyday consumer choices. For Seventh Generation, this means providing consumers the opportunity to make a positive difference through their purchases of laundry detergent, paper towels, and other household products.

Jeffrey Hollender was born in 1954 and raised in New York City. In many respects his social values and activism grew out of discontent growing up in a wealthy family on Park Avenue in the early 1960s. According to Hollender, "I grew up in 'Mad Men.' Everyone was smoking. Everyone was drinking, and I was encouraged to watch TV." His parents had a beach house on Long Island, in Westhampton, New York, near which he would surf, a welcome escape. "I turned on all that in a pretty rebellious way," he said. [2] At age seventeen, Hollender left home and headed to Santa Barbara, California, where for a short time, he lived in his car. He protested the Vietnam War. He returned to New York City after about nine months, finished high school, and headed to Hampshire College, a nontraditional college in Massachusetts, in 1974.

Hollender's discontent first motivated him to break the rules and expectations of him in his own life and over time to try to change business and consumer practices. His marketing instincts and savvy might have come from his father, Alfred, an advertising executive with a prestigious New York City advertising firm. And his inclination toward the dramatic might have been from his mother, Lucille, a former actress.

Hollender dropped out of college and began his business career in 1977 by developing a not-for-profit skills exchange program based in Toronto. The program was successful but had to be shut down as a result of Hollender's personal failing to get a work permit. After spending time on his cousin's ginseng farm in Vermont, he decided to go back and continue his entrepreneurial career in the education industry, but this time as a for-profit business in New York City. He created Network for Learning, with nontraditional classes such as "The Art of Flirting," which quickly grew, attracting sixty thousand students and turned a profit by its second year. Mr. Hollender sold the business to a Warner Communications unit for more than $2 million in 1985. [3] As a result, he became president of Warner Audio Publishing, a division of Warner Communications, a position he held through 1987. Following his tenure at Warner Audio Publishing, Hollender partnered with Vermont "eco-preneur" Alan Newman and acquired a small mail-order catalogue centered on energy conservation products known as Renew America.[4] This business provided him with the opportunity to change the society he was discontented with and it eventually became Seventh Generation in 1988.

The company's beginning was not easy, and the partners soon split. But Jeffrey Hollender had passion and kept the company. His values and unique personality moved upfront in the company and dominated its marketing and branding. This helped to differentiate the company and its products in a very competitive market.

"Many of us who have businesses run them within our cultural restraints," said Yoram Samets, an early investor in Seventh Generation who has known Hollender for two decades. "We compromise ourselves. Jeffrey has done the opposite."

Fast forward to 2010 and Hollender has served as the president, CEO, and "Chief Inspired Protagonist" of Seventh Generation, building the company to a $150 million brand and a leading authority on making a positive difference in the health of the people and planet through everyday choices. This included Seventh Generation being named the seventh most responsible brand in America in 2004 based on a study performed by Alloy Media + Marketing. [5]The commitment to sustainability was what their products were about and throughout the company—from founding CEO to product ingredient sourcing through marketing and to the end of the product's lifecycle. For Seventh Generation as a sustainable brand, the company seeks to have positive impact in the world and do it all transparently.

[1] "Consumers Claim They Are Willing to Pay Extra for Green," *eMarketer Green*, April 1, 2010, http://www.emarketergreen.com/blog/index.php/consumers-pay-extra-green;http://newhope360.com/business-directory/definitions-healthy-products-healthy-planet-hp2-sectors.
[2] Laura Holsen, "An Environmentalist's Latest Laundry List," *New York Times*, February 23, 2011.
[3] "Three Who Thrived after Early Gaffes," *Wall Street Journal*, May 4, 2010, http://online.wsj.com/article/SB10001424052748703648304575212151578380586.html.
[4] Jess McCuan, "It's Not Easy Being Green," *Inc. Magazine*, November 1, 2004, http://www.inc.com/magazine/20041101/seventh-generation.html.
[5] Seventh Generation, *2007 Corporate Consciousness Report*, http://www.seventhgeneration.com/files/assets/pdf/2007_SevGen_Corporate-Consciousness.pdf.

8.2 Marketing Focus on the Triple Bottom Line: People, Planet, and Profit

Seventh Generation's marketing has focused on offering consumers the opportunity to act on their idealism, passion, and commitment to causes larger than themselves at the supermarket each week. Consumers could get this when they purchased a Seventh Generation product.

Sidebar
Seventh Generation's Global Imperatives [1]
1. As a business we are committed to being educators and to encourage those we educate to create with us a world of equity and Justice, health and wellbeing.
2. To achieve that we must create a world of more conscious workers, citizens and consumers.
3. We are committed to creating a world that is rich in value as contrasted to a world that is rich in artifacts.
4. We will work to create Governance and social systems that increase the capacity for understanding differing perspectives and points of view.
5. We believe that our business and all businesses should engage in the personal development of everyone who works for them.
6. We are committed to approaching everything we do from a systems perspective, a perspective that allows us to see the larger whole, not a fragmented, compartmentalized world, not just what we want to see, our own point of view, our own reality, but a world that is endlessly interconnected, in which everything we do effects everything else.
7. We must ensure that globally, natural resources are used and renewed at a rate that is always below their rate depletion.
8. And lastly we are committed to creating a business where all our products, raw materials, byproducts, and the processes by which they are made are not just sustainable but restorative, and enhancing the potential of all of life's systems.

Seventh Generation Name and Brand Positioning
Seventh Generation derived its name from the Great Law of the Iroquois that states, "In our every deliberation, we must consider the impact of our decisions on the next seven generations." Seventh Generation strives to live up to that brand promise with a full line of household cleaning and personal care products—from laundry detergents to baby wipes that are safer for people and safer for the environment.

This positioning is prevalent within the company and is at the very core of their business model and marketing approach.

Sidebar
Brand
A brand is a name, term, sign, symbol, design, or a combination of these intended to identify the goods and services of one seller and to differentiate the seller from those of other sellers. Branding is about getting potential consumers to view a seller as the only one that provides a solution to their problem. A brand is an image in the consumer's mind and one that must be constantly fulfilled to remain positive.

Seventh Generation's Target Market
According to Seventh Generation, somewhere between 40 percent and 60 percent of all people in the United States have an interest in or are already purchasing some green products. Their market research studies also concluded that new moms, in particular, were more likely than others to purchase sustainable products for their new family to create a healthier home and planet.[2] The company's marketing mix reflected a focus on the "middle green" consumers and moms, particularly newer moms.

Sidebar
Survey of Consumers' Green Intentions
A 2011 study by the consultant group OgilvyEarth [3] found that 82 percent of Americans have good green intentions but only 16 percent are dedicated to fulfilling these intentions, putting 66 percent firmly in what the report called the middle green. The other two groups the report labeled were the super greens who are the 16 percent who are dedicated to green intentions and on other end of the green consumer spectrum, the 14 percent who were green rejecters who do not have any green intentions.

The *marketing mix*, also known as the four Ps of marketing, is the combination of product, price, place (distribution), and promotion. Marketers develop strategies around these four areas in marketing to enhance a company's branding, sales, and profitability. The marketing mix forms the foundation for creating a sustainable marketing strategy.

The four Ps can contribute to a company's positioning as focused on sustainability. If a product or service is competitive in terms of price, then a sustainability focus on product attributes, place, or promotion can give that product or service an advantage particularly among those consumers most interested in sustainability, such as super or middle green consumers. Sustainable marketing often requires creativity in marketing different than for traditional products, but at its core is truthfulness about the ecological and social impacts of products and services. The consumers that will be most attracted to sustainable products and services will also tend to be the most scrutinizing about ecological and social impacts and most interested in the truth and transparency.

Seventh Generation and the Four Ps of Marketing: Product, Price, Place, and Promotion
Product
There is significant competition in the household cleaning product industry. The industry is dominated by large brands, such as Procter & Gamble. In this highly competitive market, Seventh Generation's point of differentiation is that all their products are environmentally friendly, and sustainability is at the very core of the business, not an add-on.

Seventh Generation products include 100 percent recycled fiber paper towels, napkins, bathroom, and facial tissues; natural cleaning and laundry products; natural lotion baby wipes; diapers; training pants; organic cotton feminine hygiene products; and trash bags made from 55 percent to 80 percent recycled plastic. The company is committed to making products that are environmentally sustainable—from seed to shelf.

In 2009, Seventh Generation developed a product scorecard to give consumers (and their product designers) an objective scoring system for comparing different materials and product formulations to foster sustainable decision making. This tool can help consumers balance concerns relating to human health, the environment, product performance, and cost.

In terms of manufacturing, Seventh Generation does not own the facilities that produce their products. They partner with manufacturers across the United States, Canada, and Germany to produce their products for them. Through an extensive auditing process Seventh Generation monitors the manufacturers' facilities' electrical use, fuel use, greenhouse gas emissions, water use and discharge, hazardous and nonhazardous waste, and recycling to ensure they are meeting Seventh Generation's sustainability expectations. [4]

The company's business model relies on partnerships with suppliers, manufacturers, warehouses, and retailers over which they do not have full control, which creates both challenges and opportunities, especially for a company that is committed to practicing sustainability and radical transparency.

To compete effectively and to grow, however, Seventh Generation must be an innovator in the sustainability category and deliver on quality and product performance. The "green" consumer, particularly the middle green consumer, is not just looking for how well a company performs on sustainability criteria but desires a product that meets all their needs.

Packaging
Part of the product is packaging. Seventh Generation strives to create packaging that has a minimal impact on the environment. This includes reducing the amount of material used by concentrating liquid laundry products, offering refills (so far just for baby wipes, but they are working on expanding this), and redesigning the packaging to use less material. Seventh Generation favors recycled over virgin materials and

prefers materials that can be composted or recycled back into the materials stream.

In 2010, Seventh Generation undertook a major packaging initiative to reduce their postconsumer recycled (PCR) content. Previously at a 25 percent PCR content rate, they changed to have the majority of their plastic bottles contain at least 80 percent PCR content, a significant improvement.

And in 2011, Seventh Generation sought to "update its tired packaging," according to new CEO John Replogle (see more details as follows). [5] This included revitalizing its branding look and feel and modernizing its graphics. It started with laundry detergent packaging incorporating the new branding style with more recyclable, compostable, and biodegradable packaging materials (see as follows).

The new laundry detergent is a cardboard package with a plastic lining. The new bottle is made from cardboard on the outside and on the inside a plastic like film holds the laundry detergent. Once the bottle is finished, consumers can toss the whole thing out and it's 100 percent recyclable. The new packaging uses 66 percent less plastic than the traditional format.

While the new packaging is much eco-friendlier, it is being met with mixed reviews. One reviewer observed, "I'm a deeply green inclined person, but there was something about the design that missed the mark, on a psychological level. The lack of a handle made it feel strange to hold. It was only then that I realized how crucial a handle is to my laundry detergent paradigm. The package utilizes pressed recycled paper, which makes the inclusion of a handle quite a challenge." [6]

Seventh Generation needs to remember when it makes product and packaging changes that consumers do not like making tradeoffs. For more universal adoption of green products, manufacturers need to deliver fully on the same, if not better, consumer experience. This includes how well the products perform in their main purpose. For most of Seventh Generation's products this means how well they clean and how easy they are to use and at what cost.

Price

For consumers to purchase a product or service, the price of the product or service has to be lower than the value consumers derive from the product. For sustainable products with costs higher than traditional products, the additional cost and price for sustainability has to derive benefits commensurate with the additional cost for the consumer to purchase the product. Some of that value can be in the form of reduced energy use and its associated cost savings—for example, with the purchase of a hybrid car or more efficient laundry detergent—and some of the value can be psychological and emotional, such as knowing you are reducing your environmental footprint and contributing to sustainability.

Price can often be a deterrent in purchasing sustainable products or services. Of US consumers, 66 percent view environmentally friendly products as too expensive. [7] Many green products carry a premium, as they can typically be more expensive to manufacture. This is often referred to as the "green price gap." The green price gap can cause consumers to purchase based on price and not as much on sustainability criteria.

Recognizing this, Seventh Generation decreased their prices during the slow recovery from the 2008–9 recession to try to help close the green pricing gap. According to Seventh Generation's Corporate Conscience Report, they were focusing on "right pricing" and experienced improvements. "Reducing our spray cleaner price from $3.69 to $2.99 at Target lifted sales 80 percent. Our Lavender Dish Liquid, priced at $2.69, was the top-selling hand dish washing liquid at Target for 52 straight weeks. When we dropped the price on two sizes of our dish liquid from $3.99 to $3.49 and from $3.29 to $2.99 at Whole Foods Market, our sales increased 30 percent." [8] According to Hollender, "Most consumers are not willing to pay a premium, sales are highest when pricing is very competitive." [9]

Place

Seventh Generation distributes their products in natural food and grocery stores, through the Internet, and at mass merchandisers, such as Target and Walmart. Consumers who purchase eco-friendly products shop at these retailers, according to a study by Ryan Partnership Chicago / Mambo Sprouts Marketing. [10]

In an interview, Hollender revealed that to succeed at retail, their strategy was to make the financial case that the retailer's profit would be more profitable per foot of space with Seventh Generation than the products on the shelf that they were replacing. Additionally, Seventh Generation presented statistics that they brought higher value and more loyal consumers who spent more money per trip than the average consumer to the store. [11]

Promotion

In the early years of Seventh Generation, Hollender and his team relied on word of mouth and grassroots/bootstrap marketing to increase consumer awareness and encourage consumers to try their products. They did this with educational programs and events where they could encourage trial and help raise consumer consciousness and awareness of their product. Jeffrey Hollender, through his high visibility at events and in charitable and advocacy activities, was personally associated with the brand and his activities were a significant part of the early marketing efforts.

Sidebar

Grassroots Promotion and Marketing

Grassroots promotion and marketing combines some of the different promotional approaches in a focused, creative, and low-cost way that is often local or community based. It can be particularly useful for start-up ventures. It uses public relations (such as media stories), blogs, social media, and event planning and participation to drive qualified leads to company websites and physical locations for purchases.

As of 2011, Seventh Generation's promotion was still focused on events, advocacy by Hollender, consumer outreach, and educational programs as well as corporate giving. The company donated more than 10 percent of their profits to charitable programs. According to Hollender, the company donated to "the programs and practices that best exemplified Seventh Generation's innovative approach to solving the problems represented in its global imperatives. This included Change-It, Tampontification, and WAGES." [12]

- **Change-It.** A joint initiative between Greenpeace USA and Seventh Generation designed to train and sustain the next generation of "change agents" through comprehensive and active education in social and environmental justice.

- **Tampontification.** A program designed to educate about the taboo subject of menstruation and discuss through blogs why it's essential for women's health to use chlorine- and pesticide-free feminine care products. There is also an online program that encourages donations of feminine care projects to local woman's shelters funded completely by Seventh Generation and online educational information about the problem of homelessness in the United States that is designed to motivate people to volunteer at their local homeless shelters and get involved with the issue of homelessness.

- **WAGES (Women's Action to Gain Economic Security).** This organization creates jobs and empowers low-income women by organizing and incubating cooperative businesses.

In addition to these programs, Seventh Generation used social media and had an extensive website designed to educate consumers while promoting their products. The joint education and promotion efforts included the use of blogs, Facebook Fan pages, Twitter, and YouTube channels. In addition, the company's promotional efforts include downloadable coupons from their website site and a loyalty rewards program.

Other marketing initiatives included a joint promotion with noncompetitive but like-minded companies (such as Stonyfield Yogurt and Earth's Best) with a coupon booklet distributed in stores on packages via neckties.
In 2010, Seventh Generation briefly ran their first ever television advertising and print campaign, "Protecting Planet Home," focused on the super and middle green consumers and new moms. [13] The advertising efforts were very short lived and pulled from the air and their website after the departure of Hollender.

The household cleaning product market was hard to penetrate. With all the marketing efforts, Seventh Generation still had a reported low level of brand awareness with only 10 percent to 20 percent of the population aware of their products.

[1] Seventh Generation, *2007 Corporate Consciousness Report*, http://www.seventhgeneration.com/files/assets/pdf/2007_SevGen_Corporate-Consciousness.pdf.
[2] Romy Ribitzky, "Seventh Generation Embarks on First Ever National Ad Campaign," Portfolio.com, February 11, 2010, http://bit.ly/NTEMPN.
[3] "Mainstream America Unmoved by Green Marketing," SustainableBusiness.com, http://www.sustainablebusiness.com/index.cfm/go/news.display/id/22277.
[4] Seventh Generation, *2009 Corporate Consciousness Report*, http://www.7genreport.com.
[5] Marc Gunther, "Seventh Generation's New CEO," *Marc Gunther*, February 13, 2011, http://www.marcgunther.com/2011/02/13/seventh-generations-new-ceo-john-replogle.
[6] Paul Smith, "Seventh Generation's New Packaging Misses Mark," *TriplePundit*, April 22, 2011, http://www.triplepundit.com/2011/04/seventh-generations-new-packaging-misses-mark-be.
[7] GfK Custom Research, "New Report Indicates Green Sensibility Continues to Evolve," news release, September 21, 2011, http://www.gfkamerica.com/newsroom/press_releases/single_sites/008716/index.en.print.html.
[8] "Seventh Generation Corporate Consciousness Report," Seventh Generation, http://www.7genreport.com/introduction/performance.php.
[9] Jeffrey Hollender, in interview with author, August 14, 2011.
[10] Ryan Partnership Chicago and Mambo Sprouts Marketing, *One Green Score for One Earth*, http://sustainableindustries.com/resources/one-green-score-one-earth.
[11] Jeffrey Hollender, in interview with author, August 14, 2011.
[12] Jeffrey Hollender, in interview with author, August 14, 2011.
[13] "Seventh Generation Kicks Off Protect Planet Home Campaign," *Causecast*, January 13, 2010. http://causecast.org/blog/green-cleaning/seventh-generation-kicks-protect-planet-home-campaign.

8.3 Taking Seventh Generation to the Next Level: The Challenge Ahead

Jeffrey Hollender desired to grow Seventh Generation from a $150 million brand to $1 billion. How realistic was this?

According to the "'Green' Household Cleaning Products in the US: Bathroom Cleaners, Laundry Care and Dish Detergents and Household Cleaners" report published by *Packaged Facts*, retail sales of green cleaners in 2009 totaled $557 million—split between $339 million from green household cleaning products and $218 million from green laundry products—to account for 3 percent of the total household and laundry cleaner retail market. *Packaged Facts* estimated retail sales of green cleaners grew 229 percent between 2005 and 2009, more than doubling in dollar terms and more than tripling in its share of the total household cleaner market. [1] In 2009, Seventh Generation's sales were $150 million with about a 27 percent share of the green household cleaning market. [2]

Competition
As Seventh Generation's sales first began to grow, larger traditional brands began to notice. And several powerful

mainstream marketers launched green household products, including the following:

- The Clorox Company introduced Green Works household cleaners, dish, and laundry products in 2008, spending $25 million in advertising in both 2008 and 2009 behind the introduction according to Kantar Media, which tracks advertising spending. Green Works, once a $100 million brand, fell to $60 million in 2010. [3]

- Church & Dwight launched Arm & Hammer Essentials household cleaners in 2008, putting a decidedly different twist on the concept with a mix-it-yourself line. The cleaning products only include the active ingredients and the consumer adds the water at home to the bottle. This unique delivery system provides a 25 percent lower cost and 80 percent reduction in packaging than conventional cleaners. [4]

- SC Johnson & Son introduced Nature's Source household cleaners in 2009, spending $15.4 million in advertising according to Kantar Media, which tracks advertising spending. [5]

Jeffrey Hollender, commenting about the competition, said, "Competition is definitely a sign of our success especially in the face of categories that simply weren't growing for our competition." Over time, both SC Johnson's Nature's Source and Clorox's Green Works failed to meet the sales goals set by the parent companies, [6] and Seventh Generation was able to maintain its market share while competitors were experiencing a flattening out in performance since their introductory years.

According to an analysis by Stephen Powers from Sanford C. Bernstein & Company, "You see disproportionately negative impact from products like Green Works, out of the big blue-chip companies that have tried to layer a green offering on top of their conventional offering, and a relatively better performance from the niche players who remain independent." Using data from the Nielsen Company, Bernstein looked at sales for nearly 4,300 items in twenty-two categories, such as cleaning spray, liquid soap, bathroom cleaners, and detergents. It studied monthly sales from March 2006 to March 2011, the most recent data available. (Nielsen's data include mass market, grocery stores, and drugstores but exclude Walmart.) Bernstein found that the market shares of green products generally were down from their peak—especially those offered by the big consumer-products companies. But the market share of the independent brands, like Method and Seventh Generation, were starting to increase relative to the shares of traditional brands' green products in categories where they compete. [7] There were several factors at play. The mainstream companies venturing into green territory approached it much like a traditional consumer packaged goods company. They spent big money on advertising and promotion to generate awareness and trial but after the second or third year pulled back to almost zero spending. In contrast, Seventh

Generation had over two decades to build its brand. But there has to be more to it than that. Consumers may not be looking to buy just a green-looking brand from a large consumer packaged goods company but instead want to purchase green products from companies who are more substantively committed to sustainability and adhere to its principles with all their brands, not just one or two product lines. Again, this is Seventh Generation's primary competitive advantage and it was working for them but not enough to grow as large as their founder desired.

Seventh Generation Growing Pains
Seventh Generation declined in gross sales for the first time in a decade in 2009. The economic recession was a significant challenge for Seventh Generation as consumers tightened their budget and were more reluctant to pay a price premium for sustainable products. After averaging double-digit annual growth for ten years, the company's gross sales declined by 2.8 percent. The company also lost consumer loyalty with a packaging change in 2009, which created less value for the consumer and did not adhere to their strict sustainability standards. Seventh Generation reduced the number of baby wipes in their packages without reducing the size of the package, decreasing the sustainability of the product (by increasing the packaging-to-product ratio 12 percent). When they did not adequately inform consumers of this change, consumers felt cheated and it weakened the authenticity of the brand and their trusted consumer relationship.

In the midst of the 2009 problems, Jeffrey Hollender self-selected his succession heir and hired a consumer packaged goods veteran, Chuck Maniscalco, as CEO to help position the company for greater scale and long-term growth. [8] But in September 2009, Chuck Maniscalco resigned after a very short but difficult period in which it was hard for Hollender to reduce his influence on the company.

Then in October 2010, the board of directors voted to terminate Jeffrey Hollender's employment relationship and began a new search for CEO. [9] In February 2011, Seventh Generation hired a new CEO, John Replogle, who was previously president and CEO of Burt's Bees. [10]

It has been stated that the problem at Seventh Generation was that the growth plans and Hollender's founding values did not converge. At the Sustainable Brands 2011 trade event, Jeffrey Hollender, in his own words, said,
   How did I fail? How did I get myself fired?
- *I didn't institutionalize values in the corporate structure.*
- *I took too much money from the wrong people.*
- *I failed to give enough of the company to the employees who would have protected what we'd built.*
- *I failed to create a truly sustainable brand. [11]*

Changes at Seventh Generation and for Its Founder
During his time at Seventh Generation, Jeffrey Hollender made the decision to bring on investors to help financially sustain the business. Hollender sold shares and created a

board of directors, including his long time childhood friend, Peter Graham, the board chairman. It was an important move to help the company grow long term but resulted in him becoming a minority stakeholder. It's not clear whether his childhood friend Graham backed Hollender in the power struggle at Seventh Generation or turned against him. Unfortunately, Hollender, after twenty-two years with Seventh Generation, found himself out from the very company that he began.

Hollender was shocked to say the least. He reflected on this change recently: "Seventh Generation was my identity, and getting fired was like having my identity stolen away from me. Most people couldn't understand how I got thrown out of my own company. They didn't know that as we raised more equity, I became a minority owner. After that, there were always tensions between social mission and making money." [12]

In Graham's letter to shareholders and employees, he said,

As the leader of the company since its very earliest days and its philosophical guiding light for over two decades, Jeffrey has been an integral part of our brand and an obvious lynch pin of our success, our unique corporate spirit, and our much acclaimed emphasis on equity and justice in the way we conduct our business. It is no overstatement to say that without his unwavering dedication to our cause and his tireless efforts on our company's behalf, we would not be the company we are today, and indeed might not be here at all. His is a legacy worthy of the highest respect and admiration, and nothing in our recent decision should dim that in any way.

Nevertheless, recent events have forced us to choose between divergent paths. We have elected to set the company on the one we strongly feel has the very best chance of fulfilling the commitment we've made to all our stakeholders to achieve the greatest possible lasting success, financially but especially in terms of making our world a better, safer place for our children and the following seven generations. [13]

Peter Graham, Seventh Generation's chairman, said that the Seventh Generation board unanimously selected Replogle based on his track record leading a complex organization, his demonstrated commitment to corporate responsibility, as well as his strong executive and personal qualities. [14]

Hollender continues his leadership role in sustainability and is writing a new book. He is also the cofounder of the American Sustainable Business Council and a member of the board of directors of Greenpeace USA, Verite, Vermont Businesses for Social Responsibility, and the Environmental Health Fund. He speaks frequently at national venues and has advised companies on sustainability. He has published six books, including *Naturally Clean, The Responsibility Revolution,* and *Planet Home.*

Seventh Generation: The Road Ahead

The new Seventh Generation CEO faced many challenges. The company needed to ramp up its marketing efforts to break through and get noticed in the middle green market and to increase the company's brand awareness, which remained low. Also, among some of their super green customers, effective marketing would be essential to reestablish consumer trust and interest in Seventh Generation after a difficult couple of years. All of this would likely require use of marketing mediums, such as television and the print media, with broader reach than special events, educational programs, and charitable programs.

To help marketing, Replogle created a new position of chief marketing officer (CMO) and hired Joey Bergstein, who hailed from Diageo, the world's leading premium spirits company. Bergstein started his career with consumer packaged goods giant Procter & Gamble and was senior vice president of global rum at Diageo where in five years he helped to double sales while growing Captain Morgan from a US product into a global brand with a strong international presence. [15]

In marketing and other areas, it will not be easy to follow Seventh Generation's founder Jeffrey Hollender. Replogle's strengths are his leadership skills, demonstrated commitment to corporate responsibility, and a proven track record in his business career. Prior to being CEO of Burt's Bees, Replogle spent three years at Unilever, where he managed the skin care division and helped to launch the Real Beauty campaign for Dove and establish the Dove Self-Esteem Fund for young girls. Prior to Unilever, he spent eight years with Diageo as president of Guinness Bass Import Company and managing director of Guinness Great Britain. He started his career at Boston Consulting Group after he earned an MBA from Harvard, from which he graduated with distinction. He received his undergraduate degree, a BA in government, from Dartmouth College where he currently serves as a trustee. [16] According to Seventh Generation's board chairman, Peter Graham, Replogle had been charged with "ensuring Seventh Generation's untapped business potential is fully realized in the years ahead, both financially and in our continued efforts to make our world a safer place for our children and the next seven generations." [17] This would include how to grow Seventh Generation from a $150 million business. In order to do this, Replogle believed the company must innovate and refresh the tired worn out brand look making it more relevant to consumers. In a recent interview, Replogle said, "We are going to out-innovate the competition in terms of meeting consumers' needs in an environmentally-friendly way." [18] With innovation, the company must ensure that its products fully deliver on consumers' needs and provide a fair price and strong value proposition that neutralizes any green pricing gap.

What is not going to change according to company spokesperson, Dave Rappaport, senior director of corporate consciousness, is the company's deep commitment to corporate social responsibility and sustainability. Rappaport, who was hired by Hollender after working in the nongovernmental organization world, stated, "Although the company was launched by Jeff's vision, it is embraced by everyone here. It has been a part of everybody's perception of his or her roles. Down to the innovations we've created on sustainability and corporate responsibility, you will find the work of employees who took the vision to heart." He continued by stating that since letting Hollender go, the board of directors had approved the creation of a new committee on corporate social responsibility and sustainability. "With Jeffrey's departure [they] know [they] have to institutionalize all of the things" he advocated for, making sure there is management oversight and "continued direct board oversight which there was through him when he was on the board." [19]

Inherent in the culture that Hollender built is radical transparency. So consumers will be watching. With the foundation that Hollender and his team created, the company could continue to be part of a trend, even a near revolution, to nurture the planet and the health of the next seven generations, or it could lose its market presence and relevance.

KEY TAKEAWAYS

- Sustainable markets, while growing, are relatively small compared to total (mainstream) markets.
- It will be challenging to grow sustainable consumer market companies beyond relatively small (niche) markets, especially during periods of economic restraint.
- Sustainable marketing means coherence and consistency in the marketing mix—product, place, promotion, and price.
- Seventh Generation and all sustainable businesses must deliver value and performance on their sustainable goods. Price matters for all brands and consumer markets.
- Sustainable marketers need to be creative in their marketing mix to address areas that may be perceived as deficient, such as price, compared to traditional goods.
- Sustainable marketing can require commitment to sustainability throughout the organization.

EXERCISES

1. What is Seventh Generation's brand positioning, and how does the company fulfill its brand promise? Is the founder, Jeffrey Hollender, the brand or is the brand larger than the founder?
2. How can Seventh Generation grow their awareness levels? How can they best employ broader reach vehicles, such as print, television, mobile, and digital marketing? Which outlets and promotions would you suggest?
3. What marketing advice would you give to mainstream companies looking to compete in the green market?
4. In what ways were Seventh Generation's marketing plans successful and in what ways did they fail?
5. Analyze Jeffrey Hollender's four reasons explaining why he was fired. What other reasons can explain why the board fired him?
6. What are the strengths and weaknesses of new CEO John Replogle and the new CMO given their backgrounds in leading marketing efforts at Seventh Generation? Do they have a better chance than Jeffrey Hollender in growing Seventh Generation's revenue?
7. What marketing advice would you give to the new Seventh Generation CMO? What would you suggest he change, and what would you suggest he keep the same in the company's marketing mix?
8. What should Seventh Generation do with regards to pricing to generate increased market share, revenue growth, and profits?

[1] "'Green' Household Cleaning Products in the U.S.: Bathroom Cleaners, Laundry Care and Dish Detergents and Household Cleaners," Packaged Facts, http://www.packagedfacts.com/Green-Household-Cleaning-2554249.

[2] Laurie Burkit, "Seventh Generation Protecting Its Turf," Forbes, January 18, 2010, http://www.forbes.com/2010/01/18/seventh-generation-brand-awareness-cmo-network-chuck-maniscalco.html.

[3] Kari Lipshutz, "Once You Go Green, You'll Probably Go Back," AdWeek, April 22, 2011, http://www.adweek.com/news/advertising-branding/once-you-go-green-you-ll-probably-go-back-130883.

[4] "Arm & Hammer's New Cleaners Not Only Greener, They're Cheaper," EnviralMarketing.com, http://www.enviralmarketing.com/2008/10/22/arm-hammers-new-cleaners-not-only-greener-theyre-cheaper.

[5] Stephanie Clifford and Andrew Martin, "As Consumers Cut Spending, 'Green' Products Lose Allure," New York Times, April 21, 2011, http://www.nytimes.com/2011/04/22/business/energy-environment/22green.html?pagewanted=2&_r=2.

[6] Jeffrey Hollender, in interview with author, August 14, 2011.

[7] Jeffrey Hollender, in interview with author, August 14, 2011.

[8] "Big Changes at Seventh Generation," 7Gen (blog), June 1, 2009, http://www.seventhgeneration.com/learn/blog/big-changes-seventh-generation.

[9] Marc Gunther, "Seventh Generation Sweeps Out Its Founder," Marc Gunther, November 1, 2010, http://www.marcgunther.com/2010/11/01/seventh-generation-sweeps-out-its-founder.

[10] Alex Goldmark, "Seventh Generation Snags Burt's Bees CEO to Replace Founder," Good Business (blog), February 10, 2011, http://www.good.is/post/seventh-generation-gets-a-new-ceo-john-replogle-from-burt-s-bees.

[11] Priti Ambani, "Jeffrey Hollender & Seventh Generation: Lessons Learned at the End of a Chapter," Ecoprenuerist, June 27, 2011, http://ecopreneurist.com/2011/06/27/jeffrey-hollender-seventh-generation-lessons-learned-at-the-end-of-a-chapter.

[12] Issie Lapowsky, "What to Do When You're Fired from the Company You Started," Inc. Magazine, July/August 2011, http://www.inc.com/magazine/201107/how-i-did-it-jeffrey-hollender-seventh-generation.html.

[13] Marc Gunther, "Seventh Generation Sweeps Out Its Founder," *Marc Gunther*, November 1, 2010, http://www.marcgunther.com/2010/11/01/seventh-generation-sweeps-out-its-founder.

[14] Seventh Generation, "Seventh Generation Names John Replogle to Serve as CEO and President," news release, February 9, 2011, http://www.csrwire.com/press_releases/31571-Seventh-Generation-Names-John-Replogle-to-Serve-as-CEO-and-President.

[15] Steve Ratti, "Seventh Generation Adds New Chief Marketing Officer," *The Ratti Report*, August 18, 2011, http://ratti-report.com/news-new-cmo/seventh-generation-adds-new-chief-marketing-officer.

[16] "About John," John Replogle for Dartmouth Trustee, http://www.john4dartmouth.com/p/about-john-replogle.html.

[17] Marc Gunther, "Seventh Generation's New CEO," *Marc Gunther*, February 13, 2011, http://www.marcgunther.com/2011/02/13/seventh-generations-new-ceo-john-replogle.

[18] Marc Gunther, "Seventh Generation's New CEO," *Marc Gunther*, February 13, 2011, http://www.marcgunther.com/2011/02/13/seventh-generations-new-ceo-john-replogle.

[19] Alex Goldmark, "Hollender Speaks on What's Next for Seventh Generation," *Good Business* (blog), January 18, 2011, http://www.good.is/post/jeffrey-hollender-on-how-to-hold-seventh-generation-accountable.

NOTES:

NOTES:

Chapter 9:
Case: Brewing a Better World: Sustainable Supply Chain Management at Green Mountain Coffee Roasters, Inc.

LEARNING OBJECTIVES

1. Describe how sustainable supply chain management can be a source of competitive advantage.
2. Understand how one company conducts business in economically and socially disadvantaged regions of the world based on the values of its founder and senior management.
3. Explain how success in business sustainability and success in overall business performance can be related.

Getting coffee to the supermarket or the local coffee shop involves many different supply channels and business decisions with significant economic, environmental, and social implications. Green Mountain Coffee Roasters, Inc. (GMCR) has informed coffee drinkers about the environmental and social impacts of their consumption and helped to change coffee consumption and industry practices.

Bob Stiller, Green Mountain's founder and chairman, is a strong advocate that Green Mountain and all businesses can help make the world a better place by committing to sustainability values and practices. Acting with concern for sustainability in a highly competitive industry that had historically focused primarily on low cost has provided opportunities for GMCR. Green Mountain management has used achieving sustainability in its products and practices to their competitive advantage. As the company founder declares, "Our success continues to be rooted in our inclusive business model of creating an exceptional beverage experience for customers and consumers, in a socially and environmentally responsible way, leading to sustainable financial success."[1]

The focus of this case is on how Green Mountain Coffee established a strong competitive position in the specialty coffee industry by using sustainable business practices. The company helped to transform the value proposition in the coffee industry from low cost to shared value creation, meeting consumer consumption desires while addressing social and environmental impacts of the industry.

In 2010, GMCR was recognized as the largest purchaser of Fair Trade Certified coffee in the world, a reflection of the company's commitment to high-quality coffee as well as social and environmental sustainability in coffee-farming communities globally. In its 2009 corporate social responsibility report, "Brewing a Better World," the company noted, "All companies have sustainability challenges, a tension between where they are today and where they want to be with respect to sustainability issues—we're no different in that respect. What we believe makes us different is how we address that challenge—by embracing it, by running towards it, and using that tension to drive us toward new solutions."[2]

EXERCISES

1. Take a friend for a cup of coffee at Starbucks, Dunkin' Donuts, and one local coffee shop selling Green Mountain Coffee.
a. What are the different types of coffee sold?
b. At what selling prices?
c. From what countries?
d. What information is available to help educate customers about where the coffee comes from and how it is produced?
   Go to YouTube and find videos on coffee growing around the world.
a. How is coffee growing portrayed in the videos?
b. What are your impressions of how coffee growing is portrayed in the videos?
   Go to Green Mountain's homepage at http://www.gmcr.com/ and download the 2009 corporate social responsibility report, "Brewing a Better World."
a. How does GMCR define sustainability?
b. What notable sustainable business practices has GMCR undertaken for 2009?
c. How does GMCR distinguish between sustainability and corporate social responsibility?

[1] Green Mountain Coffee Roasters, Inc., *Annual Report 2009*, accessed April 16, 2010, http://www.gmcr.com/Investors/AnnualReport.aspx.
[2] Green Mountain Coffee Roasters, Inc., *Brewing a Better World: VOICES*, accessed May 30, 2010, http://www.gmcr.com/PDF/gmcr_csr_2008.pdf.

9.1 Green Mountain's Sustainable Business Model

LEARNING OBJECTIVES

1. Describe both a local and a global sustainable business practice. Explain how they are related.
2. Understand how company performance and sustainable practices can be related.
3. Describe how fair trade practice can be a source of competitive advantage in the coffee industry.

Chairman Stiller and Larry Blandford, president and CEO, in the letter accompanying the company's corporate social report, "Brewing a Better World: VOICES," declared their commitment to a sustainable business approach by

- reducing energy use,
- continuing development and marketing of Fair Trade Certified coffees,
- giving grants to coffee-growing communities,
- installing a solar power array on the roof of its Vermont distribution center.[1]

The challenge for Green Mountain Coffee Roasters (GMCR) management was trying to incorporate sustainable business practice in a market that traditionally did not take account of external costs, such as environmental and social impacts, and was focused on low costs to consumers. Green Mountain was able to develop a core competence in its ability to apply its sustainable business model across the supply chain, and the company has been able to use its sustainable business practices to differentiate itself in the highly competitive coffee industry in ways that have been difficult for rivals to copy.

How Is GMCR Doing?

Green Mountain's success is best reflected in the rise of its stock price. From 2007 to 2010, GMCR's stock rose by more than 2,700 percent, while the S&P 500 declined by 8 percent. From Green Mountain's initial IPO in September 1993, its stock had increased by 15,400 percent, significantly better than the S&P 500's 165 percent gain. [2]

Java Man Is Newest Billionaire

Bob Stiller Profile

Sometimes entrepreneurs really do become billionaires overnight. That's what happened to Robert Stiller, the founder of Green Mountain Coffee Roasters (NASDAQ: GMCR). The value of his 12% holding in Green Mountain perked up 42% last Thursday and is now worth just over $1 billion. The jump came just after his Vermont coffee company announced a strategic relationship with Starbucks (NASDAQ: SBUX). Green Mountain, also the owner of Keurig Single-Cup brewing system, will now make, market and sell Starbucks and Tazo tea K-Cups.

I profiled Stiller as Entrepreneur of the Year nearly a decade ago in a 2001 Forbes cover story. At the time, his stake in the

company was worth $89 million. I tried to reach him again this week, to no avail, but I recall his story well.

Stiller, who is probably now 67, was a born entrepreneur. His first big hit was selling rolling paper on the drug-sodden campus of Columbia University in the early 1970s. His brand, E-Z Wider, had double the width of competing brands. The paper wouldn't feed into the machine properly, causing tearing. Stiller figured out a way to prevent ripping and eventually made a small fortune. "People expected to see potheads, but we were more efficient at paper conversion than any manufacturer at the time," he told me back then. He and a partner sold out in 1980, each pocketing $3.1 million.

After cashing out, Stiller found himself at his ski condo in Sugarbush, Vermont, looking for his next opportunity. Enjoying a rare cup of good coffee at a restaurant one night, he started roasting his own beans, using a hot-air popcorn popper at one point, a cookie sheet at another, brewing batches of coffee for friends. Stiller ended up buying the store that had sold him that memorable cup of coffee in 1981 and after some twists and turns built it into Green Mountain.

One of his smartest bets was investing in, and eventually, buying the Keurig single-cup system, created by three entrepreneurs. That business is now driving much of Green Mountain's growth these days. Fiscal 2010 sales were up 73% to $1.36 billion, with majority of revenues coming from Keurig.

Stiller stepped down as chief executive in 2007 but is still chairman. In addition to his holding in his coffee business, he apparently has a stake in Krispy Kreme Doughnuts and owns a small private air charter, Heritage Flight, according to a story in a *Vermontbiz*.

Source: Luisa Knoll, "Java Man Is Newest Billionaire," *Forbes*, March 16, 2011, http://www.forbes.com/sites/luisakroll/2011/03/16/java-man-is-newest-billionaire.

Along with continued outstanding growth in sales, profits, and earnings per share, Green Mountain has received numerous industry, social, and humanitarian awards. The company reported that 2011 "was another step on our path to creating a more sustainable future. Along the way, we were pleased to be recognized for our efforts to create both profit and positive change." (See the following sidebar.) [3]

GMCR 2011 Awards and Recognition

- Readers' Choice Award for New Products of the Year (Best Cold Beverage) on *Automatic Merchandiser Magazine* for the Green Mountain Coffee Brew over Ice K-Cup Pack
- Ranked number 2 on *Fortune Magazine's* "Global 100 Fastest-Growing Companies List"
- Humanitarian of the Year Award from Medicines for Humanity (MFH)
- Largest purchaser of Fair Trade Certified coffee in the world for 2010
- Leader of Change Award from the Foundation for Social Change and United Nations Office for Partnerships
- Business of the Year Award from Northeastern Economic Developers Association (NEDA)
- One of the *Boston Globe*'s top places to work in Massachusetts, Keurig, Inc.

To view Green Mountain Coffee Roasters Information from its Annual Report, 2011, visit http://files.shareholder.com/downloads/GMCR/19039814 70x0x540307/c799e76f-7e06-418d-9bb2-b105a85ee3ea/GMCR_AnnualReport_2011.pdf

GMCR keeps track of its social and sustainability efforts in three areas: the amount of fair trade coffee (organic and nonorganic) purchased as a percentage of total coffee purchased (with a goal of at least 30 percent of all coffee purchased to be Fair Trade Certified coffee); the price it pays to farmers for premium coffee over the prevailing market price; and the dollars contributed in grants to aid its numerous supply chain partners, especially to its farmers and community partners (with a goal of at least 5 percent of profits going to aid supply chain partners and other community partners). Fair Trade USA, the leading third-party certifier of fair trade products, named GMCR the largest purchaser of Fair Trade Certified coffee in the world for 2010. GMCR purchased more than twenty-six million pounds of Fair Trade Certified coffee in 2010.

With its purchase of Fair Trade Certified (FTC) coffee, GMCR was able to identify early on and exploit market opportunities in the United States for the growing consumer interest in Fair Trade Certified organic and nonorganic coffee. With FTC coffee purchases, GMCR was able to help address the well-being of farmers in coffee exporting countries. The company did this by providing farmers and their workers a fair (also known as "living") wage and grants to help them with medical, educational, and other economic and social needs. With the purchase of Fair Trade Certified organic coffee, GMCR also attempted to reduce the environmental devastation that occurred in coffee producing countries brought on by mass clearing and mass production of coffee crops. Management used these innovative supply chain practices and associated social investments as a source of a competitive advantage in the highly competitive specialty coffee industry.

GMCR senior managers believed that once consumers understood the company's sustainability goals and practices—protecting scarce resources, strengthening communities, reducing poverty, and ensuring equity in commercial relationships—they would be more likely to purchase the company's products and thereby "partner" with the company to help build a better world. [4]

GMCR's Fair Trade Coffee Goals and Statistics

Management believed that its fair trade approach also created a "win-win" situation for the company and supply chain partners. By improving the quality of life for farmers, their families, and workers, Green Mountain sought to foster *trust* and closer working relationships in its supply chain. And management viewed this as investments that could help GMCR more effectively monitor quality and lower costs by assisting and negotiating directly with farm cooperatives. By lowering dependency on other supply chain intermediates in procuring its coffee, the company could lower supply chain logistical and procurements costs, improve turnaround time, and respond more quickly to customer preferences.

By 2009, Green Mountain was one of the largest purveyors of fair trade coffee in the United States. Fair Trade Certified coffee represented about 30 percent of Green Mountain's overall coffee pounds sold in 2009, which was a 36 percent increase over 2008.

Partnerships and Outreach in the Supply Chain

In 2008, GMCR began sharing and measuring vendor compliance to a set of guidelines. These guidelines outlined what Green Mountain expected from its vendors regarding environmental, health, and safety standards. These standards included vendor legal compliance, labor conditions, and environmental responsibility. For measuring compliance, GMCR created a set of tools, including self-assessments, surveys, on-site assessments by GMCR staff, and commissioned audits of vendor facilities. Management tested these tools by auditing its Waterbury, Vermont, facility. [5]

GMCR's goal for its coffee supply chain was ambitious: to help the people in coffee-growing communities lead healthier and more prosperous lives. To facilitate the accomplishment of this goal, GMCR's used two outreach initiatives. First, the company provided on-the-ground assistance by helping suppliers improve their ability to deliver high-quality specialty coffee to the marketplace. Areas of assistance included advice on cultivation techniques, training on cupping skills, and connecting suppliers with industry resources to help farmers strengthen and grow their business. Second, GMCR provided financial grants to nonprofits that both provided technical skills and helped communities achieve a more sustainable future. [6]

KEY TAKEAWAYS

- Sustainability practices in the supply chain can result in lower costs, shorter cycle times, and improved opportunities for product and process innovations.
- Sustainable business practices can help differentiate a company from rivals in profitable and meaningful ways.

EXERCISES

1. Visit your college cafeteria or food service area and poll students on what they know about coffee, and especially about the role fair trade coffee plays in the lives of farm workers, in their families, and in protecting the environment. What are some of the key points or lessons that you would like these students to know about GMCR and fair trade coffee?
2. Go to Green Mountain (http://www.greenmountaincoffee.com) and Starbucks (http://www.starbucks.com). How does each company demonstrate its commitment to buying and selling fair trade sustainable coffee?
3. Go to the International Coffee Organization homepage at http://www.ico.org and download its annual review for 2010 and 2011. What is the International Coffee Organization's (ICO) mission? What programs has the ICO recently adopted in support of coffee farmers in destitute coffee-growing countries? What has driven coffee prices to all-time highs? How have coffee farmers and their families' benefited, if at all, from the higher coffee prices?

[1] Green Mountain Coffee Roasters, Inc., *Brewing a Better World: VOICES*, accessed May 30, 2010, http://www.gmcr.com/PDF/gmcr_csr_2008.pdf.
[2] Green Mountain Coffee Roasters, Inc., *Annual Report 2009*, accessed April 16, 2010, http://www.gmcr.com/Investors/AnnualReport.aspx.
[3] Green Mountain Coffee Roasters, Inc., *Brewing a Better World: VOICES*, accessed May 30, 2010, http://www.gmcr.com/PDF/gmcr_csr_2008.pdf.
[4] Green Mountain Coffee Roasters, Inc., *Brewing a Better World: VOICES*, accessed May 30, 2010, http://www.gmcr.com/PDF/gmcr_csr_2008.pdf.
[5] Green Mountain Coffee Roasters, Inc., *Brewing a Better World: VOICES*, accessed May 30, 2010, http://www.gmcr.com/PDF/gmcr_csr_2008.pdf.
[6] John M. Talbot, *Grounds for Agreement: The Political Economy of the Coffee Commodity Chain* (London: Rowman & Littlefield, 2004), 44.

9.2 The Coffee Industry's Supply Chain

LEARNING OBJECTIVES

1. Define global supply chain.
2. Understand what it means to have a supply chain that is sustainable.
3. Explain the market drivers behind the growth in Fair Trade Certified (FTC) coffee and FTC organic coffee.

The Coffee Bean

Coffee has been consumed for centuries ever since the coffee bean was first cultivated and used by Arabs as a beverage in the fifteenth century. [1] First discovered and cultivated in Ethiopia, the Arabica bean found its way to coffee houses in the Middle East and spread throughout Europe in the sixteenth century. Aided by Western colonialism, religious missionaries, and explorers to other tropical and subtropical regions of the world, the Arabica bean and the less valuable Robusta bean eventually became global crops. Coffee trees only grow in tropical and subtropical climates, primarily in Africa, Latin America, and Asia. One coffee tree produces one pound of green coffee per year. There are two types of coffee: specialty and conventional (basic). Specialty coffee is made from the Arabica bean and basic from the Robusta bean. Often times these beans are blended together in the roasting process to lower costs or offer greater variety.

Coffee Industry Competitive Dynamics

The International Coffee Organization (ICO) estimated that approximately 1.4 billion cups of coffee were poured each day worldwide in 2008. [2] The United States is the single largest consumer of coffee worldwide and is the largest importer of green (before roasting) coffee, approximately 2.5 million bags per month. In 2009 Germany was the second largest importer of coffee, followed by Italy, Japan, and France. Combined, the European Union countries imported approximately 5.4 million bags a month in 2009. The largest green coffee producing countries (2007–8) were Brazil, Vietnam, Colombia, Indonesia, and Ethiopia.

More than 50 percent of Americans older than eighteen years of age drink coffee every day. This represents more than 150 million daily drinkers. Thirty million American adults drink specialty coffee beverages daily, which include mocha, latte, espresso, café mocha, cappuccino, and frozen or iced coffee beverages. The United States imports in excess of $4 billion worth of coffee per year. Americans consume four hundred million cups of coffee per day, making the United States the leading consumer of coffee in the world. (See the following sidebar.)

Coffee Statistics Report—2012 Edition
Did You Know?

- **Coffee statistics** show that coffee is the most popular beverage worldwide, with over **four hundred billion cups** consumed each year.
- Coffee industry statistics show that only **20 percent of harvested coffee beans** are considered to be a premium bean of the highest quality.
- Coffee market statistics show that coffee is grown commercially in **more than forty-five countries** around the world.
- Coffee trade statistics show that over **five million** people in Brazil are employed by the coffee trade.
- Those employed in the coffee industry are involved mostly with the cultivation and harvesting of more than **three billion coffee plants**.
- Coffee consumption statistics show that coffee represents **75 percent of all the caffeine** consumed in the United States.
- The average price for an espresso-based drink is $2.45.
- The average price for brewed coffee is $1.38.
- Men drink as much coffee as women, each consuming an average of 1.6 cups per day.
- Women seem to be more concerned about the price than men.
- Among coffee drinkers, the average consumption in the United States is 3.2 cups of coffee per day.

Source: "Coffee Statistics Report—2012 Edition," Top 100 Espresso, http://www.top100espresso.com.

Roasters compete primarily on price, brand, and differentiation. The price of green coffee is based on basic supply and demand economic factors. Supply is dependent on several factors including weather, pest damage, politics, and economics in the coffee-producing countries. Demand for coffee depends on several factors, including consumer preferences; changes in consumer lifestyles; national, regional, and local economic conditions; demographic trends; and health benefits or risks.

Key Players in the Coffee Supply Chain
An industry supply chain describes the processes (steps) by which a product is produced and ends up with (final) consumers. The green (unroasted) coffee bean travels through many steps in the supply chain (also known as the value chain) from harvest to final customer. Coffee roasters or manufacturers are the key or focal player in the coffee supply chain.

Rivals: Branding and Market and Product Segmentation
The largest US domestic coffee brands in 2007 were Folgers, Maxwell House, and Starbucks followed by several regional brands. Market segmentation is based on brands, price, cost, quality, and other variables that are based on customer (a) behavioral, (b) demographic, (c) psychographic, and (d) geographical differences. These brands either carry the coffee roaster's corporate name, such as Starbucks (an international brand) and Peet's (a regional brand), or are multimillion-dollar divisions of large multinational companies, such as Procter & Gamble, Kraft Foods (Gevalia), J. M. Smucker (Folgers, Millstone, Brothers), or Nestlé (Nespresso). Procter & Gamble and Kraft Foods dominated the coffee market with 40 percent and 30 percent market share, respectively, in 2007. [3] Starbucks was one of the largest coffee roasters with more than eight thousand stores, or 32 percent market share in the retail store category in 2007. [4]

The Specialty Coffee Retailer Association estimated that at least two-thirds of the US adult population drinks coffee at least once a week. The association estimated that there were 25,000 coffee shops in 2010, up from 9,470 shops in 2002. The coffee shops generated $14 billion in sales or approximately one-third of the $40 billion US coffee industry. [5] In addition to larger roasters, such as Starbucks, Green Mountain, and Dunkin' Donuts, small roasters included (the number in parentheses indicate the number of stores) Caribou Coffee (322), Tim Horton's (292), Coffee Bean and Tea Leaf (213), Coffee Beanery (200), Peet's Coffee (166), Seattle's Best (160), and Tully's (100). Dunkin' Donuts was by far the largest worldwide coffee and baked goods chain with more than three million customers per day in 2008. At the end of 2008, Dunkin' Donuts was close to Starbucks in number of retail stores with 8,835 stores worldwide, including 6,395 franchised restaurants in thirty-four US states and 2,240 international shops in thirty-one countries. [6]

The specialty coffee retailers competed with larger food processing companies in the supermarket segment of the industry. This category included Procter & Gamble, Nestlé, J. M. Smucker Company, Sara Lee, General Foods, and Philip Morris. Specialty coffee sales increased by 20 percent per year from 2007 to 2011 and, by 2011, accounted for nearly 8 percent of the $18 billion US coffee industry. The ICO in 2011 reported that the simplification of methods for brewing roasted coffee at home along with rising coffee prices was encouraging at home coffee consumption. Even with the growth of coffee shops, the home continued to be the preferred brewing and consumption location in all countries. The ICO reported that one of the reasons could be the development of coffee pods and capsule machines, which made it easier for consumers to make good coffee at home. [7]

Sustainable Coffee Market

The Fair Trade Certified (FTC) coffee market was established in 1988 when world coffee prices declined sharply. In 1997, the Fairtrade Labelling Organizations International (FLO) was formed as an umbrella organization to expand the scope and monitor fair trade with universal standards and labels. [8]

The Fair Trade Certified organic coffee movement attempted to reduce the environmental devastation that occurred in coffee producing countries. Fair trade was meant to counteract the practice pursued by large multinational corporations that used mass production methods for coffee farming. These methods conflicted with traditional, more environmentally friendly methods of coffee farming. The mass production techniques included clearing of large tracks of forested farmland, machine harvesting, mechanized warehouse operations, and heavy use of chemicals and pesticides to increase crop yield. Mass production farming caused severe environmental degradation and forced many small farms to close causing economic hardships in many coffee producing areas. [9] In addition, the heavy use of fertilizers and pesticides resulted in significant nitrate runoff into ground water and streams. Farmers and workers and others were exposed to highly toxic chemicals, including some banned in the United States. Concern about the adverse impacts of the change in coffee farming played an important role in the emerging Fair Trade Certified coffee market. [10]

From 1998 to 2009, 629 million pounds of fair trade products came into the United States. This included 448 million pounds of coffee or 71 percent of all fair trade products imported. Fair trade coffee imports grew 25 percent over 2008. This growth was driven primarily by increased demand for fair trade coffee in large retail outlets and restaurants, such as Whole Foods Market, Walmart, McDonald's, and Starbucks. In 2008, North American "sustainable" coffee sales were a record $1.3 billion, a 13% increase over 2007. [11]

KEY TAKEAWAYS

- Supply chains are complex open and dynamic systems.
- A supply chain is composed of multiple players of various sizes who compete on brand, price, and market segmentation.
- Fair trade and sustainable coffee is an emerging and growing market.

EXERCISE

1. Go to the Institute for Supply Management home page (http://www.ism.ws/index.cfm) and click the link to their "Ethics and Social Responsibility" page. Review their "Principles and Standards of Ethical Supply Management Conduct."

[1] "Ethiopia: Coffee History, Production, Economy Facts," Tree Crops, accessed May 30, 2010, http://www.gmcr.com/PDF/gmcr_csr_2008.pdf.

[2] Robert S. Lazich, ed., *Market Share Reporter: An Annual Complication of Reported Market Share, Data on Companies, Products, and Services* (Farmington Hills, MI: Gale, 2009), 1:191–92.

[3] Robert S. Lazich, ed., *Market Share Reporter: An Annual Complication of Reported Market Share, Data on Companies, Products, and Services* (Farmington Hills, MI: Gale, 2009), 1:191.

[4] Robert S. Lazich, ed., *Market Share Reporter: An Annual Complication of Reported Market Share, Data on Companies, Products, and Services* (Farmington Hills, MI: Gale, 2009), 2:677.

[5] "Top Ten Trends: Overview," Specialty Coffee Retailer Association, accessed April 16, 2010, http://www.specialtycoffee.com/ME2/Audiences/dirmod.asp?sid=&nm=&type=Blog&mod=View+Topic&mid.

[6] "About Us," Dunkin' Donuts, accessed April 30, 2010, http://www.dunkindonuts.com/content/dunkindonuts/en/company.html.

[7] John M. Talbot, *Grounds for Agreement: The Political Economy of the Coffee Commodity Chain* (London: Rowman & Littlefield, 2004), 33.

[8] Kathleen E. McKone-Sweet, "Lessons from a Coffee Supply Chain," *Supply Chain Management Review* (2009), accessed May 6, 2010, http://www.accessmylibrary.com/coms2/summary_0286-14185976_ITM.

[9] John M. Talbot, *Grounds for Agreement: The Political Economy of the Coffee Commodity Chain* (London: Rowman & Littlefield, 2004), 197–203.

[10] Carl Obermiller, Chauncey Burke, Erin Talbott, and Gwereth P. Green, "Taste Great or More Fulfilling: The Effect of Brand Reputation on Consumer Social Responsibility Advertising for Fair Trade Coffee," *Corporate Reputation Review* 12, no. 2 (2009): 160–61.
[11] John M. Talbot, *Grounds for Agreement: The Political Economy of the Coffee Commodity Chain* (London: Rowman & Littlefield, 2004).

9.3 Sustainability and Corporate Social Responsibility at Green Mountain Coffee Roasters, Inc.

LEARNING OBJECTIVES

1. Explain supply chain management (SCM).
2. Describe how SCM can contribute to sustainable business practice.
3. Explain the economic value added of supply chain management.

Getting Started: Green Mountain Coffee Roasters' Sustainable Business Model

Bob Stiller opened his first coffee shop in 1981 in Waterbury, Vermont, selling high-quality coffee. His concept was simple; sell only high-quality coffee to ordinary people every day. When demand for his coffee outstripped his small store, he started bagging his coffee and sold it to wholesalers, supermarkets, and by mail order. A strong following for his coffee soon developed in New England and in the Northeast. Stiller's entrepreneurial drive and passion for selling quality coffee eventually became the cornerstone of the company's purpose and guiding principles, "to create the ultimate coffee experience in every life we touch from tree to cup— transforming the way the world understands business." [1] Stiller focused his company's purpose around supply chain management (SCM).

In 2005, Green Mountain was the first company in the coffee industry to support the United Nation's Global Reporting Initiative (GRI) mission to develop globally accepted sustainability reporting guidelines. Green Mountain Coffee Roasters' (GMCR) management adopted the GRI's guidelines because the company's senior managers believed that their organization could benefit from sustainability measurement and comparison and GRI's guidelines served this purpose.

The following year, GMCR published its first *corporate social responsibility* report. Stiller noted at the time that the report would give employees a better way to understand corporate values and the way the company conducted business. It would also challenge them to do better. [2] The report made public for the first time the company's triple bottom line (TBL) goals and progress in meeting them. In 2008, a "social and environmental responsibility" committee was added for the board of directors. The committee is responsible for overseeing the company's social and environmental responsibilities. In addition, the company established the positions of vice president for corporate social responsibility and vice president for environmental affairs reporting directly to the CEO. And a corporate social responsibility team was established consisting of six individuals focused specifically on supply chain outreach, domestic community outreach, social compliance, environmental management systems, and communication. [3]

Brewing a Better World

Green Mountain's corporate social responsibility programs are organized into six practice areas that span the company's supply chain and are communicated under the banner of "brewing a better world." The six practice areas are partnering with supply chain communities, supporting local communities, protecting the environment, building demand for sustainable products, working together for change, and creating a great place to work. The company's overall corporate governance structure is available at http://www.gmcr.com/investors. In GMCR's 2011 annual report, Stiller stated, "We are particularly proud that our earnings growth has enabled us to increase the resources we direct to societal and environmental initiatives under our banner of 'Brewing a Better World.' In fiscal year 2011, the total resources we allocated to sustainability programs totaled $15.2 million. A key corporate value proposition of GMCR is ongoing support and partnership with the communities in which we operate through volunteerism, philanthropy, and other socially and environmentally responsible initiatives." [4]

Building Demand for Sustainable Products

Green Mountain successfully shifted some of the coffee industry away from a focus on price (cost to consumers) to shared *value creation* providing benefits to the company and consumers in an environmentally and socially sustainable way by stimulating greater demand for Fair Trade Certified coffee. In "Brewing a Better World," management maintained that "as the economic rewards of Fair Trade Certified™ coffee grew, more smallholder farmers would work towards Fair Trade status. And more people would be lifted out of poverty and hunger. More hectares of land under cultivation would be cultivated with care. And so on in a reinforcing circle. It could work the same in many businesses and industries—maybe all." [5]

In fiscal year 2011, GMCR delivered 95 percent revenue growth with net sales of $2,650,900,000. Approximately 84 percent of those net sales were attributable to the combination of Keurig brewing systems and related accessories and single K-Cup packs. The company sold 5.9 million Keurig brewers in fiscal year 2011. Net sales from K-Cup packs totaled $1,704,000,000 in 2011, up 104 percent, or $869,600,000 from 2010. [6]

Green Mountain's product concept was fashioned after Gillette's high-margin razor / razor blade strategy. Green Mountain sold its retail Keurig brewers at cost or licensed the technology to other roasters to enable high volume sales of its K-Cups. The goal was to place as many brewers as possible into homes, offices, hotels, and supermarkets to boost its Fair Trade Certified (FTC) model through brewer and K-Cup sales growth. Keurig brewers were sold at Bed Bath & Beyond, Macy's, Target, Kohl's, Walmart, Sears, and other well-known retailers, giving the company's fair trade business model greater exposure to a wider base of customers. By 2011, Keurig was the best-selling single-serve coffee maker brand in the United States with just over 71 percent market share.

Starbucks has been GMCR's largest rival in the specialty coffee market segment. In an attempt to stall declining retail store sales in the United States, Starbuck's launched a national campaign for its Pike's Place Roast coffee at a $1.50 per cup. Blandford saw Green Mountain's home brewing technology as a very affordable customer alternative to its competitors' retail store coffee. In contrast to Starbucks's $3 per cup for a tall latte, at-home K-Cup brewing costs consumers about 50 to 60 cents a cup. [7] Green Mountain saw its K-Cup products as a way for consumers to cut cost. *Money* magazine estimated that it would cost consumers $1,246 annually for a daily latte at Starbucks

How GMCR Built Demand for Fair Trade Coffee

In 2002, GMCR started selling Newman's Own Organics coffee in K-Cups. This collaboration gave GMCR access to Costco, BJ's, and Sam's Club. Just as important, the collaboration with Newman's Own Organics allowed GMCR to make Fair Trade Certified organic coffee available to all consumers. After the collaboration was started in 2002, Green Mountain became a leader in the organic coffee category and Newman's Own Organics became one of the fastest-growing national coffee brands in the United States.

In 2007, GMCR entered into a licensing agreement to sell Caribou Coffee that gave it access to midwestern markets. In 2009, Green Mountain acquired the brand and wholesale business of Tully's Coffee, a respected specialty coffee roaster with roots in the Pacific Northwest. In 2009, Green Mountain acquired the Timothy's World Coffee brand and its wholesale coffee business located in Toronto, Canada. This acquisition included Timothy's World Coffee, Emeril's, and Kahlúa Original brands. Timothy's gave Green Mountain entry into international markets for the first time. Timothy's sold only high-quality Arabica coffee, which was sourced globally. Through its new product development and marketing programs, Green Mountain sought to nationally expand its supermarket and college and university food service accounts. At year-end 2009, Green Mountain had more than 8,500 supermarket and 240 college and university accounts.

GMCR's Tanzanian Gombe Reserve coffee was the first coffee to receive Jane Goodall's "Good for All" seal, signifying that GMCR not only promotes better pay for farmers but is committed to protect the environment and the planet's wildlife. The coffee grown near the boundaries of Tanzania's Gombe National Park is one of the few places worldwide where coffee farmers and chimpanzees live side-by-side. GMCR's outreach program provides farmers with an incentive to preserve the forest and a chance at economic stability while giving Green Mountain access to one of the best climates for growing high-quality Arabica coffee. [8]

KEY TAKEAWAYS

- Excellence in business sustainability and excellence in overall business performance can be mutually supportive and interdependent.
- Sustainability principles and practices can promote collaborative partnerships that are mutually beneficial to supply chain communities and stakeholders.
- Being good at sustainable business management requires a systematic approach that integrates and governs all functions and elements of the company's operation and throughout its supply chain.
- Sustainable business management can be a critically important management competency, one that can help differentiate a company from rivals in profitable and meaningful ways.
- Founder and senior management commitment to sustainable business practice is important.
- Sustainability business models need to be supported and championed by senior managers.

- Sustainable business models can provide several sources of competitive advantage through branding, market segmentation, and pricing.

EXERCISES

1. Take a virtual Internet tour of a coffee farm in Tanzania, Africa. What type of coffee farming is carried out in this country? What is the quality of life like for the country's farmers? What unique environmental, social, and economic issues face the coffee farmer in this country?

2. Go to TransFair USA's website (http://www.transfairusa.org). What are TransFair USA's mission, values, and philosophy? Why is it important for a roaster's coffee to be Fair Trade Certified?

3. You have been asked to join a group of students at school or college to join a protest against Green Mountain Coffee Roasters. They are concerned about the rapid growth of the company's plastic K-Cups and the disposal of these cups into your local landfill. How would you respond to their invitation to join them?

4. What NGOs are in the country and what type of assistance do they offer coffee farmers? If you were to go on an eco-tour to a coffee-producing region of the country, what would you expect to see? How visible is GMCR's involvement in Tanzania? Are they involved? If so, how?

[1] John M. Talbot, *Grounds for Agreement: The Political Economy of the Coffee Commodity Chain* (London: Rowman & Littlefield, 2004).

[2] TransFair USA, *TransFair USA: Almanac 2009*, accessed June 8, 2010, http://www.fairtradeusa.org/resource-library/downloads.

[3] Kathleen E. McKone-Sweet, "Lessons from a Coffee Supply Chain," *Supply Chain Management Review* (2009), accessed May 6, 2010, http://www.accessmylibrary.com/coms2/summary_0286-14185976_ITM.

[4] "Home Page," Green Mountain Coffee Roasters, Inc., accessed April 10, 2010, http://www.gmcr.com/Investors/Company-Profile.aspx.

[5] Green Mountain Coffee Roasters, Inc., *Brewing a Better World: VOICES*, accessed May 30, 2010, http://www.gmcr.com/PDF/gmcr_csr_2008.pdf.

[6] CSRwire, "Green Mountain Coffee Releases First Corporate Social Responsibility Report," news release, October 3, 2006, http://www.csrwire.com/press/press_release/13663-Green-Mountain-Coffee-Roasters-Releases-First-Corporate-Social-Responsibility-Report.

[7] Green Mountain Coffee Roasters, Inc., *Brewing a Better World: VOICES*, accessed May 30, 2010, http://www.gmcr.com/PDF/gmcr_csr_2008.pdf.

[8] Green Mountain Coffee Roasters, Inc., *Brewing a Better World: VOICES*, accessed May 30, 2010, http://www.gmcr.com/PDF/gmcr_csr_2008.pdf.

9.4 Going Forward

Marketplace Challenges

Competition in the specialty segment of the coffee industry intensified as companies attempted to gain market share in this profitable and rapidly growing segment through acquisitions and by other means. This was particularly true in the single-serve coffee segment of the market. Several companies were taking greater interest in this segment and moved to acquire other companies or introduce their own brewer and K-Cup technologies. In October 2008, Green Mountain settled a lawsuit against Kraft Foods Global for patent infringement that violated its *intellectual property* rights, with Green Mountain asserting that Kraft infringed on Keurig's brewing and K-Cup technologies. Kraft paid Green Mountain $17 million to settle the suit. As part of the settlement Green Mountain licensed its brewer and cartridge technologies to Kraft. [1]

In September 2012, two patents on Green Mountain Coffee Roasters' (GMCR) K-Cups and Keurig brewer expire. These key patents are related to technology that maintained a precise amount of coffee in each pod and the means to extract its liquid. Copying the technology will not be difficult as the patents protect relatively simple inventions.

In anticipation of the patent expirations, GMCR launched new products (see more in the discussion that follows) and also aggressively pursued licensing of its K-Cup technology. Notable licensing agreements were made with Caribou, Folgers, Dunkin' Donuts, and Starbucks. However, Green Mountain Coffee Roasters' stock price plunged 16 percent after Starbucks said it would soon start selling the single-cup coffee machines. Market investors believed that this move by GMCR's main competitor would deflate demand for Green Mountain's Keurig machines. Shares of Starbucks on the same day rose by 3 percent.

Environmental Challenges

In the company's 2008 corporate social responsibility report, GMCR management stated that their top challenge was the environmental impact of their coffee packaging materials and brewing systems. To address this challenge management engaged in an in-depth life cycle assessment to understand and compare single-cup brewing versus drip brewing from a systems standpoint. Mike Dupee, Green Mountain's vice president of corporate social responsibility, in his letter in the 2008 Corporate Social Report, wrote,

> *Growth, as with any change in the status quo, generally triggers some amount of self-examination. How did we get here? Where are we going and how are we going to get there? As a values-*

based business, we ask these same questions—and our commitment to social and environmental responsibility adds another layer to the process. How do we address the management of our ecological footprint while growing at these rates? How do we manifest our commitments across a growing family of brands? How do we maintain the best aspects of our corporate culture and welcome new ideas as we spread out across new geographies and welcome more and more people into our enterprise? It is more apparent than ever that we must continue to prioritize key sustainability opportunities and challenges alongside the demands of a fast-growing business. [2]

In the 2009 CSR report, management reported on the results of their life cycle analysis. The life cycle assessment showed that the disposal of a K-Cup's packaging represented a relatively small fraction of the total environmental impact of GMCR products—the most significant environmental impacts occurred in the cultivation of coffee beans, the use of brewing systems, and the material used in the products' packaging. One area of concern with the single-serve coffee was the manufacturing requirements of the K-Cup pack, which made recycling difficult. The K-Cup pack was made up of three main elements: the cup itself, a filter, and an aluminum foil top. The pack's components were deemed as required to prevent oxygen, light, and moisture from degrading the coffee. To offset the environmental impact of the K-Cup brewing system, GMCR introduced a new line of more environmentally friendly brewers under the Vue brand name. The plastic used in Vue pack cups can be recycled wherever polypropylene / number five plastic is accepted. The Vue brewing system was viewed as another step on GMCR's long journey to reduce the environmental impact of their products. [3]

Sidebar
Can Disposable Single-Cup Coffee Be Sustainable?
Green Mountain Coffee made the popular Keurig Single-Cup brewing system in which a bit of coffee is sealed in plastic and can be popped cleanly into a single-serve coffee maker. Does it make sense to put fair-trade coffee in a disposable petroleum-based package?

Of the coffee shipped around the world by Green Mountain Coffee (GMC), 27 percent is currently fair trade certified and that number is increasing. They have partnered with Newman's Own Organics to widen the market for fair trade coffees and by putting fair trade coffees in their popular K-Cups they say they are popularizing fair trade and helping coffee growing communities. In some of their other products 19 percent of the bags are made from PLA (the corn-based bioplastic) and last year they cut their solid waste 19 percent

by composting the organic waste from their production processes. Part of their fleet runs on biodiesel. GMC offsets 100 percent of their direct greenhouse gas emissions. They partner with nonprofits such as Heifer International and provide grants focused on poverty reduction.

K-Cups however, are petroleum based plastic, with a layer of polyethylene coating an interior filter paper and an aluminum foil top. It keeps the coffee fresh, but makes recycling impossible. Small though the cups may be they are big business, with GMC reporting that 2.5 million K-Cups® are brewed every day. K-Cups® were about ½ of their net sales last year.

On the sustainability of their operation GMC states, "we understand that the impact of the K-Cup® waste stream is one of our most significant environmental challenges." They have commissioned a lifecycle analysis to compare drip brew to K-Cups®, but if they already know it is a significant challenge, in a product line representing half of their sales, it is notable that no other information on alternatives or reasonable goals are available except a statement that they "are working to identify the right definition of environmentally friendly."

People have the choice to buy the reusable filter model (although it got bad reviews for durability), but assuming that their convenience-loving customers like the no fuss product, but also care about issues like fair trade, why is such a connected company not moving faster on this high impact issue?

Source: Lillian Laurence, "Can Disposable Single-Cup Coffee Be Sustainable?," Sustainable Life Media, accessed June 25, 2010, http://www.sustainablebrands.com/news_and_views/articles/can-disposable-single-cup-coffee-be-sustainable-green-mountain-coffee.

Green Mountain management has taken many other steps in design, packaging, and energy use to reduce the environmental impact of the Keurig brewing systems, including the following:

- *Introducing nested packaging for our K-Cup® packs, which was expected to reduce distribution-related greenhouse gas emissions by more than 20%, and decrease volume of packaging by 30%.*
- *Launching two pilot programs in its Away From Home channel that divert brewed K-Cup® packs from landfills.*
- *Offering the My K-Cup® product, a reusable filter assembly that can be refilled by the consumer. My K-Piloting a K-Cup® pack for tea made with paper, a renewable resource, in 2010.*

- *Including recycling codes in its brewers to facilitate responsible disposal of the recyclable parts of its home brewing systems and to ensure compliance with the RoHS Directive, a set of European regulations designed to reduce the effect of electronic equipment on the waste stream.*
- *Providing considerable energy savings through Auto-Off features for its At Home brewing systems.* [4]

Valuation and Stock Market Performance Challenges

In October 2011, David Einhorn and his hedge fund, Greenlight Capital, publically criticized Green Mountain Coffee Roasters, attacking the company's patents and arrangement with Starbucks. [5] Green Mountain's stock promptly fell 10 percent.

Sidebar

Einhorn's concerns included the following:

1. Patent expiration: GMCR's patent on K-Cups expires in September 2012, and it could allow competitors to make pods for GMCR's Keurig machines, undercutting profit margins.
2. Starbucks, Dunkin (DNKN) and Smucker's (SJM) deals are less profitable than expected: GMCR earns around $0.15 per K-Cup it sells on its own, but filings show that K-Cups licensed to Smucker's earn around $0.06 per K-Cup. GMCR has said many times that the Starbucks and Dunkin deals would be the same, so investors should expect falling profit margins.
3. Valuation: At a P/E of 80, investors may begin to question that multiple as Einhorn attacks the stock.

The following points were made in favor of GMCR:

1. Starbucks, Dunkin, and Smucker's waited to strike a deal this year. If GMCR was about to collapse due to its patent expirations, why would Starbucks and Smucker's strike a deal? Obviously they are assuming GMCR will be around to fulfill its end of their contract.
2. Growth: Net sales soared 127% in the most recent quarter. Few, if any companies have that kind of growth. Not even Apple (AAPL) can match that kind of sales increase.

3. Expanding market share: GMCR estimates that 25% of all coffee machines sold in the quarter were K-Cup brewers. Given that this 25% is growing far above the other 75%, we think that Green Mountain will increase its market share.
4. Forward P/E: Though the P/E ratio is 80, the forward P/E is under 32, a huge fall, implying huge growth for the company. Given that the company is expected to grow earnings and revenue by 60%, is it that expensive?
5. Patent expirations are a positive: The patent expirations occurring in 2012 are a net positive for GMCR, because a lack of license fees means cheaper K-Cups, expanding demand for brewers that ARE patent-protected. Furthermore, focusing on brewers will turn them into a profit center for GMCR if it cannot earn enough from K-Cups.
6. Acquisitions have all been done to prepare for patent expirations: GMCR has been criticized for questionable acquisitions, such as Van Houtte and Diedrich. But, the net result of these acquisitions is that Green Mountain now owns its top selling K-Cup providers, which means that ironically Green Mountain is the prime beneficiary of its own expiring patents.
7. New products: GMCR is developing new products, including an espresso machine, and a new Keurig filtering system, which will come with their own patent protections.

Source: Helix Investment Management, "Who's Right about Green Mountain Coffee Roasters? Einhorn or the Street?," October 19, 2011, accessed March 3, 2012, http://seekingalpha.com/article/300640-who-s-right-about-green-mountain-coffee-roasters-einhorn-or-the-street.

Challenges Take a Toll

On May 2, 2012, GMCR shares declined 48 percent after the company reported it had sold fewer brewers and K-cups than it had anticipated in the quarter ending in March, causing the company to lower its profit expectations for the year. The fallout came as Green Mountain faces increased competition in the fall when Starbucks plans to launch a high-end espresso brewer and two of Green Mountain's patents on K-cup technology expire.

KEY TAKEAWAYS

- GMCR was able to use excellence in business sustainability as a source of competitive advantage and to help increase its profitability and market value.
- The company faces many challenges. These include continuing the following: its leadership in sustainable business practices, its strong position in the coffee industry, and its stock market performance prior to 2012.

EXERCISES

1. Describe how GMCR was able to grow and increase profitability by selling single-cup coffee. Then discuss the significance of single-cup coffee packaging and how it relates to sustainability. Is single-cup brewing compatible with sustainability? Why or

why not? Can GMCR maintain its leadership in sustainable business practice and continue to grow its single-cup coffee business?

2. Go to http://www.vuerecycling.com. How does the Vue support, if at all, GMCR's claims that its new brewer technology and its packs of plastic cup are more environmentally friendly? Is GMCR doing enough to address its environmental critiques?

3. What happens to GMCR now that its main competitor, Starbucks, is selling single-cup brewers in their stores and after its K-Cup patent expires? Will this increase the company's reliance on sustainable business practices with Vue and other similarly focused initiatives? Within the single-cup segment of the coffee market will GMCR be able to continue to distinguish itself by its sustainability effort and can sustainability efforts contribute to future profitability and stock price appreciation?

[1] Elizabeth Fuhrman, "Green Mountain Coffee Roasters Gives a One-Two Punch," *Beverage Industry*, March 2009, 32.
[2] Green Mountain Coffee Roasters, Inc., *Annual Report on Form 10-K for Fiscal Year Ended September 26, 2009*.
[3] Green Mountain Coffee Roasters, Inc., *Annual Report on Form 10-K for Fiscal Year Ended September 26, 2009*.
[4] Green Mountain Coffee Roasters, Inc., *Brewing a Better World: VOICES*, accessed May 30, 2010, http://www.gmcr.com/PDF/gmcr_csr_2008.pdf.
[5] David Benoit, "Here's the Einhorn Presentation That Killed Green Mountain Shares," *Deal Journal* (blog), October 19, 2011, http://blogs.wsj.com/deals/2011/10/19/heres-the-einhorn-presentation-that-killed-green-mountain-shares.

NOTES:

Chapter 10:
Case: Oakhurst Dairy:
Operations Management and Sustainability

10.1 Overview
LEARNING OBJECTIVES

1. Understand how operations management that incorporates sustainability principles can reduce costs and improve profits.
2. Describe how sustainable operations management practice can contribute to cost reduction and enhance a company's competitive position.
3. Highlight best practices for reducing greenhouse gas (GHG) emissions in an industry.
4. Show how lean manufacturing principles can contribute to sustainable, effective, and efficient management of a company's carbon footprint.

Oakhurst Dairy's profitability has benefitted from the company taking a leadership role in addressing greenhouse gas (GHG) emissions in the US dairy industry. [1] In the process of its carbon footprint mapping the company identified how to reduce its GHG emissions and also identified innovative ways to improve operational efficiencies, reduce operational costs (mostly energy costs), and enhance profits.

Oakhurst Dairy has changed over time. The long established northern New England dairy company no longer owns any dairy farms. It makes its money by processing milk bought from dairy farms. It owns no cows. It buys its raw milk from local dairy farmers and sells its processed milk to grocery stores and retailers such as Walmart and 7-Eleven.

The company, under the Bennett family ownership, has become one of northern New England's largest independent milk processors. Oakhurst's approach is to build brand equity and increase profits over time. This has been supported by investing in operation management practices that reduce costs and increase brand awareness and loyalty with the dissemination of information about the company's practices that reduce its carbon footprint.

Oakhurst's sustainable business approach includes (a) senior management commitment to sustainable business practices in its operations and its supply chain, (b) integration of sustainable goals and practices in the company's business systems, (c) use of operating and financial reports and communications, and (d) monitoring of environmental results and implementation of continuous improvements.

This case will highlight how the company, by adopting sustainable business practices throughout its operations, saved more than $620,000 in annual fuel costs. These are savings that have contributed directly to Oakhurst's financial bottom line. This includes savings from a $343,000 investment in solar panels at two of its facilities, resulting in annual savings of $52,500 (at a fuel cost of $3.50 per gallon) and representing a 6.5 year payback period on their investment. With an estimated life of thirty years, the solar panel investment alone will save Oakhurst $1.2 million over the life of the solar panels and lower its carbon emissions by 176 metric tons annually.

10.2 Introduction
LEARNING OBJECTIVES

1. Describe how the company was founded and how it operates as a family-operated enterprise.
2. Define how the dairy industry is organized and its larger context.
3. Understand that sustainability efforts have to be considered in the context of company organization and ownership and industry dynamics and conditions.

The founding family of Oakhurst, the Bennett family, has managed a successful dairy business based out of Portland, Maine, for ninety years. This is not a simple accomplishment. The dairy industry is dynamic and fiercely competitive, and Oakhurst has become the largest independent dairy processor in northern New England. The company is privately owned and as such its financial information is not publically available. Much of the information from this case is garnered from company interviews and a study of the company by Clean Air–Cool Planet (CA–CP). [1]

Instead of succumbing to the external economic and political forces that have reduced many family businesses to nostalgic memories of bucolic America, the Bennett family found ways to keep the dairy industry a part of the Maine economy. Oakhurst's success can be attributed in part to the company's strategy, built on the following:

- Lean manufacturing and operational efficiency
- Creation of business value through environmental stewardship
- Psychographic-centered marketing and brand equity

According to Oakhurst President William "Bill" Bennett, "We have been able to stave off being bought by maintaining a strong brand identity. People know what we do and what we stand for." [2]

Co-owner of Oakhurst with his brother Stanley, Bill Bennett took on the role of president when Stanley was diagnosed with pancreatic cancer in the summer of 2010. Stanley had led Oakhurst Dairy since 1983 when he was named president after his father's retirement. [3]

The Bennett family firmly believed that the well-being of their company and the US dairy industry were dependent on environmental stewardship. Oakhurst's proactive and interactive approach to reducing emissions has set the standard for best practices in the dairy industry. They have collaborated with interest groups, government agencies, industry competitors, and others in their sustainability efforts. [4]

Stanley T. Bennett II was one of five third-generation Bennett siblings who were keeping their great grandfather Stanley Bennett's business alive by being a preferred supplier of natural, healthy dairy products. Before his passing, Stanley T. Bennett II noted, "The cows that supply us with our product literally eat and drink and breathe the Maine environment. We have a natural self-interest in keeping that environment pure. It's something we can market that our competitors can't." [5]

Under Bill's leadership, Oakhurst has focused on ways to boost operational efficiency in the highly competitive dairy industry. With price pressure intense in the industry, success at reducing costs without sacrificing product quality and integrity could contribute to increased profitability. Finding ways to reduce energy, electricity, water, and sewage costs could enhance company profits at the same time it reduced the company's environmental impact and could enhance its favorable reputation with significant numbers of consumers.

On his brother's passing, Bill stated in the company's news release, "Oakhurst is where it is today because of Stan's leadership and foresight; he always kept an eye on the future. For a number of years, we've put a lot of thought into making sure we have a caring, experienced, and committed team in place; and this team will continue to lead us well into the future." [6]

Bill's brother John joined the company in 2004 as vice president of sales and marketing after owning and operating a successful wholesale seafood business on Portland's waterfront. Other members of the senior management team with years of service included their sister Althea Bennett-McGirr, director of customer service and consumer affairs (thirty years); Tom Brigham, executive vice president and chief financial officer (fifteen years); Paul Connolly, vice president of logistics and chief information officer (ten years); and Joe Hyatt, vice president of human resources and administration (thirteen years). [7]

Bill Bennett, reflecting on his brother's life and contribution to Oakhurst, stated, "The main reason we've been so successful over the years is because of him." Bill added that many of the recent steps the company had taken to decrease its carbon footprint, including purchasing biofuels from a local company that turns restaurant fry oil into biofuel and installing solar panels on the roofs of the company's various buildings, were because of Stanley Bennett II's leadership.[8] The challenge for Oakhurst management was to buck the industry trend toward large-scale dairy farming, processing, and distribution through consolidation of dairies while maintaining profitability. According to Bill Bennett II, "Twenty-five or thirty years ago, we were a big dairy in a sea of little dairies. Now we are a small dairy [processor]." [9]

Like its counterparts across the country, Maine dairy farmers were finding it difficult to make a profit let alone stay in business. However, compared to its northern New England neighbors, Maine was losing its dairy farms at a lower rate as a result of Maine's innovative dairy stabilization program (see sidebar "The State of Maine's Dairy Industry").

The State of Maine's Dairy Industry

In 2009, Maine's dairy industry generated more than $570 million annually for the state's economy, paid $25 million in state and municipal local taxes, and provided more than four thousand jobs. In the 1950s, Maine had 51,000 herds of dairy cattle. By 2009 it was down to 32,000 cows making 590 million pounds of milk per year (69 million gallons). By 2009 there were 315 dairy farms in Maine ranging in size from 10 to 1,700 cows. In the period from 2000 to 2004, Maine lost

106 farms. Maine has more than sixty milk processors. Six processors package fluid milk for drinking: Oakhurst Dairy, H. P. Hood, Houlton Farms Dairy, Garelick Farms of Maine, Kate's Butter, and Smiling Hill Farm Dairy. By far the largest was H. P. Hood with $2.4 billion in revenue and 3,000 employees in 2010. Dean's Foods, a National food and beverage company had revenues of $12.9 billion and lost $1.5 billion (2010). Oakhurst Dairy was the largest privately owned Maine dairy processor with 2010 revenues of $110 million and 250 employees.

Since 2004 the US dairy industry has been marked by two significant factors. The western United States has seen unimagined and unprecedented growth in total milk and average size of each dairy operation. This shift was the result of state and federal government policies that offer financial incentives in the form of tax breaks and subsidies to take unproductive land and convert it to animal agriculture, or convert land from one type of production to dairy production. Secondly, the cyclical "boom-and-bust" dynamic of dairy pricing has continued on a national scale and has become more erratic and extreme. Maine has continued to lose farms, but at a much slower rate than the rest of the Northeast. Some farms have gone out of business because of the age of the farmer or the fact there was no one to take over the farm. Most importantly, the economic impact of the remaining farms has not lost its influence on the state's economy. Many states have looked to Maine as an innovative leader in the dairy industry, first with the Northeast Dairy Compact and now with the Maine Dairy Stabilization "Tier" Program. Established in 2004, the "Tier" program provides a safety net during periods of historically low national milk prices. In contrast to the overall picture of New England dairy farming, Maine stands out and is considered a success story because of the 2004 dairy stabilization program. Since the start of the program, Maine lost 75 dairy farms, or 19 percent of the industry, in contrast to extreme losses in Vermont (52 percent) and New Hampshire (46 percent). The dairy stabilization program provides a payment from the Maine's General Fund directly to farmers when the amount that they receive from the marketplace for their milk falls below their cost of production. In Maine, the cost of production is estimated at $25 per hundred weight of milk, while the farmer can receive between $11 and $23 per hundred weight from the marketplace. If the price of milk is high, no payments are made. When it drops, the program assists the farmers. Since 2007, $30 million has been paid to Maine's dairy farmers through the tier program. According to Julie Marie Bickford of the Maine Dairy Industry Association compared to states without a milk commission, Maine is a relatively healthy dairy state.

Galen Larrabee, a dairy farmer from Knox, Maine noted that even with the tier program it hasn't been easy for Maine farmers. He noted, feed costs have gone through the barn roof—up by a third over last year at this time. Fuel costs could be doubled by the end of the year. Energy bills—mostly electricity—have been running $6,000 a month. "We spent $730,000 on grain last year. This year it will be close to a million. Fuel for the first 10 months of 2011 has been $103,000. Last year it was $72,000. We're paying our bills but there is not a lot left over." Larrabee with 490 cows is considered one of Maine's larger dairymen, but he certainly isn't unique. "Most dairy farms, about 50 percent I think, are just about breaking even," he said. "The other 50 percent are behind the eight ball." With the cost of equipment, taxes, feed, veterinary services and infrastructure all jumping higher and higher, Larrabee said, it isn't right to use the word "profit" when discussing Maine farms. "Most are just holding on." Bickford said dairy-pricing policy is a hot topic these days in the congressional halls in Washington, DC. "Maine is finally getting some traction and the USDA is listening to the idea that milk should be priced at market value. It should reflect the going rate in competitive regions," Bickford said. But as long as Maine's tier program remains in place, there is a future for dairy farming in Maine. Larrabee was encouraged by the support received from Maine consumers. "People in Maine have always spent more on dairy than other parts of the country," he said. "They want farms. They want the countryside to remain intact. They actively support us."
Source: Sharon Kiley Mack, "Maine's Innovative Dairy Program Keeping Industry Alive," *Bangor Daily News*, October 29, 2011.

KEY TAKEAWAYS

- A strong commitment to sustainability requires visionary leadership, organization-wide action and commitment, and alignment of sustainability efforts to profitability and competitive advantage.
- Sustainable business practices can improve operational efficiencies and company performance.
- Sustainability efforts have to be considered in the context of market conditions and, in the case of Oakhurst, in the context of highly competitive and challenging diary industry conditions.

EXERCISES

1. Go to YouTube and find videos on Oakhurst Dairy.
a. What market segment(s) are targeted in the videos?
b. What message(s) is Oakhurst delivering in their advertisements?
c. Why do customers buy Oakhurst Dairy products?
d. Does Oakhurst use endorsement in their advertising? If so, who is featured?

In one hundred words or less, describe the Oakhurst sustainable business model and perceived competitive advantage for doing business in the dairy industry.

[1] "Outreach and Education/Resources," Clean Air–Cool Planet, http://www.cleanair-coolplanet.org/climate_preparedness/outreach_ed.php.

[2] J. Hemmerdinger, "Maine in a Bottle: Oakhurst Dairy Homogenizes Its Marketing Message," *Portland (ME) Press Herald*, January 9, 2011, accessed January 20, 2011, http://www.pressherald.com/business/maine-in-a-bottle_2011-01-09.html; the story was revised on January 10, 2011, to correct a reference to milk prices. According to the Maine Milk Commission, dairy farmers were paid a minimum of roughly $18 per 100 pounds of milk in November.

[3] John Richardson, "Oakhurst CEO Stanley Bennett Dies," *Portland (ME) Press Herald*, February 25, 2011, accessed March 5, 2011, http://www.pressherald.com/news/oakhurst-ceo-stanley-bennett-dies_2011-02-25.html.

[4] See Clean Air–Cool Planet, *Taking All the Right Steps: A Maine Dairy Reduces Its Carbon Footprint*, http://www.cleanair-coolplanet.org/information/pdf/Oakhurst%20Dairy%20Case%20Study%2001272009.pdf. For the Oakhurst case and more information about Clean Air–Cool Planet (CA–CP), see http://www.cleanair-coolplanet.org/about and Innovation Center for US Dairy, *U.S. Dairy Sustainability Commitment Progress Report: Sustaining the Dairy Industry for Future Generations*, accessed January 9, 2011, http://www.usdairy.com/Sustainability/Pages/Home.aspx.

[5] Clean Air–Cool Planet, *Taking All the Right Steps: A Maine Dairy Reduces Its Carbon Footprint*, http://www.cleanair-coolplanet.org/information/pdf/Oakhurst%20Dairy%20Case%20Study%2001272009.pdf. For the Oakhurst case and more information about Clean Air–Cool Planet (CA–CP), see http://www.cleanair-coolplanet.org/about.

[6] Front Burner PR, "Oakhurst's Bill and John Bennett Well Prepared to Lead Respected New England Dairy," news release, February 25, 2011, http://www.frontburnerpr.com/uploads/oak_transition_feb2011_final.pdf.

[7] Front Burner PR, "Oakhurst's Bill and John Bennett Well Prepared to Lead Respected New England Dairy," news release, February 25, 2011, http://www.frontburnerpr.com/uploads/oak_transition_feb2011_final.pdf.

[8] "Stanley T. Bennett II, Oakhurst Dairy President, Dedicated to Community," *Forecaster (Falmouth, ME)*, March 1, 2011, http://www.theforecaster.net/content/pn-obitbennett-030211.

[9] J. Hemmerdinger, "Maine in a Bottle: Oakhurst Dairy Homogenizes Its Marketing Message," *Portland (ME) Press Herald*, January 9, 2011, accessed January 20, 2011, http://www.pressherald.com/business/maine-in-a-bottle_2011-01-09.html.

10.3 Greenhouse Gases (GHGs) and the US Dairy Industry

LEARNING OBJECTIVES

1. Understand the social, political, and economic impact of climate change and global warming on the US dairy industry, specifically in Maine.
2. Understand the role of industry associations and collaborative networks in addressing industry and company environmental challenges.
3. Learn about carbon footprint mapping and life cycle analysis (LCA).

Industrial growth, deforestation, and increased consumption has exacerbated global warming and changes to the climate and will continue to do so. Gases that trap heat in the atmosphere are often called greenhouse gases (GHG). Of the total GHG emitted annually in the United States, two areas in which Oakhurst have an impact—transportation fuels and agricultural byproducts—emit 14 percent and 12.5 percent of the total, respectively. [1]

There is mounting evidence that heavy concentrations of GHGs have raised the earth's temperatures from 1.2 to 1.4 degrees in the last hundred years. Also of concern is the fact that eight of the warmest years on record occurred between 1998 and 2010. [2] Rising temperatures have already had adverse effects on climate, agriculture, and people. People

and animals are affected by climate change through extreme periods of heat and cold, storms, climate sensitive diseases,

and prolonged and increased levels of smog. Scientists considering the potential impacts of climate change in the northeastern United States have identified heat waves and prolonged drought as two significant threats to the dairy industry, as heat-stressed cows generally produce less milk. [3]

The previously stated factors provided strong incentive for Oakhurst to try to reduce its GHG emissions, or carbon footprint. Acting on this concern would be in the interest of the dairy industry in Maine and beyond and society more broadly and was also consistent with the company's values in caring about the communities it served and operated in.

GHG Emissions Challenge in the US Dairy Industry

In December 2010, the Innovation Center for US Dairy published its first *US Dairy Industry Sustainability Commitment Report*. The report was a collaborative effort of leaders and experts in and outside the industry who joined together to "identify and deploy sustainability innovations that make good business sense." The report documented that the United States was the largest dairy producer in the world, producing annually 189.9 billion pounds of milk and that milk was the fourth highest dollar value agricultural product in the United States (at 8 percent of total receipts). It also identified that the dairy industry contributed 2 percent of the total US GHG emissions. Working with the Sustainability Center at the University of Arkansas, the Innovation Center conducted the dairy industry's first national GHG life cycle analysis (LCA), or carbon footprint study, of fluid milk. [4]

Formed in 2007, the Innovation Center represented an industry-wide commitment to identify best practices for lowering carbon emissions throughout the supply chain. More than five hundred dairy stakeholders including environmentalists, academics, and scientists worked on the report. The study found that "the carbon footprint of a gallon of milk, from farm to table, is 17.6 pounds of carbon dioxide equivalents (CO_2e) per gallon of milk consumed." [5] By far, the largest single source of heat-trapping gases linked to global warming from milk production are farm emissions, which contribute roughly ten pounds of CO_2e per gallon of milk. And 85 percent of those emissions come from one source—cows.

Dairy Industry Competitive Dynamics

The global demand for food is expected to double by 2050. [6] This growth will provide opportunities and challenges for the US dairy industry. The challenges for the industry include bringing milk to the consumer at competitive prices in a sustainable way when dairy prices are subject to economic cycles, changing weather patterns, and changing industry competitive dynamics.

Although the minimum wholesale price paid to farmers by milk processors is set by a complicated, government formula, milk prices constantly change across the full value chain from raw milk to processed milk to milk at the grocery store. Among the factors affecting the cost to produce a pound of milk are feed cost, cow productivity (pounds produced per cow, per day), animal nutrition, genetics, and proper farm maintenance and housing of animals. For example, an increase in feed cost without a corresponding increase in cow milk productivity will squeeze farmer profits. It is not unusual to have milk production costs above the farmer's selling price. According to Mark Stephenson, director of dairy policy analysis at the University of Wisconsin, when total milk production costs are above the wholesale price, farmers are forced to take one of a few actions. [7] These actions include the use of genetic engineering (putting human growth hormones in cow feed), investments in better cow management, culling out inferior cows, or going out of business.

Stephenson noted that weather and temperature abnormalities across the globe have dramatically affected not only the quality of feed but also the feed prices. In an industry presentation, he noted that recent changes in the La Niña pattern in the Pacific Ocean had affected weather around the globe and consequently feed prices and milk production. These changing weather patterns had raised feed prices, especially corn prices, in Australia, Indonesia, and New Zealand. Stephenson concluded that businesses in the US dairy industry are going to have to rethink their business models in an increasingly volatile industry. [8]

While a very small overall global contributor to GHG emissions worldwide, Oakhurst has successfully addressed its emissions in ways that have been beneficial to the company's profitability and reputation. This has been accomplished by installing solar panels, retrofitting the company's truck fleet, and using advanced rerouting software for its delivery trucks. With these efforts and others, Oakhurst has lowered its annual carbon emissions by more than one thousand metric tons and lowered its operating costs, primarily fuel costs, significantly. In periods of rising and highly volatile oil prices, fuel cost savings have been significant for Oakhurst. At the same time, its actions have reaffirmed the company's commitment to the environment and to consumers in Maine and beyond, which has been beneficial to its standing among consumers, particularly those who cared about the environment.

The large majority of milk consumers are most concerned about price, not carbon footprints. Reflective of this, Walmart and other large milk retailers are increasingly demanding lower pricing for the milk they get from Oakhurst and other milk processors. According to the *Wall Street Journal*, cutthroat tactics "are making a mess of the dairy aisle." [9] The article reported that "grocery stores continue to use deep discounts to attract cash-strapped shoppers, sometimes selling milk at a loss." [10] These practices and pressure from the retailers have forced milk processors to take drastic action in lowering the cost they pay for their supplies. Even Dean Foods, the largest milk processor in the

United States, has struggled to pass on price cuts to their raw products suppliers, and this has resulted in significant financial pressure on the milk processors. The recent sharp increase in milk costs has caused dramatic drops in Dean's profits and stock price. Analysts were predicting further drops in Dean's earning in 2011, which could violate the company's leverage covenant with its banks and force the company into bankruptcy. [11]

According to the *Wall Street Journal*, "Even if milk prices stabilize, however, grocers are unlikely to relax their aggressive pricing strategy. With unemployment elevated, consumers are highly sensitive to price. That has crushed profits at grocer SuperValu, which charges higher prices for a basket of goods than rivals Kroger and Safeway. SuperValu's shares have performed even worse than Dean's since the market trough in 2009." [12]

One controversial strategy to increase productivity and cut costs per gallon of milk is the use of the human growth hormone rBST in cow feed. While the US Food and Drug Administration approved the use of rBST in cow feed in 1993, the controversy was far from resolved. Some scientific studies have shown that milk produced this way is safe and has the same amount of proteins, fats, and nutrients as non-hormone-fed cows. [13] Other studies contradict these findings.

Oakhurst took a firm stand against the use of the hormone rBST in cow feed. In 1997, Stanley Bennett asked its farmers to sign an affidavit pledging not to use human growth hormone. In return they received financial incentives, and shortly after, Oakhurst began marketing its milk as free of the human hormone rBST. In 2003, Monsanto, the largest manufacturer of rBST, sued Oakhurst claiming that Oakhurst's labels deceived consumers by marketing a perception that one milk product is safer or of higher quality than other milk. At the time of the suit, Monsanto's worldwide sales revenue from rBST was $4.7 billion. Stanley Bennett countered that Oakhurst made no claim on the science involved with growth hormones. [14] He stated, "We're in the business of marketing milk, not Monsanto's drugs." After an intense legal battle, Oakhurst settled the suit. Bill Bennett recalled, "Although the fight with Monsanto was expensive, Stanley Bennett didn't waver. Stanley was very proud of our stand with Monsanto. We thought it was very important to be able to tell our consumers what was not in our milk." [15]

KEY TAKEAWAYS

- Climate change and global warming can have significant impact on industry economics, including factor costs, prices, and profitability.
- Reducing an industry's carbon footprint requires action by a host of stakeholders, including industry associations, companies, government agencies, nonprofits, educators, scientists, activists, and individuals.
- The nature of competition in the dairy industry, and all industries, is constantly changing and driven by social, economic, technical, and environmental factors.
- Addressing an industry's environmental and economic challenges often requires cooperation by industry players, governmental agencies, researchers, and community agencies.

EXERCISES

1. Go to the US Dairy Industry's website, http://www.usdairy.com/Pages/Home.aspx, and read the *2010 Dairy Industry Sustainability Commitment Report*. Why is the industry so committed to lowering greenhouse gas (GHG) emissions, especially given that only 2 percent of total US GHG emissions are due to dairy industry participants?
2. Is Oakhurst justified in paying farmers for not feeding their cows with human growth hormones?
3. Do you know your own carbon footprint? Go to the Nature Conservatory website at http://www.nature.org/initiatives/climatechange/calculator and calculate your carbon footprint. Why is it important to know your carbon footprint?
4. See the sidebar "The State of Maine Dairy Industry." How would you characterize the economic health of Maine's Dairy Industry? Why have other states looked to Maine as an innovative leader in the dairy industry? What else might be done to help save Maine's dairy farms?

[1] "Annual Greenhouse Gas Emissions by Sector," accessed January 31, 2011, http://greenlifestyleideas.com/270/the-forgotten-greenhouse-gas-emissions.
[2] "Climate Change," U.S. Environmental Protection Agency, accessed January 31, 2011, http://www.epa.gov/climatechange/basicinfo.html.
[3] Clean Air–Cool Planet, *Taking All the Right Steps: A Maine Dairy Reduces Its Carbon Footprint*, http://www.cleanair-coolplanet.org/information/pdf/Oakhurst%20Dairy%20Case%20Study%2001272009.pdf.
[4] Innovation Center for US Dairy, *U.S. Dairy Sustainability Commitment Progress Report: Sustaining the Dairy Industry for Future Generations*, accessed January 9, 2011, http://www.usdairy.com/Sustainability/Pages/Home.aspx.

[5] Innovation Center for US Dairy, *U.S. Dairy Sustainability Commitment Progress Report: Sustaining the Dairy Industry for Future Generations*, accessed January 9, 2011, http://www.usdairy.com/Sustainability/Pages/Home.aspx.

[6] Innovation Center for US Dairy, *U.S. Dairy Sustainability Commitment Progress Report: Sustaining the Dairy Industry for Future Generations*, accessed January 9, 2011, http://www.usdairy.com/Sustainability/Pages/Home.aspx.

[7] Sara Schoenborn, "Stephenson Hopeful, Realistic about 2011 Dairy Outlook," *AG Weekly*, January 27, 2011, accessed January 20, 2011, http://www.agriview.com/news/dairy/stephenson-hopeful-realistic-about-dairy-outlook/article_fc01890d-cfda-5b25-a196-50ab45dbdaa1.html.

[8] Sara Schoenborn, "Stephenson Hopeful, Realistic about 2011 Dairy Outlook," *AG Weekly*, January 27, 2011, accessed January 20, 2011, http://www.agriview.com/news/dairy/stephenson-hopeful-realistic-about-dairy-outlook/article_fc01890d-cfda-5b25-a196-50ab45dbdaa1.html.

[9] John Jannarone, "Heard on the Street: Grocers Still Milking Dean Foods," *Wall Street Journal*, February 2, 2011, http://online.wsj.com/article/SB10001424052748703445904576118502653780560.html?KEYWORDS=jannarone.

[10] John Jannarone, "Heard on the Street: Grocers Still Milking Dean Foods," *Wall Street Journal*, February 2, 2011, http://online.wsj.com/article/SB10001424052748703445904576118502653780560.html?KEYWORDS=jannarone.

[11] John Jannarone, "Heard on the Street: Grocers Still Milking Dean Foods," *Wall Street Journal*, February 2, 2011, http://online.wsj.com/article/SB10001424052748703445904576118502653780560.html?KEYWORDS=jannarone.

[12] John Jannarone, "Heard on the Street: Grocers Still Milking Dean Foods," *Wall Street Journal*, February 2, 2011, http://online.wsj.com/article/SB10001424052748703445904576118502653780560.html?KEYWORDS=jannarone.

[13] Recombinant bovine somatotropin (rBST) is a synthetic version of the bovine somatotropin (BST) hormone found in cattle. The use of rBST has met with some controversy from a variety of fronts, including the animal rights movement and some commercial dairy farmers. As a result, dairies that produce milk products without the use of rBST have begun indicating this on their labels. Though rBST has been banned in several countries, the Environmental Protection Agency in the United States has determined it to be safe to consume. See "What Does rBST Free Mean?," wiseGEEK, accessed March 3, 2011, http://www.wisegeek.com/what-does-rbst-free-mean.

[14] Drew Kaplan, "Monsanto Sues Oakhurst Dairy over Advertising," Health Freedom Alliance, June 18, 2010, accessed February 11, 2011, http://healthfreedoms.org/2010/06/18/monsanto-sues-oakhurst-dairy-over-advertising.

[15] John Jannarone, "Heard on the Street: Grocers Still Milking Dean Foods," *Wall Street Journal*, February 2, 2011, http://online.wsj.com/article/SB10001424052748703445904576118502653780560.html?KEYWORDS=jannarone.

10.4 Oakhurst: Improving Business Value through Sustainable Practice

LEARNING OBJECTIVES

1. Understand how the success of carbon reduction strategies depends on the commitment of a corporation's management and the ability of management to effectively align company efforts to corporate values, strategy, and profitability.
2. Explain why it is important for a company's commitment to sustainability to be reflected in a company's core values, strategy, and operations.
3. Describe how sustainable business practices can facilitate and enhance operational efficiencies and effectiveness.

Keep it "CLEAN," Keep it "COLD," Keep it "MOVING." [1]
The Oakhurst motto

Stanley T. Bennett purchased a dairy from the Leadbetter family in Portland, Maine, in 1921. [2] The grove, or hurst, of oak trees near the original dairy gave Stanley the idea for the name, Oakhurst Dairy. Sixty years later, about twenty-five dairies were operating in Portland. Today, only a few dairies remain in Portland and in New England, and the few that remain are the survivors of consolidation that has swept the dairy industry nationwide. The Bennetts have differentiated their company by making caring for the environment a core value and defining component of the Oakhurst brand. With a strategy of Maine-centric branding, operating efficiencies, and a deep commitment to the environment the company has carved out a market niche that has helped the small dairy processor survive against dairy processors and retailers many times larger.

As a member of the US Dairy Industry's Sustainability Council, Bill Bennett was a contributor to two of the industry's Innovation Center reports: (1) *US Dairy Sustainability Initiative: A Roadmap to Reduce Greenhouse Gas Emissions and Increase Business Value* (December 2008) and (2) *The Sustainability Commitment Report* (December 2010). Bennett joined the Dairy Industry's Sustainability Council as part that organization's efforts to map, study, and recommend programs for greenhouse gas (GHG) reduction in the industry. Oakhurst Dairy was featured in two case studies illustrating carbon reduction best practices by the Innovation Center's reports: (1) *Case Study—Solar Thermal Systems: Dairy Processor Carbon Reduction through Energy Efficiency (D-CREE)* and (2) *Oakhurst: Sustainability in Practice*.

Products and Marketing

Oakhurst sells a full line of dairy products to customers in northern New England and eastern Massachusetts. Approximately 90 percent of Oakhurst's sales come from milk. Customers include large chains, such as Walmart and Market Basket, and small- to medium-sized independent grocery and convenience stores, foodservice outlets, schools, restaurants, and independent distributors. In addition to milk,

Oakhurst sells branded cream, sour cream, cottage cheese, butter, ice cream, Portland mixes, juices, drinks, and water.

Oakhurst spends more than $2 million annually on its advertising and promotion, featuring in its branding strategy "the natural goodness of Maine."[3] According to dairy farmer Eddie Benson, "Oakhurst has helped to build a market for Maine milk." He noted, "They have done a really good job of promoting Maine-grown products and marketing milk to people in Maine." [4]According to Julie-Marie Bickford, executive director of the Maine Dairy Industry Association, "Oakhurst in its markets emphasizes the local factor, more than the larger dairies. They use the Maine cachet, linking to the idea that milk comes from local farms." [5]

Cheryl Beyeler, executive director of the Maine Dairy and Nutrition Council, when asked about Stanley's knowledge of the Maine consumers, "Maine consumers don't always follow national trends, and I think Stan was acutely aware of that." [6]

Facilities and Operations

Oakhurst's sole manufacturing facility and primary warehouse are located at its headquarters in Portland. It owns three additional distribution facilities in Maine, one in New Hampshire, and one in Massachusetts. Every day approximately ten 7,500-gallon tanker trucks deliver raw milk to Oakhurst's 65,000-square-foot processing plant in Portland, Maine. And every day between 130,000 and 150,000 gallons of milk are processed. The milk comes from eighty farms throughout Maine and northern New England. Many of these farms are family owned and operated and sell their milk exclusively to Oakhurst. [7] Oakhurst has been buying its milk from some of these farms for more than seventy-five years.

In 2010, Oakhurst processed approximately twenty-two million gallons of fluid milk per year in addition to other dairy products and beverages. [8] At twenty-two million gallons of fluid milk per year, Oakhurst emits approximately a little under sixty-six million pounds, or thirty thousand metric tons, of carbon dioxide equivalent (CO_2e) annually. A metric ton is equivalent to 1,000 kilograms or about 2,200 pounds. Oakhurst used an estimated 27,500 million BTUs in milk production, packaging, and transporting.

Oakhurst samples the milk from each farm, each tanker is tested for antibiotics, and upon completion of the testing, the milk is off-loaded into raw milk storage silos. From the silos, the milk is piped to the processing area where it is separated to the proper level of butterfat. Fluid milk products are then homogenized, pasteurized, and fortified with vitamins. The product is piped into pasteurized tanks from which it is sent to filling machines in the packaging area. Cultured products like buttermilk or sour cream are standardized to the proper fat level and then sent to a cultured tank, where they are held until the culturing process is complete. After completion of the culturing process, the product is sent to another filler in the packaging area.

Eight packaging machines controlled by a computer system direct the products through a network of valves and stainless steel pipes so that each product gets to the proper filler at the right time. Each packaging machine fills a different size or style package. Quality testing is conducted every step of the way through the processing and packaging areas. Oakhurst was one of the first dairy processors to voluntarily adopt the most modern and rigorous set of federal quality standards known as HACCP (Hazardous Analysis Critical Control Points) and is one of only twelve dairies in the country currently implementing these exacting quality standards. After filling, each product is cased and moved to refrigerated warehouses where it is put away for storage until shipped to customers. In warehouse locations and on trucks, the temperature is constantly monitored to ensure the product's quality. [9] According to Bill Bennett, "The whole process, from cow to supermarket can be as short as 3 days."

Crafting and Executing a Carbon Reduction Strategy

Stan and Bill Bennett's quest for improving their company's carbon footprint and the quality of life in the communities in which it operates have guided the company's [10] decisions for nearly three decades. Oakhurst has focused on significantly reducing its carbon footprint primarily by lowering its use of fossil fuels and improving its operations by implementing lean manufacturing principles. Oakhurst's GHG emission factors include the use of electricity, natural gas, diesel fuel, heating oil, and refrigerant in the transporting, processing, packaging, and distributing of its milk to customers.

Maine's Governor's Carbon Challenge (GCC)

When Governor John Baldacci of Maine put into place a first-in-the-nation Governor's Carbon Challenge (GCC), a voluntary carbon dioxide emission reduction program, in 2004, Oakhurst was one of the first companies to sign on to the program. The goal of the GCC program was to encourage organizations to develop strategies to reduce direct emissions from on-site fuel combustion and company-owned vehicles as well as from indirect sources, such as purchased electricity. [11]

Oakhurst set a goal of a 20 percent reduction in carbon emissions by 2010 (15 percent direct GHG emissions and 5 percent indirect) using Oakhurst's 1998 carbon footprint as the baseline. With the help and encouragement of a nonprofit, Clean Air–Cool Planet (CA–CP), an inventory of Oakhurst energy consumption by operations was completed. It was determined that the company's 1998 carbon footprint was 12,594 metric tons of CO_2e. Oakhurst's carbon footprint began with raw product entering the processing plant and ended with the delivery of packaged milk to the store via truck. [12]

Operational and Logistical Efficiencies
Plant Expansion and Operational Improvements
In 2005, Oakhurst brought online a new, state-of-the-art, $10 million plant at its headquarters in Portland. [13] Working with an energy consultant and CA–CP, the facility integrated a number of energy efficient technologies, systems, and procedures. These included installing insulated cold tanks and a hot water recovery system. The hot water recovery system lowered cost and significantly reduced water use. The processing of milk uses large quantities of hot water for pasteurization and for cleaning cases and equipment. The hot water recovery system saved 2,500 gallons of heating oil per year and reduced carbon emissions by twenty-five metric tons (There are 22.384 pounds of CO_2e *per gallon* of *diesel* fuel). [14] *National Geographic* estimated that fifty-three gallons of water are used from the farm to the table for every glass of milk consumed.[15]

Switch to Biofuel
Also in 2005, Oakhurst, working with CA–CP, calculated that by switching their truck fleet from diesel to B20 (a 20 percent soy and 80 percent petroleum blend), it could lower carbon emissions. As a result of this estimate, management converted more than one hundred trucks and tractors to biodiesel fuel without any modifications. By 2006, Oakhurst Dairy operated the largest private fleet of its kind in New England to run on soy-based biodiesel. The switch reduced Oakhurst carbon emissions by 1,332 tons. [16] Bill Bennett noted, "Maine bio-fuels take the oil from the restaurants, converts it to biofuel, then we put it in the trucks that are delivering (milk products) to those same restaurants." [17]

Rerouting Software
In an additional effort in 2005 to lower its carbon emissions, Oakhurst invested in "rerouting" software for its delivery trucks. With the new software the company was able to reduce the number of its delivery routes from ninety-two to sixty-seven. By doing this, Oakhurst saved 88,000 gallons of diesel fuel and lowered its carbon emissions another 894 metric tons. [18]

Computerized Vehicle Routing and Scheduling (CVRS) for Efficient Logistics: Example Project Costs and Savings
Estimated typical costs and savings for a single-site CVRS project implemented to reduce transport costs by improving efficiency. Note that clearly, as each project is different, the costs and savings shown are only indicative, although they are representative of those experienced in practice.

Solar Panels, Portland Facility
In the spring of 2008, Oakhurst, with the help of CA–CP and Ascendant Energy, installed seventy-two solar hot water panels, approximately 2,500 square feet, on the roof of its Portland facility, making it one of the largest installations of its kind in the northeast. By preheating water, the hot water panels reduced heating oil use at the facility by more than five thousand gallons per year, lowering carbon emissions by fifty-one metric tons. [19] The payback period for the $220,000 investment in the Portland facility was estimated at eight years using 2008 fuel costs of $2.40 per gallon. [20]

Solar Panels, Waterville Facility
In 2009, Oakhurst installed a solar photovoltaic (PV) energy system on the roof of its Waterville facility. The 216 solar PV panels generated approximately forty-five thousand kilowatt hours (kWh) of electricity annually, or approximately 15 percent of the building's electricity use. The installation saved another five thousand gallons of fuel oil annually, or fifty-one metric tons. Other benefits accruing to the installations were the extension of the life of the company's boilers. [21]

Hybrid Delivery Trucks
In 2009, Oakhurst purchased a hybrid delivery truck, the first of its kind in use in the dairy industry. Oakhurst estimated saving nine gallons of fuel per day with the hybrid truck and lowering CO_2 emissions by fifty-two thousand pounds annually. [22]

Aerodynamic Truck Side Skirts and Fleet Management
In 2009, Oakhurst started installing aerodynamic side skirts to twenty-five of its large semitrailer delivery trucks. The skirts lowered annual diesel fuel cost by 6 percent to 8 percent. Each semitrailer truck traveled an average of thirty thousand miles per year. When completely equipped, the twenty-five-truck fleet would produce approximately 7.6 million fewer pounds of CO_2e annually, or 154 metric tons. [23]

Other cost-saving, waste-reduction, and carbon-lowering steps adopted by Oakhurst in the management of its truck fleet included recycling of oil filters, antifreeze, and waste oil; installing equipment in refrigeration units to improve efficiency; purchasing retreads, which often record better gas mileage and require less oil to manufacture; installing idle regulators to reduce emissions; and installing truck speed governors. [24]

Oakhurst's carbon and waste reduction actions were not isolated events or one-time investments. The company's culture fosters continuous learning and improvement. For example, Oakhurst had followed traditional industry practice of leaving truck refrigeration units running at the end of the day to keep product inventory from spoiling. Under new operational guidelines, Oakhurst now removes product from refrigeration trucks at the end of the day, and the refrigeration units are shut down, reducing annual CO_2 emissions by 120 metric tons. [25]

Measuring Results

In October 2007, CA–CP awarded Oakhurst its Climate Champion Award for corporate action on global warming. The company was selected for demonstrating an enterprise-wide commitment to reducing heat-trapping gases, for willing to be transparent in its efforts, and for helping support effective policy in the region. Also that month, Oakhurst became the first recipient of the Environmental Hero Award presented by *Heart of New Hampshire Magazine.* [26] In September 2007, as part of an effort to begin tracking GHG emissions in a select portion of its supply chain, Walmart singled out Oakhurst Dairy as one of a small percentage of the retailer's sixty thousand suppliers that were taking steps to reduce their carbon footprint. [27]

In 2008, CA–CP, Oakhurst's nonprofit environmental partner (see http://www.cleanair-coolplanet.org), published a case study on Oakhurst's environmental initiatives. CA–CP reported in the case study that by implementing a variety of initiatives since 2002, Oakhurst was able to reduce its CO_2e emissions by 1,630 metric tons annually, which is equivalent to taking 262 cars off the road for a year. [28] Also in 2008, Oakhurst was recognized by Maine's Department of Environmental Protection and the governor's administration

for meeting part of its GCC goal ahead of schedule Governor Baldacci stated at the time, "Whether it's solar, wind, tidal or innovative wood products, we must be aggressive in our pursuit of energy alternatives. Oakhurst is showing great leadership with its solar project, which further underscores the company's commitment to a cleaner planet and a stronger Maine." [29]

By the end of 2010, Oakhurst had met the GCC. Also in 2010, Oakhurst's Sustainability Committee set new carbon reduction and other resource conservation and efficiency goals for energy, water, solid waste, and transportation. The carbon reduction goals set for 2014 using 2008 as the baseline year are as follows:

- Water—20 percent
- Plant energy—20 percent
- GHG emissions—20 percent
- Transportation—20 percent
- Solid waste—5 percent [30]

Culture and Code of Ethics and Respect

Oakhurst's senior management team strives to build an organizational culture that supports its sustainability strategies and practices in the long term. In addition to partnering with CA–CP, Oakhurst hired a sustainability consultant to work with the senior managers to examine Oakhurst's social and environmental practices and to design organization change tactics to improve those practices. The consultant worked with the Bennett family to help transform and inspire employees to adopt and integrate sustainability practices into Oakhurst's operational culture. As part of this effort, internal teams were established to help bring sustainability to the forefront of Oakhurst Dairy's culture. These teams helped to establish and manage sustainability efforts including calculating carbon footprint, setting and tracking reductions, reporting to the Carbon Disclosure Project and Maine's governor's challenge. As part of the continuing training program, Oakhurst hired another consultant to help them draft a code of ethics and respect in the workplace.

KEY TAKEAWAYS

- Passionately communicating and reinforcing a clear vision and policy from the top down for a carbon reduction strategy and aligning efforts with efficiency improvements and cost savings can lead to company-wide results.
- A beneficial very first step to sustainability efforts is to measure a company's carbon footprint.
- It is important to establish systems to regularly review carbon reduction performance indicators and to constantly track, assess, and monitor progress toward carbon reduction goals and their impact on costs and profits.
- Building core competencies in sustainability can enhance business operations and profitability.

EXERCISES

1. How did Oakhurst survive as the only family dairy in northern New England? What was the role of the company's sustainable business practices?

2. How did Oakhurst benefit from its relationship with the NGO Clean Air–Cool Planet (CA–CP)? In addition to earning a number of community awards for its sustainable business practices and initiatives, what other benefits did Oakhurst receive? Is its brand name more highly respected?

3. How can detailed targets, calculations, and monitoring of sustainability efforts contribute to effective management?

4. What are the company's main challenges in 2012 and beyond?

5. Do you expect Oakhurst to continue to be an independent dairy in 2020?

[1] "Home Page," Oakhurst Dairy, http://www.oakhurstdairy.com.

[2] J. Hemmerdinger, "Maine in a Bottle: Oakhurst Dairy Homogenizes Its Marketing Message," *Portland (ME) Press Herald*, January 9, 2011, accessed January 20, 2011, http://www.pressherald.com/business/maine-in-a-bottle_2011-01-09.html.

[3] Elaine Pofeldt, "Oakhurst Dairy," Center for Small Business and the Environment, http://www.aboutcsbe.org/docs/oakhurstdairy.pdf.

[4] J. Hemmerdinger, "Maine in a Bottle: Oakhurst Dairy Homogenizes Its Marketing Message," *Portland (ME) Press Herald*, January 9, 2011, accessed January 20, 2011, http://www.pressherald.com/business/maine-in-a-bottle_2011-01-09.html.

[5] J. Hemmerdinger, "Maine in a Bottle: Oakhurst Dairy Homogenizes Its Marketing Message," *Portland (ME) Press Herald*, January 9, 2011, accessed January 20, 2011, http://www.pressherald.com/business/maine-in-a-bottle_2011-01-09.html.

[6] John Richardson, "Oakhurst CEO Stanley Bennett Dies," *Portland (ME) Press Herald*, February 25, 2011, accessed March 5, 2011, http://www.pressherald.com/news/oakhurst-ceo-stanley-bennett-dies_2011-02-25.html.

[7] J. Hemmerdinger, "Maine in a Bottle: Oakhurst Dairy Homogenizes Its Marketing Message," *Portland (ME) Press Herald*, January 9, 2011, accessed January 20, 2011, http://www.pressherald.com/business/maine-in-a-bottle_2011-01-09.html.

[8] Elaine Pofeldt, "Oakhurst Dairy," Center for Small Business and the Environment, http://www.aboutcsbe.org/docs/oakhurstdairy.pdf.

[9] "Home Page," Oakhurst Dairy, http://www.oakhurstdairy.com; J. Hemmerdinger, "Maine in a Bottle: Oakhurst Dairy Homogenizes Its Marketing Message," *Portland (ME) Press Herald*, January 9, 2011, accessed January 20, 2011, http://www.pressherald.com/business/maine-in-a-bottle_2011-01-09.html.

[10] J. Hemmerdinger, "Maine in a Bottle: Oakhurst Dairy Homogenizes Its Marketing Message," *Portland (ME) Press Herald*, January 9, 2011, accessed January 20, 2011, http://www.pressherald.com/business/maine-in-a-bottle_2011-01-09.html.

[11] Clean Air–Cool Planet, *Taking All the Right Steps: A Maine Dairy Reduces Its Carbon Footprint*, http://www.cleanair-coolplanet.org/information/pdf/Oakhurst%20Dairy%20Case%20Study%2001272009.pdf.

[12] Clean Air–Cool Planet, *Taking All the Right Steps: A Maine Dairy Reduces Its Carbon Footprint*, http://www.cleanair-coolplanet.org/information/pdf/Oakhurst%20Dairy%20Case%20Study%2001272009.pdf.

[13] "Home Page," Oakhurst Dairy, http://www.oakhurstdairy.com.

[14] Clean Air–Cool Planet, *Taking All the Right Steps: A Maine Dairy Reduces Its Carbon Footprint*, http://www.cleanair-coolplanet.org/information/pdf/Oakhurst%20Dairy%20Case%20Study%2001272009.pdf.

[15] "Hidden Water," *National Geographic*, April 2010, http://ngm.nationalgeographic.com/2010/04/last-drop/royte-text.

[16] Clean Air–Cool Planet, *Taking All the Right Steps: A Maine Dairy Reduces Its Carbon Footprint*, http://www.cleanair-coolplanet.org/information/pdf/Oakhurst%20Dairy%20Case%20Study%2001272009.pdf.

[17] "Stanley T. Bennett II, Oakhurst Dairy President, Dedicated to Community," *Forecaster (Falmouth, ME)*, March 1, 2011, http://www.theforecaster.net/content/pn-obitbennett-030211.

[18] Clean Air–Cool Planet, *Taking All the Right Steps: A Maine Dairy Reduces Its Carbon Footprint*, http://www.cleanair-coolplanet.org/information/pdf/Oakhurst%20Dairy%20Case%20Study%2001272009.pdf.

[19] Clean Air–Cool Planet, *Taking All the Right Steps: A Maine Dairy Reduces Its Carbon Footprint*, http://www.cleanair-coolplanet.org/information/pdf/Oakhurst%20Dairy%20Case%20Study%2001272009.pdf.

[20] Innovation Center for US Dairy, *Case Study—Solar Thermal Systems: Dairy Processor Carbon Reduction through Energy Efficiency (D-CREE): New England Dairy Taps Solar Energy and Hot Water Recovery to Reduce Energy Costs and Carbon Footprint*, accessed January 9, 2011, http://www.usdairy.com/Sustainability/OurCommitment/Documents/CaseStudy-SolarThermalSystems.pdf.

[21] Clean Air–Cool Planet, *Taking All the Right Steps: A Maine Dairy Reduces Its Carbon Footprint*, http://www.cleanair-coolplanet.org/information/pdf/Oakhurst%20Dairy%20Case%20Study%2001272009.pdf.

[22] "Home Page," Oakhurst Dairy, http://www.oakhurstdairy.com.

[23] "Home Page," Oakhurst Dairy, http://www.oakhurstdairy.com.

[24] "Home Page," Oakhurst Dairy, http://www.oakhurstdairy.com.

[25] Clean Air–Cool Planet, *Taking All the Right Steps: A Maine Dairy Reduces Its Carbon Footprint*, http://www.cleanair-coolplanet.org/information/pdf/Oakhurst%20Dairy%20Case%20Study%2001272009.pdf.

[26] Clean Air–Cool Planet, *Taking All the Right Steps: A Maine Dairy Reduces Its Carbon Footprint*, http://www.cleanair-coolplanet.org/information/pdf/Oakhurst%20Dairy%20Case%20Study%2001272009.pdf.

[27] Elaine Pofeldt, "Oakhurst Dairy," Center for Small Business and the Environment, http://www.aboutcsbe.org/docs/oakhurstdairy.pdf.

[28] Clean Air–Cool Planet, *Taking All the Right Steps: A Maine Dairy Reduces Its Carbon Footprint*, http://www.cleanair-coolplanet.org/information/pdf/Oakhurst%20Dairy%20Case%20Study%2001272009.pdf.

[29] Clean Air–Cool Planet, *Taking All the Right Steps: A Maine Dairy Reduces Its Carbon Footprint*, http://www.cleanair-coolplanet.org/information/pdf/Oakhurst%20Dairy%20Case%20Study%2001272009.pdf.

[30] "Home Page," Oakhurst Dairy, http://www.oakhurstdairy.com.

10.5 Going Forward: Opportunities and Challenges

LEARNING OBJECTIVES

1. Show how to set up a successful carbon reduction strategy in a capital intense, mature industry.
2. Show how one company created business value through a carbon reduction strategy.

While meeting its 2010 carbon reduction goals and still growing in sales and profits, 2011 looked to be another challenging year for the Bennett family. The death of Stanley Bennett, the rising cost of energy, and the sluggish US economy were presenting challenges for Oakhurst. According to Bill Bennett, competition is tough, and margins are thin; with fuel prices rising rapidly, 2011 will be a difficult year. [1] Government-set milk prices had been less than the cost of milk production for a couple of years. Many farmers had to make ends meet by selling hay, crops, or livestock for beef and blamed producers, including Oakhurst, for low prices. While Bill Bennett reflected that the "gripes against Oakhurst aren't fair…the company pays at least market rates and even pays incentives to farmers who keep clean operations and take extra steps to minimize livestock overcrowding and milk contamination." [2]

Oakhurst believed that its energy reduction and other sustainability programs had been successful, having an impact on reducing its carbon footprint while improving overall company profits. But the company wanted to do more. Bill Bennett highlighted how "the biggest single impact of dairy on the environment is not the energy we use at the plant but methane gas, over 75 percent released from the cows," [3] Bennett and his team were encouraging their suppliers to start using methane digesters that harvest the energy in cow manure, but none have been able to invest in the technology yet. Bennett was also investigating feed additives designed to improve cows' digestion, noting that "doing the right thing environmentally is always the right thing for your bottom line." [4]

Jer-Lindy—Case Study

Jer-Lindy Dairy

Jerry and Linda Jennissen's 140-cow herd in Minnesota is industrious, pumping out around 1,100 gallons of milk per day. But that's not the only thing they're producing. The 3,500 gallons of manure Jennissen's animals leave behind turns out to be an asset of comparable value when it is converted into power through an anaerobic digester.

The technology first came to the Jennissen's farm through a grant from the Minnesota Project, a program that encourages sustainable and profitable farming. The project hoped to partner with a mid- to small-sized farm to find the technology to make a digester work financially. Digesters have proven effective on farms with more than 300 cows, but approximately 96 percent of Minnesota dairies have between 50 and 200 cows.

"Digester technology is evolving fairly rapidly, and it needs to," Jerry Jennissen says. "We viewed it as an opportunity, and we believe that we can make it work."

By partnering with a nearby processor to add whey to the mix, the Jennissens hope to double gas production.

The digester extracts methane gas from the manure and converts it into power, which is used to run a generator. The electricity is sold on a grid. The remaining solids are separated out and used as bedding, and remaining liquids are used for fertilizer. Jennissen believes it is only a matter of time before technology like this comes to farms of all sizes.

"Things are changing so rapidly. Our digester was the third one in the state of Minnesota," Jennissen says. "There are five now, one year later. I know of several more that are currently operating or in the planning stages."

Source: Innovation Center for Dairy U.S. Dairy, *Sustainability in Practice,* http://usercontent.s3.amazonaws.com/companydocs/docs/company_docs_1295995594.pdf.

In announcing plans to celebrate the company's ninetieth year in business, Bill Bennett stated, "Our story is of one of growth, innovation, service and success. We have been able to remain family-owned and independent while competing against dairies significantly larger than we are because we have a strong brand identity and people know what we stand for and that they can count on us to deliver a high-quality product." By striving to protect and enhance "the natural goodness of Maine" through its sustainability strategies and community practices, Oakhurst has enhanced its profitability and gained a competitive advantage, a competitive advantage built on creating customer value that competitors find difficult to match. Still Bill Bennett faced many challenges as he planned for the future. While Oakhurst's opportunities and challenges with its upstream partners (milk suppliers or farmers) align with Oakhurst's previous strategic commitment to sustainability, can Oakhurst make this happen in the future? What are the possible tradeoffs in doing this with Oakhurst's suppliers and partners? Can Oakhurst continue to capitalize on its brand of promoting "the natural goodness of Maine" when milk prices are squeezing farmer profits and forcing some out of business?

KEY TAKEAWAYS

- Commitment to sustainability requires continuous innovation with constant attention to alignment of sustainability efforts with corporate values, strategy, and profitability.
- Environmental initiatives often come with an up-front investment presenting internal hurdles that, when overcome, can be worth the effort and expense.
- Investing in sustainable operations can help to make a business more efficient and profitable and can generate brand loyalty.

EXERCISES

1. What challenges face Oakhurst in 2011 and beyond? How do Oakhurst's efforts to reduce carbon emissions through operation changes help address the challenges?

2. How can your college or university lower its operating costs through sustainability efforts? If your school or college does not know their carbon footprint, suggest the Clean Air–Cool Planet (CA–CP) webpage (http://www.cleanair-coolplanet.org/toolkit/inv-calculator.php) to an administrator and consider downloading their carbon footprint calculator.

3. The Natural Resources Defense Council's November 2007 Report (see http://www.nrdc.org/policy) stated, "Although there are some exceptions, in most cases, locally produced food proves the best choice for minimizing global warming and other pollutants. In fact, another study showed that when you combined all locally grown food, it still produced less carbon dioxide emissions in transport than any one imported product. The effects all this pollution can have on our health may be reflected in high rates of asthma and other respiratory symptoms, as well as increased school absence days for children." How does Oakhurst's sustainable business model help to support the Natural Resources Defense Council's findings that buying local not only helps Maine farmers but also helps the environment?

4. What can you do to reduce your own carbon emissions? Could this reduce your costs and help you save money?

[1] J. Hemmerdinger, "Maine in a Bottle: Oakhurst Dairy Homogenizes Its Marketing Message," *Portland (ME) Press Herald*, January 9, 2011, accessed January 20, 2011, http://www.pressherald.com/business/maine-in-a-bottle_2011-01-09.html.

[2] J. Hemmerdinger, "Maine in a Bottle: Oakhurst Dairy Homogenizes Its Marketing Message," *Portland (ME) Press Herald*, January 9, 2011, accessed January 20, 2011, http://www.pressherald.com/business/maine-in-a-bottle_2011-01-09.html.

[3] Elaine Pofeldt, "Oakhurst Dairy," Center for Small Business and the Environment, http://www.aboutcsbe.org/docs/oakhurstdairy.pdf.

[4] Elaine Pofeldt, "Oakhurst Dairy," Center for Small Business and the Environment, http://www.aboutcsbe.org/docs/oakhurstdairy.pdf.

NOTES:

NOTES:

Chapter 11:
Case: Accounting for Sustainability:
How Does Timberland Do It and Why?

Sustainability reporting is about being radically transparent. That means talking about the bad just as much as the good…we want to be transparent and get feedback from others on how we're doing, or how we could be doing better. And our hope is to have a dialogue on how we can scale good solutions for our industry and then even broader beyond that.

Betsy Blaisdell, Timberland manager of environmental stewardship

LEARNING OBJECTIVES

1. Discuss Timberland's approach to sustainability.
2. Understand how corporate social responsibility relates to sustainability.
3. Discuss what it means to be a leader in sustainability and sustainability reporting and what the challenges and benefits of leadership can involve.

The purpose of this case is to introduce students to the current state of sustainability reporting in business. Timberland provides a leading example of the different ways that sustainability reporting can be performed. The case also discusses what sustainability means to Timberland and how sustainability reporting supports its environmental and social goals and progress.

11.1 Sustainability Reporting at Timberland

LEARNING OBJECTIVES

1. Understand the motivations for sustainability reporting.
2. Explain the role of different stakeholders in sustainability reporting efforts.
3. Discuss different sustainability reporting methods and reports.

How Did Timberland Get Started on Sustainability Reporting?

As a publically traded company, Timberland was required to report on its financial performance and make disclosures about the business regularly to shareholders and the general public. However, this type of reporting traditionally does little to communicate to stakeholders the sustainability actions that the company undertakes.

Through its efforts in support of employee service and on other areas related to the social responsibility, Timberland developed a strong reputation and following in the national and global corporate social responsibility (CSR) leadership communities. This attracted the attention of the NGO Ceres, which was leading a national coalition of investors, environmental organizations, and other public interest groups working with companies to address sustainability challenges. Ceres's mission is to "integrate sustainability into business practices for the health of the planet and its people." Ceres was one of the first organizations to formally introduce and advocate for the concept of sustainability reporting. Ceres believed that Timberland was a good candidate for publicly disclosing sustainability-related information specifically because of their unique employee service program. In addition to reporting metrics on employee service, the "beyond the traditional reporting" for Ceres also included the compliance area. This included reporting on the Timberland workplace and at the factories of their suppliers around the world, including issues such as child labor and unfair working conditions.

In 2001, Timberland released its first annual corporate social responsibility report. The nineteen-page report focused heavily on service related activities of the organization, including City Year. The following year, a second annual corporate social responsibility report was released. This was a more comprehensive thirty-eight-page report that included a more detailed discussion on environmental and social activities.

Starting in 2004, the annual CSR reports from Timberland began to feature the Global Reporting Initiative (GRI) sustainability reporting guidelines and featured sustainable performance indicators (SPIs). Sustainability reporting helped the company become a recognized industry leader on sustainability efforts, and this helped to strengthen the brand's name, recognition, and value.

Beginning in 2008, Timberland started reporting on key CSR performance indicators on a quarterly basis. The main report is presented in a dashboard format, which contains SPIs in each of the four CSR strategy categories.

Sidebar
Sustainability Reporting
Sustainability reporting is a statement to stakeholders and the general public about an organization's environmental and social impact and what the organization is doing to improve its impact. It is about being accountable for the ecological and social impacts that an entity has and also the solutions the entity develops around sustainability.

What Does Timberland's Sustainability Reporting Include?
Timberland's reporting and communications for sustainability includes the following:
- Full CSR reports released every other year that summarize their efforts in sustainability for the previous twenty-four months; their CSR reports are reported on their website http://responsibility.timberland.com
- Quarterly key CSR performance indicator reports and quarterly CSR dialogues
- Stakeholder engagement forums called Voices of Challenge on http://community.timberland.com, a web 2.0 platform that allows all types of stakeholders to interact with Timberland

Timberland also shares its social and environmental values and product attributes with consumers through retail messaging and product information. Their Green Index rating is intended to give consumers clear and easy to understand information about the impact their footwear choices have on the environment.

Quarterly Reporting
Timberland Quarterly Sustainable Performance Indicators
The quarterly dashboard is organized around the four Timberland CSR pillar areas: energy, product, workplace, and service. For example, average grams of volatile organic compounds per pair of footwear is a sustainable performance indicator in their product category. In each pillar area, there are three category measures and three to six total indicators reported. All together there are fifteen indicators measured between 2007 through the present.

The dashboard provides a consistent and cohesive way to engage internal and external stakeholders on CSR. It enables

Timberland to be accountable for progress against stated goals. Internally, it also allows for prioritization of resource allocation against key sustainability initiatives.

Green Index
In 2006, Timberland introduced an industry-first "nutrition label" on all of its footwear boxes in an effort to provide consumers with greater transparency about the company's environmental and community footprint and the environmental impact of the specific Timberland products consumers are purchasing.

The Green Index program is the company's primary mechanism for pursuing "cradle to cradle" product design. This index measures and communicates critical aspects of environmental performance in a format that allows Timberland to guide product design and help consumer choice. The Green Index measures three areas of product impact:
- Climate impact—greenhouse gases produced in making raw materials and during footwear production that contribute to climate change. Timberland's climate impact rating measures the emissions of greenhouse gases from the production of each material through the manufacturing of the final product.
- Chemical used—chemicals used in material and footwear production.
- Resource consumption—the score decreases as Timberland uses materials that require less land and water and fewer chemicals to produce.

The data are compiled to give a product an index score from ten to zero, with ten being a high impact and zero being no impact at all.

The Timberland CSR Team
Timberland has a team of employees dedicated to CSR in the company. It consists of a vice president of CSR, four managers, a team of fourteen code-of-conduct employees, and two community service employees. The CSR team works closely with senior management, including the CEO.

In December 2006, the company created a formal CSR committee within its board of directors. This group consists of four board members who are responsible for guiding all CSR strategy development. To accomplish this task, the committee meets regularly with the CSR leadership team to help set the strategic agenda and hold the team accountable for their actions.

Two members of the current CSR team are Beth Holzman, the company's CSR strategy and reporting manager, and Betsy Blaisdell, the manager of environmental stewardship. Beth Holzman was a manager at Ceres before joining Timberland and interacted with Timberland in that capacity. Betsy Blaisdell had previous experience working in the New Hampshire state government and performing environmental research at the University of New Hampshire. The CSR team's responsibilities include developing the metrics to report and standardizing the reporting. It also includes collecting information, preparing reports, communicating information to senior management, and interacting with stakeholders.

A key objective is to ensure that the sustainability reports are used and integrated into the other departments at Timberland. As Betsy Blaisdell describes it, "Everybody wants to do the right thing at Timberland. And so for us, it's taking something that can be a really complex environmental metric, like kilograms of CO_2 for a pair of shoelaces, and translating it into: this is the best choice, this is a good choice, and we really discourage you from using this approach."

Another key objective is to standardize the reporting method and information in order to make reporting easier and more cost effective within Timberland but also within the industry. The goal is to create standardized sustainability metrics and standardized measures of environmental performance for Timberland's products. The goal of standardization being that instead of Timberland collecting the information through their own business systems, suppliers would provide the information into a registry that Timberland and other companies could access.

Driving Forces behind Sustainability Reporting

In many respects, former CEO Jeffrey Swartz was the leader on CSR reporting efforts and a driving principle of the company's sustainability reporting efforts has been radical transparency. For Timberland, radical transparency is about talking about the bad as much as the good. It is about being provocative, sharing information with the intent of receiving a reaction and response from stakeholders. It includes communicating things that are material and important to the company.

For example, Jeffrey Swartz was the champion of Timberland's "nutrition" labeling for shoes. His view was that if consumers could go into a supermarket and look at a couple different boxes of cereal and know what's good or bad for them, why couldn't they do that going into a footwear

store or going into a large retailer and see similar information reported?

On their website "Voices of Challenge," Timberland managers share very difficult challenges and concerns related to sustainability and ask for candid feedback through blogs and social media. And consumers and NGO organizations have asked challenging questions to Timberland through this resource.

As Betsy Blaisdell describes it, "I think we're always pushed further ahead by external stakeholders. And I'd say we're largely influenced by requests that we get externally for improving or shifting our reporting. We had a major issue with Greenpeace a couple years ago. It had to do with transparency in our leather supply chain in Brazil and it really pushed us to have an industry dialogue about how can we take our protocol for assessing the environmental performance of our tanneries, and push that further back down the supply chain. That led to more transparency. And that was purely an external push from Greenpeace that led to that." For Timberland consumers are always the most important stakeholder group to reach, but the reality, at least for now, is that very few consumers actually read, understand, and act on the sustainability reports.

According to Betsy Blaisdell, "There is evidence that significant numbers of consumers do read the nutrition label on the footwear. But very few probably fully understand what it means…it's hard for them to really use it because it's not relative to anything. It's not like they can compare a Timberland product with a Nike product right now and say, OK, price, performance, and aesthetics alike, I'll take this shoe over this shoe. So I think it's nice to do for consumers, but it's not necessarily impacting their purchasing decisions, which is where we would love to take it."

Other stakeholder groups that are leading Timberland to expand its sustainability reporting are the investor community, peer businesses, and other companies, including stores and retail outlets that Timberland sells its product to. Outside the United States, there is more governmental involvement around sustainability reporting. For example, in France the government is moving to pass legislation that would require the nation's companies to begin measuring the environmental life cycle impacts of their products. France is leveraging what some industry groups in Europe have already developed. The French government recognizes that businesses have been ahead of government on sustainability reporting, and this is the case of Timberland in the United States.

- Unlike financial reporting for publically traded companies, there are limited experience and standards for sustainability reporting.
- The key drivers of sustainability reporting are company values and desire to engage proactively with external groups, senior management personal priorities, and environmental action leadership groups, such as Ceres and Greenspace.
- Timberland's sustainability reporting includes biannual reports, quarterly performance dashboards, and eco-labels.
- Timberland provides for stakeholder involvement in its sustainability efforts through its "Voices of Challenge" site providing the opportunity for 360-degree feedback.
- Timberland has a separate CSR department of approximately twenty employees with leadership from the board of directors and the CEO.
- Radical transparency and stakeholder engagement are the driving forces for sustainability reporting at Timberland.

EXERCISES

1. Discuss Timberland's interpretation of radical transparency. Is radical transparency a requirement of sustainability reporting?
2. What do you think of the company using the "Voices of Challenge" as part of its sustainability reporting process? Do you think it is wise to provide the opportunities for stakeholders to have a voice in the direction of the company's efforts?
3. Discuss Timberland's sustainability reporting choices. Review their most recent biannual report and quarterly performance dashboard at http://responsibility.timberland.com/reporting/report-archive. What recommendations would you make to Timberland about their reporting efforts?

11.2 Business Value of Sustainability Reporting

LEARNING OBJECTIVES

1. Understand the key benefits of sustainability reporting.
2. Explain the difficulty of quantifying the benefits of sustainability reporting.
3. Discuss the key challenges in sustainability reporting and how they might be overcome.
4. Describe the different dimensions or perspectives of sustainability materiality and why they are important.
5. Explain the importance of materiality in determining what to report on in sustainability efforts.

Benefits

Timberland has a goal of being the reference brand for sustainability and sustainability reporting, and they do not limit that to within their own industry. The company wants to be a leader, the brand that's pushing the edge on transparency and reporting.

There is evidence that the efforts on sustainability and branding around sustainability reporting are affecting Timberland profitability, market share, and customer loyalty. Timberland's highest-margin products—contributing the most on a dollar of sales basis to profitability—are the company's Earthkeepers products and this is suggestive that consumers are willing to pay a premium for a low environmental impact product.

There is also anecdotal evidence of sustainability reporting contributing to Timberland's market performance; however, the company has struggled to put a hard dollar value on this. Timberland's marketing managers and public relations professional report that sustainability efforts and the various sustainability reports Timberland have released over the last several years has resulted in an increased number of positive media impressions. Timberland receives other kinds of anecdotal evidence in market research and focus groups with consumers that sustainability initiatives generate brand heat. Brand heat is a marketing term to describe the positive feelings when exposed to a brand name. There is even less evidence that brand heat actually leads to a purchase. A challenge for Timberland is quantifying and linking sustainability to the financial bottom line.

Challenges

One of the hardest challenges for Timberland was determining the right metrics to report on. Timberland, in part, used the indicators from the Global Reporting Initiative (GRI) as a starting point. However, the GRI has many performance indicators and many were not relevant to Timberland's stakeholders or material to Timberland.

For Timberland the most important areas to report on, measure, and act on are those that are material to the company. Timberland's areas of focus for materiality are the environment, consumers, and other stakeholders, including government. Timberland prioritizes measurement and action on the areas that are at the intersection of these three dimensions of materiality.

Dimensions of materiality at Timberland.
For example, Leather and rubber use is highly material to Timberland's business operations. These two inputs have significantly more impact on the environment than any other inputs because of the volume of leather and rubber used in the manufacturing process and by the very nature of the materials. These manufacturing inputs are material to the environment, to customers, and to stakeholders and as a result are areas of focus and reporting for Timberland.

This strategy helps the company focus on the areas that have the greatest impact. For example, customers might think Timberland should focus on packaging, such as footwear boxes, because it is one of the aspects of the product that they most interact with. The environmental impact of their use of leather and rubber is much more material (significant) to the company's ecological and social impact than its use of cardboard for shoeboxes, as the boxes come from recycled sources and also can be easily recycled.

Another major challenge for Timberland is the constant tension between measuring more metrics due to demands from different stakeholder groups and the resources required by Timberland to provide those metrics. This was a lesson learned by Timberland as the company started its sustainability reporting efforts. At the beginning, Timberland struggled with trying to provide more and more sustainable performance indicators due to stakeholder requests. The company expended significant resources to collect and report on the different disclosure requests that they received, which distracted the company from undertaking the activities necessary to lead to substantive improvements in its environmental and social impact.

Efforts at Standardization and Integration
Initiating sustainability reporting and developing the appropriate communication methods has been a significant undertaking for the company over the past decade. Sustainability reporting had to be done largely outside of Timberland's regular business units and systems. A separate reporting software system was developed for storing sustainability performance indicators (SPIs), but, at the time, it was too complex for the corporate social responsibility (CSR) reporting system to be integrated with the company's accounting and finance system tools or product design systems. They were all developed on different software platforms and did not communicate.

The other reporting and management systems were not designed to include sustainability measures, as it was not part of standard business practice. For example, in designing a new product, there was limited product design reporting system ability to take into consideration the sustainability impacts of different designs, as they were not developed for environmental reporting.

Just recently (2011), business decision software systems companies, such as SAP, and the designers of product life cycle management systems are developing systems software that have environmental modules. This means that what were two or three separate systems before can now become more of one integrated system to include environmental and, eventually, social impact along with product design and financial analysis.

Timberland is moving toward being able to upload CSR metrics into their financial information and product design systems. Their environmental and financial information systems are starting to "talk" to one another. Timberland can take into consideration reductions in energy or material usage reductions from both an environmental and financial perspective.

The benefits include not only being able to better tie environmental efforts with bottom line considerations but also enabling the CSR team to reach and impact key decision makers in finance and product design who were outside the Timberland CSR reporting system. The sharing of information and reporting systems integration allows different business units and functional areas to begin to speak a more common language and take a more systems and full-cost and benefit perspective in their decision making about financial, product design, and sustainability actions.

Timberland is focusing its sustainability reporting efforts increasingly on this integrated systems perspective, using a core set of metrics to help identify problems and then identifying root causes and finding the best solutions. The company can then link the problem and solution to the financial performance of the firm.

As Betsy Blaisdell describes it,
> *The environment will be embedded in the financial statement. I think we are experiencing the merging of the two right now. I think 20 years from now, the business value will have been demonstrated and that environmental metrics will become a part of the financial statement, the links will have been created, in that CSR will be a part of everybody's role, versus a distinct stand-alone department.*

My hope is that in 20 years, this is just a part of the business—the normal business school program. It's a part of the normal business acumen. And that folks are educated and have a carve-out, or have distinct responsibilities within their regular

business job to make sure that the commerce and the justice piece go hand in hand, versus living in different parts.

KEY TAKEAWAYS

- What is most important to track and report out in sustainability reporting are activities with material impact on the environment, consumers, communities at large, and business profits.
- What is not tracked and reported on will be difficult for business managers to act on.
- It is difficult to quantify the benefits of sustainability in general and sustainability reporting in particular.
- Sustainability reporting can enhance business reputation and branding.

EXERCISES

1. Discuss some of the challenges faced by Timberland in relation to its sustainability reporting. What are some of the benefits they have experienced?
2. Do you think sustainability can generate "brand heat"? Why or why not? Go on Facebook and look for an example of a "green" product that is generating positive discussion. Do you see any ways that the company is commercially capturing the value of that discussion (such as a link or app that would lead to a sale of the product)?

11.3 Looking Forward: New Corporate Parent and New Corporate Social Responsibility Leader

On June 13, 2011, V. F. Corporation (http://www.vfc.com/about) announced the purchase of Timberland for over $2.2 billion. V. F. already owned and operated several well-known apparel brands such as the North Face, Wrangler, and Lee. In announcing the purchase V. F. CEO Eric Wiseman commented, "The Timberland brand is synonymous with high-quality outdoor footwear and apparel. We believe the unique rugged outdoor positioning of Timberland will perfectly complement the premium, technical positioning of The North Face brand. This acquisition will continue the transformation of VF's portfolio, propelling VF's outdoor and action sports businesses to 50% of total revenue."

V. F. offered $43 for each Timberland share, a premium of 43 percent to Timberland's closing price the day before the offer. On the announcement day, Timberland shares climbed $13.21, or 44 percent, to $43.20. Timberland stock had traded between $15.07 and $45.72 from June 10, 2010, to June 10, 2011, and was at $30 before the offer. The owners of about three quarters of Timberland's stock, including Chairman Sidney Swartz and CEO Jeffrey Swartz, entered into a voting agreement and gave written consent for the deal on July 26.

V. F.'s shares rose by 10 percent after the deal was announced, which added about $1 billion to the V. F.'s market capitalization. This was atypical as shares in the buying company usually fall due to stockholders expectations that most acquisitions end up destroying value. V. F. says it intends to both grow Timberland's sales and increase

Timberland's sales efficiency. In 2010, Timberland's operating margin was 9 percent, which was considerably lower than V. F.'s operating margin of 20 percent. [1]

V. F. has not been a recognized leader on corporate social responsibility (CSR) or sustainability. The company is at an early stage of addressing climate change and other issues related to climate change. According to the Climate Counts Company Scorecard on V. F., the corporation has started to measure its company-wide impact it has on global warming (i.e., its greenhouse gas emissions or climate footprint) and has made some efforts to reduce its impact on global warming (i.e., its greenhouse gas emissions or climate footprint) through the North Face (http://www.climatecounts.org/scorecard_score.php?co=58). It has, however, shown minimal public information that it supports public policy that addresses climate change and provides limited information on its company-wide efforts to address climate change.

On June 28, 2011, after the announcement of V. F.'s purchase of Timberland, the company hired a new vice president for corporate social responsibility, former Dell executive Mark Newton. Newton is joining Timberland following eight years with Dell, most recently as executive director of global sustainability, where he was responsible for balancing the company's growth strategy to minimize impacts on natural and human resources across the value chain. During his tenure with Dell, he directed global policy development, stakeholder engagements, and corporate strategies on environmental and social issues. Prior to joining Dell, Newton led environmental technology programs at

Apple and Motorola. He sits on the advisory boards of Clean Production Action and Carbonfund.org.

Newton will lead the CSR global team. [2] He will report to Timberland's CFO Carrie Teffner and be responsible for the following:

- Overseeing Timberland's effort to demonstrate environmental leadership and reduce the company's environmental impact as a global brand
- Ensuring that the human rights standards set forth by the company's code of conduct are adhered to and enforced by all Timberland vendors and suppliers worldwide
- Creating a global standard for community service through innovation, regional relevance, and employee engagement
- Executing against Timberland's commitment to transparency and reporting by engaging a diverse set of stakeholders

Jeff Swartz's last day as CEO of Timberland was September 13, 2011. In his final blog post he wrote the following:

Recently, I listened to the acquirer's CEO addressing Timberland employees, in an open air town hall meeting (we take the 10 minutes of New England summer time seriously here, and so when we can meet outdoors, we do). It tore my guts out, to sit in the community gathering as a listener, watching my colleagues watching the new boss, wondering what changes are in store for our brand, our business, our community…an environmental activist in our ranks rose, way in the back, to ask the new guy, the Boss to Be, about sustainability.
"Tell us, please, why sustainability is important to you."
And the man with whom I negotiated hard and long for the best possible deal for shareholders stood his ground, and answered, authentically and naturally. "The answer is simple—we believe that sustainability is good for the business and good for the world environmentally."

He went on; the answer got more detailed and more concrete. But I had stopped listening.

For 30 years, we've been trying, fighting, struggling, to choreograph the intricate interaction between shareholder value, consumer demand, and social accountability. I have the scars, and the long list of failed efforts, incomplete outcomes, unrealized dreams and frustrated ambitions before my eyes all the time that reflect this passionate effort. And yet in this poignant moment of transition, from a business run by my family for three generations to a business to be run by relative strangers—here is the CEO of a 10B$ powerhouse, talking about sustainability simply and easily—good for business, good for the earth. And he means what he says. And it strikes me, hard, as I sit there—30 years later, a vitally important conversation has shifted. Maybe, there comes a time to say, "my job here is finished." [3]

KEY TAKEAWAYS

- V.F. Corporation has had limited efforts in sustainability, but the acquisition of Timberland provides it with the opportunity to be a global leader in business sustainability.
- The stock acquisition of Timberland provided great value to the stockholders of V. F. Corporation.

EXERCISES

1. Prepare a memo for V. F. that summarizes Timberland's experience with CSR and sustainability reporting. What are the benefits and difficulties of the different activities within reporting? What are the main lessons that have been learned?
2. Review V. F.'s corporate website. Prepare a two-page memo to the company's CEO outlining whether V. F. should more broadly adopt Timberland's CSR reporting, identifying which of its brands would most likely benefit the most from sustainability reporting.
3. Upon reviewing former CEO Jeff Swartz's final blog post, do you agree or disagree with his finding that the business world has shifted to sustainability?
4. Review Timberland's timeline included at the end of this chapter. Do you think including environmental and social indicators in the timeline paints a fuller picture of the history and actions of the company? Why or why not?

Table 11.1 Timberland Timeline

Year	Key Events	Sustainable Performance Indicators				
		Economic	Ecological	Social		
		Revenue / Net Income (in Millions of Dollars)	Stock Price (First of Year and Adjusted for Splits)	GHG Emissions Inventory (Metric Tons)	Employees	Community Service Hours
1955	Nathan Swartz bought the remaining interest in Abington Shoe Company and welcomed his sons into the company, manufacturing private label shoes for leading brand manufacturers for almost 10 years.					
1973	The Swartz family developed the "Timberland" brand name. Timberland created its first guaranteed waterproof boot under the Timberland name.					
1975	Company produces 25,000 Timberland brand boots and approaches the $1 million mark in sales.					
1978	The Swartz family changed the name of the company to the Timberland Company.					
1980	Timberland footwear introduced into first international market—Italy.					
1987	Timberland went public on the American Stock Exchange.		$1.80 (June 30, 1987)			
1989	Timberland partnered with City Year, Inc., the Boston-based youth "urban peace corps," to support community service. Since then, Timberland has provided over $10 million to City Year helping them to expand their service program to 13 cities across the United States.	$156/$6	$1.84			
1992	To sustain the communities in which its employees live and work, Timberland developed what later became the Path of Service program, a progressive corporate policy offering employees 16 hours paid leave to perform community service. Timberland launched its "Give Racism the Boot" awareness campaign supporting diversity and standing up against oppression internationally.	$291/$13	$1.14			

Year	Key Events	Sustainable Performance Indicators				
		Economic	Ecological	Social		
		Revenue / Net Income (in Millions of Dollars)	Stock Price (First of Year and Adjusted for Splits)	GHG Emissions Inventory (Metric Tons)	Employees	Community Service Hours
1997	Timberland increased the benefit of paid employee volunteer time to 40 hours. Timberland introduced apparel for kids.	$796/$47	$4.72		5,100	17,500
2000	The company was listed as one of the "100 Best Corporate Citizens" by Business Ethics Corporate Social Responsibility Report. Timberland issues its first annual corporate social responsibility report.	$1,091/$124	$12.47		5,400	34,200
2006	The company set a new standard for product transparency and increased its efforts to minimize environmental impact by introducing new, more eco-conscious packaging for its footwear products and a "nutritional label"—product information label that details aspects of the company's environmental and community footprint. The company unveiled a solar panel installation at its distribution center in Ontario, California. At the time, the system was one of the 50 largest in the world, generated 60% of the power for the distribution facility, and reduced the facility's greenhouse gas emissions by an estimated 218 metric tons per year.	$1,568/$106	$32.92	25,599	6,300	80,600
2009	Shrinks the carbon footprint of its US stores by an additional 11% by switching 70% of its North American stores to LED lighting. Timberland and Soles4Souls launch nationwide in-store shoe donation program.	$1,286/$57	$11.68	16,273	5,700	82,300
2010	Timberland ranks #2 on Climate Counts' list of companies making aggressive strides in fighting climate change.	$1,429/$97	$18.19	15,889	5,600	75,900
2011	Timberland stock reaches highest price ever at $45.72 on April 28. VF Corporation announces purchases of Timberland for $2.2 billion on June 13.		$24.79			

Sources: "Our History," Timberland, http://www.timberlandonline.co.uk/timberland-corporate-timeline/about_timberland_corporate_timeline%2Cdefault%2Cpg.html; "Home Page," Timberland, http://www.timberland.com/category/index.jsp?categoryId=4089424; "About Timberland," Timberland, http://www.timberlandonline.co.uk/timberland-corporate-timeline/about_timberland_corporate_timeline%2Cdefault%2Cpg.html; "About Us: Timeline," Timberland, http://www.timberland.com/category/index.jsp?categoryId=4089424.

[1] Marc Gunther, "Timberland's Jeff Swartz: 'This Is Hard,'" *Marc Gunther* (blog), June 14, 2011, http://www.marcgunther.com/2011/06/14/timberlands-jeff-swartz-this-is-hard.

[2] "Timberland Hires CSR Vice President," Environmental Leader, http://www.environmentalleader.com/2011/06/28/timberland-creates-role-of-csr-vice-president.

[3] Jeff Swartz, "Endings and Beginnings," *The Bootmakers Blog*, September 13, 2011, http://blog.timberland.com/jeff-swartz/endings-and-beginnings.

NOTES:

Chapter 12:
Case: Sustainable Investing:
Pax World Helping Investors Change the World

We at Pax World understand that investing is rooted in one's aspirations for a better, more secure future—it's really all about tomorrow. Moreover, we believe that Sustainable Investing is an investment approach that is particularly focused on the future—a methodology that searches for better-managed companies that are better positioned for long-term business success. We think our Sustainable Investing approach is right for the times, and is right for our investors.

　Pax World (*http://www.paxworld.com/about-pax-world/why-invest-pax*)

LEARNING OBJECTIVES

1. Understand socially responsible investing (SRI) and its relationship to sustainability.
2. Describe how SRI compares with traditional investment approaches.
3. Explain the key elements of SRI.
4. Understand the size of the market for SRI, both absolute size and relative size to total investment market.
5. Discuss SRI market growth prospects.
6. Explain the key challenges of implementing a socially responsible approach to investments.

In a speech to the Boston Economic Club on June 15, 2010, Joseph Keefe, president and CEO of Pax World Management, LLC, stated,

> *We need a new design. We need to take this moment in time to imagine what the Next Economy might look like—an economy that is both post-Sustainability Crisis and post-Financial Crisis. It seems clear to me, first of all, that over the next few decades, market capitalism will need to undergo a Sustainability Revolution equal in significance to the Industrial Revolution that ushered in the modern period. In order for this to happen, corporate behavior, market behavior and investor behavior will need to change. In each case, they will need to become more sustainable—which means, among other things, to behave in a way that focuses more on the long term. Investors can play an important role in this great transformation, as well they should: the transition from an industrial age economy powered by coal and oil to a sustainable economy powered by clean energy and new technologies will unleash a new era of economic and investment opportunities. Sustainable Investing, as I am using the term, is not only a strategy to hasten this historic transformation, but also to harvest the potential investment returns associated with it. [1]*

[1] Joseph F. Keefe, "Sustainable Investing and the Next Economy" (speech, Federal Reserve Bank of Boston, June 15, 2010), http://www.paxworld.com/about-pax-world/viewpoint.

12.1 Introduction to Socially Responsible Investing (SRI)
LEARNING OBJECTIVES

1. Describe what is meant by socially responsible investing (SRI).
2. Explain what a mutual fund is and what can be of interest to individual investors.
3. Understand why many investors were reluctant to invest in SRI funds.
4. Describe how Pax World helped to convince individuals to invest in SRI funds.

Socially responsible investing (SRI)—also known as sustainable investing—refers to investment strategies that seek to not only provide financial return but also be consistent with moral values and have positive societal impact. SRI can be as straightforward as an investor who avoids investing in any industry they find morally questionable—such as a tobacco manufacturer—to as complex as a billion-dollar fund that screens in or out many different types of investment opportunities based on key performance indicators in environmental and social areas.

SRI recognizes that corporate responsibility and societal concerns are valid and important criteria for investment decisions. While SRI refers to a spectrum of investing activities, in general, SRI will be referred to as a broad-based approach that invests in companies that manage themselves in ways related to sustainability, including environmental protection and human rights. However, as mentioned previously, SRI can also be morally based and avoid so-called sin industries, such as those involved in alcohol, tobacco, gambling, animal testing, or weapons.

SRI roots back to biblical times, as Jewish law provided specific guidance on ethical investment. In colonial times, Quaker and Methodist immigrants to the United States brought with them the concept of values-based investing exercised by their refusal to invest in slavery or war. In the 1700s, Methodist reverend John Wesley (1703–91) outlined his basic tenets of social investing—including not to harm your neighbor through your business practices and to avoid industries, such as tanning, because of their potential to harm the health of workers.

Modern SRI can trace its roots to the 1960s and 1970s in the United States as concerns over civil rights, the Vietnam War, gender equality, the environment, and nuclear power all emerged. [1] Pax World Funds was created in 1971 as the first SRI mutual fund by Luther Tyson and Jack Corbett, both of whom worked for the United Methodist Church, for investors who did not want to invest in companies involved in the Vietnam War.

SRI investment grew dramatically in the 1980s as significant societal events—for example, apartheid in South Africa, the nuclear disaster in Chernobyl, and the oil spill in Alaska by the Exxon Valdez—led millions of people and organizations to invest in companies that were more socially and environmentally responsible. Other social phenomenon in the 1990s, such as Nike's use of sweatshops, increased respect for indigenous populations, and tropical deforestation, further supported investment in SRI. By 1995, SRI had grown to fifty-five mutual funds with $12 billion in assets under management. Most recently, climate change has motivated new waves of SRI investment by both institutional investors and individual investors.

SRI mutual funds now span a wide range of investments opportunities, including domestic and international securities. In addition to mutual funds, a growing number of financial products are becoming available that target SRI, including hedge funds and exchange traded funds (ETFs).

The performance of SRI funds has slowly convinced investors that there is not a significant trade-off—and there even may be some positive correlation—between social and financial performance. At the end of 2009, a review of 160 socially responsible mutual funds found that 65 percent of the funds had outperformed their benchmarks—funds with similar investment objectives. [2]Between 1995 and 2010, SRI had grown significantly.

As of 2010, there were 250 mutual funds using SRI criteria in the United States, with assets of $316.1 billion. [3] These funds increasingly compete with traditional mutual funds and SRI-focused funds, such as Pax World Funds, and increasingly compete with the mutual funds industry giants, such as Fidelity Investments, Vanguard, and T. Rowe Price, who have started SRI funds as part of their family of funds. Investors in the traditional funds are increasingly likely to move at least some of their assets to an SRI investment approach. How fast they do this and how much of their investments they direct to SRI funds and to mutual fund companies that only engage in SRI, such as Pax World, will depend on how important a sustainability- and moral values–based approach to personal financial investing becomes for households in the United States and in other nations and also on SRI fund performance and marketing.

Mutual Fund Industry
At the end of 2010, there were 7,581 mutual funds in the United States with combined assets of $11.8 trillion, according to the Investment Company Institute (ICI), a national trade association of investment companies in the United States. This is about 80 percent of the size of total US annual economic activity (gross domestic product) of $15 trillion. Worldwide assets invested in mutual funds totaled $24.7 trillion.

Mutual funds are investment vehicles that are made up of a pool of funds collected from many investors for the purpose of investing in securities, such as stocks and bonds. Anyone who invests in a mutual fund receives shares of the fund. Each share represents an interest in the fund's total investments, often times called its investment portfolio. Portfolios include equity (ownership) shares in a large number of publically traded companies and bond holdings. Bonds are similar to loans and are issued by companies and public entities, such as cities and states, and purchased by mutual funds and other investors.

The value of mutual fund shares rise and fall depending on the performance of the underlying securities (stocks and bonds) in the portfolio. Similar to a shareholder in a corporation, an investor receives a proportional share of income and interest generated by the portfolio mutual fund units, or shares. Shares can typically be purchased or redeemed (sold) directly from the mutual fund company at the fund's current net asset value (NAV) per share.

In 2010, more than fifty-one million US households invested in mutual funds, or about 44 percent of all households. The median number of mutual funds owned by households was four and the median amount that fund-owning households invested in mutual funds was $100,000.

Mutual funds have advantages compared to direct investing in individual securities, including increased diversification, daily liquidity, professional investment management, service and convenience, and ease of comparison. One of the main advantages of mutual funds is that they give diversification to investors with relatively modest amounts to invest. Disadvantages of mutual funds include management fees and less control over timing of recognition of capital gains or capital losses.

In the United States, all mutual funds are registered with the US Securities and Exchange Commission (SEC). The SEC was formed after the stock market crash of 1929 in response to abuses in the widely unregulated financial securities markets. Its mission is "to protect investors, maintain fair, orderly, and efficient markets, and facilitate capital formation." [4] Under the 1940 Investment Company Act, which governs the mutual fund industry, a mutual fund consists of the shareholders and a board of directors (if organized as a corporation) or board of trustees (if organized as a trust) who are fiduciaries charged with acting in the best interests of the shareholders. A fiduciary duty is the highest standard of care. A fiduciary is expected to be extremely loyal to the persons to whom it owes some responsibility; the fiduciary must not put its personal interests before its duty and must not profit from his position as a fiduciary, unless the principal explicitly consents.

The board of directors or trustees is charged with hiring a professional money manager or investment adviser to manage the assets of mutual fund. The fund manager, also known as the fund sponsor or fund management company, invests the mutual fund's assets in accordance with the fund's investment objectives. A fund manager must be a registered investment adviser. The fund manager's responsibilities include portfolio management, legal compliance, operations, and marketing. Mutual fund managers generate revenue by charging investors fees, usually as a percentage of funds managed. These fees are called management fees. The fees normally vary from .3 percent to 1 percent of funds under management. [5] Multiple mutual funds that are managed by the same fund manager and that have the same brand name are known as a "fund family" or "fund complex." The two largest mutual fund companies have total assets well above $1 trillion (see Table 12.1 "Five Largest Mutual Fund Companies by Assets under Management, November 30, 2009").

Table 12.1 Five Largest Mutual Fund Companies by Assets under Management, November 30, 2009

Top Five Fund Families	Assets under Management (in Billions of Dollars)
Vanguard	1,313.39
Fidelity Investments	1,215.41
American Funds	926.68
JPMorgan	449.41
iShares	360.07

The largest single mutual fund, American Fund's Income Fund of America, had net assets of just under $69 billion in 2011. The largest SRI mutual funds' single funds are small in comparison, Parnassus' Equity Income Fund has $3.7 billion and the Pax World Balanced Fund has $1.8 billion. The traditional mutual fund companies have also started SRI funds, which are included in their total but these funds are a small portion of their family of funds.

Types of Mutual Funds

The types of mutual funds vary according to a fund's investment objective. A fund's investment objective will usually seek capital gains (gains from the sale of portfolio securities), income (interest and dividends earned on the portfolio securities), or a combination of both. A mutual fund's portfolio is structured and maintained to match the investment objectives stated in its prospectus.

The following is a list of common categories of mutual funds:

- **Money market.** A money market fund seeks the safety of principal by investing in high-quality, short-term securities. This type of fund is designed with the aim that an investor's principal should not decrease in value.
- **Growth.** A growth fund invests primarily in the common stock of well-established companies. This type of fund may invest for long-term capital gains.
- **Income.** An income fund invests in debt securities. Hence this type of fund is designed for investors who desire periodic income payments. There are, however, substantial differences and varying degrees of risk among income funds depending on the credit quality of

the debt issuer, the maturity of the debt instrument, and the prevailing interest rates.

- **Balanced.** A balanced fund, as the name implies, invests for both growth and income. The fund will invest in both equity and debt securities. A balanced fund seeks to provide long-term growth through its equity component as well as income to be generated by the portfolio's debt securities.

SRI Industry

As of 2011, the Forum for Sustainable and Responsible Investment, SIF (formerly the Social Investment Forum), identified $3.07 trillion in total assets under management using one or more of what SIF defined as the three core SRI strategies—screening, shareholder advocacy, and community investing. [6] This includes mutual fund investing. Between 2007 and 2010, SRI experienced a 13 percent growth rate from $2.71 trillion in 2007. About one out of every $8 under professional management in the United State—or 12.2 percent of the $25.2 trillion in total assets under management tracked by Thomson Reuters Nelson—was involved in SRI. Three Core Approaches in SRI [7]

There are three core approaches in SRI. First, screening is the practice of evaluating investment portfolios or mutual funds based on social, environmental, and good corporate governance criteria. This includes both positive and negative screens. Positive screening, or "buy" indicators, involves including strong corporate social responsibility (CSR) performers, avoiding poor CSR performers, or otherwise incorporating CSR factors into the process of investment analysis and management. Generally, social investors seek to own profitable companies that make positive contributions to society. "Buy" lists may include enterprises with, for example, strong environmental practices, products that are safe and useful, and operations that respect human rights around the world.

Conversely, many social investors avoid investing in companies whose products and business practices are harmful to individuals, communities, or the environment. This is a negative screen, or "don't buy or sell" indicator. It is a common mistake to assume that SRI "screening" is simply exclusionary, or only involves negative screens. Positive SRI screens are being used more and more frequently to invest in companies that are leaders in adopting clean technologies and exceptional social and governance practices.

Second, **shareholder advocacy** involves socially responsible investors who take an active role to encourage corporations to improve their social and environmental practices. These efforts include talking (or "dialoguing") with companies on issues related to environmental, social, and governance (ESG) issues. Shareholder advocacy also frequently involves filing shareholder resolutions on such topics as corporate governance, climate change, political contributions, gender or racial discrimination, pollution, and labor practices. Shareholder resolutions are then presented for a vote to all owners of a corporation.

The process of dialogue and filing shareholder resolutions generates investor pressure on company management; often garners media attention; and educates the public on social, environmental, and labor issues. Such resolutions filed by SRI investors are aimed at improving company policies and practices, encouraging management to exercise good corporate citizenship, and promoting long-term shareholder value and financial performance.

Third, **community investing** directs capital from investors and lenders to communities that are underserved by traditional financial services institutions, such as banks. Community investing provides access to credit, equity, capital, and basic banking products that these communities would otherwise lack. In the United States and around the world, community investing makes it possible for local organizations to provide financial services to low-income individuals and to supply capital for small businesses and vital community services, such as affordable housing, child care, and health care. Community investing is the fastest growing area of SRI. From 2007 to 2010, community investing grew more than 60 percent, from $25 billion to $41.7 billion in assets.

Among the mutual fund companies that use an SRI-type approach, Pax World is commonly recognized as the third largest (http://ussif.org/resources/mfpc).[8] Parnassus Investments (http://www.parnassus.com), based in San Francisco, has about $6 billion in assets under management. Calvert, which includes both SRI and more traditional investing, has sustainability-focused funds of approximately $5 billion (http://www.calvert.com/sri.html). All the SRI funds, as with other investment funds, were larger in assets before the financial crisis of 2008–9. Pax World experienced nearly a 40 percent decline in assets under management during the sharp stock market decline.

Smaller SRI funds have been consolidating over time. For example, Sentinel Funds (http://www.sentinelinvestments.com) bought Citizens Funds in 2008. And further consolidation is expected as some of the big, traditional mutual fund firms enter the market and try to buy SRI mutual fund firms or consider launching their own suite of SRI-like products to compete with Pax World Investments and other SRI funds in response to increasing numbers of institutional and private investors asking for funds with social objectives.

KEY TAKEAWAYS

- Socially responsible investing (SRI) refers to investment strategies that seek moral values and social impact and provide financial return.
- Mutual funds are investment vehicles that allow investors to receive professional management, diversification, and liquidity for a relatively small investment.
- Pax World helped start SRI and the sustainable investing industry by forming the first SRI mutual fund in 1971.
- In starting the industry, investors had to be convinced that attention to social and environmental concerns had positive influence on company financial performance.
- There is evidence to suggest a positive link between social and environmental performance and company financial performance.
- Three core SRI strategies are screening (both positive and negative), shareholder advocacy, and community investing.

EXERCISES

1. Discuss the spectrum of investing that is classified as socially responsible investing (SRI). Go to a company's website and see what actions they take related to sustainability, such as environmental practices or water usage. After reviewing, does that change your view of the company? Are you more or less likely to invest in the company now?
2. In 2006, Parnassus Investments (http://www.parnassus.com) added an exclusionary screen to exclude investing in businesses involved with Sudan when the international community recognized the Darfur region conflict as genocide. Do you agree or disagree with these criteria for a SRI investment? What might be unintended consequences of a screen like this?

[1] "History of SRI," SRI Conference, http://www.sriintherockies.com/about/historyOfSRI.jsp.
[2] Jason M. Ribando and George Bonne, *A New Quality Factor: Finding Alpha with Asset4 ESG Data* (New York: Thomson Reuters, 2010).
[3] "Sustainable and Responsible Investing Facts," USSIF, http://ussif.org/resources/sriguide/srifacts.cfm.
[4] "The Investor's Advocate: How the SEC Protects Investors, Maintains Market Integrity, and Facilitates Capital Formation," US Securities and Exchange Commission, http://www.sec.gov/about/whatwedo.shtml.
[5] "Socially Responsible Mutual Fund Charts: Financial Performance," USSIF, http://ussif.org/resources/mfpc.
[6] "Sustainable and Responsible Investing Facts," USSIF, http://ussif.org/resources/sriguide/srifacts.cfm.
[7] This is taken from "Sustainable and Responsible Investing Facts," USSIF, http://ussif.org/resources/sriguide/srifacts.cfm.
[8] Because of the broad definition of socially responsible investing (SRI), it is difficult to do a standard accounting of all the funds that engage in SRI and SRI-like investing.

12.2 Pax World

LEARNING OBJECTIVES

1. See what external factors influenced the creation of Pax World.
2. Define the structure of Pax World.
3. Understand what challenges Pax World has faced.

Background

Pax World Investments, Inc., helped to start the socially responsible investing (SRI) industry that exists today. Pax World was founded in 1971 as the first socially responsible mutual fund in the United States. Two United Methodist ministers, Luther Tyson and Jack Corbett, based in Boston and Maryland, wanted to start an investment fund for their church assets that did not support the Vietnam War. They were antiwar clergy, and they specifically did not want to use church funds to invest in weapons and weapons manufacture. The ministers still cared about the financial return of the investment of the churches' funds to help fund the operations of the churches and did not have the expertise to invest the churches' funds themselves. They needed an investment manager who would invest their churches' funds based on the churches' financial and social objectives. The ministers ended up finding Tony Brown, an investment adviser based in Portsmouth, New Hampshire, which is an hour north of Boston, who was willing to work with them. Mr. Brown was, at that time, with the financial firm Fahnestock, which later became Oppenheimer Funds, and he started managing the churches' money. It was the first social responsibility directed investment fund and later it grew to become Pax World Funds.

Pax World Funds was named to represent the social objectives of its investment fund, Pax being the name of the Roman goddess of peace and world to represent the broad global perspective of the ministers and the investment fund. The initial investors in the Pax World Fund were the two churches, private investors identified by Tony Brown, and Tony Brown himself. The total initial funds invested totaled $101,000 (about $600,000 in 2011). The first fund later became the Pax World Balanced Fund, which is still in existence today. It is Pax World's largest mutual fund accounting for more than 90 percent of its total assets under management and one of the largest SRI mutual funds in the world.

Very soon after the first Pax World mutual fund was started, the ministers got the idea that if they could screen out weapons manufacturers they could and should also screen out other things that they did not think were appropriate for church fund investment. They choose to add tobacco industry companies and firms that had a record of pollution to the list not to invest in. Social screens were new for the investment industry at the time, including for Tony Brown. Mr. Brown had to figure out a way to do the screens for the first SRI fund. He hired a recent college graduate to do the screens for the initial fund. The staffer started doing the screening as best they could from public information on companies' products and services and business practices. There was no experience in this and very little research out about how to do this effectively, and there was only a small amount of publically available data about company social impacts. So the Pax World and the industry first social screener sorted through the industry and company data that was publically available and screened out of investments in defense and tobacco industry companies and well-known polluters.

Pax World's Organization
Pax World is organized as required by federal law as a mutual fund trust company with the Securities and Exchange Commission (SEC). The fund is required to have a registered investment adviser and uses Pax World Management, LLC, as its investment adviser (the management company) for the funds. The two entities are independent but related. Pax World Funds has eight board members with the chair of the board and five of the other board members independent of Pax World Management, LLC.
Since 2005, Joe Keefe has served as president and CEO of both Pax World Funds and Pax World Management, LLC. The 75 percent owner of Pax World Management, LLC, is a holding company for the Shadek family (of New Jersey) with Larry Shadek, the lead family member and chair of the board.

The family bought their ownership share of Pax World in 1996. Since 2008, Pax World Management, LLC, employees have purchased 25 percent of the company from the owners. There are four members of the board of Pax World Management, LLC, Joe Keefe, Larry Shadek, another member of the Shadek family, and Chris Brown, the Pax World, LLC, chief investment officer. Every year Pax World Management has to have their investment management contracts renewed with Pax World Funds. In order to get their contract renewed, the company has to show the fund's board that the funds are performing well, that costs are reasonable, and that the funds are being well managed.

As of 2011, Pax World Management had forty-eight employees organized in six departments (see as follows). This included a portfolio management group headed by a chief investment officer with five (Women's Equity, Balanced & Growth, High Yield, International, and Small Cap) fund managers, five analysts, and two traders. The sustainability research is in another department with five researchers. In addition to the portfolio management and sustainability research, the other major functional areas are compliance, finance and administration, shareholder services, and marketing and sales. Compliance involves being in accordance with established guidelines, specifications, and agreements with customers and shareholders.

Pax World's Portfolio
As of 2011, Pax World Funds had eleven mutual funds and two exchange traded funds (ETFs) with assets under management totaling $2.4 billion. The Balanced Fund was started in 1971. The Growth Fund and the High Yield Bond Fund were started in late 1990s. The newest funds were the ESG Managers Portfolios, ESG Shares (ETFs), Pax World Small Cap Fund, Pax World International Fund, Pax World Global Women's Equality Fund, and Pax World Global Green Fund.

Overall Pax World offers four different investment products areas:
1. *Pax World Funds*—a family of actively managed mutual funds across a range of asset classes.
o   Pax World Balanced Fund
o   Pax World Growth Fund
o   Pax World Small Cap Fund
o   Pax World International Fund
o   Pax World High Yield Bond Fund
o   Pax World Global Women's Equality Fund
o   Pax World Global Green Fund

2. *ESG Managers Portfolios*—a series of multimanager asset allocation funds with asset allocation, manager selection, and portfolio construction by Morningstar Associates.
3. *ESG Shares*—the first family of ETFs devoted exclusively to a sustainable investing approach.
4. Separately managed accounts for institutional investors.

Pax World's Balanced Fund

Pax World's largest fund, their Balanced Fund, is the oldest SRI fund in the industry. It is the second-largest single SRI fund (at $1.8 billion) after the Parnmassus Equity Income Fund ($3.7 billion) as of September 30, 2011. [1]

Pax World's Balanced Fund has a $250 minimum investment requirement and an expense ratio of 0.96 percent. As of September 30, 2011, compared to the overall market (S&P 500), Pax World's largest fund has tended to underperform in the short term but outperform over the longer term. When compared to just other balanced funds (the Lipper Balanced Funds Index), the fund has tended to underperform financially at times.

Table 12.2 Comparison of Pax World Balanced Fund to Comparable Investment Benchmarks

Total Returns » Month Ended September 30, 2011 » Quarter Ended September 30, 2011	Cumulative Returns (%)				Average Annual Returns (%)			
	1-Month	Quarter	Year-to-Date	1 Year	3-Year	5-Year	10-Year	Since Inception
Balanced Fund—Individual Investor Class	−7.92	−13.77	−8.90	−1.04	0.98	−0.34	3.24	8.14
Balanced Fund—Institutional Class 1	−7.89	−13.69	−8.71	−0.74	1.23	−0.11	3.36	8.17
Balanced Fund—R Class 2	−7.93	−13.78	−9.04	−1.23	0.73	−0.53	3.14	8.11
60% S&P 500 Index / 40% Barclays Capital US Aggregate Bond Index	−3.93	−7.04	−2.65	3.05	4.44	2.25	4.29	—
S&P 500 Index	−7.03	−13.87	−8.68	1.14	1.23	−1.18	2.82	—
Lipper Balanced Funds Index	−5.36	−9.62	−5.41	0.30	3.94	1.53	4.13	—
Pax World Balanced Fund—Individual Investor Class	−7.92	−13.77	−8.90	−1.04	0.98	−0.34	3.24	8.14
60% S&P 500 Index / 40% Barclays Capital US Aggregate Bond Index	−3.93	−7.04	−2.65	3.05	4.44	2.25	4.29	—
S&P 500 Index	−7.03	−13.87	−8.68	1.14	1.23	−1.18	2.82	—
Lipper Balanced Funds Index	−5.36	−9.62	−5.41	0.30	3.94	1.53	4.13	—

According to Morningstar, one of the leading providers of independent investment research in the world, in the eleven years from 2000 to 2011 Pax World's Balanced Fund performed in the top quartile among all (not just SRI) funds in its category five of the year, in the bottom quartile five of the years, and in the second lowest quartile in one year.

Pax World's Challenges
Marketplace Acceptance

A significant challenge for Pax World has been to attract investors to their fund. Wall Street and the traditional investment marketplace were at first skeptical of social screens and SRI in general. The Wall Street perspective was that social screens "shrink" the investment universe by screening out investment opportunities based on values—such as not investing in companies with poor environmental records—rather than on financial performance. It was believed that it was far more difficult for SRI funds to achieve strong market performance in terms of returns on investments, capital gains, and investment income. This pervasive perception was the biggest early barrier SRI.

The performance over time of the SRI funds compared to the universe of funds has convinced increasing numbers of investors. At the end of 2009, a review of 160 socially responsible mutual funds found that 65 percent of the funds outperformed their benchmarks—funds with similar investment objectives—and a United Nations Report concluded, "There is mounting empirical evidence that companies with better corporate governance practices carry less risk and outperform poorly governed companies over time; that companies with strong environmental performance carry less risk and outperform environmental laggards over time; that companies with good workplace practices enjoy higher productivity, higher morale, lower turnover and increased profitability." [2]

Walking the Talk

Pax World experienced its own internal challenge in regards to ethics and social responsibility. On July 30, 2008, the SEC fined Pax World Mutual Funds $500,000 because it failed to follow its own SRI criteria from 2000 to 2005. The settlement between Pax World and the SEC concluded an investigation that had commenced in December 2004, prior to CEO Joe Keefe's arrival at the company. Pax World's funds had invested in some of the kinds of companies they were supposed to avoid. For example, the Pax Growth Fund owned shares of a major oil and gas exploration company, even though it had failed three of Pax's social screens. And the Pax High Yield Fund owned bonds issued by a company that had major revenue from gambling and liquor. The SEC found Pax had violated its own restrictions by purchasing at least ten securities that screening criteria prohibited; in addition, Pax failed to screen 8 percent of its new security purchases between 2001 and 2005. Continuously from 2001 through early 2006, the Pax Growth Fund and the Pax High Yield Fund held at least one security that violated criteria. All

told, the fund company held forty-one securities that either weren't screened or didn't pass its screens. [3]

The following comments were made by some of the people involved in the incident:

> *"Mutual fund companies marketing socially responsible funds need to be responsible themselves," said David Bergers, regional director of the SEC's Boston office.*
>
> *"Advisers simply cannot tell investors they are going to do one thing with their funds and then not follow through on those promises," said Linda Chatman Thomsen, director of the SEC Division of Enforcement, in a statement.*

Pax World Management Corporation, the then investment adviser to Pax World Funds and predecessor to Pax World Management, LLC, the reorganized management company, entered into a settlement order with the SEC dated July 30, 2008. Under the terms of the settlement, Pax World agreed to a cease and desist order and a civil penalty of $500,000 under Section 206(2) of the Investment Advisers Act, which is a section involving negligent conduct, not intentional wrongdoing.

Pax World, under the leadership of Joe Keefe, undertook a vigorous response, and the SEC chose to recognize Pax World's substantial remediation efforts and cooperation in its order. In addition, the Pax World Balanced Fund, which held approximately 95 percent of Pax World assets during this time period, did not purchase any unscreened securities and was not cited in the order.

The portfolio managers of the two funds involved—the Growth Fund and the High Yield Fund—as well as the head of the social research department and Pax World's outside counsel and chief compliance officer all left the firm. Pax World completely overhauled its compliance procedures to ensure that its portfolio managers can only buy securities that have passed their social and environmental criteria. As part of a top-to-bottom reorganization and modernization of their business operations, Pax World put in place new sustainability screening and other compliance procedures, controls, and technology.

In a 2011 interview, CEO Joe Keefe said of the mistakes made, "I can tell you that today Pax endeavors to meet best practices in all aspects of our business and operations. And we have a compliance culture that I would match up against any in the industry. Like all companies (and all individuals) we are not perfect, but we learn from our mistakes, are proud of the progress we have made and are constantly striving for improvement."

KEY TAKEAWAYS

- Pax World was started in 1971 to address a gap between a group's interest in taking into account social considerations into investing and what was available in the marketplace.

- The Pax World Balanced Fund is the oldest socially responsible investing (SRI) mutual fund and the second largest (in terms of assets) in the United States.

- Pax World is organized in accordance with federal law and has two parts: (1) Pax World Funds—the mutual fund company—and (2) Pax World Management, LLC—the Securities and Exchange Commission (SEC) registered investment adviser that oversees the operations and marketing of the Pax World Funds.

- Pax World Funds currently has eleven mutual funds and $2.4 billion in assets under management.

- Challenges for Pax World have been marketplace acceptance of SRI as an investment strategy and compliance issues in following their own SRI criteria.

EXERCISES

1. How have investors' views of social and environmental activism changed from 1971 to 2011?
2. How has Pax World's largest fund, the Balanced Fund, performed compared to the universe of funds, other balanced funds, and compared to other socially responsible investing (SRI) funds? What might explain the differences in performance?

[1] "Socially Responsible Mutual Fund Charts: Financial Performance," USSIF, http://ussif.org/resources/mfpc.

[2] UNEP Finance Initiative, *Show Me the Money: Linking Environmental, Social and Governance Issues to Company Value* (Geneva, Switzerland: United Nations Environment Programme, 2006).

[3] Mark Jewell, "Pax Fined for Failure to Screen Investment Funds," *USA Today*, July 30, 2008, http://www.usatoday.com/money/economy/2008-07-30-1549841276_x.htm.

12.3 Pax World's Approach to Investing

LEARNING OBJECTIVES

1. Describe Pax World's approach to sustainable investing.
2. Discuss the investment process at Pax World.
3. Describe how and why Pax World changed its investment criteria from screening out to defining what to invest in.

Pax World had primarily relied on exclusion, for example, negative screens, for avoidance of undesired companies to invest in. However, the resistance to the screening out of some companies among traditional investors led Pax World, in 2006, to change their approach from socially responsible investing (SRI) to "sustainable investing."

To Pax World, sustainable investing is similar to and has its origins in SRI, but it is fundamentally different. For Pax World, sustainable investing involves fully integrating environmental, social, and governance (ESG) factors into investment analysis. So where SRI had tended to define itself by **what not to invest in**, sustainable investing defines **what to invest in**.

Pax World's new methodology allows it to invest in companies that have superior sustainability or ESG performance. By investing in "sustainable" companies, Pax World seeks to reduce risk and deliver competitive long-term investment performance.

Table 12.3 Differences between Sustainable Investing and SRI

Sustainable Investing	SRI
Performance-based orientation	Values-based orientation
Inclusionary approach—seeks to identify leaders in sustainability	Exclusionary approach—negative "screens" for avoidance of "sin stocks"
Striving for broad market acceptance	Niche ("alternative") investment style

By combining rigorous financial analysis with equally rigorous ESG analysis, there is an increased level of scrutiny that helps them construct portfolios made up of companies that

- are leaders in their industries,
- are better managed and more forward-thinking,
- are better at anticipating and mitigating risk,

- meet positive standards of corporate responsibility,
- focus on the long term.

The goal is for all the funds to beat the performance of group peer funds, not just other SRI funds. For each of Pax's funds, this means outperforming on an average return on investment basis funds with similar investment objectives. Pax World's view is that rigorous financial and ESG analysis will lead to superior fund performance over time. This emanates from the Pax World perspective that companies that do well on both analyses and that execute well on both financial and ESG measures will be the best performers in terms of return for mutual fund investors.

Pax World's Investment Process

Investment analysis is very detailed and difficult work. Pax World's investment process is a well-defined, systematic, four-step process: (1) top-down analysis, (2) financial analysis, (3) ESG analysis, and (4) portfolio construction. This process takes Pax World from assessing the broad universe of investment opportunities to assessing a selection of investments for its funds. The ESG analysis of the four is the least established and most qualitative.

Deciding how to invest funds starts with a top-down analysis of domestic and international economies. This involves analysts identifying long-term economic, social, and political trends and their investment implications. This global economic analysis can include the interest rate environment, consumer sentiment, and unemployment. The top-down analysis helps to determine the broad sectors of the economy for Pax World funds to invest in and, more specifically, to overinvest or underinvest in relative to benchmarks by fund type average.

The major themes in 2011, for example, included aging population demographics in developing nations (including the United States, Japan, and many European nations), the growth of emerging markets (such as China, India, and Brazil), and strong demand for and limited supply of natural resources (which puts price pressure on many commodities). The top-down analysis also includes identification of some shorter-term factors. In 2011, this included the economic recession and low consumer confidence.

The 2011 themes suggested that Pax World funds invest in industries that benefit from (e.g., sell in or to) aging demographics, commodities, and emerging markets over and above the percentages in the benchmark fund. Specific industries to invest in the 2011 market, for example, would include construction, mining and utility equipment companies with a majority of their sales in emerging nations, and consumer product companies with more than 50 percent of sales in emerging markets.

Fundamental Financial Analysis

The next step involves fundamental financial analysis. This is in-depth financial analysis on an individual company basis to identify companies that appear to offer above-average relative growth rates, sound business models, strong competitive positioning, and attractive valuations. Pax World financial analysts target individual companies or stocks in their specified industry sectors. Each financial analyst is responsible for three sectors.

Company financial fundamentals are reviewed mostly using financial information that is available for all publically traded companies and required by governmental regulatory bodies including the Securities and Exchange Commission (SEC) in the United States. Companies within industries are compared based on their profitability, growth, valuation, and quality. Income statement and balance sheet information for companies, including returns on equity and assets, long- and short-term growth in earnings, price-to-earnings ratio, and debt-to-capital ratio are considered along with other financial information.

Pax financial analysts determine overall rankings of companies in targeted industries by using a weighted composite measure. In most cases, the top twenty-fifth percentile of performers in the targeted industries are identified for potential investment. In addition, financial analysts review the financial performance of all the holdings regularly.

ESG Analysis

If a company passes the financial test and is among the top twenty-fifth percentile in a targeted industry it will go to the sustainability research team, and they will do an environmental, social, and governance (ESG) analysis. ESG analysis involves an evaluation based on ESG criteria. The ESG analysis includes review of company ESG performance with three views—past performance, current policy, and future trajectory. A company with poor prior performance, improved current policy, and positive future trajectory would be more favorably rated than a company with static moderate performance. The review by ESG analysts results in companies passing, failing, or passing but requiring monitoring. For example, Pax World was monitoring BP just prior to the BP Gulf of Mexico oil spill in 2010.

Environmental considerations include whether there has been company violations of environmental laws (such as the Clean Air Act and Clean Water Act in the United States), the company's record of management of emissions, climate change–related policies and actions, and renewable energy use or development. On social issues, consideration is given to human rights issues in countries in which companies operate, for example, treatment and rights of women and workforce issues, such as worker safety, child labor laws, and minimum wages. On governance, the key issues assessed include board independence (e.g., the percentage of outside directors), diversity of board (including percentage of females on the board), and executive compensation practices and policies.

The sources of information used for the ESG analysis include company reporting in annual reports and in separate sustainability reports. The latter are increasing in numbers as companies, particularly larger companies and companies in Europe, are providing sustainability reports. Other key sources of information include government data (e.g., from the US government's Food and Drug Administration [FDA], Occupational Safety and Health Administration [OSHA], and Environmental Protection Agency [EPA]); news coverage and composite reporting of news coverage from Dow Jones Factiva (http://www.dowjones.com/factiva/index.asp); other third-party sources, such as MSCI ESG Research (http://www.msci.com/products/esg/about_msci_esg_res earch.html), Goldman Sachs, and the Corporate Library (http://www2.gmiratings.com); and nongovernmental organizations (NGO), such as Silicon Valley Toxics Coalition (http://svtc.org/resources/reports).

Smaller companies are harder to get information on, as are many companies in the developing markets. Some countries require a lot of disclosure and some don't; it varies greatly. In general, publically traded companies in the United States and Western Europe are required to disclose information on financial, environmental, and social factors that will affect their market value but there is significant discretion in doing this.

Big companies, such as General Electric, Exxon-Mobil, Starbucks, and Walmart, have a lot of ESG information available through media attention, NGOs, and other watchdog groups. They're pretty transparent and increasingly so. But as you go down the capitalization scale, smaller companies are not as transparent, so it can be harder to research a smaller company or a company in an emerging market. These are some of the factors Pax World

Management ESG analysts have to deal with. It gets more or less complicated depending on what company they are researching.

The ESG analysis team's long-term goal is to be able to assess a larger number of companies on ESG performance (not just those provided to them in the top twenty-fifth percentile according to traditional financial criteria) and, over time, to be able identify companies that are strongest in ESG performance and based on that identifying if the company should be considered for Pax fund investment by the financial analysts. This would enable a more interactive and dynamic investment selection process with more active ESG consideration.

In order to get to this, and to be able to identify companies in percentiles of ESG performance, ESG analysts have to be able to more formally and fully quantify their analysis. While the ESG analysis has made substantial progress in being more quantitative, structured, and rigorous from its start in 1971, the ESG analysis remains limited to quantitative final assessment of pass or fail, without precise definition or measurement of ESG performance. Part of this is a result of the limited data available and the difficulty of collecting the data that might be available, but it might more strongly reflect the relative newness of ESG analytics compared to traditional financial investment analysis, which has been developing for more than one hundred years. This is true at Pax World and with SRI funds in general.

An example of a company that made it through Pax's financial review process, but not the ESG process, is Suez Environment. Suez is a utility company based in France that operates largely in the water treatment and waste management sectors (http://www.suez-environnement.com/en/homepage), providing drinking water to seventy-six million people worldwide.

Suez was identified as being in a growing industry and emerging as an industry leader with strong financials in that industry. The company failed the ESG review based on a number of negative factors, including employee tampering with water supply testing, high incidence of worker injury, and antitrust investigation by the European Union.

Portfolio Construction
Portfolio construction involves choosing a select number of companies that emerge from the combination of financial and ESG analysis and that meet both the financial and sustainability criteria and, as a portfolio, the overall investment guidelines of individual funds (e.g., targeted

percentages for bonds and stocks). This entire process is repeated as new insights are developed or economic conditions change.

Every company in the Pax World mutual fund portfolio is reviewed from a financial and ESG perspective on a periodic basis, mostly annually.

KEY TAKEAWAYS

- Pax World follows an investment approach called sustainable investing—the full integration of environmental, social, and governance (ESG) factors into investment analysis and decision making.
- To Pax World, sustainable investing means what to invest in as opposed to socially responsible investing (SRI), which means what not to invest in.
- The Pax World investment process includes (1) top-down analysis, (2) financial analysis, (3) ESG analysis, and (4) portfolio construction.

EXERCISES

1. How has Pax World's investment approach changed and what were the driving forces?
2. Do you feel that Pax World's sustainable investing approach is a better approach than their interpretation of socially responsible investing (SRI)? Why or why not?
3. Will sustainable investing enable Pax World to differentiate their funds?

12.4 Pax World Looking Forward

The increasing investments in socially responsible investing (SRI) mutual funds reflect enhanced awareness of the potential positive influence of sustainability in businesses financial performance. This is in contrast to when Pax World first started in 1971, when most investors and investment managers believed that companies would incur costs with social- and environmental-minded efforts. Now more and more investors believe that over the long term, sustainable business practices can help to lower costs and risks, can open up market opportunities, and can have a net positive financial impact on business performance and returns on investment. And for Pax World, its approach to SRI is increasingly well recognized and respected. According to Morningstar, the Pax World Balanced Fund "has terrific socially responsible investing bona fide. It is the flagship offering of fine all-SRI shop. Manager Chris Brown has been at the helm for 13 years, so he's more seasoned than a healthy majority of SRI skippers (and a healthy majority of allocation managers). And Brown steadfastly applies a rigorous set of environmental, and social, and governance factors while running the portfolio."[1]

Still, critical to the success of Pax World and its growth—as with any mutual fund company—is financial performance. As Joe Keefe, Pax World Investments CEO and president, commented,

> For Pax World, because we're a mutual fund company…I would say the number one component critical to our success is the financial performance of our funds. We have a fiduciary obligation to our shareholders to try to get them market or above-market returns and to manage their risk. So that's

> fundamental to what we do….If we grow, we do two things. First of all, we are successful as a business. And we are a business, so we're trying to make money and make a profit. But we also are a mission-driven business, and as we grow assets, not only will we become more profitable and successful from a business perspective, but we will have more impact. And that's what, ultimately, this has to be about. We want to change corporate behavior. We want markets to produce better outcomes, not just financially, but from a social and environmental perspective. And the larger we get, the more leverage we have, the more we can change investor behavior, and the more we can change corporate behavior.

For Pax World, increasing the funds under management is not just for their own profitability, and it's not growth for its own sake; it's toward Pax World's mission, which is changing corporate America. Pax World's growth and changing corporate America are tied together because the more successful Pax World Funds and Management are from a business perspective, the more leverage they will have to be more successful from a social and environmental perspective. They reinforce each other. They're integrated, which is what triple bottom line (TBL) and sustainable companies try to achieve—the successful integration of environmental and social factors into their business models.

Investment in SRI mutual funds and public awareness of the importance of environmental, social, and governance (ESG) factors in financial performance accelerated from 1990 to 2010, as there were increasing numbers of examples of companies that suffered significant financial losses by not being attentive environmentally, such as was the case with BP and the Gulf of Mexico oil spill in 2010.

Individuals are at the same time personally experiencing the financial benefits of their environmental practices, such as reducing energy and materials use. Increasing numbers of people are beginning to see environmental stewardship as a financial positive rather than a cost, and this influences their investment decisions over time.

A similar dynamic could be suggested about concern about treatment of workers and good corporate governance. Most individuals had doubts about the financial relevance of the treatment of workers and good governance. Now there is increasing evidence that companies that treat their workers well have higher productivity and lower absenteeism (as stated in a McGill University study published by Harvard Business Review, http://www.portfolio.com/business-news/2010/05/19/harvard-publishes-study-that-shows-treating-workers-well-boosts-bottom-line), and on the governance side, many investors have personally experienced the fallout from the 2008–9 financial crises that resulted from unethical business practices that could have been avoided with stronger governance.

Pax World's shareholders, like most mutual fund investors, are not interested in short-term performance. This is compatible with Pax World's approach and use of ESG factors that can tend to play out over the long term to affect company financial performance and to help minimize risk. That does mean that in every year Pax's funds do better than or as well as a non-ESG funds. But as Joe Keefe says, "We believe over time we can outperform other funds because environmental, and social, and governance factors have what they call materiality. In the financial world, all that really means is relevance. They are relevant to how companies perform. So we think focusing on them is really important." Pax World has traditionally been primarily a retail mutual fund, with a majority of its funds under management for individual and household investors. However, Pax's institutional presence is increasingly important. Many of the so-called individual or household investors are coming to Pax through institutional investment platforms, such as through an option for pension funds, through personal financial planners and investment adviser recommendations, and through platforms provided for investors through larger financial players, such as Schwab, Fidelity, Merrill Lynch, and UBS. Increasing Pax World's institutional presence is not a question of retail or institutional because the two are integrated.

An increasing number of large institutional investors and the major consultants that work with them are incorporating SRI into their portfolio as evidenced by the significant increase in

SRI recently. Individuals tend to either invest directly or, now more often than not, they invest through a broker, financial adviser, or a financial planner. And individual brokers and financial planners tend to be individuals who have to do a lot of research on their own, and they don't necessarily have all the most recent findings on SRI performance. Thus on the individual and household investment side, Pax World growth is being driven a lot by the investment advisers as the intermediary to the end customer. Pax World's task then becomes to convince a financial planner to include Pax World in what they recommend to their client.

On the "pure" institutional side, Pax World continues to have religious institutional investors and pension funds. Looking forward Pax World plans to attract more and more investment from institutional investors because the institutional investment world is ahead of the individual investment world in embracing sustainable investing in many respects. There are reasons for this, including having the track record of performance being similar to traditional funds. As Keefe commented, "Eventually, individual investors will catch up, but institutional investors in general are ahead of the curve right now in embracing our investment approach. Institutional investors study market trends. They have a lot of research and data at their disposal, and they're seeing a lot of the research, a lot of the data, that underscores the materiality of ESG, or the financial relevance of environmental, social, and governance factors."

Even with all the positives for Pax World and the more general acceptance of SRI-like funds, many believe that it will still require the next generation of investors to have Pax World and SRI get closer to 50 percent of mutual fund holdings. Personal investments are "sticky"—they don't change that easily. And the SRI approach to investing, incorporating the ESG into the analysis, is very different from the traditional approach.

But the data show high growth recently, suggesting the hockey stick model of growth might be at work. There are two things going on. The first is that the generation of baby boomers is inheriting wealth from its parents. And that generation is more likely to want to have some alignment between its values and its investments because they are the ones who grew up during the Vietnam era. Second, you go to the generation behind the baby boomers, and according to Keefe, "they are even more inclined toward concern about the environment and SRI-type-investment, because the notion to them that your investments can be somehow out of whack with the rest of your values and the rest of your lifestyle does not make sense. They want to have that alignment. When we were growing up, certainly our parents' generation, but to some extent ours, would say something like, well, great, but your investments should just be making money. Then, if you want to change the world, give it to charity. Get involved in your community, protest. Now investing and values needing to be integrated into their investment decisions by boomers and others, and this is the hockey stick—SRI is ramping up fast."

As the SRI industry grows and its prospects look more promising, the traditional mutual fund companies are moving aggressively into SRI. This is happening through traditional families of funds starting new funds on their own or acquiring existing SRI funds. With this trend, Pax World could get purchased or lose market share within the SRI industry to the larger mutual fund company participants.

It is increasingly important for Pax to differentiate what they do. This was accomplished with the adoption of the sustainable investing approach in 2006. And Pax World has added new funds that are innovative, including the Global Women's Equality Fund, which is the only mutual fund in America that focuses on investing in companies that treat women better, that invest in women, and that recruit and promote them. Pax World added the Global Women's Equality Fund because of their belief that there are connections between having more women in management and more women on your board and financial performance.

On the issue of women's equity and other issues, Pax World also differentiates themselves from traditional mutual fund companies by its many investor initiatives. With regards to women's equity, this includes collaboration with the United Nations Principles for Responsible Investment (UNPRI) and the Calvert funds to encourage greater gender equality on boards of directors and in senior management and to promote improved disclosure. (As of 2011, only 13 percent of *Fortune* 500 board chairs are held by women.) Pax World launched a campaign to promote greater gender diversity on corporate boards by encouraging investors to vote no on proxies for board membership that did not contain a sufficient number of women. During the 2011 proxy season, Pax World withheld votes from, or voted against, 264 director slates for insufficient gender diversity, sending notification letters to those companies explaining why and offering guidelines to improve diversity.

Pax World is an increasingly active shareholder representing investors with proxy voting. During the 2011 proxy season, Pax World also signed on to eighteen environmental initiatives, many of which focused on the oil and gas industry.

For example, Pax World joined other investors in writing to oil and gas companies engaged in offshore oil drilling, requesting information regarding the companies' policies and programs to manage operational risks and steps taken to improve them.

Pax World has participated in multiple initiatives led by Ceres (a national coalition of investors, environmental organizations, and other public interest groups working with companies to address sustainability challenges), encouraging Congress and state legislators to take action on environmental standards. These included decreasing emissions of air pollutants and greenhouse gasses, passing comprehensive clean energy legislation, and urging the EPA to raise fuel economy standards for motor vehicle fleets.

Pax World also joined with other investors in the Investor Network on Climate Risk urging California voters to oppose Proposition 23, a statewide ballot initiative that would have stopped implementation of the state's landmark clean energy bill. The proposition was rejected in the fall 2010 election. In addition, Pax World signed on to an initiative led by the organization As You Sow, urging companies to take responsibility for recycling postconsumer product packaging. The companies receiving the letter included General Mills (whose share holdings represented 1.8 percent of the Pax World holdings in the Growth Fund), Procter & Gamble (1.4 percent of the Growth Fund and 0.9 percent of the Balanced Fund), and Unilever (1.6 percent of the Global Women's Equality Fund and 1.9 percent of the International Fund). Pax World also cofiled a shareholder resolution led by Domini Social Investments with Southwestern Energy (1.4 percent of the Growth Fund) requesting that the company publish a report on the risk of hydraulic fracturing as a means of obtaining natural gas. The company agreed to improve its disclosures and work with stakeholders to develop a model disclosure format for other natural gas firms; the resolution was successfully withdrawn.

Pax World's focus looking forward is not as much on their SRI industry competitors, like Parnassus, but on growing the overall SRI market and changing corporate America. Their main competitors looking forward are Fidelity Investments, Vanguard, T. Rowe Price, and others of the large traditional mutual fund families whose investors are increasingly likely to move at least some of their assets to an ESG-like investment approach. In many respects, Pax World's main challenge is to try to win those people over who are not familiar or were previously not comfortable with sustainable investing and to try to convince people that their values do not have to be compromised when it comes to their financial investments. And this will require strong financial and ESG performance at Pax World, particularly with evidence that companies with better ESG performance have better financial performance.

As Keefe commented, "There are studies suggesting that, over time, funds and investors that use the ESG approach do better than the market. And I believe, over time that will clearly be the case....I think once you start measuring up 10-year track records versus 10-year track records, I think you're going to see that this investment approach holds up very well....there's all kinds of research now suggesting that environmental, social, governance factors are relevant....over time, we're going to be able to convince more and more people of that."

And for Pax World, if they grow, they can have greater societal impact—with the company's business success and societal impact being intimately tied together. For Pax World, there are opportunities to change corporate behavior on greenhouse gas emissions and climate change, on gender issues, and on all kinds of social and environmental issues that will help markets produce better outcomes. But to do that, Pax needs to grow its asset base.

Europe certainly is ahead of the United States right now in embracing sustainable investing. In fact, most of the governments in Europe, for their own government pension funds, have a mandate for it. But Pax World would have to get licensed in Europe and it's a complicated and costly process. The company would have to launch new entities and they are not like Fidelity and some of the larger mutual fund companies that are large enough to establish themselves outside the United States.

According to Keefe, "The main opportunities for us right now are, one, opening up conversations that were hard to open up before in the US, with investment advisers, the intermediary platforms, and institutional investors. Those conversations are starting to happen now. In fact, we have a hard time keeping up with it all."

To open up these opportunities, Pax has newsletters and their own marketing and sales teams to e-mail and visit the financial planners and financial advisers. The company also does webinars and podcasts. There are also opportunities with particular demographic groups, such as female investors. With research showing that women are more likely to want to align their investments with their values than men (http://www.northerntrust.com/wealth/11-summer/women-in-wealth.html). Research shows that women are controlling a larger share of investment dollars. On the institutional side, there are opportunities with private foundations and their endowments and pension funds. The strategy is to launch the products that the investment community wants, to attract investors, and to communicate with those investors, which often is through their advisers and intermediaries.

The biggest challenge for Pax World continues to be overcoming the conventional wisdom in the financial industry that if you base investments on moral values, you're going to have to significantly sacrifice financial performance in order to do the right thing.

KEY TAKEAWAYS

- Pax World differentiated their socially responsible investing (SRI) by adopting a new approach, which includes selecting companies to invest in by positive environmental, social, and governance (ESG) performance as compared to using screens to limit investments.
- Pax World and other SRI-focused funds will have to continue to differentiate and distinguish their SRI products to compete in the industry as SRI is increasing and now larger traditional investment funds are starting to compete in the industry.

EXERCISES

1. What lessons from Pax World's experience are there for the socially responsible investing (SRI) industry and for sustainable businesses more generally?
2. How can Pax World continue to grow and be an SRI industry leader? What are its current strengths and weaknesses in the industry?
3. How can Pax World be a mutual fund industry leader, not just SRI industry leader? What will it have to do well? What are the emerging market opportunities? What will it have to avoid?
4. *SRI market analysis.*

TABLE 12.4 ALL BALANCED FUNDS							
Morningstar Category	**1 Year**	**3 Year**	**5 Year**	**10 Year**	**Equity (%)**	**Bond (%)**	**Cash (%)**
Median	−0.16	3.85	1.46	4.20	56.48	33.10	6.39
Average	−0.23	3.87	1.49	4.30	52.22	33.87	10.01
Number of funds	506	458	403	257	531	531	531

TABLE 12.5 ALL SRI BALANCED FUNDS							
Morningstar Category	**1 Year**	**3 Year**	**5 Year**	**10 Year**	**Equity (%)**	**Bond (%)**	**Cash (%)**
Median	−0.16	3.18	0.83	3.35	56.99	33.55	5.14
Average	−0.35	3.21	1.06	3.47	55.99	34.40	7.70
Number of funds	30	23	23	14	30	30	30

The previous charts show the financial performance of all balanced mutual funds versus only SRI-balanced mutual funds (including Pax World) for the period ending September 30, 2011. Compare the one-year, three-year, five-year, and ten-year financial performance of the two different categories. Does this evidence support or refute assertions that SRI funds outperform the overall market? What might be some reasons for the difference in performance? How does this example compare with other examples of SRI performance in the chapter? What conclusions can you draw on the comparison? What are the implications for the future growth potential of SRI funds and Pax World funds specifically?

[1] "Pax World Balanced Individual Investor," Morningstar, September 2011, http://quote.morningstar.com/fund/f.aspx?t=PAXWX.

NOTES:

Chapter 13:
Case: Strategic Mission–Driven Sustainable Business:
Stonyfield Yogurt

LEARNING OBJECTIVES

1. Look at the role a sustainability-focused mission and strategy can play in identifying organizational purpose and guiding a business.
2. Understand the complexity of managing what can be at times competing and conflicting environmental, social, and business demands and values.
3. Describe how sustainability-focused strategy can contribute to competitive advantage in local and global markets.

13.1 Introduction

LEARNING OBJECTIVES

1. Define the meaning of corporate strategy.
2. Explain how strategy relates to competitive advantage.
3. Understand the indicators or metrics to measure and assess competitive advantage.

Stonyfield Farm, Inc., or Stonyfield, is an organic yogurt manufacturer located in Londonderry, New Hampshire. The company was founded in 1983 at Stonyfield Farm and got its start using its herd of seven jersey cows to produce organic milk. The milk was then manufactured on-site into organic yogurt using founder Samuel Kaymen's family recipe. During the first year, Stonyfield sold $56,000 worth of product. By 2010, Stonyfield had grown to be the number one selling organic yogurt brand in the United States and the third-largest selling yogurt brand in the world with more than $375 million in revenue and with profits exceeding the industry average.

This case describes and examines Stonyfield's sustainability strategy and its execution. This includes description of the key elements in the implementation of Stonyfield's sustainability strategy and practices and discussion of how a well-executed sustainability-focused strategy can benefit a business, giving it acompetitive advantage. The case concludes with consideration of Stonyfield's future direction; the CEO's rationale for selling the company to Groupe Danone, a $17 billion food and beverage conglomerate; and exploration of how the relationship between Stonyfield and Danone resulted in an improvement in sustainability efforts for both organizations.

Sidebar

What Is Strategy?

Strategy, according to Jack Welch, the former CEO of General Electric, is identifying and making clear cut choices about how to compete. For management scholar Michael Porter at Harvard Business School, strategy requires answering the following questions:

- How are we going to be unique?
- How are we going to use this unique position to create a competitive advantage?
- How are we going to sustain this competitive advantage over time?

Strategy can be thought of as the actions chosen that direct an organization to a future goal. Its purpose is to position an organization to achieve its objectives through a planned allocation of resources that take into account the state of the external environment and internal resources and accountability to stakeholders.

Competitive advantage provides a company an advantage over its competitors. There are two primary types of competitive advantage—comparative advantage and differential advantage. Comparative advantage, or cost advantage, is a firm's ability to produce a good or service at a lower cost than its competitors. A differential advantage is created when a firm's products or services differ from its competitors' products or services and are seen as providing new or greater value than a competitor's products by customers, for example, introducing organic yogurt that contributes to the health of people and the planet.

Strategic management is the process by which an organization selects its strategy, the tools that are used to promote the strategy, and the manner by which management leads the organization, and it is specifically how leadership is aligned with strategy.

As part of strategy development, organizations will develop a mission statement. Mission statements are a short statement of the purpose of a company or organization. They provide the framework or context within which the company's strategies are crafted and executed. Mission statements commit an organization to what its key stakeholders and leaders want it to achieve. The mission statement articulates the company's purpose, for those in the organization, for consumers, and for all stakeholders. Mission statements will broadly describe an organization's capabilities, customer focus, and core value proposition.

This case highlights the decisions that Stonyfield has had to make that balance business reality with sustainability ideals and how the company's focus on strategy and mission, **especially a** sustainability-focused mission, has helped the company achieve an effective balance without sacrificing the values of its founders. Throughout the case, connections are made between the concepts of strategy, discussed in the previous sidebar, and the actions of Stonyfield to plan, develop, and execute its strategy.

KEY TAKEAWAYS

- Strategy consists of the actions chosen that direct an organization to a future goal.
- Competitive advantage can be achieved with strategies that help company's differentiate their products or services and contribute to profitability.
- Compounded growth rates compared to competitors is one measure of competitive success.

EXERCISES

1. Go to the website of a company and try to identify the company's main strategy.
2. For the same company, try to identify indicators of the company's competitive position. Does the company appear to have a competitive advantage? Use company data and figures to answer the question.

13.2 Stonyfield Farm: A Sustainability-Focused Start-Up

LEARNING OBJECTIVES

1. Understand how the founders and their values shaped the development of Stonyfield.
2. Understand the demands on the entrepreneurs when starting the business.
3. Provide examples of how Stonyfield executed its business strategy.

Background

From its inception, Stonyfield was founded with a sustainability mission. This mission has persisted throughout the company's history. It commits the company to **healthy food**, **healthy people**, **healthy planet**, and **healthy business**.

In 1979, Samuel Kaymen, a former engineer and self-declared "back-to-the land" hippie, and his wife Louise started the Rural Education Center (TREC) in Wilton, New Hampshire. TREC was a nonprofit organization devoted to teaching homesteading skills with an emphasis on organic food production. The Kaymen's founded TREC to help turn around the struggling New England dairy industry and halt the decline of family farms and as a response to the rising industrialization of the food system. Samuel, one of the country's early authorities on organic agriculture, had perfected a recipe for an organic yogurt the previous year. His organic yogurt tasted better than other yogurts available on the market and would form the basis for the Stonyfield brand. In 1982, Gary Hirshberg was recruited by Samuel for the TREC's board of trustees to help generate financial support. Gary had previously served as a water-pumping windmill specialist and also worked for the Massachusetts-based nonprofit ecological advocacy group known as the New Alchemy Institute, which focused on organic agriculture and renewable energy systems. When Gary joined, the center and farm were deep in debt and close to bankruptcy. Under Gary's leadership, TREC decided to expand farming at the center and to produce organic yogurt to sell to support the operations of the center.

Gary said of the decision to choose to enter the yogurt business, "Samuel made this really incredible yogurt. It was really the best yogurt I had ever eaten. So we were all sitting around talking about how we were going to make some money and somebody said 'why don't we sell the yogurt?' We all kind of laughed. He also made wonderful beer and pickles, but eventually we decided to go with the yogurt." [1]

In 1983, the company Stonyfield Farm was born in an old barn at the center. Samuel was appointed chairman and Gary was named CE-Yo (chief executive of yogurt). The company was started with a $35,000 loan from the Institute for Community Economics with $25,000 coming from the Sisters of Mercy. On April 9, 1983, Stonyfield produced their first fifty-gallon batch of yogurt.

Sidebar

A Trip to Disney World [2]

In 1982, Gary Hirshberg, while serving as the executive director for the nonprofit the New Alchemy Institute, went to visit the recently opened Disney World's Epcot Center. This experience changed how Gary viewed influencing the general public on environmental issues. At Epcot Center, he observed twenty-five thousand people walking through the Kraft artificial cheese exhibit, which featured a technologically driven view of farming including test tube–based plants (a stark contrast to the ecologically driven agriculture solutions taught at the New Alchemy Institute). Gary was struck that the daily attendance at the Kraft exhibit was equal to the annual visits at the New Alchemy Institute. This experience led Hirshberg to change his view on environmental education and ultimately, he concluded that, for him personally, he would be more effective in spreading environmental awareness in a business context. The incorporation of Stonyfield Farm would provide him the opportunity to test this in the real world.

Sidebar

Profile of a Social Entrepreneur: Gary Hirshberg

Gary Hirshberg serves on several corporate and nonprofit boards including Applegate Farms, Honest Tea, Climate Counts, Stonyfield Europe, Glenisk, and the Danone Communities Fund. He also is the chairman and cofounder of Stonyfield Café, a natural fast food restaurant company. He has received eight honorary doctorates and was named a Gordon Grand Fellow at Yale University in 2009 and was named one of "America's Most Promising Social Entrepreneurs" by *BusinessWeek*. Gary was also featured in the 2009 documentary *Food, Inc.* [3]

Within the first year, Gary and Samuel decided to close TREC, which ironically the business was originally meant to support, and focus their energies on building a socially driven business—selling healthy food that was healthfully produced. For the first seven years, Samuel and Gary's families lived on-site in adjacent apartments in the 1852 Wilton farmhouse.

The house and barn provided office space and the "Yogurt Works" (the manufacturing facility).

Making their social mission a reality while building a profitable business proved to be extremely challenging for the two social entrepreneurs and their families. But with the deep and passionate commitments of the two founders working long hours, family support, and extensive grassroots marketing, the fledging company was able to survive.

Like many entrepreneurial start-ups, the business was built with a lot of family equity, the two families did most of the work themselves—milking cows, making yogurt, calling customers, and delivering the yogurt. Louise Kaymen noted, "Without the Kaymen kids doing cow chores, making yogurt, shrink-wrapping orders and getting up at all hours of the night, we would not have been able to 'hang in there' in those first years." [4] By the end of 1983, Stonyfield sales were $56,000 and the company was selling at a rate of 150 cases of yogurt per week.

Sidebar

Early Marketing: Yogurt or Camel Manure? [5]

Gary found creative and low-cost ways to market Stonyfield's yogurt. For example, when Andy Moes, radio cohost of Boston's well-known "Joe and Andy Show," told his audience he'd rather eat camel manure than yogurt (which at that time was not as popular a food as it is today), Gary saw this as an opportunity and stopped by nearby Benson's Animal Farm in New Hampshire to collect some camel manure. Gary and his wife Meg drove down to the radio station with a packed quart of yogurt and a packed quart of camel manure and demanded that Andy choose to eat one. Andy eventually ate the yogurt and conceded, "I admit it. This yogurt does taste better than camel manure." Stonyfield received instant airplay and had found a creative way to not only sell yogurt but also get their message of the health benefits of yogurt across to a wide audience.

Later Marketing

Stonyfield thrived on innovation. It constantly looked for innovative products that would drive sales and bottom line profit. It was one of the first companies to exploit market segmentation for its yogurt product line. Stonyfield segmented its markets by age, gender, demographics, and psychographic factors. It educated customers on the impact of its products and company actions on people's health and the environment.

For example, Stonyfield product categories have included yogurts formulated specifically for women, infants (YoBaby), and kids (Planet Protectors low-fat yogurt). The company has introduced new yogurt recipes and limited edition yogurts, such as low-fat eggnog yogurt, breakfast and desert yogurts, and frozen yogurts. Through its innovative marketing and product development, Stonyfield has been able to be an industry leader in taking yogurt from a side dish, consumed by a small number of health food "junkies," to an everyday food for the American diet.[6]

In response to growing production, the company decided in 1984 to stop on-site production of milk, sold its herd (now up to nineteen cows), and switched to purchasing milk from local farmers. The company ended 1985 with ten employees, new yogurt flavors, $317,200 in sales, and production of 1,100 cases per week.

Demand for the company's organic yogurt was growing faster than the company's ability to supply it, so in 1986, the company relocated from the farm and contracted with a copacker in Massachusetts. Shortly thereafter, the copacker went bankrupt and the bank seized the packer's and Stonyfield's assets, including equipment, raw materials, and finished product. This event almost ruined the company, but by accessing some additional family funds, Samuel and Gary restarted yogurt production back in the old barn in Wilton. The company managed to maintain their customer relationships but Stonyfield ended the year with a loss of $400,000 and was essentially bankrupt. However, Gary was able to secure a Small Business Association–backed bank loan and convinced private investors (family, friends, and others) to further invest in Stonyfield. Meg Hirshberg recalled that "during the nine painful years it took us to reach profitability, we endured countless disasters, mishaps, and near-death experiences. That meant there were countless times we could have rid ourselves of the misery we called a business."

With the infusion of capital in 1988, Stonyfield production and operations moved into a twenty-one-thousand-square-foot facility in Londonderry, New Hampshire. This proved to be a very good business decision and a turning point for the company. Stonyfield ended 1989 with forty-two employees, $2.5 million in sales, and production of 8,050 cases of yogurt per week. By 1990, Stonyfield had made number 113 on *Inc.*'s list of the five hundred fastest growing companies in the United States, and the following year, Stonyfield's annual sales had grown to $56 million.

In 2001, Samuel retired from Stonyfield (but still remained on the board of the company) as the company took a new strategic direction by forming a partnership with Paris-based Groupe Danone (Danone), the largest fresh dairy company in the world. This meant that Gary Hirshberg was in charge of the company.

Danone, a $17 billion multinational company in 2001, whose brands included Evian bottled water and Danone/Dannon yogurt, initially purchased 40 percent of Stonyfield shares. This was followed with share purchases in late 2003 and again in 2006, with the additional share purchases bringing Groupe Danone ownership to an 85 percent interest in Stonyfield.

This was a strategic purchase that benefited both companies and was a unique partnership. Gary Hirshberg still remained chairman, president, and CEO with relatively few restrictions on his ability to lead the company and Danone eventually ended up with near full ownership of a profitable and growing subsidiary. Hirshberg, in a unique strategic arrangement to maintain his status as Stonyfield's leader and main decision maker, retained 60 percent of voting shares in the company.

Gary discussed that the relationship with Danone involved three things: "I set agreed-upon growth and profit targets that we both agree to; I agreed that I wouldn't expand into any other segments other than yogurt without their approval. And also, any capital improvements over $1 million, I needed their approval. But otherwise, I'm free to do whatever I want."

Frank Riboud, Groupe Danone's chairman and chief executive officer, said, "We want Stonyfield to leverage Groupe Danone's strengths while retaining its own unique culture and management. We believe it is important for Stonyfield to continue to grow its market share while maintaining its commitment to social responsibility."

Sidebar
Stonyfield's Shareholders

By 2006, Stonyfield had grown into a $263 million business with 297 private investors. A large number of the company's private investors—many of whom were friends, family, and employees—were eager to realize a return on their investments after many years of investment. The Danone purchase provided a desired exit strategy for Stonyfield's investors.

Gary Hirshberg had previously considered an initial public offering (IPO) for Stonyfield or selling shares directly, but neither of these financing options provided him the ability to meet financial obligations to investors without giving up control of the company. He courted twenty different companies until he finally found the right fit with Danone. Under the agreement with Danone, he could sell a majority stake while simultaneously maintaining control of the company. This was a breakthrough agreement—one that critics thought would never be possible—and is referred to in merger and acquisition circles as the "Stonyfield deal."

At the time, Gary's wife, Meg, expressed a sense of relief regarding Danone's investment. Meg's mother had invested considerably over time to help her son-in-law's business survive and then grow. Meg said, "My mother is now at ease in her retirement. Her risky investment in Stonyfield secured college educations for all her grandchildren. Our family is as close as ever and feels great collective satisfaction at having been part of building a successful business."

Gary noted that "Danone's investment provided Stonyfield investors a healthy return on their investments. It also gave Stonyfield the knowledge to make its business more efficient, to launch in other countries, to continue to grow its mission-driven initiatives and to participate in the rapidly growing organic and natural dairy industry segment." [7]

The initial buyout of Stonyfield by Groupe Danone did not include direct investment in the company, it only was a purchase of selling investor's shares in the company and therefore resulted in no real additional financial resources for Stonyfield. The purchase and partnership did allow Danone to share knowledge about increasing production and market share with Stonyfield.

It was not until 2006 that the synergistic relationship between Danone and Stonyfield became more readily apparent. Danone began to invest considerable resources in the company and approved $66 million to expand Stonyfield's plant in Londonderry to keep up with growing product demand.

Stonyfield Goes Global

Danone had a significant role in Stonyfield entering the global marketplace in 2006. The European organic food market was growing rapidly, from €10 billion in 2005 to €18.4 billion in 2009. [8] Danone and Stonyfield worked together to create a subsidiary, Stonyfield Europe as an independent entity within Groupe Danone's Fresh Dairy Products division. Franck Riboud, the chairman and chief executive officer of Danone, stated that "the European market for

organic dairy products is growing, but it remains a fairly discreet presence. With Stonyfield Europe, we hope to capitalize on the success and unique expertise of Stonyfield Farm to speed up its development."

Upon its creation, Stonyfield Europe immediately announced the acquisition of more than a third of family-owned Irish firm Glenisk, a recognized leader in organic dairy in Europe. Glenisk was established in 1987 and was owned by its founding family. The firm's organic milk and yogurts had sales growth of more than 10 percent when Stonyfield Europe acquired a portion of it in 2005. [9]

Danone and Stonyfield also created Stonyfield France. Stonyfield France's goal was to create a brand suited to French tastes consistent with Stonyfield's successful "healthy people, healthy planet" messaging. The French market had tremendous potential as French consumers eat four times as much yogurt as American consumers; however, organic yogurt was viewed as appealing to only a small niche market of more socially minded French consumers. The result was "Les Deux Vaches des Fermiers du Bio" (the two cows of organic farmers); the website is http://www.les2vaches.com. [10]

Danone not only helped Stonyfield expand overseas but also helped in North America with the creation of Stonyfield Canada. In 2006, Stonyfield Canada opened a head office and a manufacturing plant in Boucherville, Quebec. All the organic milk for Stonyfield Canada comes from organic farms in Canada and their products are distributed through a wide array of retailers throughout Canada, including Walmart, Loblaws (the largest food retailer in Canada), and Sobeys (the second-largest food retailer in Canada).

Continued growth in the US market and the expansion of Stonyfield globally helped Stonyfield grow significantly—from a $73 million company in 2001 to a $366 million company in 2010. Throughout this period of high growth the company kept to its sustainability mission of offering healthy food to enhance the health of people while promoting a healthy planet. There was strong synergy, as the high growth was a result of the sustainability focus, and the sustainability mission benefited from the growth.

KEY TAKEAWAYS

- Stonyfield was founded on and has kept to its sustainability mission.
- The company was founded to support environmental education and outreach through organic yogurt sales.

- Danone's arrangement (deal) with Stonyfield was an unusual partnership that benefited both organizations and was based on both companies' interests in sustainability and market and profitability growth.

EXERCISES

1. Entrepreneurs must demonstrate a strong, genuine, continuous, and personal commitment to a cause-related mission and action plan. Why was Stonyfield started as a company? What roles did the two entrepreneurs play in taking Stonyfield to the company that it is today?
2. Were Gary and Samuel presiding over something really innovative or unique in the business world or were they just adding a few novel twists to business as usual?
3. How did Stonyfield use alternative marketing tactics to grow its business?

[1] David Phillips, "Bringing the Cultural Revolution," Business Library, December 2003, http://findarticles.com/p/articles/mi_m3301/is_12_104/ai_111508193/pg_2/?tag=content;col1.

[2] Gary Hirshberg, *Stirring It Up: How to Make Money and Save the World* (New York: Hyperion, 2008), 2–4.

[3] "CSR Heroes: Gary Hirshberg of Stonyfield Farm," *Just Means* (blog), April 5, 2010,accessed August 2, 2011, http://www.justmeans.com/CSR-Heroes-Gary-Hirshberg-of-Stonyfield-Farm/12086.html. Also see Will Marre, "Stonyfield Farm's Gary Hirshberg Is a True Pioneer of Sustainability and Giving Is Winning," *Giving Is Winning* (blog), December 30, 2010, accessed August 2, 2011, http://willmarre.com/blog/stoneyfield-farms-gary-hirshberg-is-a-true-pioneer-of-sustai nability-and-giving-is-winning.

[4] "Our Story in a Nutshell / Milestones," Stonyfield Farm, Inc., http://www.stonyfield.com/about-us/our-story-nutshell/milestones.

[5] Gary Hirshberg, *Stirring It Up: How to Make Money and Save the World* (New York: Hyperion, 2008), 89–90.

[6] "Our Story in a Nutshell / Milestones," Stonyfield Farm, Inc., http://www.stonyfield.com/about-us/our-story-nutshell/milestones.

[7] Meg Cadoux Hirshberg, "Brother, Can You Spare a Dime? Family Money Can Be a Lifeline: At the Very Same Time, It Can Be the Most Expensive Money in the World," *Inc. Magazine*, November 2009.

[8] "BioFach Session 'The European Market for Organic Food,'" Organic World, http://www.organic-world.net/news-organic-world.html?&tx_ttnews%5Btt_news%5D=463&cHash=706047cd74d37a75b3535c3f8396655d; David Phillips, "An American in Paris: Stonyfield France Launches 'Les Deux Vaches' Brand with Grassroots Environmental Messages," Business Library, October 2006, http://findarticles.com/p/articles/mi_m3301/is_10_107/ai_n16808775.

[9] Lorraine Heller, "Danone and Stonyfield Create European Organic Dairy Firm," Food Navigator, June 20, 2006, http://www.foodnavigator.com/Financial-Industry/Danone-and-Stonyfield-create-European-organic-dairy-firm.

[10] David Phillips, "An American in Paris: Stonyfield France Launches 'Les Deux Vaches' Brand with Grassroots Environmental Messages," Business Library, October 2006, http://findarticles.com/p/articles/mi_m3301/is_10_107/ai_n16808775.

13.3 Stonyfield's Social Mission

LEARNING OBJECTIVES

1. Discuss Stonyfield's mission and how it guided organizational strategy, operations, and marketing.
2. Understand the different types of initiatives Stonyfield undertakes to support its sustainability strategy.
3. Understand the role that profitability plays in a social mission–oriented organization's ability to achieve its mission and **operational excellence**.

As social entrepreneurs, Gary and Samuel deeply cared about the environment and family farms long before they founded Stonyfield. Gary knew from the start that he needed more than a vague aspiration that Stonyfield could make money and save the world. He developed a mission statement to help guide the company. This mission has evolved over the years for Stonyfield but has been consistently focused on sustainability and has remained a foundation that guides company strategy and all decisions and practices.

On mission statements, Gary stated, "Every world-saving (and money-making) business needs a stated mission—a rallying cry that focuses efforts, helps set priorities, and gives all hands a meaning and a purpose. So one night I sat down with a bottle of cabernet and wrote a mission statement that has barely changed since." [1]

Table 13.1 Stonyfield's Mission Statement

Gary's Draft Mission (1983)[2]	Stonyfield's Current Mission Statement (2011) [3]
To provide the very highest-quality, best tasting, all natural, and certified organic products. To educate consumers and producers about the value of protecting the environment and supporting family farmers and sustainable farming methods. To serve as a model that environmentally and socially responsible businesses can also be profitable. To provide a healthful, productive, and enjoyable workplace for all employees, with opportunities to gain new skills and advance personal career goals. To recognize our obligation to stockholders and lenders by providing an excellent return on their investments.	**Yogurt on a mission** *We're no greenhorns when it comes to green business. We were on a mission to make the planet healthier even before we were making yogurt. Today, we make it our mission to work towards all sorts of healthy.* Our mission: We're committed to healthy food, healthy people, a healthy planet and healthy business. **Healthy food.** We will craft and offer the most delicious and nourishing organic yogurts and dairy products. **Healthy people.** We will enhance the health and well-being of our consumers and colleagues. **Healthy planet.** We will help protect and restore the planet and promote the viability of family farms. **Healthy business.** We will prove that healthy profits and a healthy planet are not in conflict and that, in fact, dedication to health and sustainability enhances shareholder value. We believe that business must lead the way to a more sustainable future.

In the beginning, as the company struggled to sustain itself financially, Stonyfield fulfilled its mission primarily directly through its product. Organic yogurt was a product that was produced without pesticides and other harmful chemicals and was therefore better for the environment and healthier for consumers. While Stonyfield had a much broader vision of its social purpose, it simply did not have the financial resources to devote to any other actions to express its social values other than through its product.

From the beginning, the company had to balance business realities with sustainability aspirations. Stonyfield started as all organic but soon had to switch to "natural" milk due to lack of sufficient organic milk supply as its production needs grew. By the mid-1990s, the company was back up to 85 percent organic, with some fluctuations afterward depending on the supply of organic milk. By 2007, the company had returned to its former 100 percent organic (for a significantly larger production base) and has remained there ever since. A more in-depth discussion of natural and organic takes place later on in the case.

Also very early on, Stonyfield learned that they had to match up the business realities of producing a good that consumers wanted to buy while still holding true to their values. For example, at one point, a garden salad–flavored yogurt was introduced, and while the company had high hopes for the flavor and it being a healthful option, it was not popular with consumers and had to be discontinued.

The next generation of sustainability (beyond the organic yogurt product) effort did not occur at Stonyfield until 1990 with the launch of the company's Adopt-a-Cow program

(later renamed Have-a-Cow). The program was formed to educate consumers on the link between food and the environment and the value of supporting family farmers and sustainable farming methods. It had taken seven years, but the company was finally arriving at a place where it could start fulfilling its original broader social mission and the key was having had some financial success. [4] Stonyfield achieved profitability in 1991 and that allowed for new sustainability initiatives for the company.

In 1991, the company opened a farm visitors' center to help further promote awareness of the family farm and also produced the first *Stonyfield Yogurt Cookbook*. The cookbook combined marketing with education on the nutritional benefits of organic yogurt.

In 1993, with sales of $12.5 million and strong profitability, Stonyfield was in a position to actively engage in significant environmental initiatives. This included a comprehensive recycling program, an energy retrofit of their facility, and work with the nonprofit Oxfam America to promote sustainable agriculture worldwide. Also in 1993, the company launched a Profits for the Planet program that contributed 10 percent of profits to efforts that helped protect and restore the earth.

As Stonyfield expanded its sustainability programs, it also held true to its values for its products. For example, one new product, the "Frookwich"—vanilla frozen yogurt sandwiched between two whole-wheat, fruit juice–sweetened cookies—was popular with consumers but had quality problems. The cookies become soggy relatively quickly. Stonyfield discontinued the product rather than compromise their values by adding an artificial ingredient that would have prevented the product degradation.

Stonyfield also was the first dairy processor to secure agreements with its milk suppliers to ensure that milk did not come from cows treated with the controversial synthetic bovine growth hormone rBST (or rBGH) after the FDA approved its use. In 2005, Stonyfield became a certified organic producer and all of its products were certified and labeled under the USDA organic seal.

Other examples of product stewardship tied to Stonyfield's mission included the switch from plastic pint containers to more environmentally friendly unbleached paper pint containers for the company's frozen yogurt and ice cream.

Stonyfield also assumed a leadership position in addressing climate change. In 1997, Stonyfield became the first US manufacturer to offset 100 percent of the CO_2 from its facilities' energy use. Stonyfield also partnered with the Union of Concerned Scientists in 1997 to raise awareness of global climate change and developed a guide called *Reversing Global Warming: Offsetting Carbon Dioxide Emissions* to help other businesses take steps to reduce their carbon footprint. In 2001, Stonyfield entered, in a significant way, the political arena to give the company a voice in setting national policy on environmental issues. This involved using a public relations and Internet campaign to educate consumers about the negative effects of the White House's proposed energy bill. Stonyfield used this opportunity to teach consumers and the general public about energy efficiency and other positive steps they could take to reduce their environmental impact. In 2002, Stonyfield, after the release of the US Department of Agriculture National Organic Standards, published a guide to help consumers understand organic products and the positive impact that supporting organic agriculture could have on the environment. To improve the eating habits of children, the company sponsored organic and all-natural snack vending machines in schools from California to Connecticut.

Also in 2002, the company provided free smoothies to commuters stepping off Boston subways to thank them for choosing public transportation. This was part of Stonyfield's marketing efforts tied to the company's social mission.
Another "subway marketing" example was in Chicago. In order to keep a new account for a large Chicago supermarket chain, Stonyfield needed to increase its market share from 0.08 percent to 3 percent in three months. Gary Hirshberg himself crafted Stonyfield's "hand-to-mouth" marketing strategy and distributed free cups of yogurt to Chicago Metro transit riders. Eighty-five thousand containers of yogurt were handed out with a coupon that read, "We salute your commuter ridership and thanks for doing your part to help save the planet." The coupons reminded transit riders that traveling by train instead of car kept forty-five pounds of particulates per year from spewing into the atmosphere. The strategy worked. Stonyfield received media coverage in every local newspaper and NBC's *Today* show Chicago affiliate. Market share jumped to 2.5 percent, enough to keep the account and build a stable market position in Chicago. An added bonus was the hand-to-mouth offensive only cost $100,000, or just 1 percent of the $10,000,000 an advertising agency wanted to charge in order to try to achieve the same share. [5]

In 2006, Stonyfield formally put into place its Mission Action Plan (MAP) program under the direction of Gary's sister and vice president of natural resources, Nancy Hirshberg. MAP set detailed plans and goals for the company's environmental strategies and programs. It was designed as a company-wide initiative to engage all employees in achieving Stonyfield's environmental mission and the company's philosophies and culture. The management saw MAP as part of a transformative change for the company and employees on both a professional and personal level.

Under Nancy's leadership, high-level teams in each of Stonyfield's high areas of environmental burden were formed. These areas included sustainable packaging, zero waste, facility GHG emissions, and transportation. Each environmental team was required to complete an annual action plan that set long-term and near-term goals and outlined the steps to achieve the goals. The plans needed to be approved by Gary, Nancy, and Stonyfield's chief operating officer (COO).

A portion of management compensation was directly tied to meeting plan objectives. MAP turned what was once an ad hoc and sporadic process into a company-wide management system lead by senior leaders across the organization.

MAP required a team charter and specifics on required behavioral and other changes. For example, training was provided, which included measuring the number of computer users using energy savings software settings.

Stonyfield managers were responsible for developing "green leaders"—their employees. Employees received training on environmental issues and ethics.
Teams used specific criteria and assessment tools to measure outcome performance. Outcome measures had to be

SMART—specific, measurable, attainable, realistic, and tangible. MAP included a resource assessment and a plan homepage aimed at identifying and correcting any gaps between current human resource skills and what was needed to accomplish the plan (training and team building). MAP required teams to identify obstacles and issues to plan achievement and recommendations to address them.

MAP was a management system and process that helped managers and employees rally around Stonyfield's sustainability-focused mission. Stonyfield's overarching mission was driven by five "sub-missions" that paved the way for making sustainability an everyday reality for the company. The five sub-missions built on one another in a continuous flow of interactions throughout the organization. Stonyfield's sub-missions constituted essential elements of Stonyfield's mission, organizational culture, values, and way of doing business. The following were the five sub-missions:
1. Superior products for market leadership
2. Education through products and services
3. Cause-related marketing for success
4. Delivering the mission publically and privately
5. Providing the best possible returns to stockholders

Sub-Mission 1

The Company will sell only superior products, the prerequisites for becoming a market contender and a rallying point for employees to maintain top quality.

By 2010, Stonyfield was the number one selling US yogurt brand and number three worldwide. Stonyfield used a differentiation strategy that separated it from much larger rivals and was highly valued by its customers. It sold only superior, high quality, 100 percent certified organic yogurts and dairy products. No artificial ingredients, colors, flavors, sweeteners, or preservatives were used in its products. All ingredients were sourced from suppliers who did not use toxic, persistent pesticides, chemical fertilizers, synthetic hormones, antibiotics, or genetically modified organisms (GMO).

Stonyfield's sourcing strategies differentiated the company from competitors. It paid farmers a premium for not treating their soils with chemicals that killed microbial soil life on nonorganic farms and helped to keep more than 180,000 agricultural acres free of toxic pesticides and chemicals known to contaminate food, soil, water, and air. [6]

Sub-Mission 2

The Company will use its products and services to educate people about a cause they care about.

Gary felt that a lot of people didn't trust companies, but by Stonyfield having a worthy mission statement and following it, the company could be different and could be trusted. Trust needed to be earned and built on making good on Stonyfield's mission. This required not only delivering on its pledge of selling superior products but also educating people about a cause they cared about and what Stonyfield was doing to help them address the cause. One of the main ways Stonyfield got its educational message out was on its yogurt lids and product packaging. Stonyfield printed its messages on millions of yogurt lids each month. The lids told customers about nonprofit environmental efforts, farming and health issues, and other causes. Stonyfield put its messages on more than three hundred million lids annually.

In addition to lids, Stonyfield delivered its messages through its web page; visitors center; community-sponsored events; product and naming contests; publications; management and employee presentations; and participation in governmental, environmental, educational, and business conferences and events.

Sidebar
Family Farms
A founding premise of Stonyfield Farm holds that the small family farm in comparison to the large, concentrated animal farming operation (CAFO) is generally a better farming system…Large numbers of animals in a confined area concentrate the animal waste products posing an environmental and health risk. On smaller farms, animals generally receive more personal attention and live longer lives under less stress…Family farmers live on the land that they steward. Thus, we believe, they are generally inclined to care about what goes into the soil, water and air where they live and raise their children. Family farms provide open spaces, which preserve rural character and provide fields and forests for wildlife. They also provide jobs and support rural economic vitality, as well as opportunities for business ownership and independence.
Source: "Stonyfield Mission Statement," Stonyfield Farm, Inc., http://www.stonyfield.com.

For Stonyfield, while it supports a wide range of social causes, a driving principle is the importance of family farms. The Have-a-Cow program discussed previously is a tangible example of the company using its resources to help educate the public on family farms and the vital role they play in linking food to person.

Sub-Mission 3

The Company will prove that a cause-driven enterprise can also succeed as a business.

From many perspectives, Stonyfield's approach to business was different. The company paid a minimum of 50 percent above the going rate for conventionally grown raw materials, and in some instances, it paid up to two and half times the price. Because of the higher price for ingredients and supplies, its gross margin was lower than its industry rivals' gross margin. Gary Hirshberg compared Stonyfield's business model and gross margins to Danone's: "They [Danone] don't really understand our business model. They don't really know anything about organics. They know about yogurt, but we have a much more expensive product than them. And while we charge more than them, I can tell you my gross margin is much, much poorer than theirs. Organic milk costs 70 percent more than conventional milk. I can't charge 70 percent more for a cup of yogurt. Organic sugar can be at times 100 times more than conventional....But yet my net margins are actually the same as or better than theirs." [7]

Partly offsetting the higher cost of raw materials and supplies, Stonyfield's sold its organic yogurt at a 20 percent price premium over nonorganics. But this was not enough to make up for higher material and supplies costs. To address the impact on bottom line profitability Stonyfield also ran a leaner and more efficient operation than rivals. Many of the cost savings and productivity improvements were achieved through the company's sustainability initiatives and methods. Gary wrote that organic is "quite simply, the best way to do business....It's true for anyone who wants to run a truly cost-efficient business the only kind that can survive long-term—and still leave behind a habitable planet for our children." [8] Stonyfield used several sustainability strategies and practices to lower its transaction cost or cost of doing business and its impact on the environment:

- **Efficient transportation.** Package improvements and software that limited maximum truck speed resulted in a 46 percent absolute reduction in transportation GHG emissions from 2006 to 2010 and saved the company $7.6 million. Package improvements, including package redesign, resulted in eighteen fewer tractor-trailer loads of plastic per year. Whenever possible, the company shipped its packages by train to reduce GHG emissions.

- **Zero waste initiative.** The company practiced the four Rs of waste reduction: redesign, reduce, reuse, and recycle, which resulted in solid waste being reduced by 39 percent from 2007 to 2010 and $450,000 in annual savings. Package redesign, including packaging made from plants and environmentally friendly material resulted in annual savings of $3.2 million.

- **Operations extensively planned.** By adding solar panels to facilities, investing in more energy-efficient and waste reduction equipment and processes, and implementing better scheduling and operational

processes, facility energy and GHG emissions were reduced by 11 percent from 2007 to 2010 saving $2 million annually.

Sub-Mission 4

The Company will deliver on its mission privately and publicly.

By exploiting market opportunities based on crafting and applying sustainability principles and practices, Stonyfield delivered on its mission privately and publicly. It built core managerial and organizational capabilities and distinctive competencies that advanced Stonyfield while benefiting the community. Its success was partially based on building trusting, collaborative relationships and partnerships across its entire supply chain. In addition to selling superior products and finding innovative ways to lower its cost of doing business, Stonyfield focused on the health of cattle, the employees, and the environment. It supported small-scale dairy operations localized in New Hampshire and taught sustainable farming techniques through its educational efforts. Farmers were offered educational programs in how to preserve their soil, how to minimize runoff, and how to grow vegetables and fruits without the use of chemicals.

Stonyfield's mission statement and practices stressed the importance of providing meaningful work and jobs that had a higher purpose than money. A mission focused on sustainability and other important causes helped to attract and retain high-quality employees who shared this mission and vision for the company.

Stonyfield's MAP teams and employees "walked the talk" regarding their environmental goals and programs and actions. Employees conducted all Stonyfield events, activities, and purchases in a manner that were consistent with the company's mission and values, including environmental sustainability, employee health, sustainable agriculture, and social responsibility. Because the MAP teams had several working groups, there were numerous goals, such as the following:

- By 2011, eliminate 70 percent of junk mail (from 2008 levels).

- By 2012, all onsite events will be zero waste.

- By 2013, all food served at Stonyfield will be organic and healthy. [9]

Stonyfield's sustainability accomplishments and business achievements extended well beyond the operational boundaries of the company. In March 2011, Stonyfield funded Preserve Gimme 5, a nationwide contest to find avid recyclers. The contest identified "local heroes" of recycling nationwide and accomplished its goal "to inspire recycling efforts across the country and to showcase and acknowledge individuals who were avid recyclers."

Sub-Mission 5

The Company is fully committed to providing stockholders with the best possible return on their investments.

Stonyfield believed that commitment to sustainability principles enhanced profits and contributed to society in many different ways. Profits were neither wrong nor immoral, and doing business in a sustainable way would pay financial and social dividends to investors.

KEY TAKEAWAYS

- Effective sustainability strategies are based on operational and functional core capabilities and distinctive competencies.
- Organizations can achieve business excellence by crafting and implementing sustainability-focused missions.
- Competitive advantage can be achieved by being good at being a sustainability-focused business with core and distinctive competencies built on sound sustainability principles and practices.
- Stonyfield's sub-missions supported operational excellence in the organization.

EXERCISES

1. What is Stonyfield's mission? Why is it important for companies to have a clearly articulated mission statement?
2. Describe Stonyfield's environmental performance in terms of management of resources and waste, including energy use, application of materials science, clean technology, emissions control, and recycling. Cite specific examples of added value or cost reduction from the company's management of resources and waste.

[1] Gary Hirshberg, *Stirring It Up: How to Make Money and Save the World* (New York: Hyperion, 2008), 23.

[2] Gary Hirshberg, *Stirring It Up: How to Make Money and Save the World* (New York: Hyperion, 2008), 23–24.

[3] "Our Mission," Stonyfield Farm, Inc., accessed August 2, 2011, http://www.stonyfield.com/about-us/our-mission.

[4] "Meet the Cows," Stonyfield Farm, Inc., http://www.stonyfield.com/healthy-planet/organic-farming/have-cow/meet-cows.

[5] Gary Hirshberg, *Stirring It Up: How to Make Money and Save the World* (New York: Hyperion, 2008).

[6] Siel Ju, "Interview with Stonyfield CEO Gary Hirshberg: 'Everybody Can Win,'" *Mother Nature Network* (blog), June 16, 2010, accessed August 2, 2011, http://www.mnn.com/lifestyle/responsible-living/blogs/interview-with-stonyfield-ceo-gary-hirshberg-everybody-can-win.

[7] "Stonyfield Farm & Groupe DANONE Announce Partnership Organics, Health and Nutrition Brings Yogurt Makers Together for Unique Combination of Cultures," Dannon, last modified October 4, 2001, accessed August 2, 2011, http://www.dannon.com/pages/rt_aboutdannon_pressrelease_Archive_StonyfieldFarmGroupeDANONE.html.

[8] Diane Brady, "The Organic Myth Pastoral Ideals Are Getting Trampled as Organic Food Goes Mass Market," *Bloomberg Businessweek,* October 16, 2006, accessed August 2, 2011, http://www.businessweek.com/magazine/content/06_42/b4005001.htm.

[9] "Our Story in a Nutshell / Milestones," Stonyfield Farm, Inc., http://www.stonyfield.com/about-us/our-story-nutshell/milestones.

13.4 Organics and Natural Foods Industry

LEARNING OBJECTIVES

1. Define organic and what is meant by natural foods and how they compose an industry and market.
2. Describe yogurt's position in the organics and natural foods industry.
3. Explain Stonyfield's positioning in the industry.

Organic food and beverages are produced without pesticides and synthetic fertilizers and are different from "natural" foods. Food labeled "natural" cannot be labeled organic unless they meet US Department of Agriculture (USDA) standards. The USDA organic certification system includes various levels of organic. The highest level is 100 percent organic; the next highest level is "organic" if 95 percent of ingredients are organic. [1]

Natural foods, and yogurt in particular, have moved from being requested by a small group of committed individuals and only available in specialized health food stores to broad

appeal available in virtually all supermarkets and grocery food stores. Throughout the 1990s and 2000s several social, economic, and technological trends impacted sales growth and industry dynamics in the organic and natural food segment of the food and beverage industry. Some of these trends include the following:

- Increased consumer awareness of nutritional benefits of eating a healthy diet
- Aging population and changing consumer tastes and preferences for organic food, especially yogurt
- Increased recognition by large companies with substantial market power that being in organics and

natural foods was not only good for profits but also good for their public image and relations and that it should be a part of their sustainability initiatives

Sidebar
USDA Organic Labeling Standards
In 2002 the U.S. Department of Agriculture (USDA) established an organic certification program that required all organic foods to meet strict government standards. These standards regulate how such foods are grown, handled and processed. Any product labeled as organic must be USDA certified. Only producers who sell less than $5,000 a year in organic foods are exempt from this certification; however, they're still required to follow the USDA's standards for organic foods. If a food bears a USDA Organic label, it means it's produced and processed according to the USDA standards. The seal is voluntary, but many organic producers use it. Products that are completely organic—such as fruits, vegetables, eggs or other single-ingredient foods—are labeled 100 percent organic and can carry the USDA seal. Foods that have more than one ingredient, such as breakfast cereal, can use the USDA organic seal plus the following wording, depending on the number of organic ingredients:

100 percent organic. *To use this phrase, products must be either completely organic or made of all organic ingredients.*

Organic. *Products must be at least 95 percent organic to use this term. Products that contain at least 70 percent organic ingredients may say "made with organic ingredients" on the label, but may not use the seal. Foods containing less than 70 percent organic ingredients can't use the seal or the word "organic" on their product labels. They can include the organic items in their ingredient list, however.*

Source: "Organic Foods: Are They Safer? More Nutritious?," Mayo Clinic Staff, last modified August 31, 2011, http://www.mayoclinic.com/health/organic-food/NU00255/METHOD=print.

In 2010, the US organic food market was a $26.7 billion industry, up 8 percent from the previous year and rising from $1 billion in 1990. Organic foods represented a 4 percent share of the $673 billion US food industry. [2] Organics had significantly outpaced the 0.6 percent growth rate for the total food industry. Organic fruits and vegetables were $10.6 billion or 40 percent of the total organic food industry and nearly 12 percent of all US fruit and vegetable sales. Organic dairy was the second-largest organic category with $3.9 billion or 6 percent of the total US dairy market.

Since 2002, the North American organic food and beverage industry had experienced major industry consolidation causing significant change to its market structure. When the USDA passed the US National Organic Labeling Standard in

2002 large food companies were quick to react. The standard allowed food companies to voluntarily label products as "USDA-Organic" if they met the USDA standard. Although labeling was voluntary, it became a major marketing tool for the large conventional food companies, such as General Mills, Kraft, Dean, Pepsi, Kellogg, and Cargill, among several others.

Labeling helped to validate the organic movement. To enter the market quickly, the majors began acquiring the better-known and more successful organic and natural food start-ups. Industry analysts reported that the major food companies could quickly add to their bottom-line profits by acquisition, despite the organic industry's origins as a form of resistance to the mass production and mass marketing methods employed by the majors.

Major food companies paid a significant premium for the smaller organic companies. Premiums were based on the higher sales growth. The acquisitions provided majors with insights on how to achieve customer loyalty and find new growth opportunities—two areas in which the smaller organic food manufacturers were outperforming the larger major food companies. [3]

Notable acquisitions were (acquiring company in parenthesis) Honest Tea (Coke), Ben & Jerry's (Unilever), Cascadian Farms (General Mills), Kashi (Kellogg), Tom's of Maine (Colgate-Palmolive), and Naked Juice (PepsiCo). [4] Thus the rapid entry by major companies into organics segment of the industry caused a shakeout where several of the smaller organic and natural food companies were acquired or forced out of business..

The organic food industry has continued to grow. Two companies who are standouts in organic food markets are Whole Foods Market and Walmart. Founded in 1980, Whole Foods Market reported $9 billion in sales for 2010. Whole Foods was the leading US retailer for organic and natural foods with 304 stores in the United States, Canada, and the United Kingdom. Walmart has made a major investment in organic foods in its retail and club stores in what is viewed by many as a tipping point for the organic industry and a favorable signal for continued long-term industry growth.

Walmart's entry into organic and natural foods threatened the organics supply chain, as it lowered prices paid to family farms. Another issue is climate-change impacts on water and crops, which are expected to continue to drive organic ingredients prices up. Another trend impacting the organics market is the aging US population, with its growing concern about health.

Yogurt Industry

Overall demand for yogurt has been growing and new yogurt categories have been rapidly emerging, especially products aimed exclusively for women, kids, and the elderly. [5] For example, since 2002, product introductions targeted to children included Breyers' YoCrunch, Stonyfield's YoBaby and YoKids, and Yoplait's Scooby Doo–inspired "Ro-gurt."

By 2011, Greek yogurt emerged as the single most competitive battlefield in the $6.8 billion yogurt industry. *Euromonitor International* projected Greek yogurt sales to nearly double to $1.5 billion in 2011, up from $60 million in 2006. [6] Analysts reported that sales of Greek yogurt were increasing faster than for regular yogurt because many consumers perceive Greek yogurt—thicker, creamier, less sweet, and with more protein—to be healthier than regular yogurt.

Two companies drove most of this growth, Chobani, owned by privately held Agro Farma, Inc., and Fage, S.A., a Greek dairy company. The trend toward Greek yogurt started in early 2000s when Fage entered the US market, but Chobani is the market leader going from nonexistence four years ago to 2010 sales of approximately $500 million. Kraft Foods discontinued its yogurt business in 2007 only to reenter the industry in 2010 with its Greek yogurt Athenos.

Rapid Greek yogurt growth caught General Mills (owner to the US Yoplait rights) and Danone by surprise. Danone and General Mills were fierce rivals with number one and two in US yogurt sales, respectively. Consumers not only found Greek yogurt to be a healthy alternative to regular yogurt, but they were willing to pay a premium price for it.

KEY TAKEAWAYS

- Organic food and beverages are produced without pesticides and synthetic fertilizers.
- Sales of organics in the United States have significantly outpaced the growth rate for the total food industry.
- Major food companies trying to benefit from the growth in the organic market have paid a significant premium for smaller organic companies.

EXERCISE

1. Go to Professor Philip H. Howard's web page at https://www.msu.edu/~howardp./organicindustry.html and look at all of Howard's five diagrams. How has the structure of the organic food industry changed over the time frame covered by the five partial network diagrams (from the earliest network diagram to the latest)? If you were the owner of a small, privately owned organic food company what lesson can you learn by studying all five diagrams?

[1] "Organic Foods: Are They Safer? More Nutritious?," Mayo Clinic Staff, accessed August 31, 2011, http://www.mayoclinic.com/health/organic-food/NU00255/METHOD=print.

[2] "Industry Statistics and Projected Growth," Organic Trade Association, http://www.ota.com/organic/mt/business.html.

[3] Christine MacDonald, "Big/Green: Eco-Conscious Brands Are Increasingly Being Bought Out by Giant Corporations. Can We Trust Them?," *Sacramento News and Review*, July 21, 2011, accessed August 2, 2011, http://www.newsreview.com/sacramento/big-green/content?oid=2838435.

[4] Philip H. Howard, "Consolidation in the North American Organic Food Processing Sector, 1997 to 2007," *International Journal of Sociology of Agriculture and Food* 16, no. 1: 13–30, accessed April 3, 2009, https://www.msu.edu/~howardp.

[5] Ted Reinstein, "It's Crazy Out There," Thebostonchannel.com, April 23, 2011, accessed August 17, 2011, http://www.thebostonchannel.com/index.html.

[6] Stuart Elliott, "Chobani, Greek Yogurt Leader, Lets Its Fans Tell the Story," *New York Times*, February 16, 2011, accessed August 17, 2011, http://www.nytimes.com/2011/02/17/business/media/17adco.html.

13.5 Stonyfield's Strategy and Execution

LEARNING OBJECTIVES

1. Understand the importance of an organizational commitment to and focus on strategy in sustainable business.
2. Describe how sustainability strategy can guide business decisions and help sustainable businesses achieve environmental and profitability goals.
3. Explain how successful implementation of sustainability strategy requires strong execution that includes finding the right balance between achieving environmental goals and economic and business realities.
4. Understand that a sustainability-focused strategy is about constant innovation and change and doing things significantly different from traditional ways of doing business.

Stonyfield provides an example of a company that embodies many of the best practices in sustainability and business. The company's partnership with Danone illustrates how a business can focus on sustainability as a business model and meet planet, people, and profit objectives and that it can do this not only locally but also globally. Globalization and sustainability may often be considered as contradictory, specifically in the context of buy-local movements and the energy required to transport products across the globe, but Stonyfield's experience suggests otherwise.

The Stonyfield "story" is not one of straight line success. There have been a lot of bumps in the road and there are challenges that will have to be addressed in the future. Throughout its history, Stonyfield has had to carefully analyze and consider business decisions that have sustainability implications. They have constantly had to make choices and consider tradeoffs that may not be the "sustainable ideal" but reflect the operational practicalities of doing business in the world as it exists today. To accomplish this, Stonyfield has created and used emerging tools and techniques of sustainable business (discussed throughout this textbook), including carbon foot printing, life cycle assessment, and supply chain analysis.

Stonyfield has always stuck to its sustainability compass as embodied in its mission statement but has sometimes had to take different paths than its founders may have idealized. This is seen right from the beginning when Stonyfield switched from organic milk to "natural" milk as their production needs in New England outweighed the ability of the local market to supply it. What is noteworthy is that Stonyfield never accepted this alternative as the way things are and invested considerable resources in strengthening

supplies of organic milk so that in 2007, almost two decades later, the company was back to 100 percent of what it believes to be the most healthful option for people and the planet—organic milk.

Supply chain dynamics will always be an area of challenge and opportunity for Stonyfield. While Stonyfield has the desire to combine organic with local family farms, it is not always possible for them to source organic from local sources. Stonyfield currently sources from multiple locations as part of its business strategy to avoid supplier failures in any one area. Although all organic milk for its US operations currently comes from family farms in the United States, Stonyfield must source from elsewhere also. Some ingredients—such as cocoa, banana, and vanilla—simply do not grow in the United States, so those must be sourced from other countries.

An example of a more recent action the company took that again showed its constant balancing of business reality and sustainability ideals was in 2010. Stonyfield switched their multipack cups to PLA (a plant-based plastic). While this may seem like a "no-brainer" win for the environment, as the cups previously had been made from a petroleum-based plastic, it actually was not that simple.

In the United States, the only current manufacturer of PLA, NatureWorks (a division of Cargill), uses corn, which has many other sustainability issues to consider. Table 13.2 "Plant-Based Plastics Use Considerations" illustrates some of the potential issues and Stonyfield's considerations in choosing the product.

Table 13.2 Plant-Based Plastics Use Considerations

Issue	Stonyfield's Consideration of the Issue
Corn is a food, and by using corn to make containers instead, it can make food less affordable.	NatureWorks only uses a small fraction of the overall US corn supply and does not change demand significantly enough to alter the price of corn.
Corn can be genetically modified and grown using pesticides and synthetic fertilizers. In other words, it's a nonorganic cup that embodies all the industrial practices that Stonyfield stands against.	Stonyfield considers the corn only as a stepping stone as PLA can be made from other plant sources. They plan on switching as more environmentally sustainable products appear in the market place. In addition, to help address some of the harm from the agricultural practices used to produce the corn, they purchase offsets called Working Landscape Certificates (WLC). The money from these offsets go to farmers who agree to follow strict sustainable production standards so that non–genetically modified organism (GMO) corn is produced equal to the amount of GMO corn used to make Stonyfield's packaging.

Issue	Stonyfield's Consideration of the Issue
Is the PLA packaging recyclable or compostable?	PLA can be composted, but in the form used by Stonyfield, it is not. PLA can be recycled, but currently, the infrastructure is not in place to do so. Stonyfield considered this but through using Life Cycle Analysis, found that the disposal of the product is a very small contributor to its impact; the materials going into producing the product have much bigger impact. Stonyfield has pledged to make their use of PLA a closed-loop system.
Is PLA safe?	PLA is approved by the US Food and Drug Administration. Stonyfield has contractually obligated its supplier for the PLA not to contain any harmful additives (including carcinogens and reproductive toxins), and it routinely tests for compliance.

Source: "Multipack Cups Made from Plants," Stonyfield Farm, Inc., http://www.stonyfield.com/healthy-planet/our-practices-farm-table/sustainable-packaging/multipack-cups-made-plants.

While PLA is not a perfect "sustainable" packaging, Stonyfield carefully considered a broad array of issues and decided that the environmental benefits from switching to PLA outweighed the negatives. The benefits being that it reduced the carbon footprint of their multipack packaging by almost 50 percent, which will save 1,875 metric tons of CO_2 per year and reduced their overall packaging carbon footprint by 9 percent. To help further mitigate some of the drawbacks of PLA, Stonyfield has committed to not only offsetting the current impact but also learning from the use of the packaging to make it a more sustainable in the future.

Sidebar
Considerations in Using Plant-Based Plastics
Watch the video at http://vimeo.com/15674301 to learn more about the process that Stonyfield undertook in considering PLA as a packaging material.

The business relationship between Danone and Stonyfield provides an example of a strategic alliance focused on sustainable business objectives and capabilities. It provides one model for how a large and small business can strategically interact to achieve singular and collective sustainability and profitability objectives. It also suggests how business sustainability efforts can involve large multinational corporations seeking to enhance their sustainability efforts with acquisitions and, in this instance, a particularly creative and collaborative acquisition. It is interesting to note that this was not an example of an "unsustainable" company purchasing a sustainable one to transform its entire business model but an example of a good fit between two companies that had congruence on social mission.

Danone was not a stranger to the concepts of corporate social responsibility. In 1972, founder and CEO Antoine Riboud stated, "Corporate responsibility does not stop at the threshold of the company's factories or offices. The enterprise creates and provides jobs that shape people's entire lives. It consumes energy and raw materials, and in so doing alters the face of our planet. The public is charged with reminding us of our responsibilities in this industrial society." This statement formed the basis of the Danone model: economic performance, attention to people, and respect for the environment go hand in hand. In fact, Danone had a history of social and environmental initiatives long before it acquired Stonyfield.

The Danone-Stonyfield relationship is an example of a win-win partnership. As discussed previously, Gary Hirshberg needed to provide a buyout, a return for his many investors, but did not want to "sell out" and have the company acquired by an organization that would use Stonyfield as a brand to be exploited and have its values compromised. The Danone deal allowed Hirshberg and Kaymen to pay off their original investors and gave Stonyfield access to a strong distribution network, financial capital, marketing muscle, and the global market.

The partnership was of benefit to Stonyfield in that it not only provided financial resources but also provided strategic resources and knowledge to allow Stonyfield to expand its operations globally and, in the process, further spread the mission of healthy food, people, planet, and business.

For Danone, it was a "win" as well; the company was committed to sustainable agriculture but did not have expertise in the organics market. The Stonyfield partnership allowed Danone to acquire a valuable business asset with its growing revenue and profits. But more importantly it gave them access to knowledge about the organics market and Stonyfield's sustainability-focused manufacturing expertise. As a result of the Stonyfield acquisition, Danone is now the world leader in organic yogurts with a 7.4 percent market share. It is important to note that organics are only one part of Danone's sustainable agriculture portfolio as its other business lines promote integrated farm management (which limits the use of pesticides and fertilizers) and other programs that integrate nature with agriculture (such as the Bleu-Blanc-Coeur program).

At the time of the acquisition, Gary noted, "Anyone with enough money can buy a company, but it takes a real commitment to our core principles of organic farming to nurture it and make it work." His statement was in response to some who believed that Stonyfield's mission and way of doing business was threatened by Danone's ownership. Gary disagreed with his critics, many of whom were former friends and business associates.

Bloomberg News reported that it was not coincidental that Kaymen decided to retire in 2001 when Danone first invested in Stonyfield. According to the report, Samuel was against any large conglomerate owning Stonyfield. [1] Critics questioned whether "big businesses" could be trusted in buyouts of "eco-conscious" brands. Can a new corporate parent be trusted to continue the ethical and environmentally sustainable practices that earned its new subsidiary a loyal following? Especially while these large corporations generally preserved the brand names and folksy advertising styles, how do we know that "the stuff inside the box, bag or carton hasn't changed"? [2]

In contrast to critics, Gary Hirshberg believed that working with big companies was an imperative for all sustainability-focused companies. To combat global warming, pollution, and other environmental concerns, large business involvement is essential. He stated, "The happy news is that we've got a $23.5 ($26.7) billion industry. The sad news is that we're 2.6 percent of total U.S. food. If we're going to make the change that we need to make in the time we need to make it…then we need to work with companies like Groupe Danone because they're not going to go away."

Furthermore, Gary noted that being part of a large conglomerate had only advanced his career-long effort to support family farmers and challenge giant agribusiness. In many ways only big business could achieve the economies of scale and harness needed resources to address society's most pressing environmental and social problems.

Still others felt that the entry of large companies into organic-focused markets brought other problems, such as trying to feed the masses in an industry where supplies were vulnerable. Even Walmart and Costco were having difficulty finding adequate suppliers of organic ingredients, especially given their low-priced business model. Critics saw it as an "organic ethical paradox." That is, the organics movement succeeded beyond the proponents wildest dreams, but success had imperiled their ideals. To the organic traditionalists it "simply wasn't clear that organic food production could be replicated on a mass scale."

One of the most transformational ways that Danone and Stonyfield are contributing to sustainability may also be one of the least apparent. It is their investments in sustainable agriculture and local organic farming. The two companies are providing programs and resources to help farmers through the difficult and costly transition from conventional to organic and sustainable farming practices. This can be seen in the Danone Ecosystem Fund, particularly with its Molay-Littry plant in France (Reine Mathilde project), which is working to transition local farmers to organic in the region. It is also seen in Gary's decision to open a 3,800-square-foot Stonyfield Café at Chelsea Piers, New York City's major amateur sports and entertainment complex. In addition to the café's dairy bar, parfaits, and frozen yogurts, the menu featured macaroni and cheese, salads, and flatbread pizzas with ingredients purchased from farms in New York State. This was not Gary's first effort to expand Stonyfield's mission into restaurants. In 2001, Gary cofounded O'Naturals restaurant in Falmouth, Maine, to further support local farms and to promote healthy foods and healthy living. His restaurant vision was to free people from the world of junk food by providing families with quick, natural, and organic meals served by staff passionate about the food they served.

While on the face of it this could seem benevolent, it is also strategic. Stonyfield has consistently run into challenges with regards to the limited supply of organic ingredients. By developing a stable supply chain that can keep up with their growth, this can be addressed over time. When viewed from a sustainability perspective, it is beneficial for the environment (a less harmful means of agriculture), beneficial for society (local farmers can generate higher income from organic), and beneficial for business (stable supplies reduce costs and enhance profitability).

Sidebar
Gary Hirshberg's Advice on the Role of Business in Society
Gary shared his journey and the lessons he learned in his 2008 book in what he called his "hard-headed" conclusions:

- It's going to take a lot more than moral rectitude and virtuous principles to set us on a truly sustainable path.

- Business is the most powerful force on the planet; it got us into this mess and is the only force strong enough to get us out.
- Most environmental problems exist because business has not made solving them a priority.

- Only when the solutions to our environmental problems are accompanied by profitable, commercial (business) strategies for enhancing them will the business world get on board. [3]

KEY TAKEAWAYS

- Managing a successful business based on a sustainability-focused mission and business model requires the deep and passionate commitment of founders and leaders.
- Sustainability-based business ventures need to be creative enterprises that balance competing business, social, and environmental demands.

EXERCISES

1. Discuss the relationship between Stonyfield and Danone. Are the guiding principles of what is important to Stonyfield's sustainability mission and strategies at risk under Groupe Danone's ownership?
2. List three to five main contributing factors in Stonyfield's success. Discuss how these factors led to Stonyfield's success. What, if any, specific aspects of Stonyfield's contributing factors, sustainability mission, strategies, and approaches have the greatest potential for transferability to other businesses?
3. Throughout the case there are several examples where a sustainability action has positive and negative implications. Discuss the powdered milk and PLA cup decisions in terms of features and benefits.
4. Are Gary Hirshberg's "hard-headed" conclusions little more than moral platitudes or are they really hard-earned, practical, positive (e.g., what is), and normative (e.g., what should be) lessons on how to globally scale sustainable products benefit of the plant, people, and profits? Find two or three examples of how other companies have applied Hirshberg's conclusions on a global scale to benefit the planet.
5. Corporations are important elements of the communities in which they operate. As a corporate citizen, an organization should be moved to interact with and contribute to its local, regional, national, and global communities, especially as related to environmental, health, and business issues. Describe Stonyfield's resulting corporate partnerships. Note operational strategies, tools, or methods used to foster corporate citizenship within the local and extended corporate community. Explain how sustainability principles are demonstrated by management and encouraged throughout the organization.

[1] Meg Cadoux Hirshberg, "Brother, Can You Spare a Dime? Family Money Can Be a Lifeline: At the Very Same Time, It Can Be the Most Expensive Money in the World," *Inc. Magazine*, November 2009.

[2] Christine MacDonald, "Big/Green: Eco-Conscious Brands Are Increasingly Being Bought Out by Giant Corporations. Can We Trust Them?," *Sacramento News and Review*, July 21, 2011, accessed August 2, 2011, http://www.newsreview.com/sacramento/big-green/content?oid=2838435.

[3] Siel Ju, "Interview with Stonyfield CEO Gary Hirshberg: 'Everybody Can Win,'" *Mother Nature Network* (blog), June 16, 2010, accessed August 2, 2011, http://www.mnn.com/lifestyle/responsible-living/blogs/interview-with-stonyfield-ceo-gary-hirshberg-everybody-can-win

13.6 Moving On

On January 12, 2012, Gary Hirshberg announced he was stepping down as CEO but will stay on as chairman of Stonyfield. Walt Freese, former CEO of Ben & Jerry's, was named to replace him. In making the announcement, Gary Hirshberg said, "The company is in great shape and the change leaves him time to focus on U.S. food and agriculture policy, especially food labeling." Freese was chief marketing officer for Ben & Jerry's before he became CEO. Before that, he served as president of Celestial Seasonings in Boulder, Colorado, and held senior management roles with Kraft General Foods and Nestle. Freese said, "This is what I want my life to be about…working for businesses that both can be strong and vibrant financial enterprises and contribute in a meaningful way to the world. This just seems to me to be the perfect fit."

13.7 Conclusion

This case study provides insight into the challenges and complexities of producing a sustainable product in a sustainable way and highlights the benefits from taking a strategic approach to sustainability. The story of Stonyfield includes tensions between sustainability vision and business realities. Through innovation and a strategic approach, Stonyfield effectively narrowed the gap between vision and reality by making thoughtful decisions while constantly adhering to its organizational mission. Stonyfield has always been strongly committed to its mission and has always aspired to improve on its sustainability practices. If the company could not, for whatever reasons, get things "right" with regards to its sustainability objectives the first time, it continuously strived to improve and get it right or better over time, constantly working for people, planet, and profits.

EXERCISES

1. Write a memorandum to the new CEO of Stonyfield about the importance of focusing on the sustainability mission of the company. The memo should include detailed discussion with specifics of how Stonyfield has benefited from a focus on sustainability at the strategic company level and how it can continue to benefit from a focus on sustainability.

2. In a separate memorandum to the CEO of Stonyfield's parent Danone, discuss the risks and opportunities of having Gary Hirshberg step down as CE-YO of Stonyfield. The memo should include discussion of how much of the company's success has been based on the leadership and commitment of Mr. Hirshberg to sustainability and how an effective leadership transition can be achieved with Mr. Freese.

3. Discuss the likelihood of Stonyfield having a strong influence on Danone's sustainability practices over the long term. Describe the challenges for Danone in adopting Stonyfield's mission-driven approach to sustainability. Describe the main opportunities for Danone in adopting Stonyfield's sustainability practices throughout the international company.

NOTES: